Adrian Nicole LeBlanc is a frequent
Magazine. Her work has been publi:
Village Voice and other magazines.
Smith College, a Master's of Philo
Oxford University, a Master of Law !
currently a Visiting Scholar at the New York University School of Journalism. She has also been the recipient of numerous awards including a
Bunting fellowship from Radcliffe, a MacDowell Colony residency and
a Soros Media Fellowship from the Open Society. Adrian Nicole
LeBlanc lives in Manhattan and *Random Family* is her first book.

'An extraordinary non-fiction saga which follows four young Latinos
from the South Bronx. They make out, fall out, give birth, get high
and break down without ever lowering the volume. LeBlanc's portrait is
intimate without being voyeuristic . . . With this ghetto-blaster of a book,
sympathetic and unsentimental, she makes us think deeply about
America's desperate urban poor'   *Independent on Sunday*

'*Random Family* portrays an America that many choose to ignore, in
which people struggle daily just to survive . . . A fascinating and com-
passionate chronicle of life there'   *Time Out*

'A startling portrait of how demanding it is to be poor'
     Books of the Year, *Economist*

'A remarkable first book. *Random Family* is so filled with indelible
images and heartbreaking moments I cannot praise it enough . . . Rather
than looking for a story, *Random Family* gives us a whole way of life'
     Daily Telegraph

'LeBlanc's work shines. What really marks out *Random Family* as such a
monumental work of narrative journalism isn't the scale of its dramas
but the depth of its empathy. Poverty is the oldest story in town, and the
trick is to write about it in a way that makes us look at it anew. LeBlanc's
reportage does just that, and shows us exactly what we're missing. Read
it and wonder why'   *Scotsman*

'A fine piece of observational journalism . . . *Random Family* has the plot
of an action-packed blockbuster, vivid with passion and high crime . . .
Although it concerns one neighbourhood in the Bronx in the 1980s and

Random Family

LOVE, DRUGS, TROUBLE,
AND COMING OF AGE IN THE BRONX

Adrian Nicole LeBlanc

HARPER PERENNIAL

Harper Perennial
An imprint of HarperCollins*Publishers*
77–85 Fulham Palace Road
Hammersmith
London W6 8JB

www.harpercollins.co.uk/harperperennial

This edition published by Harper Perennial 2004

9 8 7 6 5 4 3 2 1

First published in Great Britain by Flamingo 2003
First published in the US by Scribner 2003

A catalogue record for this book is available from the British Library

ISBN 0 00 716343 6

Set in Electra

Printed and bound in Great Britain by Clays Ltd, St Ives plc

For my parents,
Eve Mary Margaret Mazzaferro
and Adrian Leon LeBlanc

... Some say that Happiness is not Good for mortals & they ought to be answerd that Sorrow is not fit for Immortals & is utterly useless to any one a blight never does good to a tree & if a blight kill not a tree but it still bear fruit let none say that the fruit was in consequence of the blight.

WILLIAM BLAKE, letter to WILLIAM HAYLEY
London, October 7, 1803

PART I

The Street

CHAPTER ONE

Jessica lived on Tremont Avenue, on one of the poorer blocks in a very poor section of the Bronx. She dressed even to go to the store. Chance was opportunity in the ghetto, and you had to be prepared for anything. She didn't have much of a wardrobe, but she was resourceful with what she had—her sister's Lee jeans, her best friend's earrings, her mother's T-shirts and perfume. Her appearance on the streets in her neighborhood usually caused a stir. A sixteen-year-old Puerto Rican girl with bright hazel eyes, a huge, inviting smile, and a voluptuous shape, she radiated intimacy wherever she went. You could be talking to her in the middle of the bustle of Tremont and feel as if lovers' confidences were being exchanged beneath a tent of sheets. Guys in cars offered rides. Grown men got stupid. Women pursed their lips. Boys made promises they could not keep.

Jessica was good at attracting boys, but less good at holding on to them. She fell in love hard and fast. She desperately wanted to be somebody's real girlfriend, but she always ended up the other girl, the mistress, the one they saw on the down-low, the girl nobody claimed. Boys called up to her window after they'd dropped off their main girls, the steady ones they referred to as wives. Jessica still had her fun, but her fun was somebody else's trouble, and for a wild girl at the dangerous age, the trouble could get big.

It was the mideighties, and the drug trade on East Tremont was brisk. The avenue marks the north end of the South Bronx, running east to west. Jessica lived just off the Grand Concourse, which bisects the Bronx lengthwise. Her mother's tenement apartment overlooked an underpass. Car stereos thudded and Spanish radio tunes wafted down from windows. On corners, boys stood draped in gold bracelets and chains. Children munched on the takeout that the dealers bought them, balancing the styrofoam trays of greasy food on their knees. Grandmothers pushed strollers. Young mothers leaned on strollers they'd parked so they could concentrate on flirting, their irresistible babies providing excellent introductions and much-needed entertainment. All along the avenue, working people shopped and dragged home bags of groceries, or pushed wheelcarts of meticulously folded laundry. Drug customers wound through the crowd, copped, and skulked away again. The streets that loosely bracketed Jessica's world—Tremont and Anthony, Anthony and Echo, Mount Hope and Anthony, Mount Hope and Monroe—were some of the hottest drug-dealing blocks in the notorious 46th Precinct.

The same stretch of Tremont had been good to Jessica's family. Lourdes, Jessica's mother, had moved from Manhattan with a violent boyfriend, hoping the Bronx might give the troubled relationship a fresh start. That relationship soon ended, but a new place still meant possibility. One afternoon, Jessica stopped by Ultra Fine Meats for Lourdes and the butcher asked her out. Jessica was fourteen at the time; he was twenty-five. Jessica replied that she was too young for him but that her thirty-two-year-old mother was pretty and available. It took the butcher seven tries before Lourdes agreed to a date. Two months later, he moved in. The children called him Big Daddy.

Almost immediately, the household resumed a schedule: Lourdes prepared Big Daddy's breakfast and sent him off to work; everyone—Robert, Jessica, Elaine, and Cesar—went to school; Lourdes cleaned house and had the evening meal cooked and waiting on the stove by noon. Big Daddy seemed to love Lourdes. On weekends, he took her bowling, dancing, or out to City Island for dinner. And he accepted her four children. He bought them clothes, invited them to softball games, and drove them upstate for picnics at Bear Mountain. He behaved as though they were a family.

Jessica and her older brother, Robert, had the same father, who had died when Jessica was three, but he had never accepted Jessica as his; now only Robert maintained a close relationship with the father's relatives. Elaine, Jessica's younger sister, had her own father, whom she sometimes visited on weekends. Cesar's father accepted him—Cesar had his last name on his birth certificate—but he was a drug dealer with other women and other kids. Occasionally he passed by Lourdes's; sometimes Cesar went to stay with him, and during those visits, Cesar would keep him company on the street. Cesar's father put him to work: "Here," he would say, passing Cesar vials of crack taped together, "hold this." Drug charges didn't stick to children, but Big Daddy cautioned Cesar about the lifestyle when he returned home. "Don't follow his lead. If anybody's lead you gonna follow, it should be mine." Big Daddy spoke to Cesar's teachers when Cesar had problems in school. Jessica considered Big Daddy a stepfather, an honor she had not bestowed upon any other of her mother's men. But even Jessica's and Cesar's affection for Big Daddy could not keep them inside.

*   *   *

For Jessica, love was the most interesting place to go and beauty was the ticket. She gravitated toward the enterprising boys, the boys with money, who were mostly the ones dealing drugs—purposeful boys who pushed out of the bodega's smudged doors as if they were stepping into a party instead of onto a littered sidewalk along a potholed street. Jessica sashayed onto the pavement with a similar readiness whenever she descended the four flights of stairs from the apartment and emerged, expectant and smiling, from the paint-chipped vestibule. Lourdes thought that Jessica was a dreamer: "She always wanted to have a king with a maid. I always told her, 'That's only in books. Face reality.' Her dream was more upper than herself." Lourdes would caution her daughter as she disappeared down the dreary stairwell, "God ain't gonna have a pillow waiting for your ass when you fall landing from the sky."

Outside, Jessica believed, anything could happen. Usually, though, not much did. She would go off in search of one of her boyfriends, or disappear with Lillian, one of her best friends. Her little brother, Cesar, would run around the neighborhood, antagonizing the other children he half-wanted as friends. Sometimes Jessica would cajole slices of pizza for Cesar from her dates. Her seductive ways instructed him. "My sister was smart," Cesar said. "She used me like a decoy, so if a guy got mad at her, he would still come around to take me out. 'Here's my little brother,' she would say. 'Take him with you.' " More often, though, Cesar got left behind. He would sit on the broken steps of his mother's building, biding his time, watching the older boys who ruled the street.

Jessica considered Victor a boyfriend, and she'd visit him on Echo Place, where he sold crack and weed. Victor saw other girls, though, and Jessica was open to other opportunities. One day in the fall of 1984, when she should have been in school, she and Lillian went to a toga party on 187th and Crotona Avenue. The two friends were known at the hooky house on Crotona. The girls would shadow the boys on their way to the handball courts or kill time at White Castle burgers, and everyone often ended up in the basement room. The building was officially abandoned, but the kids had made a home there. They'd set up old sofas along one wall, and on another they'd arranged a couple of beds. There was always a DJ scratching records. The boys practiced break dancing on an old carpet and lifted weights. The girls had little to do but watch the boys or primp in front of the salvaged mirrors propped beside a punching bag. At the toga party, Jessica and Lillian entered one of the makeshift bedrooms to exchange their clothes for sheets. Two older boys named Puma and Chino followed them. The boys told the girls that they were pretty, and that their bodies looked beautiful with or without sheets. As a matter of fact, they said, instead of joining the party, why don't we just stay right here?

Puma dealt drugs, but he was no ordinary boy. He had appeared in *Beat Street*, a movie that chronicled the earliest days of hip-hop from the perspective of the inner-city kids who'd created it. The film, which would become a cult classic, portrayed self-expression as essential to survival, along with mothers, friends, money, music, and food. *Beat Street* showcased some Bronx talent, including Puma's group, the Rock Steady Crew. Puma had cinematic presence, and he was a remarkable breakdancer, but when he met Jessica his career was sliding to the bottom of its brief slope of success. The international tour that had taken him to Australia and Japan was over, and the tuxedo he'd worn break dancing for the queen of England hung in a closet in its dry-cleaning bag. He'd spent all the money he had earned on clothes and sneakers and fleets of mopeds for his friends.

Jessica was glad for anybody's attention, but she was especially flattered by Puma's. He was a celebrity. He performed solo for her. He was clever, and his antic behavior made her laugh. One thing led to another, and next thing you know, Jessica and Puma were kissing on top of a pile of coats. Similar things were happening between Lillian and Chino on another bed.

Both girls came out pregnant. Jessica assured her mother that the father was her boyfriend, Victor, but there was no way to be certain. The following May, Jessica and Lillian dropped out of ninth grade. They gave birth to baby girls four days apart, in the summer of 1985. Big Daddy clasped Jessica's hand through her delivery. At one point, Jessica bit him so hard that she drew blood. The grandfather scar made Big Daddy proud.

Jessica named her daughter Serena Josephine. Lourdes promptly proclaimed her Little Star. It was understood that Lourdes would have to raise her; Jessica didn't have the patience. Even if she hadn't been young, and moody, Jessica wasn't the mothering kind. Lourdes wasn't, either—in fact, she wished she'd never had children—but circumstance had eroded her active resistance to the role. She'd been raising children since she was six. First, she'd watched her own four siblings while her mother worked double shifts at a garment factory in Hell's Kitchen. She'd fought their neighborhood fights. She'd fed them and bathed th[?] put them to bed. Now Lourdes's own four, whom she had been able to manage when they were little, were teenagers slipping beyond her reach.

Robert and Elaine had been easy, but Lourdes felt their fathers' families were turning them into snobs. Robert returned from his weekend visits with his grandmother smoldering with righteousness. Lourdes could tell he disapproved of her involvement with Santeria, but who was her son to judge? How holy had it been, when Jessica was pregnant, for Robert to chase her around the apartment, threatening to beat her up? Her daughter Elaine's arrogance occupied a more worldly terrain. On Sunday nights, she alighted from her father's yellow cab, prim in her new outfits, and turned up her cute nose at the clothes Lourdes had brought home from the dollar store.

Jessica and Cesar were Lourdes's favorites, but they ignored her advice and infuriated her regularly. When Lourdes stuck her head out of the living room window overlooking Tremont and called her children in for supper (she used the whistle from the sound track of the movie *The Good, the Bad, and the Ugly*), she was usually calling for Jessica and Cesar; Robert and Elaine were apt to be at home. Robert and Elaine worried about getting into trouble, whereas Jessica and Cesar had as much fun as they possibly could until trouble inevitably hit. Robert and Elaine were dutiful students. Jessica and Cesar were smart, but undisciplined. Jessica cut classes. Cesar sprinted through his work, then found it impossible to sit still; once, he'd jumped out of his second-story classroom window after Lourdes had physically dragged him around the corner to school.

Jessica and Cesar also looked out for each other. One night, Jessica went missing and Lourdes found out that she had been with an off-duty cop in a parked car; when Lourdes kicked Jessica in the head so hard that her ear bled, it was Cesar who ran to the hospital for help. Another time, during an electrical fire, Jessica ushered Cesar to the safety of the fire escape. Jessica knew how to appease Lourdes's brooding with cigarettes and her favorite chocolate bead candy. Cesar, however, had fewer resources at his disposal. He had learned to steel himself against his mother's beatings. By the time he was eleven, when his niece Little Star was born, Cesar didn't cry no matter how hard Lourdes hit.

For Lourdes, Little Star's arrival was like new love, or the coming of spring. As far as she was concerned, that little girl was hers. "When I pulled that baby out—Jessica was there—the eyes!" Lourdes said. "The eyes speak faster than the mouth. The eyes come from the heart." A

baby was trustworthy. Little Star would listen to Lourdes and mind her;
she would learn from Lourdes's mistakes. Little Star would love her
grandmother with the unquestioning loyalty Lourdes felt she deserved
but didn't get from her ungrateful kids.

Meanwhile, Jessica made the most of her ambiguous situation. She
told Victor that he was the father: she and Victor cared for one another
and he had attended the delivery; he also gave Jessica money for Little
Star's first Pampers, although his other girlfriend was pregnant, too.
Secretly, however, Jessica hoped that Puma was the father, and she was
also telling him that the baby was his. Puma was living with a girl named
Trinket, who was pregnant, and whom he referred to as his wife; he also
had another baby by Victor's girlfriend's sister. Despite the formidable
odds, Jessica hoped for a future with him.

Publicly, Puma insisted Little Star was not his. But she certainly
looked like his: she had the same broad forehead, and that wide gap
between her dot-brown eyes. The day Jessica came home with a videotape
of the movie *Beat Street*, Lourdes had heard enough about this breakdancing Puma to go on alert. She settled on her bed with Little Star, Jessica, Elaine, and their dog, Scruffy. In one of the early scenes of the film,
a boy who looked suspiciously like Little Star did a speedy break dance at
a hooky house. Then he challenged a rival crew to a battle at the Roxy, a
popular club.

"Hold that pause," shouted Lourdes. "That's Little Star's father! I will
cut my pussy off and give it to that dog if that ain't Little Star's father!"
Jessica laughed, pleased at the recognition. Puma could say what he
liked, but blood will out.

Puma's confidante was a short, stocky tomboy named Milagros. Milagros
had known Puma forever and considered him family. Puma was the first
boy she'd ever kissed. Kissing boys no longer interested Milagros. Puma's
stories of Jessica's sexual escapades, however, intrigued her; Milagros had
noticed Jessica as well, when they both attended Roosevelt High School.
Milagros knew that Puma still saw Jessica, but she kept it to herself.
Meanwhile, Milagros and Puma's live-in girlfriend, Trinket, were
becoming friends.

Milagros and Trinket made an unlikely duo. If a river ran through the
styles of poor South Bronx girlhood, these two camped on opposite
banks. Milagros, who never wore makeup, tugged her dull brown hair
into a pull-back and stuck to what she called "the simple look"—T-shirts,

sneakers, jeans. Trinket slathered on lipstick, painted rainbows of eye shadow on the lids of her green eyes, and teased her auburn hair into a lion's mane. Trinket was looking forward to becoming a mother, whereas Milagros proclaimed, loudly and often, her tiny nostrils flaring, that she would never have children and end up slaving to a man.

In the fall of 1985, some of Jessica's friends returned to school. Bored and left behind, Jessica became depressed. She would page Puma, and once in a while he would call her back. Sometimes Jessica went looking for him in Poe Park, a hangout near Kingsbridge and Fordham Road, where the Rock Steady Crew occasionally performed. Usually, though, she found Puma at work, standing on a corner not far from the hooky house. Jessica had little chance of running into Trinket at his drug spot because Puma urged his wife to stay away. Alone with Puma, Jessica broached the touchy subject of what was between them: "Give time for her features to develop and you'll see, it'll look like you." She thought the space between Serena's eyes was a giveaway. On the small span of her infant face, the gap made her look as though she'd landed from another galaxy. Jessica also thought that Little Star had Puma's magnetism. "There's something about her that brings her to you," she said.

Jessica harassed Trinket with crank phone calls. The calls were Jessica's trademark: she would whisper, "I have Puma's kid," and then hang up. Eight months into her pregnancy, Trinket decided to confront Jessica. Whoever was or wasn't a baby's father, the business of claiming love tended to be a battle between girls. The next time Jessica called, Trinket told her she wanted to see the child. Jessica gave her Lourdes's address. Milagros went along as Trinket's bodyguard.

"Where's the baby?" Trinket asked. Serena hung forward in a baby swing. Her enormous head seemed too heavy for her scrawny body. Jessica propped up her baby girl to give Trinket a better look. She also produced additional evidence — "Love" and "Only you" written on photographs of Puma, in his own hand. The assessment took less than fifteen minutes. Milagros said good-bye to Jessica and hurried after Trinket, who burst into tears once they were safely back on the street.

Privately, Trinket didn't blame Puma for fooling around with Jessica. "Jessica had this sexuality about herself and her domineering ways," Trinket said. "I was so closed-off." Trinket attributed her inhibitions to having been molested by one of her mother's boyfriends. Jessica had also been sexually abused, by Cesar's father from the age of three, but Trinket didn't know this. Jessica seemed so comfortable in her body. She flirted easily with girls and boys, men and women, alike. Jessica appeared to have no boundaries, as though she were the country of sex itself. Puma told Trinket that that baby could belong to anyone; he said that Jessica had been with everybody; she was no one's girl. Trinket consoled herself with the thought that maybe Jessica's promiscuity had resulted in a baby that had features from different boys.

A month later, in January 1986, Trinket gave Puma his first son. Her position as his wife was secure.

Jessica then began dating Puma's brother, Willy. Willy and Puma were often together, but Jessica claimed she didn't know they were related until Willy took Jessica to his mother's apartment and she spotted Puma's photograph on a wall. In fact, the brothers shared a striking physical resemblance: Willy looked like Puma with a mustache, although instead of Puma's wiry expressiveness, Willy had a bit of a hangdog look. Both had a way with the ladies, though; Willy, who was twenty-two, had already been married, and had fathered four kids.

That winter, Cesar's father called Lourdes—he was broke, homeless, and heroin sick—and Lourdes took him in. The family treated him "like a king," he recalled, but he soon left, unable to resist the drugs.

Jessica's depression grew. She started gouging small cuts on her inner thighs. Nobody wanted her—she had been neglected by her own father; then by Puma; and even by Willy, her second choice. She said, "I was never loved the way I wanted to be. Nobody in my family ever paid any attention to me." That spring, after receiving a vicious beating from Lourdes, Jessica tried to kill herself by swallowing pills, and Big Daddy whisked her to Bronx Lebanon Hospital. The drastic action worked, but only briefly. "They paid attention to me for about two days afterwards," Jessica said scornfully. After she had her stomach pumped, the doctor informed her she was pregnant again—with twins.

Jessica claimed that Willy was the father, but once again, there was no way to be certain. When Jessica had been carrying her first child, Lourdes had indulged her cravings, buying her the orange drink *morir soñando*—"to die in your dreams"—and preparing her oatmeal with condensed milk, vanilla, and fresh cinnamon stick. This time, however, Jessica's pregnancy didn't grant her special status in the household.

Jessica and Willy tried to get ready for the babies. Jessica's older brother Robert got Willy a job at the paint store where he worked; Jessica sold clothes at a store on Fordham Road. If a man came in looking for an outfit for his girlfriend, it was Jessica's job to model it. Jessica generated so much business that her boss let her keep some of the clothes. Her best-selling item was called The Tube. "You could roll it down and wear it as a miniskirt, and if you roll it up and hook a belt, it could be a dress," Jessica explained. "Or a tube top if you fold it, or if you twist it, you could make a headband." Day after day, men came in for an outfit for their women and departed with three or four, fully accessorized. Many of the men asked Jessica out. Her boss started bringing her into the back and asking her to model the new lingerie; he rewarded her with a gold-nugget necklace and matching earrings, and took her out to eat. Before long, Jessica had to quit.

Willy had left his job as well, and soon they were both back to their old ways. Willy's girlfriends included one of Trinket's cousins, a school-girl named Princess. It was Princess's turn to receive Jessica's calls.

"I'm pregnant from Willy," Jessica said.

"You're a ho," said Princess. Next call, Princess snapped, "You're pregnant from that bum in Poe Park," which was worse than saying the baby's father was an immigrant.

Willy may have lacked Puma's lightning energy, but that September he quickly agreed to put his last name on the birth certificates: Brittany arrived at 5:01 P.M., several weeks early and two minutes ahead of her twin sister, Stephanie. They were scrawny, with that prominent forehead, a tuft of thin, black hair, and a sweeter trace of Willy's hangdog look. Jessica had a C-section scar; Puma was an uncle; Willy was a father; Serena had two baby sisters; and Lourdes was a grandmother again.

Jessica and the twins moved in with Willy at his mother's, but even with the babies, Jessica had no legitimate place. Her relationship with Willy's family was shrouded in shame. Puma's mother accepted Serena, but some of his sisters considered Jessica a home-wrecker, and privately called her worse. She holed up with the babies in Willy's bedroom, and he sometimes got physical when he was drunk. Trinket paraded through with Puma's precious son, trailed by Milagros. Milagros said, "Jessica was always sad and alone. She would be in the room by herself. Nobody talked to her. They all loved Trinket. They knew what Jessica did." Milagros made a point to stop and say hello. Sometimes she visited without Trinket, and she and Jessica started becoming friends.

Puma ignored Jessica around his family, but they still got together on the sly. Once, he slipped Jessica a note. She met him at a nearby bus stop. He bristled: "Hearing you with my brother, don't you know how bad that feels!" Jessica was moved that Puma cared. Puma discouraged Willy's affection, though:

"Why you going out with her? She's a slut."

"You picture her the way you want," Willy would reply defiantly. "I'll picture her with me." But it was hard for Willy to hold on to his private image of Jessica when the real girl had such wide appeal.

By November, Willy had also become involved with a girl who lived upstairs. One rainy night, after an awful fight, he kicked Jessica out. Desperate, Jessica called Milagros from a pay phone: she was standing with the twins, drenched, on the street. She had two plastic bags that held all of her things, two two-month-old babies, and no welcoming place to go.

The call didn't surprise Milagros. Plenty of people moved house to house—she had herself—and girls with babies had it extra hard. They would move in with boyfriends and their mothers, but more people created more problems, and the welcomes wore out when the money thinned at the end of the month. Mothers' husbands or boyfriends' brothers or grandfathers and uncles couldn't stop their roving hands. Or a boy could get too possessive when a girl moved into his bedroom and mistake her for a slave, or the mother-in-law wanted a baby-sitter for her other children instead of a daughter-in-law, or the family was just plain mean. Some grandmothers were unable to tolerate another crying baby; some had already lost their own babies—young ghost mothers gone to crack. Or they resented the young lovers, especially if they had no love of their own.

Sometimes girls turned to men like Felix, a friend of Lourdes's who lived on Mount Hope Place, just around the corner from East Tremont. Lourdes would send her daughter to Felix when she needed cash. Occasionally Felix gave Jessica money as well, but Jessica hated going there alone. Sometimes Lillian went along, but Felix drank, and the girls would have to fend him off. Worse-off girls stayed in abandoned buildings, with other teenagers and adults on the run from other crowded apartments. But even for a girl who gave up what she had to— sex or pride or the mere idea of independence—the rate was unpredictable, and for gorgeous, sexually untethered girls like Jessica, the length of the welcomes at other women's apartments seemed especially short. It didn't help that Jessica wasn't in any hurry to clean or cook. Girls with attitude discovered that the shirt your man's sister gave you suddenly turned into a loan, and when a twenty went missing, nobody said it but everybody was staring at you. Even if your man backed you up, you were left in the house while he went to the street. A little brother or sister or nephew or niece might bring you a plate of food or keep you company, but it was impossible to feel at ease.

That night, Milagros did what she'd done for other girlfriends countless times: she took Jessica in. Milagros was living with Puma and Trinket, but she told Jessica to take a cab and meet her at her mother's apartment, in Hunts Point, where Milagros had been raised. Hunts Point was a heavily industrialized area, even rougher than East Tremont. Streetwalkers worked the barren blocks after the warehouses shut. Career junkies dragged themselves to Hunts Point when every other option failed, nine lives lived, waiting to die. Milagros waited for Jessica outside her mother's building and paid the driver. She scooped up the babies and led Jessica up two flights of stairs. She fed Jessica and the twins. The twins fell asleep, but she and Jessica broke night. Milagros's bedroom window overlooked the Bruckner Expressway, and cars and trucks rushed in and out of the city, headed west, to New England, or upstate. They talked till the sun rose, their voices mixing with the traffic din.

Milagros readily devoted herself to Jessica, and Jessica didn't discourage her. When Jessica retreated to Lourdes's a few days later, Milagros offered to keep the twins so that Jessica and Willy could try to work things out. Trinket knew Milagros well enough to recognize the foolishness in such an offer. "Here she comes with her big ass to save the day for another unstable person," Trinket complained. To Milagros she said, "You're making Jessica's life easy. How responsible is that?" Milagros's mother worried that Jessica might take advantage of her daughter's generosity. On the other hand, she herself had been effectively raising a little boy from the building named Kevin, whose mother spent her time running the streets. Milagros assured her mother that she was watching the twins only temporarily.

Things at Lourdes's were getting out of hand. The apartment was filling up—a sure predictor of trouble. A friend of Big Daddy's named Que-Que, whom Lourdes claimed as a long-lost brother, was regularly crashing on the couch. Lourdes had been partying heavily with him and a woman downstairs who practiced Santeria. Willy occasionally brought money for the girls and spent the night with Jessica. Milagros also stayed with Jessica, on the weekends or after work. She had a job as a teller at a check-cashing place. Elaine had moved back from her father's, after a male relative had molested her, and Lourdes ridiculed her for having thought she could survive away from home. Elaine had briefly dated Willy's brother, until Jessica brought her to the hooky house and introduced her to Angel, a wily drug dealer with a good sense of humor and a moped. No one had much time for Cesar, who was running wild.

The line between having fun and getting into trouble wasn't always clear. Lourdes and Big Daddy had always partied on the weekends, but now Lourdes was using during the week as well. She'd also been shirking her wifely duties, and Big Daddy was getting fed up: she disappeared for hours, then whole afternoons, and then it got to the point where she sometimes stayed away all night. She returned in the morning just in time to cook Big Daddy's breakfast and send him off to work, after which she took herself to bed. There were other danger signs: Lourdes, who was vain, cared less about her appearance; her house was no longer spotless; cereal and SpaghettiOs replaced cooked meals.

Big Daddy was a good-looking young man with a job, and he felt entitled to the privileges of his advantages; he'd tired of acting like a husband to a woman seven years his senior who was behaving more like a teenage girl than a wife. He did not mind that Lourdes used cocaine as long as she still had sex with him five nights out of seven, but now she gave excuses; he remembered asking, "You mean I gotta give you twenty to cop to give me some?" Lourdes saw it differently. She needed money—every woman did—but his touch felt unbearable. Although he denied it, she was convinced that he'd cheated on her, and she was sick and tired of serving him.

Big Daddy found better-paying work as a janitor. For a while, he was also dealing cocaine, but he quit because he said that Lourdes kept dipping into his supply. According to his calculations, she was snorting a gram or two a day; she insisted that she knew how to pace herself and that she never used more than half a gram. When Jessica and Milagros wanted to go out, they gave Lourdes cocaine to baby-sit.

By the spring of 1987, the house was packed: Besides Jessica, Serena, Cesar, Robert, Elaine, Lourdes, Big Daddy, Lourdes's alleged brother, Que-Que, and the guests, there was Elaine's boyfriend, Angel, and Shirley, Robert's girl. Elaine was pregnant. Shirley was also pregnant, and her father had kicked her out. Ordinarily, Lourdes used her welfare benefits to pay the basic bills, while Big Daddy covered all the additional necessities and any luxuries. But with the company and the drugs, they could not keep up.

That summer, Big Daddy finally issued an ultimatum: the drugs or him. Lourdes physically attacked him as he began to pack his things; she then went into a seizure, but Big Daddy still left. Lourdes assured her worried children that the separation wasn't permanent—she just needed time to herself. Jessica, who had been sleeping out on the couch, moved into Lourdes's room. Soon afterward, Cesar returned from school and found a man stepping out of the bathroom in a towel. His mother was combing her long black hair, which was wet. "What about Big Daddy?" Cesar asked, devastated. "He only left three days ago. That's not even enough time to work it out!" Jessica was sent back to the couch, resentful and furious. She said, "Big Daddy really loved my mother. My mother left him for an asshole who didn't even pay the rent."

Milagros took the twins for a while, but Little Star stayed behind. Days could pass without her seeing sidewalk, even though lots of people came and went—everyone who was living there, their friends, and friends of friends. When Lourdes was out of bed, she badgered her daughters to take the child outside—both to give her a break and Little Star some fresh air. Sometimes Jessica brought Serena with her on her rounds: to the bodega, to the pay phone, to Puma's drug spot. If someone offered Jessica a ride, though, she left her daughter with whatever friend was willing to keep an eye on her.

That summer, Serena started to cry whenever she peed, and after a few weeks, Lourdes threatened to hit Jessica if she didn't bring Serena to the hospital to be checked. When Jessica and Elaine finally took her to the emergency room, the doctors discovered that she'd been sexually abused. She was two years old. Jessica was detained. A police officer interviewed her and explained that he could not release Serena into her custody. Lourdes had to sign for her.

At home, anger shouted down the sadness: threats sailed; guilt was leveraged; everyone and no one was responsible. Serena had been unsupervised in the company of so many different people it was impossible to know whom to blame. There was that dark-skinned friend of Cesar's who was simple and liked to play with the girls when they were in the tub, and the family friend's brother who'd taken Serena into an apartment to use the bathroom one night while she was hanging around with Jessica on Crotona. How about the boyfriend of Lourdes's who would go into the bedroom at night when the girls were making too much noise and hit them until they cried themselves to sleep? Lourdes ordered the young men who came in and out of her apartment to the hospital for physical inspections. Underneath all the indictments and posturing, however, bad mothering was considered the true culprit: Lourdes blamed Jessica; Jessica blamed herself. And somehow, Serena got lost in the noise. All the women in Serena's life had been sexually abused at one time or another, and their upset seemed to be less about the child's trauma than the overwhelming need, precipitated by the crisis, to revisit their own.

Soon afterward, Lourdes ran away. She made it only as far as Que-Que's brother's girlfriend's, but at first the children didn't know where she was; later, they often couldn't reach her. Elaine got a job at C-Town, a grocery store across the street. She cleaned, cooked, and attempted to retain control over what remained controllable. Robert was still working in Manhattan as a paint-store clerk. On weekday evenings, he took a plate of whatever Elaine had prepared and shut himself in his room with Serena. "The twins had each other. Serena had no one," Robert later said. Lourdes would pass by Tremont when the welfare check arrived, but she refused to come upstairs; Elaine would meet her down by the mailboxes in the lobby. Lourdes kept the small cash allotment and gave Elaine all but $50 worth of the food stamps. Even so, everyone was getting skinny—except for Robert, who stockpiled food in his bedroom and padlocked the door when he went out. Jessica cajoled the girls' fathers to bring by Pampers and milk, but they didn't always come through.

For a time, Cesar and Jessica grew closer. He remembered that "Elaine, she be in her own whole world. My brother was in his little world. Me and Jessica was in the same world." Their world was the street. If she was in a good mood, Jessica was beautiful. She generously shared whatever she had. She set Cesar up with her girlfriends and gave him pointers on how to please women. They had sex with their dates in the same room. "We was real open with each other, it didn't bother us," Cesar said.

At the end of the summer, Lourdes returned home. Que-Que, no longer a long-lost brother, now slept in her bedroom. Robert and Cesar each had a bedroom because they were male; Elaine had reclaimed Jessica's old room, with her boyfriend, Angel; Little Star had a daybed in Lourdes's room; Jessica was still on the couch. When the twins were there, Jessica put them in a crib next to her; they both cried a lot.

Without Big Daddy's contributions—$500 a month in cash, in addition to a running tab at the bodega—Lourdes had to scramble again. No woman with four children could survive on welfare, and now Lourdes also had four grandchildren, another on the way, and a drug habit to support. Jessica and Lourdes fought, ferociously and often. Both women wanted to be taken care of; neither wanted to baby-sit. The cocaine helped Lourdes, but there was never enough of it.

Life at Lourdes's now moved in lockstep with the life of the street. The first week of each month, after the welfare check came in, was best—a time to buy things, to feel some sense of agency. Outside, the drug dealers also enjoyed a surge in business. Lourdes stocked the shelves with food and bought what the house needed from the dollar store—King Pine for cleaning and cocoa butter for healing scars and the comforts of air freshener and hair conditioner. She clanked around the kitchen, blasting Latin oldies, cooking rice with *gandules* and frying her pork chops seasoned with the fresh herb she called the Puerto Rican leaf. She cooked well. Friends and neighbors dropped by, and Lourdes fed everyone.

Everything changed toward the end of the month when the money ran out. Lourdes took to bed. Elaine cooked rice, which Cesar flavored with ketchup. He stole fruit for his family from a nearby Korean market or snatched bread from a grocery store's delivery bin. Milagros brought the children diapers and food. She remembered seeing Cesar drink their Similac, then refill the bottles with sugar water, as he'd seen his sisters do. For longer and longer stretches, Milagros lugged the twins back to her mother's, one under each arm, their skinny limbs dangling.

That winter, in 1987, Lourdes hit bottom. All the jewelry was in the pawn shop. The phone company shut off the phone. Usually, Lourdes managed to pull things together at holiday times. As far back as her children could remember, she had prepared dozens of *pasteles*, her specialty dish, which the bodega by the Grand Concourse would sell for her. She'd spend the extra cash on food and gifts. She would buy each of her children a brand-new outfit, and on Christmas Eve, they would all dress and take the subway to Manhattan to have Christmas dinner with Lourdes's mother, uncles and aunts, and their kids. It was a happy night.

That Christmas, however, they remained in the Bronx, with Lourdes curled up in bed. Even the birth of Elaine's baby boy—Lourdes's first grandson—barely roused her spirits. Occasionally, she shuffled out of her room and made coffee and peed. The dog's messes dotted the narrow hallway, and if Lourdes stepped in a puddle, she'd yell at her children, then call Scruffy sweetly. Scruffy would run with such excitement toward her that he would skid into her legs when he tried to stop. She'd punt him down the hall. By January, Scruffy had learned to cower at the sound of Lourdes's voice.

At the lean end of the month, Elaine's boyfriend, Angel, set Jessica up on a blind date with a drug dealer named Boy George. Jessica was Angel's gesture of thanks to George for giving him work. Angel had met George years earlier, on Watson Avenue. Angel was selling crack then, doing pretty well, and George was just coming up. But Angel, like many neighborhood kids, had enjoyed the lifestyle that accompanied dealing and had started using drugs. Then the money couldn't come fast enough, and now Angel had Elaine and a baby son to support. Boy George, however, had been disciplined. He never touched his product; he rarely drank. In the midst of the hype of the crack boom, he'd had the smarts to concentrate on heroin, and his business was thriving. Years later, looking back, Jessica said, "That was the date that changed my whole way of life."

CHAPTER TWO

It was a double date: Elaine and Angel, Jessica and George. Jessica had agreed to meet this George under one condition. "If he's ugly, bring me home at ten," she said. The evening of January 23, 1988, Lourdes sat by the window gazing down over Tremont. "George pulled up in a car that was like the ocean," Lourdes said. He saluted her through the sunroof of a charcoal-gray Mercedes-Benz 190. Jessica took one look at him and rescinded her curfew. He was so handsome that she was willing to surrender the next day or two.

George's black leather cap matched the black leather trench coat. He'd cropped his dark brown hair close and kept his goatee neatly trimmed. His brown eyes were intent. Like her daughter, Lourdes recognized an opportunity when she saw one, but Lourdes was experienced enough to make a bid for something more reliable than love. Suddenly, she suddenly remembered she could not baby-sit. George understood the cue: he gave Lourdes some high-quality cocaine and $1,000. It wasn't the first time he'd heard a defensive response like hers, *Baby, you can keep my daughter out all night.*

"She just sold her to me for a thousand dollars," George later said. "I could have been a serial killer and sliced her up, and she just sold her to me for a thousand dollars." A thousand dollars was nothing to George. At the time that he and Jessica met, his heroin business grossed over $500,000 a week.

Lourdes's recollection of meeting Boy George did not include this unmatronly trade-off, but she did recall having a vision whose warning she later shared with Jessica, and Jessica failed to heed: "There will be a man in your life. He is from another road, a high, tight, dangerous road. And if you cannot stay on that road, you should not stay with that man." That night, however, Lourdes sniffed coke and baby-sat.

Out in the Mercedes, George popped in a cassette of Guns N' Roses and sped off. Jessica was intrigued: George listened to rock and roll, like a white boy. He liked R&B music, but the lyrics, all the whining about hardship and heartache, irritated him. George took them all to the movies, to *Eddie Murphy Raw*, and treated them to dinner. Then he suggested they go clubbing. Jessica had dressed conservatively. ("You know how when you go on a blind date you don't really know what to wear?" she later said.) She asked George to stop by her mother's so she could change.

When she reappeared, George asked, "What happened to the girl who I went out with? You sure you the same girl?" Jessica called her club-style dressing *puta*. Contact lenses had replaced her eyeglasses. Her hair, which had before been pulled into a bun, now fell around her neck in a soft, loose mane. She'd slipped out of the long skirt and blazer and squeezed into a pair of Spandex leggings and a low-cut body blouse. She'd kicked off the plain pumps and slid on knee-high boots. He wasn't certain he liked the change, but he was impressed by her gameness. Clearly, this was a girl he could take places.

George took her to Club 371, his employees' haunt. A long line of people waited to enter. He strode to the front. Girls eyed him. "I'm gonna get beat up!" Jessica whispered to Elaine excitedly as they followed him in. The hostess seated the foursome in the VIP section, and a waitress appeared with a bottle of Moët. The dance floor smelled of perfume instead of sweat. Jessica got up and performed a little dance for George in front of their table; everyone treated George like a king. They were the only Puerto Ricans; everyone else was black. Boy George preferred not to hire Puerto Ricans. He believed his own kind were more likely to betray him.

The night ended in two $500 suites at the Loews Glenpoint Hotel, in Teaneck, New Jersey. Jessica recalls that George really talked to her, as few dates ever had. He not only asked questions about her hopes and fears, he actually listened to her answers. She told him what she had never told Lourdes: that Cesar's father had sexually abused her for years. George ordered room service. He fed Jessica strawberries in the king-size bed. "I felt like a princess," she said. Finally, life resembled life as Jessica imagined it ought to be: "I felt loved. My knight in shining armor." Jessica was most overwhelmed by the fact that despite all he'd paid for, George didn't expect to have sex. Instead, he held her.

The following afternoon, while George paid the bill, Jessica waited near a waterfall in the lobby for her sister and Angel. The spread of the brunch buffet dazzled her: sliced fruit fanned out on silver trays, cheese cubes stacked near tubed cold cuts, orange juice chilled in heavy crystal glass. There were huge green olives and bread baked into animal shapes. The food banquet filled a large cloth-covered table beneath two ice swans in a melting embrace.

Back on Tremont, Jessica lingered in the passenger seat of Boy

George's idling car after Elaine and Angel went upstairs. She could feel the neighbors' eyes on her in the Mercedes and she loved it. George said, "Get your moms and your daughters ready, I'm taking you out to eat." He'd return and collect them in an hour. He told her to be on time. He did not like to wait.

Jessica stripped and jumped into the shower. She told her mother to dress and get the girls ready. Lourdes pulled on jeans and a clean T-shirt, dressed the three girls in what she could find and brushed their hair. She assumed they'd eat locally—perhaps a seafood place on City Island, but more likely White Castle or take-out Chinese. But George liked surprises. He'd even switched cars, exchanging the Mercedes for one of his BMWs. He took them to an upscale Cuban restaurant in Manhattan, Victor's Café.

Signed photographs of celebrities and boxers decorated the walls. The maître d' recognized Boy George. Lourdes hid behind the menu. For the price of one meal, she noticed, she could feed her five grandchildren for a week.

"Get whatever you want," George told her. "Don't worry about what it costs." Unasked, the waiter uncorked a bottle of Moët.

The ride home was slow and dreamy. Jessica didn't often drink, and she was giddy from the champagne. They got stuck in traffic, but the BMW felt airtight, like a little house. George invited Jessica to open the glove compartment. He had photographs there from a recent trip he had taken to Hawaii. The farthest Jessica had traveled was to Bear Mountain, an hour north of the city, on the picnics her family had taken with Big Daddy.

A man selling roses approached George's window. Each stem was wrapped in cellophane and tied with a crimson bow. George bought one for Jessica and one for Lourdes. The man moved toward the next car. George called him back and said, "As a matter of fact, mister, give them all to me." The man passed three buckets' worth of roses through the tinted window. Jessica received them like a beauty queen. Roses covered her lap, and her mother's, and some fell to the floor. They brushed the feet of her daughters, who'd fallen fast asleep, their bellies full.

Not long after their first date, Jessica paged Boy George from a pay phone on the Grand Concourse. Snow was falling. Jessica hadn't heard from him. She did not have a winter coat. The damp had crept from her penny loafers into her bunched-up athletic socks.

She punched in her beeper code—176. Most girls used the number of the street nearest their block, as did the managers of Boy George's drug crew. Sometimes the beeper numbers were messages, a dialect—911 (for an emergency), 411 (you have or need information), 3333*14 (Hi, baby), 3704*14 (Hi, ho). Similarly, if you read the screen upside down, 3704*550 roughly translated to "asshole" and 038*2**06*537 to "Let's go to bed" (69 being a possible further specification of that). Boy George used 666. He got a kick out of the satanic implication of the code. He was known for having an evil temper, and by then had been involved in several shootouts, yet he never missed a chance to intimidate. One of Boy George's workers returned the call from Grande Billiards. George went on with his pool game.

"I'm calling for Boy George," the worker said.

"Oh, hello," Jessica remembers answering in her softest voice, just loud enough to be heard above the traffic. "I was wondering if you could do me a favor." Jessica had opened many conversations in her life exactly like this. She'd request money, then explain for as long as necessary, facts toppling more facts like a snake of falling dominoes: she needed a ride; she didn't have money for a cab; she needed a ride to a friend's house to collect $20; the girl owed her the money; she needed the money to buy milk for her hungry girls.

Boy George took the receiver. His voice was calm but sharp. "Listen, if you are calling me just for money, don't call. Don't you call me for money."

"Mnnn," Jessica said.

"Where you at?"

"A Hundred and Seventy-sixth and the Concourse."

"Stay there. Someone will be by to pick you up."

The worker delivered her to Grande Billiards. She didn't go in. She waited in the backseat of the car. Eventually, Boy George joined her, with three friends. Again, she asked him for money.

His voice turned impatient. "I only like to say things once. If you calling me for money, don't call."

"Fuck you," Jessica snapped.

In retrospect, Boy George thought he should have served her with a proper beating. Instead, he ordered the driver to head for Lourdes's building. He dragged Jessica from the car and frog-marched her up the stairs. He noticed that she was wearing the same pair of jeans that Lourdes had worn to Victor's Café.

"Whose jeans are those?" he asked.

"They mine," said Jessica.

"Why did your mother have them on then?"

"It's not like what's mine is mine. We the same size. We—"

"Shit," he said. For the time being, he gave her a polo shirt he'd bought from the Gap.

On George's next visit to Tremont, he and Jessica sat on the sagging couch in the living room. The twins, in their crib by the drafty window, cried inconsolably. Scruffy barked. The TV blared. Cesar rolled through with some of his tough-looking friends. George despised disorder. He remembered thinking, "What the fuck is going on here? This is no type of an environment for a female to raise children in."

"I'm tired," Jessica said.

"Then go to sleep," George said practically.

"You sitting on my bed right now," Jessica said with a trace of impudence.

"It's one of those foldout things?"

No, it was just a couch. Someone had carved initials into the wood frame. The cushions had done double duty as a mattress for years. George inspected the kitchen. Chunks of plaster were missing from the wall. He opened the cabinets—roaches. He checked the refrigerator. There wasn't even milk to shut those children up. "There was nothing," he recalled. "There was nothing in that subway station."

Several hours later, two of his employees returned to the apartment. They lugged bags and bags of groceries from Food Emporium. Cesar rushed to his bedroom window and looked down to the street. Two Jeeps, parked on Tremont, were still stuffed with food.

"There was so much food that the bags didn't fit in the kitchen," Cesar said. "There was food in my room under the bed." Chicken, pork chops, and steak filled the refrigerator and the freezer. There was turkey and ham. Lourdes sobbed as each grocery bag passed under a lucky horseshoe she had nailed above the door. "No one ever done this for me," she said, even though the bounty was intended for Jessica and her girls.

"He got everything," Jessica said. "Everything." There had never been enough, and now, when a need was suddenly met, the assistance inspired suspicion and scorn. It was as if the gesture exposed a vulnerability so great that it immediately had to be dismissed. Jessica and Lourdes combed through each bag marveling, but also assessing whether George had overlooked anything. He hadn't. He'd even bought a flea collar for Scruffy.

CHAPTER THREE

Not everyone survives being rescued. Cesar's nemesis lived in the tenement next door. Rocco was half-Italian and nine years older than Cesar, with thick, dark brown eyebrows that accentuated the funny repertoire of expressions animating his rubbery face. The first time they spoke, Cesar, who was then twelve, was crying on the stoop with his head in his arms. The public display of vulnerability surprised Rocco: Cesar was famous around the neighborhood for taking punches with as much spirit as he dished them out. Rocco had heard the stories—how Father Tom from the Christian Church had barred him from game night for breaking windows, stealing pool balls, and whacking other kids with the cues. Rocco had once watched Cesar take on a much older boy easily twice his size: Cesar barreled into him with everything he had and didn't stop swinging until the guy left him in a heap. "He always had a black eye or swollen lips and was always running, with kids chasing him," Rocco said, bemused. That afternoon, Rocco asked what was wrong; it turned out Cesar had a terrible toothache—probably from the candy he sometimes ate for breakfast. "I think from there I started liking that crazy little kid," Rocco said. He would know Cesar for many years, but he never saw him cry again.

The friendship took a while to develop. Rocco was training as a boxer, busy with his girlfriend, running around with a crew of guys his age, edging in and out of crime. Cesar was busy sprinting around the warm-up track of a criminal life—roofing other children's balls, stealing bikes, fighting, fighting, fighting. Sometimes Cesar watched Rocco practice boxing in the back alley or in the basement; occasionally they played handball together on the corner of Anthony, at Cesar's elementary school.

One summer night, Rocco was going to night pool, and Cesar, who'd just graduated from sixth grade, tried to tag along. The older boys were strapped—carrying guns—because they were a group of Puerto Ricans and the swimming pool was in Highbridge, a predominantly Dominican neighborhood. Cesar begged to go, but Rocco said he was too young for trouble. But then a few months passed, and Cesar sprang up. "Damn,"

Rocco said, "you got big, how old are you now?" Cesar lied and told Rocco he was sixteen.

By the spring of 1987, as things fell apart at Lourdes's, the boys were hanging out in earnest. Rocco had time for Cesar, and Cesar gave Rocco a second childhood. When Rocco had been Cesar's age, his father wouldn't even let him outdoors on summer nights; now they dropped eggs on unsuspecting pedestrians and hopped turnstiles and jumped onto moving subway cars and stole Chinese takeout and chased girls. "I was twenty-two, going on twelve," Rocco said. He'd rap on Cesar's bedroom window from the fire escape. When they had money, they'd eat a late breakfast of beef patties in coco bread at Skeebo's, a Jamaican restaurant on Tremont, then head up to Moody's, Rocco's favorite record store. Rocco taught Cesar boxing moves and brought him along to Gleason's, his boxing gym in Brooklyn. Cesar jumped at any chance to prove worthy of Rocco's friendship.

Rocco's role model had been his uncle Vinny. Vinny was a longtime heroin user with throat cancer and a fairly successful illegal career. Unlike Rocco's father, who did nothing but work and come home tired, Vinny exuded seventies cool—dark shades, long black hair slicked back into a ponytail, jailhouse tales and tattoos. Vinny had had a tracheotomy; his raspy voice reminded Rocco of the Godfather. When Vinny told his nephew, "I'm never gonna die," Rocco believed him: his uncle Vinny had been in and out of prison, shot at, stabbed, even hit by a city bus. Vinny told Rocco that he could succeed at crime as long as he stayed away from drugs and didn't trust anyone.

"Vinny raised me to be streetwise," Rocco said.

Cesar said, "Rocco raised me to be a criminal."

By the time Big Daddy left, Cesar and Rocco had renamed themselves 2DOWN and graduated to more serious crimes. Cesar didn't make it to junior high.

As it turned out, Cesar and Rocco were to be separated by a crime that neither of them had committed. During the long free days and endless nights, 2DOWN joined with other boys in other crews named Showtime and ABC. Both Cesar and Rocco happened to be in Echo Park one fall afternoon when an argument over a basketball erupted into a shooting spree. Usually, the cops weren't so concerned about hoodlums shooting at one another, but this time a bullet had grazed a two-year-old. When the police started rounding up the kids in the neighborhood with reputations,

Lourdes scuttled the boys to Spanish Harlem, where Cesar's father kept an apartment. After only one night, however, Rocco suggested they move on: Cesar's father had an outstanding warrant, and Rocco worried that he might try to get rid of it by turning them in.

The following morning, Cesar returned to the Bronx; Rocco went to work out at Gleason's, where his trainer, who'd read about the shooting in the paper, convinced Rocco to go to the police. Rocco was interrogated and released, and when he caught up with Cesar, he convinced him to follow his example. Shortly afterward, however, two Showtime boys were arrested for the shooting, and the word on the street was that Rocco had ratted. Cesar was incredulous. Until that point, his trust in Rocco had been total; now his disappointment was complete.

After his break with Rocco, Cesar continued to hang out with Show-time and ABC. He was loyal, and now he carried a snub-nose .38. Guys invited him along when they needed backup for their beefs—or someone crazy enough to stay up front. But then, one night in Manhattan, a fight broke out in a Times Square arcade while Cesar was playing pinball; he tried to run, but the police caught up with him and confiscated his gun. Once he was no longer armed, the older boys weren't so interested. Cesar was learning—by painful trial and error—that lots of boys talked a good game about the thug life, but when it came to taking action, they came up short.

That winter was bleak; after the family's dizzying encounter with Boy George, the cupboards were soon bare again. Jessica clung fiercely to her fantasy of being rescued. Cesar recalled how she paged Boy George constantly: "My sister burned that beeper up." In the spring of 1988, George finally called her back and gave her a job. He needed more millworkers to process his new shipments of heroin. Cesar helped Elaine bag groceries at C-Town, and she gave him food money, but she had other problems: Angel had been arrested on a drug charge and was stuck in a Massachusetts jail. After Elaine bailed him out, Angel went to work at George's mill. Even Milagros worked the table. Cesar asked George to hire him, but George refused; Cesar was too young.

Street life warmed up with the weather and, more than ever, Cesar wanted to get away from his block. Trouble never finished. He wanted to avoid the messes he'd started, the awkwardness with Rocco, the familiar boredoms, and the burden of having to fight anyone who bad-mouthed his family. Sometimes he rode his bike to visit Hype, a boy he'd met months earlier at a party. Hype ran with The Andrews Posse—TAP—

whose turf was at the other end of Tremont, but he also did his own thing. Hype's independent streak appealed to Cesar, and the feeling seemed mutual. Cesar was also on the lookout for new girls.

Girls tended to stay close to home, as if they were literally tethered to their blocks. Some hung around in front of their mothers' buildings. Others weren't allowed outdoors at all. Girls were anchored by younger siblings or their own kids or the unspoken laws of being girls. "Girls don't go as far," said Tito, one of Cesar's Tremont friends. "Boys want to see the sights. We like pioneers." Beautiful sights were girls on their way to buy groceries for their mothers, or girls wheeling laundry to the Laundromat, or girls taking little kids to the park. Boys roamed. Girls stayed inside and cooked and baby-sat. Girls had responsibilities. Boys had bikes.

One afternoon that fall, Cesar wheeled his bicycle into the hall and carried it down the four flights to the street. He pedaled by the triangular white building on the Grand Concourse that reminded him of a slice of cake, glided down the slope on the other side of Tremont, and headed west.

Strangers stood out in Coco's neighborhood: religious missionaries, immigrants hawking clothes, the occasional reporter scribbling about recent disasters and the stymieing toll of chronic injustice and bad luck. Music was always playing somewhere—salsa, merengue—and there were always customers looking for drugs. The dealers stood on the corners; some wore nameplates around their necks, like gold-dipped nametags for upscale mug shots; others wore coveted charms of guns and dollar signs, and medallions—as big as oversize cookies—of patron saints. The boys tended to hang around the dealers, while the older men sat on milk crates in front of their stoops repeating tired stories, their watered-down hopes dribbling out as the sun warmed their beer. Cesar called attention to himself just by appearing. He sported a red leather jacket with a collar trimmed in what looked like real rabbit fur. Coco was an ebullient girl with a taste for excitement. She noticed him immediately.

Like Cesar, Coco was looking for distraction—anything but the same people doing the same old things. She wasn't a church girl and she wasn't much of a schoolgirl, either, but she wasn't raised by the street. She was a friendly around-the-way girl who fancied herself tougher than she could ever be. She liked action, although she preferred to watch from the periphery. Boys called her Shorty because she was short, and Lollipop because she tucked lollipops in the topknot of her ponytail; her teacher called her Motor Mouth because she talked a lot. Coco's friendly face held the look of anticipation even in repose.

That afternoon, she and her best friend, Dorcas, were looking out of Dorcas's mother's third-floor bedroom window, as they often did after school—knees balanced on Dorcas's mother's sinking bed, elbows planted on the ledge. The window overlooked University Avenue, a main artery that ran through Morris Heights, where Coco lived. The bedroom window gave the girls a good view of the bodega on 176th near Andrews Avenue, "right where they sell drugs at," Coco said. Sometimes Coco propped herself up and out of the window altogether, her square upper body pushing out from the brick wall as if she were a wooden figurehead jutting from the bow of a ship. But her brown eyes weren't squinting to see the horizon. Coco lived in the present; she was looking down, over the street. The bodega's appeal for the girls was the boys their own age fooling around out front: boys talking to other boys, boys eating Cheez Doodles, boys idly bouncing basketballs, boys in cleats, boys with their boom boxes, on the way to Roberto Clemente Park for handball or to Aqueduct to finish twelve-hour shifts dealing drugs.

In other windows were grown women—mothers in their twenties and grandmothers in their thirties, older women weathered by years of poverty's slamming seas. These women rested their fattening elbows on flattened pillows, cushioning the edge of the window frames. The much older women—the great-grandmothers in their fifties—had lost interest in the drama: they kept the curtains closed. Coco, however, courted consequence; she was still a girl, and she still assumed a connection between what she was doing and what she wanted and what might result. And what she wanted right then was the fine light-skinned boy in the red leather coat on the street below, straddling his bicycle seat.

Cesar's friends called him Casper because he was so white. His graffiti tag names, which he'd scrawled in fat letters on most of the buildings near his mother's block, were LC (Lone Cesar) and PBC (Pretty Boy Cesar). He also used Big Rock, but he preferred PBC. He covered a mole on his substantial forehead with the band of his baseball hat, which he always turned to the back. He was self-conscious about his ears. He thought they were too small and that they stuck out. Coco knew only what she saw—an agile boy with full lips, serious brown eyes, and a flat nose, who knew how to dress. Cesar's sneakers were scuffless. His clothes were pressed and clean.

"Damn," Coco said to Dorcas. "That guy look good." He wore his curly blond hair short, in an Afro. He walked sexy, dipping his slender hips as he loped. He squinted as though he had just sucked on a lime. Coco could not quite keep him in view because he kept moving and cars kept driving by, getting in the way. He went into the bodega, then reappeared. She lost him in the cluster of boys by the battered pay phone. She caught sight of him again. Then he was gone.

Some days later, Coco and Dorcas left their window post and stood out in front in the shade of Dorcas's mother's building, across the street from the bodega. The move was strategic; they stood at boy-level now. Coco may have been shameless about flirting and flaunting her chubby body, but she liked whom she liked and, in her own time, she would let the lucky boy know. When Cesar showed up again, she smiled her crumpled smile and gave him her best eye—a raccoon eye, because Coco outlined her eyes with liner, applied as thick as crayon. But Cesar didn't seem to notice her. Coco's boyfriend, Wishman, foiled the next attempt, and Cesar had left by the time she'd shooed him away.

Coco next saw Cesar when she was walking to the store. Cesar blasted out of a nearby pool hall, chasing a man he stood no chance of catching. As he passed her, he spit out a Now and Later candy in a spray of blood, and a stream of obscenities followed. It turned out that the man had wrongly accused Cesar and his friends of overturning his car, which he'd parked in front of the pool hall, and when Cesar had cursed the man out, the man had pistol-whipped him. Now Cesar was scrambling for backup, trying to mobilize The Andrews Posse. The challenge was, as always, to get the boys organized. "Ooh," Coco remembered thinking, "my baby's gonna fight." Coco was a member of TAP's unofficial auxiliary. Boys needed girls at times like these as decoys. Police were less likely to stop a boy accompanied by a girl. Coco grabbed the arm of a boy her sister used to like.

And that's when Cesar noticed Coco—which placed her in a quandary: she didn't want Cesar to think she had a boyfriend besides Wishman, but if she let go of the other boy's hand, he could get into trouble, and that would be her fault. To her relief, the moment dissolved in the ensuing commotion, all the yelling and jostling and undirected threats. Everyone assembled, eventually, but by then the pistol-whipper had long since fled.

Yet the incident did its deeper work: the outburst relieved frustration and gave the bored teenagers something new to talk about. Revenge provided an excuse to connect, and another sort of hormonal communication replaced the desire for a fight. Cesar did not speak to Coco, and Coco kept the most important questions to herself. Did he have a girlfriend?

What did he think of her? Darkness descended over University and it was growing cold, but the headlights from the cars felt summer bright.

The smallest hope had a way of vaulting Coco into overdrive; just on speculation, she broke up with Wishman. She needed him out of the way in case Cesar wanted her. Wishman acted unconcerned, but Wishman's mother, Sunny, told Coco she was sorry to hear of the split. She liked Coco: Coco struck her as the type of girl who could anchor a restless boy like Wishman without expecting too much. Sunny had hoped for this match, since trouble seemed the destination of this particular son. Sunny, who was large and easygoing, could tell that Coco had heart—that she could hold her own in a fight—but she also possessed a sweetness. Coco wasn't greedy. She didn't curse. She was happy to feed Sunny's baby and change a diaper and go to the store to buy Sunny a loosie when her Newports ran out. Sunny would never tell Wishman what she thought—she did not want him all into her business, either—but she memorialized her hope for his softer landing by taping Coco's photograph to the refrigerator door. Now Wishman would be reminded of Coco every time he got a drink.

Coco lived in the heart of the inner city, but to her it was more like a village: her world was made up of roughly five square blocks. Its emotional center was her mother's apartment on the top floor of a six-story building off University Avenue. Just down the street was a high-rise housing project that staggered back toward the Deegan Expressway. The projects were another country; Coco traveled there only with her mother, Foxy, and her stepfather, Richie, who liked to do battle on the handball courts. Coco visited other outposts more often: the emergency rooms of North Central and Bronx Lebanon, where Coco waited for hours whenever her younger brother had a seizure or her older brother had an asthma attack; her grandmother's apartment, a five-minute walk away; the apartments of friends, who were mostly relatives by blood, and who hosted birthday parties, baby showers, christenings, and coming-home parties whenever the prison let somebody's son or boyfriend out. There was Burnside Avenue, where Coco went shopping whenever her mother had money for the big purchases—shoes and coats. There was Fordham Road, where she attended school.

And yet there were important distinctions within this circumscribed world. Church people generally lived their lives separate from the people who hung around outside. Some working people kept their kids on lockdown to protect them from the street; some kids stayed outdoors, afraid of what awaited them inside. Everyone traversed the same stairwells and corner stores and bus stops, but sometimes moving in opposite directions. There was a kind of swing shift: the hanging-out folks straggled home as the working people headed out; the working people returned just as the streets were heating up. Even within households, these tensions persisted: Foxy worked full-time, while Richie, her longtime boyfriend, was a heroin addict; Coco loved the street, but her older sister, Iris, was a homebody.

Trying to do right wasn't necessarily rewarded: the bulk of the housework fell to Iris. In fact, Iris also shouldered a fair share of the parenting: Foxy managed a clothing store called the Rainbow Shop, and she didn't get home most nights until ten or eleven. Iris cooked, fetched Coco from the corner, and fielded phone calls from the schools, where Coco and Hector, the youngest, were always getting into fights. Foxy liked to say, "I have to kick Iris's ass outside and kick Coco's to stay in."

That fall, however, Foxy was easing up on Coco because she had more pressing worries; Iris was pregnant, at fifteen, and threatening to move out. Foxy liked Iris's boyfriend, Armando—the teenagers had met at a summer youth program, and Armando was devoted and responsible—but Foxy didn't see how she could manage without her eldest daughter; Iris made it possible for Foxy to work.

Iris didn't want to abandon her mother, but she longed for peace—a peace she hadn't even known was possible until she'd spent two quiet weeks with a family upstate one summer, as a camper with the Fresh Air Fund. She hated the constant fighting at her mother's; someone was always taking someone else's something, someone needing or getting hit or crying or complaining or bickering. Iris had enjoyed the refuge of Foxy's sister Aida, who lived in New Jersey, but Aida had recently started using drugs, overwhelmed by problems of her own. Before she fell in love with Armando, Iris hid out in the bedroom she shared with Coco and entertained herself by rearranging the furniture and changing the clothes on her Barbie dolls. Now, she hid out in Armando's room.

Iris also hated Foxy's boyfriend. Richie was unemployed, and because Iris stayed indoors, she got the brunt of his restlessness, some of which he subdued with heroin. Iris was tired of serving him—preparing his coffee, watching his nature shows instead of cartoons, and after he nodded out, dousing his cigarettes. Once, Richie overdosed in the bathroom while Foxy was at work. Coco screamed hysterically, and their older brother, Manuel, ran to get a neighbor, but Iris prayed that Richie wouldn't make it.

Iris had hated her own father, too. She remembered doing cartwheels in the hall at school when she received the news that he had died. Coco, who was eight at the time, scratched her face until she bled. She had been his favorite. When Coco was younger, and he tossed her in the air, Iris would try to distract him, so he would drop her. Or Iris would hide beneath the bed with the cat, tease the cat to the point of torture, then throw it at her father's feet and watch him get clawed. She cooled his diabetes medication in the freezer. When Foxy finally kicked him out, Iris was secretly pleased. But as far as Iris was concerned, Foxy had simply traded one useless man for another. Now Iris's pregnancy made her more outspoken, and she disrespected Richie to his face.

Coco, on the other hand, concentrated on Richie's positive qualities. He was handsome—light-skinned, with blue eyes—and he and her mother matched: Foxy had green eyes and platinum-blond hair. They looked beautiful together when they danced, and he made her mother happy sometimes. Richie also took the time to teach Coco the Hustle. He was intelligent; he read books; he registered Coco for her first library card, and he helped her with her homework. Ever since Iris had come out pregnant, Richie had been warning Coco to guard herself and aim for a better life.

Exactly how she was supposed to do this was unclear, but Coco might have instinctively understood that success was less about climbing than about not falling down. Since there were few real options for mobility, people in Coco's world measured improvement in microscopic increments of better-than-whatever-was-worse. These tangible gradations mattered more than the clichéd language of success that floated blandly out of everyone's mouth, like fugitive sentiments from a Hallmark card. Girls were going to "make something of themselves" as soon as the baby was old enough; boys were going to "do right" and "stay inside"; everyone was going back to school. But better-than was the true marker. Thick and fed was better than thin and hungry. Family fights indoors— even if everyone could hear them—were better than taking private business to the street. Heroin was bad, but crack was worse. A girl who had four kids by two boys was better than a girl who had four by three. A boy who dealt drugs and helped his mom and kids was better than a boy who was greedy and spent the income on himself; the same went for girls and their welfare checks. Mothers who went clubbing and didn't yell at their kids the next tired day were better than mothers who did.

Whenever Richie asked Coco about her plans for the future—whenever he asked her even a simple question—she'd say, "I don't know," and he'd say, " 'I don't know' is gonna be your middle name." Richie wanted Coco to think ahead, but his advice was vague: "Always have a plan A, and behind that, always have a plan B." When it came to garnering heroin money, Richie worked the entire alphabet. He had once fallen off a fire escape while attempting to rob a neighbor and broken both his wrists and ankles. He had then filed a lawsuit against the landlord, claiming that the fire escape was unsafe. But Coco could see that even the most inventive plans routinely failed and that Richie's needs still often came down to Foxy's salary. Sometimes Coco would hand over her allowance to stop the arguing; she couldn't stand to see Foxy upset and Richie heroin-sick.

That chaotic autumn, Coco's only plan was Cesar, who had yet to speak to her.

At first, Cesar noticed Coco the way he noticed all kinds of girls. She was pretty, "real short and thick." He wanted to have sex with her. His friend B.J. told him to forget it: Coco was a virgin. Cesar wanted her even more.

The high days of virginity put a girl in demand. For the girls, it was not simply a state but an asset that gave them a rare and coveted form of power; virginity could put sneakers on your feet. Ideally, it was something that a girl could make up her own mind about, something that really mattered. And, unlike good looks or real fathers or money, virginity was democratic. Even skanky girls who had it—while they had it—possessed something tangible and clean. For boys, catching a virgin was an accomplishment. It was like winning the dice games—hope skimming the sidewalk, playing calculated odds. Getting a virgin, they told one another, meant a lifelong open door: girls always held a soft spot for their first.

"Yo, forget about her, man," B.J. said to Cesar, "she won't give no sex up." Wishman had not had any luck.

And Wishman had tried. Coco had once given sex to Kodak, he reminded her. He'd say, "You let Kodak. You know I shoulda been your first." Coco agreed. It had mortified her that her brief, disappointing encounter with Kodak had been broadcast along her block like a street fight or a bust. She had since resolved to keep her romantic interests to herself. Coco may no longer officially have been a virgin, but she was as close to a virgin as you could get. Her pact of privacy did not exclude confiding in Dorcas about Cesar, however, both because Coco was no good with secrets and because they were best girlfriends, best friends for life.

Cesar wasn't the only boy who had noticed Coco's chunky figure and appealingly sassy attitude. Her body had long generated unspoken acknowledgments. But now she'd entered the dangerous age, stepped into the open marketplace, and the desire behind men's eyes came out in compliments and crude remarks. Smooth offers chased appraising glances. Boys lobbed aggressive comments, begging for a response. Older women warned her off:

You think he's so wonderful? He ain't so wonderful, ask him where he been!

Let me tell you, baby, he might buy you sneakers but he ain't gonna pay the rent!

Check you out, Shorty!

Look at the way she walk!

Whatchu do, paint on those pants?

Their banter supposed that men never passed up sexual opportunity and that young girls were good for little more than waving the chance at them. Men will be men. Boys were worse. Girls were naive, stupid. To Coco, the women's warnings sounded like jealousy, as if they wanted their dire predictions to come true. They seemed eager for the girl to lose what made her powerful. If older girls and women were supposed to have the knowledge and teach girls about love, the way they went about it wasn't right. Coco noticed such discrepancies.

Cesar thought Coco sounded like a challenge, and he loved challenges. His friends were always daring him to do crazy things. Once, to Rocco's great amusement, Cesar had undressed at the dry cleaner's and walked home, along Tremont, in his underwear. Cesar already had a way with women—real women (his mother's friends), young women (Jessica's friends), and girls his age. He varied his approach—from nice guy to bully—depending upon the girl. He bet B.J. $100 that he could have sex with Coco within two weeks: her panties would be the proof. And although he had never even spoken to her, Cesar promised B.J. that Coco would deliver the evidence herself.

Freed from school one afternoon, Coco and Dorcas headed for the bodega on Andrews Avenue. Coco had her black hair pulled up severely, with a dollop of Vaseline on her bangs to tame the curl, and two lollipops stuck in her ponytail. Her skin shone. She used Vaseline as a moisturizer, but also to protect her from scarring if she got into a fight. Conspicuous signs of wear were shaming in the ghetto, which was partly why Coco liked her clothes neat and new. "That was one thing, my mother always tried to keep us in style," Coco recalled. She preferred shirts that exposed her midriff, and tight pants or short-shorts that showed off her thighs. The pants in style were called chewing gums because they stretched. Foxy bought Coco a pair in every color—blue, red, green, yellow, black, and pink. Foxy got a 30 percent discount on everything she bought at the Rainbow Shop. Coco was extremely proud of her thickness, which the chewing gums did right by. She said, "I used to rock those, they used to cling to my butt, I used to love it." That day, Coco wore a turquoise Spandex pair. She swished her way into the bodega. The cleats on her tiny feet clacked against the floor.

"Yo, what's up with that girl?" Cesar asked.

"Yo, what's up with your friend?" B.J. asked Dorcas. "My friend thinks she's nice."

Coco returned to the sidewalk, and Dorcas filled her in. "Why can't he talk for himself?" Coco said pertly.

"I can talk for myself," Cesar said.

"So what happened then, why you telling my friend?" Coco asked. She pursed her lips in one corner, lifted her thick eyebrows, and leaned into her hip. On a woman the position would have looked caustic, but not on Coco. Her nose was small and turned up. Her eyes looked happy and playful; there was hope in them, maybe even trust. Cesar held a pack of Mike and Ikes and sunflower seeds in his big hand. A smile formed on those bee-stung lips. Within seconds, the words spilled out.

"We began to conversate," Coco recalled. Soon, Coco began cutting school.

Cesar found himself actually liking Coco, and so he defaulted on his bet with B.J. He liked her more each time they spoke, and they'd spoken every day. They always had things to talk about. He spent less time robbing and mugging, preferring to visit with her instead. A girl could save a boy from the street, but Cesar wasn't looking to be saved, and Coco wasn't looking to rescue him. She liked the excitement and wasn't thinking further than that. She waited for Cesar in the lobby of Dorcas's mother's apartment building. They talked and talked and then they began to kiss and kiss. They kissed in Dorcas's mother's lobby, in stairwells, on sidewalks, against graffitied walls and ravaged trees. They kissed with Cesar sitting on the hood of a car, bent over Coco's uplifted chin. They began to make love and Coco stayed silly and happy, not scared and sad like other girls he'd been with. She was spontaneous, which was like being with a new girl every day. "It was never the same-old with Coco," Cesar said. "She was adventurous." Cesar wasn't ashamed to introduce her to his friends. Once, Cesar brought a friend to Dorcas's mother's apartment for Dorcas, but the friend wasn't interested. "She was *too* fat," Coco said, and

Dorcas's clothes were stained and worn-out. So Coco outfitted Dorcas in new clothes that Foxy had brought home from the Rainbow Shop. Coco's generosity exasperated Foxy—perhaps because it was a flaw they shared. Then Cesar found a fat friend for the spruced-up Dorcas, and everything worked out.

A few months after Coco and Cesar got together, after kissing throughout one early-winter afternoon, Cesar announced, "Coco, I want to take you somewhere."

"Where?" she asked.

"I want you to meet my moms."

It was a big moment. Coco had never been in Cesar's mother's house. Cesar had not spoken much about his family.

On University, Cesar flagged down a livery cab. They climbed in. Off they went, sinking into the cushiony backseat for the bumpy ride to the east end of Tremont Avenue.

Lourdes placed her hands on her hips and raised one eyebrow as she scrutinized the short girl who sat beside her Cesar on his queen-size bed. The weight of Lourdes's beeper made the string of her apron sag. There had been plenty of girls in and out of this bedroom, but she could tell that her baby cared for this one: he'd tucked a picture of Coco in the edge of his mirror. The girl's feet were swinging. They didn't even touch the floor.

In the silence that followed Cesar's introduction—"Ma, I want you to meet my girl"—Coco noticed that Cesar had inherited his mother's bubble lips. "From all the girlfriends he brung here, from all the girls you seem like you okay, you a nice person," Lourdes intoned. "But let me tell you, I'm going to tell you one thing. One thing I don't like about you." The darkness of Lourdes's eyes emphasized the paleness of her skin. She wore her waist-length black hair in a single braid. The lady knew how to make a pause count for something.

"How you going to say you don't like me, for you just met me?" Coco asked sincerely.

Lourdes ignored her and continued, "That eyeliner, it's got to go. It don't go with your eyes." She paused again. "To be honest with you, baby, it looks like shit." The insult was a gesture of inclusion. "What's your sign?" Lourdes added solemnly.

"Sagittarius," said Coco.

"No wonder! Cuz I'm a Sagittarius!" Lourdes exclaimed. With that exchange, Lourdes and Coco became coconspirators on the subject of

Cesar, whom they both loved. Lourdes found a fresh audience for her old stories, and Coco, just coming up, found a veteran guide for the bewildering turns her life was about to take.

Jessica, who was also home the day Coco met Lourdes, was the most beautiful girl Coco had ever seen: light-skinned, with dead hair like a white girl's, the bangs and feathered edges blown forward like a commercial for shampoo. She also had a perfect body: a big butt without a stomach, nice breasts, and nails polished by a manicurist in a beauty salon. Her wide smile was like Cesar's—sexy—crowded with those same white, even teeth. She smelled like a rich girl—not of the sharp scents you got at the dollar store, but of a name-brand perfume. She was friendly, which surprised Coco, because a girl with all that could have been a snob. Even across the room, the way Jessica spoke felt pressed up close. The day they met, she wore thigh-high black leather boots with pointy toes.

"You could kill mad roaches with those boots," Cesar said.

"Right?" Jessica said, her laughter breathing out like a sleepy joke.

Jessica tried to chat with Coco, but Cesar kept interrupting, and he finally closed the bedroom door. "I don't want you and Jessica hanging out," Cesar told Coco. Cesar liked Coco exactly the way she was. Jessica was an entryway to a lifestyle he didn't want Coco to even understand.

Jessica's life was getting bigger. She was one of Boy George's girlfriends now. She'd head out to the store for milk and not come back for five days. George had already taken her to Puerto Rico and to Disney World. "Here comes your portable sister," Lourdes would quip to Cesar whenever Jessica materialized. She no longer traveled by bus or foot like she used to; she came and went by cab.

CHAPTER FOUR

B oy George's earliest childhood memory is of hot water burning him during a kitchen-sink bath. His next is looking out a window over Tremont and seeing his cat get hit by a car. He remembers crying for the dead cat. "I loved pets. I tried to keep dogs, but they were always getting hit, too," he said. Electrical fires were also common in his neighborhood. Once, while he and his little brother, Enrique, were watching *Laverne & Shirley*, the TV burst into flames. That day, George managed to save his cat. From the sidewalk, he and Enrique and the new cat watched their apartment burn.

After his father left when George was six months old, his mother changed apartments frequently. The family lived on St. Lawrence, on Prospect, on Tremont, east and west. They stayed in the Soundview Projects. They had an apartment across from Woodlawn Cemetery. "We were always moving around," George said. He recalls no childhood friends. Enrique was a sickly, fearful boy. George was the solid one. He was decisive. Said Enrique, "My mother is a heartbroken person. My own heart gets broken quick. But when it comes to heartbreaking matters, George knows how to deal with it professionally. He was the bravest in the family."

George quickly grasped the importance of solving the small problems that can quickly become big problems in the ghetto. Poverty raised the stakes of even ordinary activities, such as walking down the street. George instructed Enrique how to carry himself in public, how to be cautious without looking cautious: "He would always say to me, 'Choose what you want in life. You got to be serious when you do things. You have to stop being a little faggot boy.'" George also taught his brother how to read. He would tell Enrique, "Look, you don't know the words? Break it down."

George said that his mother, Rita, beat them, sometimes with an extension cord. Most mothers hit their children; what was more disturbing to George was the unpredictability of Rita's rage. He ran away for the first time when he was ten. Enrique dropped blankets and clean clothes out the window when his brother appeared on the sidewalk below. George wandered around the wastelands of Hunts Point. He slept on a bench in

St. Mary's Park and washed his face in the dribble of a fire hydrant. He also slept in abandoned cars and once camped out on a bus. At the time, he must have been terrified, but George recast the hardship as an opportunity. "I wasn't a mama's boy no more. I was out on the street by myself. I had to fend for myself. I had to make money for myself," he said. "That taught me responsibility."

When he was twelve, his mother requested a PINS from family court. PINS, the acronym for Parent with a Child in Need of Supervision, gave a judge final say in a child's care and discipline. A PINS was one of the early markers of a troubled kid's life, and it usually meant there had been steady trouble for a while. The authorities sent George to a diagnostic center called Pleasantville, where he stayed for three months. George crossed paths with Mike Tyson, who had also landed in the system. They once argued over a pool game but became friends afterward. George was transferred to St. Cabrini's, a group home in New Rochelle, New York, where he was to stay until he and his mother worked things out. He lived there for three years that he later called the most important in his life.

George welcomed the new routine at the group home, and he was relieved to be away from his mother's dramatic mood swings and capricious violence. He also enjoyed the companionship of the male counselors and credited St. Cabrini's with turning him into a man: "When you're home with your moms and stuff, it's you and your mom and your brother, that's it. I had a chance to spread out, wide, like a wide-angle lens. I got hip to everything that I would need to get hip to and I started analyzing and analyzing."

The four-bedroom ranch housed eight boys. George was the youngest, not yet thirteen. The house sat in the corner lot of a residential street of a working-class neighborhood aspiring to the middle class. The rich folks lived on the hill. St. Cabrini's had a lawn, and fruit trees. George enjoyed his first exposure to raccoons and skunks. He missed the Bronx but resigned himself to life in New Rochelle. "Well, you long to be home, but the reality of the matter is that you're not—that's one," he said. "Two, if the other fellas see you crying and all that—whining—that's gonna be one sign of weakness that they are going to prey on forever and a day. So why cry over spilled milk? You're spilled already."

The Cabrini kids attended the local schools. Most of the residents, who were poor and minorities, kept to themselves, but George didn't aim just to get by. He deployed his sharp sense of humor to make himself a place in his class, and he became known as a practical joker. He joined the New Rochelle High School football team. The local newspaper published his photograph. Invitations came to him for parties held by the popular kids, and he always brought the Cabrini boys along. "George never forgot that his friends were his friends," a counselor remembered.

During one party, George and a few of his Cabrini buddies made off with some silverware. That same night, they burglarized a few other homes. The next day, the police caught up with George at a pawnshop, where he was negotiating with the proprietor. George chose to take the rap for the entire group. He spent thirteen months in detention at Valhalla, a secure juvenile facility upstate, and from there he was sent back to the Bronx.

George returned to his mother's and briefly attended Morris High School, but the arrangement didn't work. She had remarried, and George had his own rules. Morris High School did not hold his interest, and apparently, he wasn't alone; during those years, only 40 percent of its incoming students were sticking around to graduate. He dropped out of school, onto the street again. "I put it on full turbo," he said.

George later tried to explain his ambition: "You can't read about it in books, and you can't look at it in movies. I was born with something inside of me that says, 'George, that's a pretty girl. Go and get her. George, that's a pretty suit—go and get that suit. George, this is something out here, it's *for* you. We don't know exactly how long you'll have it, or how wide a span it'll get, but you could get it and all you gotta do is just put your mind to it. Don't think of nothing else. And ask about it, *think* about it, think *with* it, act like if you were it and change the shoes around like it was you. And then you'll see.' And when you get a feel that you're almost that thing, you reach out and grab it and it's yours." He paused. "You have to have a lot of sleepless nights, but Lord behold, it'll paint a picture."

George's first opportunity, however, seemed to have as much to do with happenstance as with ambition. During those months he lived at home, he sometimes passed by a doughy, bearded guy named Joey Navedo on his way to school; Joey ran a cocaine operation, and one of his spots wasn't far from George's mother's apartment. Joey was a successful businessman. He woke early to ensure that his spots were open and running efficiently. But he was also a sadist with crazy amounts of money. Joey's idea of a practical joke was to fly toward his dealers with his foot on the gas and a bazooka aimed out the window of his latest car. His Thanksgiving turkeys and bags of toys at Christmas did little to allay the threat of his presence; Joey terrorized the neighborhood.

George asked Joey for work, and Joey hired him as a lookout at his spot on 156th and Courtlandt. "I idolized the guy," said George. "He was running around in Benzes and all that good stuff—Porsches, BMWs, he had it all." He had even given one of his girlfriends a silver Cadillac. "I said, 'Shit, I want to be just like him.' " It was Joey who gave him his street name. "It's different," Boy George said. "It's not like calling somebody Chino, or calling them Red or Lefty or Fingers. When you say Boy George, you're talking about the singer or you're talking about me."

Boy George soon became friendly with another of Joey's workers, a boy named Talent. Talent had a female relative who worked in the heroin trade. George decided to switch over from selling coke to selling dope: "Less time and faster money." Boys arrested with heroin received less jail time, too. George worked for the Torres brothers, who dominated the South Bronx market, becoming a lookout on Watson Avenue. He was soon promoted to the position of pitcher, which involved handing out glassines. Before long, he had hooked up with Talent's relative and become a manager. George oversaw the sale of a brand called Blue Thunder at a spot on 166th and Washington.

It was a profitable, desolate location. Rusted stoves jutted out of broken windows. Scrap yards interrupted block after block of garbage lots. At night, packs of wild dogs roamed the streets. The businesses, other than narcotics, were run by tired men in garages that resembled crumbling caves: there were mattress shops, where soiled mattresses were hocked and reupholstered, and auto-repair shops, which did the same with cars. Gunshots and shouts of "Radar!" were regularly heard in the streets. (*Radar* was one of the ever-changing code words warning customers and dealers of approaching police.) The only uplifting sounds, aside from children's voices, came from the determined gospel choir of a nearby storefront church.

Boy George had scaled the hierarchy quickly; he soon learned how to talk the talk, even when he didn't know what he was talking about. One Hundred Sixty-sixth and Washington was an excellent place for the driven young teenager to further prove himself. Lots of managers rolled out of bed at noontime, but Boy George got up early, like his mentor, and made sure the spot was open for the day. He didn't spend the day smoking weed on the corner, or visiting girls. In a business full of deception and conning, George projected reliability and trust. He kept close tabs on the street dealers and maintained the supply. If he received $30,000 worth of work, $30,000 was returned; 166th and Washington cleared an average of $65,000 a week. George paid his people from his 10 percent and delivered the remainder to Talent's relative. At one point, there was a turf war, an innocent bystander ended up dead, and George's reputation was secured. He was only seventeen.

George recruited several of his old Cabrini friends. He also pulled into the driveway of his old group home to show off his first Mercedes and invited the counselor on duty out to eat. "He knew how to present himself," the counselor recalled, "and knew when people were playing a con game on him."

George's living situation was still precarious, though. For a while, he moved in with Talent and his mom, but he also fell in with girls who gave him a place to stay. George and Joey Navedo sometimes shared breakfast at a Crown Donuts, where George had his eye on a smart green-eyed girl named Miranda who worked behind the counter. Miranda lived near his friend Rascal's mother's building. For their first date, George took Miranda and her baby son with him to Rikers Island; while he visited a friend, she napped in the parking lot. George sometimes stayed with Miranda, but Miranda soon discovered that he had another girlfriend— who was pregnant—and she kicked him out. George's other girl, Vada, lived with her mother in Rascal's building. George moved in and Vada gave birth to a son. George named him Luciano. Another girlfriend, Isabel, gave George a second son, but George considered Vada his main girl—his wife.

Meanwhile, Joey Navedo exposed Boy George to other features of the good life. They visited Great Adventure, a New Jersey theme park. Joey introduced George to Victor's Café, the Cuban restaurant where he would later take Jessica and Lourdes. Joey also hooked up George with his jeweler at Norel's, a store in Chinatown. The boys sampled the seats of the exotic cars at car shows and inspected the fine custom work on other drug dealers' expensive cars. They practiced shooting at a firing range in Mount Vernon. They skied the Poconos. George paid attention. He said, "Like a lint brush, I pick up." From Joey, George learned to anticipate the sudden opportunities that characterized the drug business and to be prepared to act decisively. Joey's preferred managerial tool was fear. George picked that up, too.

"It's like a fisherman with a little boat, that's the drug dealer," George later said. "I want to catch the whale. I want it big. I don't want to go through the steps. I want it big because I know I can handle it. Where's the fisherman gonna fit that damn whale? He's gonna have to tug it! But he wants to bring in the mother lode, the catcher, everybody eats, everybody's happy, we can relax. I didn't need a high school diploma to do what

I did. I did what most people are too scared to do, and that's to take control of something very powerful."

In June 1987, the Drug Enforcement Administration, in conjunction with the New York Police Drug Task Force, brought the Torres brothers down. Boy George moved swiftly. Instead of delivering $65,000 to his connection, he set up a processing mill. He bought heroin, mannitol (a dilutant), a glass table, six chairs, a triple-beam scale, and glassine envelopes. Then George, Miranda and a friend, Rascal and one of Rascal's girlfriends, and an older Jamaican man named 10-4 gathered around the table and settled in. The next day, 166th and Washington reopened for business with Boy George's new brand. He named his heroin Obsession. The Obsession logo, stamped on the glassines in red ink, was a miniature king's crown.

10-4 handled the administrative details of the expanding operation, including payroll and personnel. George had met 10-4 during his tenure with a brand called Checkmate. 10-4 drove a livery cab. Before hooking up with George, he had shuttled another well-known Bronx drug dealer on his rounds. Drug dealers often used cabs to make deliveries because livery cabs—a common mode of transportation in the ghetto—were less conspicuous than pricey cars. George had been one of 10-4's biggest tippers. 10-4's war stories impressed George, and whenever he needed a cab, he requested him; 10-4 was his dispatcher code. Sometimes George kept 10-4 on hold for days. 10-4 worked the relationship. A seasoned hustler, he supplemented his income running welfare schemes. Before driving cabs, he'd been fired from the post office for stealing envelopes with donations to religious charities. 10-4 had a knack for helping Boy George with what he needed—phony guarantors for leasing cars; friends in real estate who'd rent apartments under other people's names, to be used for mills; fraudulent business certificates. It was 10-4 who bought Boy George his stamp for Obsession. Shortly after George launched the brand, 10-4 became the organization's right-hand man.

Business grew steadily. Boy George and Joey Navedo stayed in touch. George appreciated that Joey treated him as a peer. Joey provided an introduction to a contact for weapons; he also lured a buyer for some low-quality heroin George needed to unload. Joey even escorted the man to the meeting place, the Baychester Diner, and oversaw the exchange himself. To have found a friend and business ally in the man who had given him his street name seemed to Boy George an auspicious sign.

But Joey Navedo's generosity extended in both directions: for years, he'd been moonlighting as a confidential informant, filing reports with the New York Drug Enforcement Task Force and the DEA. Perhaps Joey's flamboyant disregard for the law had something to do with his confidence in his usefulness to investigators, which granted him a measure of immunity. Duplicity was a taxing fact of ghetto life. The high expectation of betrayal raised the premium on loyalty.

By the time George met Jessica, in 1988, he owned five selling locations and was the youngest major-league heroin dealer in the South Bronx. Obsession ranked as one of the market's most popular brands. He parked a Ferrari, a Lamborghini, a Bentley, and a Porsche in his garages. Through a phony business of 10-4's called Tuxedo Enterprises, George leased a stable of Jettas, Maximas, and other cars for daily use. James Bond, one of George's heroes, inspired the $50,000 worth of special features added to the 190 Mercedes in which he'd taken Jessica on their first date: radar detectors manned the car's front and rear; the license plate slid into a side compartment and a strobe light blinded anyone following him; secret compartments in the door panels and the floor hid weapons and suspicious amounts of cash. One device gushed gobs of oil from the tail, while a hidden switch flipped a box in the trunk that sprayed nail-like tacks.

Meanwhile, the case file for Obsession was growing thick.

During the eighties, a good amount of the heroin on the New York market was controlled by bosses of Chinese social associations known as tongs. The dope traveled through gangs like the Flying Dragons, to which one of George's suppliers belonged. Drug dealers at Boy George's level usually purchased their bulk heroin from middlemen, who controlled quality and flow and marked up the price of their dope 30 to 50 percent. Low-quality heroin, or a lengthy dry spell, damaged the brand, but street dealers had to accept what they could get. The potency of the dope weakened the further it moved down the line.

Relationships with direct sources were nearly impossible for dealers like George to acquire because preventing such connections was crucial to the middlemen's livelihood. But like so much about the drug trade, the game as it was imagined by nonparticipants and described in the press sounded far more organized and sophisticated than what really happened on the street. Dealers made dumb mistakes. Employees overslept. Lookouts watched for girls instead of for undercover cops. Lots of people worked drearily long hours and barely scraped by. Some boys spent down a day's wages on junk food for themselves and their friends. Other workers smoked up their earnings or took an advance on the product and never climbed out of debt. The business earned its reputation for violence, but plenty of people went down for foolish mistakes and capriciousness. For most, living large remained a fantasy. Those who did well in the trade—who survived it and had something to show for it later—tended to be not only ruthless and calculating but lucky. For a time, George was all three.

In April 1988, George's supply underwent a dry spell; he urged 10-4 to keep trying to reach one of his Chinese sources, a guy named Ryan, but Ryan and his people were looking for dope as well. During this time, a young Puerto Rican named Dave introduced George to a man named Pirate, who Dave claimed could help George out. George invited the Chinese in on the deal, and each contributed $300,000 for the much-needed heroin. Boys from both crews surrounded the duplex where the exchange had been scheduled, heavily armed in case something went wrong. And then something did go wrong: Pirate entered the building with the money, but then snuck out an unknown rear exit. Who was double-crossing whom wasn't initially clear, and the situation could have quickly turned into a massacre. But George managed the delicate situation professionally: he reimbursed the Chinese their $300,000 and absorbed his own loss; he should have cased the building himself before the deal went down. "Excuses are for assholes," he often said.

According to Rascal, George drove Dave to the Henry Hudson Parkway, where he made him kneel, then shot him in the head; George told Rascal that if he hadn't gone after Dave, the Chinese would have gone after him. Rascal also claimed that George hired a man named Taz to take care of Pirate, and that soon afterward, Pirate disappeared. George's quick response to the slipup cleared the way for direct dealings with the Chinese connection.

George himself had no patience for overdue accounts: "Don't fall for tricks, about 'Oh, I'll see you tomorrow, blasé blasé blasé,' when you are dealing with someone who owes me money. You say, 'Listen, homie, I want to eat today. So I'm not going to wait to tomorrow to eat. I want to eat right now. I'm hungry. Pay up, dude. That's it.'"

George and the Chinese source, whom he privately called Fried Rice, conducted their business efficiently, scheduling their meetings in the parking lots at Kennedy Airport, on various corners in midtown Manhattan, and in commercial neighborhoods all over Queens. Once the routine was established, Boy George delegated the responsibility to his friend Rascal and another boy who worked for him named Danny. Rascal and Danny were supervised by 10-4.

Rascal and Danny collected the bricks from the source. The bricks were the size of the small boxes of soap from the vending machines at a Laundromat. 10-4 followed twenty or so minutes later with the cash. Or the cash went first, and 10-4 awaited the drop. He once collected in a booth at an International House of Pancakes. Over the telephone, they referred to the bricks as "girls," as in "How many girls do you need?" The $100,000 girls brought back $240,000.

Bricks of heroin were diluted and packaged for retail sale at the mills. Renting a dealer a room for a mill was a better way to make money than renting out your apartment as a stash house: the risk was high but temporary. George rented apartments, or rooms of apartments belonging to his employees, their mothers, girlfriends, or friends. Mills lasted from a week to several months, and the workers moved along if the apartment got hot. Heat usually came from too much human traffic, or from the fumes, which might draw a neighbor's attention and—if bribery or threats didn't work—the police.

George's mills were heavily armed. Robbers worried George. Mills were an obvious source of cash, and robbing drug dealers had become its own lucrative business; dealers rarely reported their troubles to police. At one point, after an attempted robbery at a mill on 213th Street, George briefly relocated to the Manhattan Marriott Marquis.

At first, Boy George had paid someone $50 to deliver the heroin to his store, or spot. Now, delivering the dope to his block managers was a full-time job. Rascal and Danny fed the stores. By this time, George ran five: 166th and Washington, where he had gotten his start; 122nd and Second Avenue; the block-long abandoned building on 139th and Brook; 153rd–156th and Courtlandt, a playground in a public housing development; and 651 Southern Boulevard, better known as St. John's. George, respecting local custom, closed the spots while children walked to and from the school nearby.

Spot managers broke the milled bricks into smaller bundles, and dealers stored them where they could—in mailboxes, under the wheels of parked cars, inside baby strollers, or wrapped in a diaper in a girl's baby bag. The severity of criminal charges depended upon the weight of the drugs one carried, so no one wanted to work around bulk. Accordingly, the lookout carried nothing but information. The steerer brought the customer to the dealer. The dealer took the money. Another steerer sent the customer to a pitcher, who delivered the glassines.

The managers also stored the bricks at a main stash house, usually an apartment or rented room. Ideally, a manager wanted access to several empty apartments within one building to split the stock and the risk. Some managers paid a building super for an empty or illegal unit or bought temporary access from a tenant who'd moved. Some covered the rent for a single mom and threw in milk and cereal money for the kids. If the tenant used drugs, managers could take over the place for little more than a handful of glassines of heroin or vials of crack. Some managers bullied their way into the apartments of former girlfriends—whom they called project holes—and refused to move out.

Profits varied by location: Washington Avenue and Courtlandt and 122nd each generated $40,000 daily; $150,000 was normal for St. John's. George explained that it was "in the right place—good, good junkies, good access of all kinds." Good access meant right in the ghetto, but also right by an exit off the Bruckner Expressway, which made it easy for suburban commuters to pull in, buy their drugs, and get out again. The squalid residential building was in Hunts Point on a stretch that lawenforcement officers called the Westchester Strip. Cars idled three deep, and the constant clog of traffic made surprise visits by the cops almost impossible. Four lookouts were stationed on the sidewalk outside the building; others perched on nearby fire escapes. Two runners steered the long lines of pedestrians into the building; you didn't stop at #1C unless you wanted some of what Boy George's people sold. Cement framed the apartment's thick metal door. Behind the hole in the door stood a pitcher, who handed out Obsession glassines.

Red, yellow, and green bulbs flashed from a homemade panel nailed to the floor. Upstairs, in another apartment, the dealer placed the tiny bags of heroin on a makeshift dumbwaiter and sent them down. The pitcher could only escape the first-floor apartment by going up: he was locked in during the shift, and sheet metal, pipes, and bars barricaded all the windows. Boy George briefed the pitcher. He didn't speak loudly, but he explained the rules only once: "If I look out the window and I could see a cop, I give it the yellow switch. You see it, and you slow down. If there's no movement in the upstairs apartment—no signals coming—you know something's up and you bum rush. Bum rush. If I hit the red switch, pack everything up, get in the dumbwaiter, and go. Green's green, dude. The material come down and the money go up. That's all you need to know, ready? Breakfast or lunch or dinner? We'll send a runner for a hero and one of those big, big Cokes."

At the end of the day, the manager deducted his 10 or 20 percent of the day's profits and paid his lookouts, pitchers, dealers, and any other employees from that. Rascal and Danny collected the rest and delivered it to 10-4 for counting—often in sneaker boxes, a familiar sight around the neighborhood. Business was so good that even with several counting machines and everyone skimming, 10-4 fell garbage bags behind. Every week, he paid himself $12,000 and Rascal and Danny $2,500 each and brought the rest to George. George stored some of his money in safes in empty apartments. Sometimes he crammed duffel bags full of cash in the trunk of a car he'd parked in a long-term garage.

By the spring of 1988, business got even better: George's sources rewarded him for his savvy handling of the Pirate fiasco and let him buy more weight directly, which increased his profit by an extra $100,000 for every brick. Suddenly, George needed new mills and extra workers to process the dope; this was when he hired Jessica.

Jessica may have been desperate for money, but love was what she wanted. She wasn't planning on laboring long as a mill girl. She still had her eye on the boss.

CHAPTER FIVE

J essica was equipped with a beeper and briefed about the company codes. Double 0—00—represented work. Add five to the number before the 00 and that's the time she was due in; arrival times were staggered to reduce suspicion and avert potential robberies. When two mills were open, the number 1 or 2 designated which table she was to report to. Millworkers, like lawyers who worked long hours at big law firms, were collected and delivered home by car service. On Jessica's first day, she rode to work in luxury.

She reported to a mill in an apartment on Holland and Burke, and the apartment impressed her as well. The place had carpeting, a kitchen set, a bedroom set, and a huge TV. Two large glass tables had been pushed together. Garbage cans filled with lighter fluid flanked each end, in case the police arrived (the heroin would be shoved into the cans, and sulfuric acid—kept on the table—would be dumped on top in an optimistic attempt to destroy the evidence). Guns rested on the table in case of stick-ups—.357s and .38s, a .45, Uzis, an automatic shotgun, and a Mossberg.

Preparing heroin was tedious and exacting. The millworkers tended to be girls and women, girlfriends and ex-girlfriends and sisters of ex-girlfriends of male employees. George hired by word of mouth; he held the person who referred a girl responsible for any trouble that followed her. At one end of the table, a worker crushed the brick while it was still in its packaging before cracking it, like an egg, into a metal cup and crushing the chunks into powder. At the other end of the table, someone weighed out mannitol, measuring the chalky substance on what would become a fixture of evidence in the decade's drug trials and a popular reference in gangsta rap: the triple-beam scale.

If the supply had recently undergone a dry spell, less cut was added, and the bags were made bigger to jump-start the sales. As soon as business picked up, however, the bags shrank and the heroin got weaker. If George was at the mill, he added the cut himself. The success of Obsession owed much to its potency; George diluted his dope just like other dealers, but the product he was getting was remarkably pure—87 percent. He compared it to the difference between dollar-store soda and Coke.

The heroin would then be ground in a coffee grinder and repeatedly strained until it was sufficiently fine; then another woman, using playing cards like salad forks, would toss the mannitol with the heroin. Potent heroin was toxic, and the other workers routinely cleared out of the room at this point. Some wore surgical masks to diffuse the noxious smell. The glassines had been stamped ahead of time with the Obsession logo by somebody's sister or mother or grandmother, who did it as piecework at home. Finally, after the heroin had been carefully measured into the glassines with a plastic coffee stirrer from McDonald's, Jessica taped the bags closed. In 1987, soon after Boy George first launched Obsession, his mill processed one hundred to two hundred grams of heroin per day, five days a week. By the time Jessica was hired, the mill regularly processed seven hundred grams every sit-down, or shift.

When George wasn't around, the table could almost feel like family. Workers listened to music and gossiped. A woman might leave the table for the kitchen and cook for everyone. Some sniffed cocaine to stay awake throughout the long shifts. The atmosphere stiffened when George arrived. Some drug dealers believed the best way to protect themselves was to remain hidden, but George had little interest in invisibility. His management style was a familiar combination of bribery and threat. He lorded over the millworkers like an ornery factory owner. He docked workers $300 for showing up late and fired them after one absence—although he often took them back. George also believed in incentives. He sent his table managers and prodigious workers on fully paid vacations to Puerto Rico and Disney World.

George's ex-girl Miranda was managing the table the first night Jessica reported in to work. At the time, Jessica struck her as unremarkable. She worked slowly, and it baffled Miranda why George was bothering with a scrawny girl who complained about the vinegary smell of the heroin. Then Jessica got her temporarily fired. Miranda and another worker were ragging about George's predilection for expensive silk shirts, and Jessica reported the gossipers to George. George rehired Miranda, but from then on, she resolved to keep a close watch on her new coworker. Jessica's mill gig proved short-lived, however; she lasted less than a week.

George promoted Jessica to errand girl and started seeing her regularly. She was pretty, interested without being nosy, quick to recover from his insults, and sharp enough to adjust to the wider world he was inhabiting. He also gave her a place to live: after one of his apartments became hot, he'd rent another and move Jessica into the hot one to cool it down. She shopped for groceries and collected his dry cleaning. Jessica wished for some commitment, but she accommodated him. Sometimes she accompanied him in public, but she often passed the time without him just as she had without the other boys—talking on the phone, cleaning, waiting, watching TV.

George frequently traveled to Puerto Rico, where his wife, Vada, now lived with their son. Sometimes he brought Jessica along; once, he even put her up at the house. George told Vada that Jessica worked for him, but Vada was skeptical: "She must be a good worker if you brung her all the way here." After George gave them both money and sent them off to a mall together, Vada kept needling Jessica: "You sure you work for him? You must be a pretty special worker, his most *favorite* worker." When they got back, Vada reported loudly to George, "Shoo! This girl can talk to men. You shoulda seen the way she was handing out her number!"

"Why you got to say that?" Jessica whispered.

"Why does it matter to you?" Vada answered, not whispering back.

George's rules at home were as strict as those he imposed at the mills: no visitors—not family, not friends. Never give out his telephone or beeper or cell numbers. No one needed to know where he was headed or where he'd been. No one needed to know his real name if they called asking for him by any of the aliases he used—Tony, or Manny, or John—just take a message. Under no circumstances was she to reveal who he was or where she was or where he lived or which of the other apartments were or were not occupied.

Jessica knew the routines of lying and bluffing and keeping secrets. She was better suited to her life as a concierge than as a mill girl. She loved to interact with people, she had a pleasing phone voice, she was personable and organized. She graciously accepted deliveries. She met George's rigorous standards for a clean house. "He always liked everything spotless— house, clothing. He never liked to see anything dirty," Jessica said. "He'd bring home a whole lotta videos and I would just watch TV. I didn't have to get a job. I was to cook and clean and take care of the things, and I would get an allowance at the end of the week."

For the first few weeks, the allowance was excellent—$1,000 or more. George surprised Jessica with jewelry. He didn't want her gold to be thin and bendable, with clasps that broke. It had to be thick. If Jessica liked a necklace—a heart of sapphires, say—George said to his jeweler, "We'll take that, but make it different." He added rubies to her diamond Rolex. He bought her a belt buckle with *Jessica* studded in emeralds. Poverty, which limited neighborhood people to shopping at the same cheap neighborhood stores, meant looking like everybody else. He wanted Jessica customized, like his cars.

Boy George also demanded color coordination. "He matched me up," Jessica said. No white clothes in winter, nothing stained or borrowed, no jeans with the yellow sheen from the cheap soap at the Laundromat, no vinyl belts sewn to the waist of the pants. He drove Jessica to Greenwich Village and introduced her to the $50 rule. Nothing under $50 was to be taken off the rack. No $10 stores, no V.I.M., no Jimmy Jazz, no Payless. He was generous with his money. After he bought her things, he didn't demand sex.

Sex seemed to be less of a lure for George than it had been for other boys. When he was in the mood for it, however, George expected Jessica to do what she was told. Jessica performed the striptease scene from *Nine ½ Weeks*, but George was picky. "We just have to do, exactly, everything that was done," she said. He also liked to act out scenarios from hard-core films. Still, his interest in Jessica was erratic. He wanted her with him, then he didn't. She could shop all day and club all night and then he expected her to be locked down for a solid week. George could be a loving husband in the morning and a landlord the same afternoon: "Get out of here," he'd suddenly say. "I don't want to see your ugly fucking face." Jessica couldn't appease him as she had Lourdes or her other men. It wasn't about giving George what he wanted; subjecting her to the whims of unpredictability seemed to be the point.

As tenuous as her living arrangement was, however, Jessica considered it an improvement. She had everything she needed materially. She had her own bed, space for her own things. Her proximity to someone extraordinary made her special, too. Being one of George's girls was as good as being the wife of an ordinary boy. "Before meeting him, I never had any hope," said Jessica. "The only dream I've ever had was being married, being committed to one man, living in a little house with a fence and little, you know, playground in the back, and a lotta kids." She already had the children but neither father had wanted her. Even her children's love lived elsewhere; when they visited, Brittany and Stephanie cried for Milagros and Little Star cried for Lourdes.

Periodically, George beat Jessica and kicked her out. She'd stay at her mother's, but more often with Milagros, who was then living in an apartment George rented in Riverdale. Milagros had quit her job at the check cashier's to raise the twins. Jessica had promised to pay Milagros $2,000 a month in child support, but George had only paid once. Milagros managed to get by on welfare, supplementing her income by working for George or Puma in a pinch. If Jessica stayed over, they put the girls in strollers and headed to a nearby twenty-four-hour mall. Jessica adored makeup; pharmacies were her favorite stores. She loved beauty products and stocked up on potions and perfumes. She treated the girls to outfits and ribbons. Milagros was too practical to indulge in frills.

Jessica and Milagros always stopped at Toys "R" Us and ended the night at McDonald's, or in the apartment listening to music and playing cards. George had lots of pornography and occasionally Jessica and Milagros sampled his vast collection. They cracked up over the inventive positions and creative coupling in the videotapes. They snorted cocaine. When Jessica would tease Milagros suggestively, Milagros would shoo her away, embarrassed but pleased. Whenever George was ready to take her back, though, Jessica was ready to go. She left her daughters behind with Milagros. Jessica said, "I did just what my mother did to me."

Around this time, Miranda bumped into Jessica in a Manhattan club. The well-dressed bitch—Miranda used the word admiringly—standing beneath the flashing lights of Roseland showed no trace of the skinny aspirant from the heroin mill: she'd fattened up. Jessica had a body now—thickened thighs, breasts you noticed, beauty-parlor hair. With the radar of a wounded lover, Miranda understood the significance of Jessica's ascent in rank. The twenty-two-karat-gold *Boy George* nameplate around her neck flashed a victory sign. Jessica was no longer George's around-the-way girl, hidden in a stash house. She had been promoted yet again: Jessica was one of Boy George's mistresses now.

During the summer of 1988, Boy George ran into Cesar, who was standing with Rocco on Tremont Avenue. Cesar and Rocco hadn't mended their friendship, but they were on speaking terms. George had a gash on his hand. He explained to Cesar and Rocco that he'd been in a street fight with a guy who really knew how to move.

"So what did you do?" Rocco asked.

"Jumped him," George said. The next time, however, George wanted to do better than improvise. He remembered that Rocco had boxed and asked him about finding a trainer. "Who's the best guy at Gleason's?" George asked.

"Panama," said Rocco. They agreed that Rocco would introduce them.

"Tell him he's got to get me to fight Mike Tyson," George said. When Rocco relayed the message, Panama scoffed. But the next time Panama saw Rocco, he embraced him—Panama had hooked up with George. "I could have told the guy [Panama] to kiss my ass and he would have done it," Rocco said. George had started training, but Panama, in his new gold jewelry, looked more like the champion. George even flew Panama to visit his parents in Panama; George had once been similarly expansive with one of his Chinese suppliers, setting him up in a rental house on the beach in Puerto Rico with limousines and party girls.

A carton overflowing with barely used boxing boots sat beside Panama's desk in his office, not far from a locker jammed with training shorts: George wore them once and gave them away. "You don't know, you don't know," Panama said to Rocco, shaking his head at the extravagance. George wanted to win the Golden Gloves and Panama believed George had more than a decent chance. George called Panama "Papi" and "Dad." Another trainer approached Rocco and asked, "You got any more friends like that?"

George treated his regimen seriously. "He'd always like healthy foods," said Jessica. "Vegetables and, you know, things that would cleanse your body, like teas." He popped vitamins. Instead of soda, he drank cranberry juice. He cycled and jogged. His new schedule left less time than ever for Jessica. Danny became his surrogate.

"George, I want to go to the movies," Jessica would say.

"Have Danny take you," George would reply.

"George, I have an appointment."

"Beep Danny."

"George, I want to go shopping."

"Have Danny take you, I have things to do."

George did not keep his other girls from her. There was no need to. When a guy had money, girls were everywhere. "One-night-stand girls who came back for more," George explained, "girls who clung to me like a cheap suit. Then there were girls who were my regular jewels of the Nile, more upper class than these regular girls." One of George's block managers got sex from a girl for allowing her to sit in his car—without even having to take her driving. Other girls gave it up for a pair of sneakers, or a pack of Pampers, or cigarettes, or a take-out meal. Sex was currency. Sex was also the boy's right and his main girlfriend's problem. Jessica perceived the challenge the same way the women around her did—girl versus girl. Jessica did not ask George questions about what he did all the hours he spent away from home. "I'm not the type to ask questions because I don't like to be asked questions," Jessica said. But she did try to intimidate the competition. When girls paged George, Jessica phoned them back. "Don't beep my man," she'd say, or, "Don't you be calling my husband." Boy George would learn of her defiance and yell, "What are you doing beeping my girls back? You're not allowed to beep my girls back."

If George was in the shower, she would jot down the numbers from his beeper screen and dial the girls up a few days later. It was an old habit she couldn't resist. "Is Georgie there?" she'd ask in her sexiest voice.

"George? Who's this?"

"I'm his girl. He told me if I needed to reach him I could call him here."

If a girl paged him on a beeper that he'd left at home, Jessica returned the call immediately. "Hello?" the girl asked expectantly. Jessica let the hope dangle before hanging up.

After Boy George's exotic trips, the calls would pour in.

"Is John there?" the latest girl would ask.

"No, he's not, may I take a message?"

"You his sister?"

"No," Jessica would answer, pausing, "I'm a *friend*."

In phone conversations with these girls, George sounded like the George who'd whisked her away from Tremont on that first date—mannered, attentive, confident. To one girl who expressed interest in seeing him, he said coyly, "Well, if you could put up with me." Jessica wanted to grab the receiver and scream, *Bitch, if I can't put up with him, you gotta be fucking Wonder Woman!* But she just kept quiet, listening in. A girl who did confront her boyfriend was likely to be reminded that there was plenty of pussy everywhere.

Jessica knew when George had a date: he wore slacks instead of jeans. "Why don't you just wear jeans if you going out with the boys?" she'd tentatively inquire.

"Why don't you fucking shut the fuck up?" he'd reply.

Jessica understood the consequence of breaking George's rules—vicious beatings—but she broke his rules fairly regularly. She knew a beating had been bad if she came to consciousness at his mother's; George brought her there because Rita worked at a hospital. Jessica would wake to Rita's frowning face. "What did you do this time?" Rita would whisper; she also feared her son. When there was serious damage, such as the time George cracked Jessica's skull, he turned her over to a private doctor who was paid generously in cash. Jessica called the doctor for other health-related problems, such as the time the twins had diarrhea that nothing seemed to cure. The doctor always asked after George, whom he jokingly called "the old baby."

George threatened Jessica with worse beatings than those he'd already administered. "If I can trust you, I can kill you," he was fond of saying. Jessica knew what he was capable of. That June, the word was that he'd set up Todd Crawford, one of his employees. As witnesses later told it, George had heard that Todd was planning to rob an old friend of George's named Snuff. Snuff and George had been classmates at Morris High School together; now Snuff dealt crack at George's lucrative 122nd Street spot. Snuff was one of the few people George's own age whom he considered an equal. George arranged for a mutual friend to invite Todd and his girlfriend to King Lobster, a City Island restaurant, for dinner. While they ate, Taz, the sometime enforcer, waited in a car in the parking lot. As Todd opened the door of his car, Taz shot him four times in the back. Todd had ordered shrimp scampi for his last meal. George hired Taz full time, paying him $1,000 a week. "Being taken out for shrimp scampi" became a nervous inside joke.

Jessica cautioned her girlfriends about calling her at the apartment, since she was not supposed to give out the number. If George answered the telephone, they shouldn't hang up; Jessica got punished for hang-ups. She instructed her friends to pretend it was a wrong number. It was tricky, because George disguised his voice as a way of testing Jessica. "Sal's Pizzeria!" he would say, but with George, the humor always had an edge.

When Jessica answered, there was no need to use his name; her friends' voices were hushed:

"He in?"

"Where he at?"

"You alone?"

Usually, she was. She saw George late at night if she saw him at all. George would have given Jessica money if she'd asked, but Jessica was more interested in winning his love. "Less money for her meant more money for me," George said. He teasingly referred to Jessica's need as her "attention attraction." It would be years before he understood that Jessica's desire for attention had the strength of a weed pushing through cement.

Late that summer, Jessica was staying in one of George's rentals, a basement apartment at the bottom of a flight of stairs on Henwood Place. George sometimes used Henwood as a drop for shipments of guns. The guns came up from Virginia. A runner by the name of Wayne drove them to the Bronx. Wayne was scheduled to make a delivery during another of George's trips to Puerto Rico. George instructed Jessica to stay in the apartment until the shipment arrived. Instead, Jessica broke out. She had decided to go dancing with her thirteen-year-old cousin, Daisy. Daisy's pretty young mother, who had divorced Lourdes's brother, worked as a cocktail waitress and partied after work. Daisy spent a lot of time alone and bored. She was in awe of her older cousin.

"She makes you feel good about yourself. She's beautiful, but she doesn't make you feel that she's the most beautiful, that's what I love about Jessica," Daisy said. Daisy stunned audiences in her own right, with her coltish body, unmarked face, and mane of curly brown hair. Daisy was at the dangerous age, already cutting school and noticing boys. She rode the train uptown to visit Jessica; sometimes she cabbed there, and Jessica paid the fare.

The night Wayne was due in with the weapons, Jessica and Daisy went out to the Herpes Triangle, three popular clubs clustered beneath the elevated subway tracks on Westchester Avenue. Wayne arrived, found no one at Henwood, and paged George. Meanwhile, George had just landed at the airport, unannounced; he didn't have a set of house keys, and Jessica still hadn't returned by the time George caught up with Wayne at the apartment. It infuriated George that Jessica had not upheld her part of their arrangement—her doing whatever he told her to do and him paying for everything. But George knew where to find her: Rascal shuttled him to the Herpes Triangle. Danny sat morosely in the passenger seat. George paged Jessica, punched in the number of his cell phone, and waited.

Jessica scooted outside as soon as she received George's page. She didn't dare call from inside the club with the music; she dialed his cell from a pay phone on the street.

"Where you at?" George asked.

"I don't know, I can't tell, the signs is all messed up," Jessica lied. Just then, Daisy stepped outdoors in search of Jessica, and Jessica flagged her down. George caught sight of her waving arm.

"I just want you to do one thing for me," he said in the tone of voice that made Jessica's heart race. "I just want you to turn around and look down the other side of the street."

Jessica had a choice: George could beat her at home, or right there on the sidewalk. She chose home and joined George in the backseat of the car. Her decision didn't matter; before they reached Henwood, he'd already started punching her. Then she realized that she had left her keys in her coat back at the club. George administered what she later called a double beating—during the ride back to the club, and on the trip back to the apartment again. Then he shoved her bloodied body onto the sidewalk and ordered Danny to bring her inside. As an afterthought, George told him to chop off Jessica's hair.

"I forgot scissors," Danny lied. He gently dragged Jessica down the stairs into the building and whispered, "He treats you so bad. I wish I could take you and the kids away." All Jessica wanted to do was go to sleep.

Jessica continued to violate house rules. Even when she stayed home, she opened the door to visitors. One day, George called from Puerto Rico in a fury after learning that a gold belt buckle with Snuff's name inscribed on it in diamonds and rubies was missing from the Henwood apartment. As it happened, there were any number of possible suspects: Danny, Rascal, another worker named Dean who had passed through to pay a debt, a friend of Jessica's named Beatriz, who had relatives in the building, George's brother, Enrique, and George's mother, Rita. George made it clear that he considered all of them responsible. By nightfall, his announcement that he was on his way back to New York had sent the apartment into an uproar: Rascal and Rita were turning over the couch and pulling it apart, while Enrique was frantically rummaging through closets and drawers. Jessica sat in the tub fully clothed with the water running, on the verge of hysteria. "George is going to kill me, you don't know," she said. When Rascal learned that Beatriz had been in the apartment earlier, he understood: George didn't like Beatriz.

George arrived at Henwood and interrogated everyone. He doubted that his blood family would rob him. Rascal and Danny earned plenty of money. Dean was already in the doghouse for getting arrested three months earlier with $22,000 of Boy George's money and one and a half pounds of his heroin; it seemed unlikely Dean would have done anything so stupid as rob George intentionally. Jessica then confessed that Beatriz had also been present. Dean later testified that George beat Jessica and decided to have Beatriz killed, using Dean as bait. George told him: "Jessica's going to call her, and you take her out." Whether Jessica ultimately made the call was never proven, but the date was somehow arranged.

It was raining when Dean collected Beatriz that evening, in one of George's company cabs. Beatriz's aunt waved down to her niece from the fifth-floor window and watched the chauffeured sky-blue car pull away. In the backseat, Dean passed Beatriz cocaine that George had provided—"to keep her happy." Drug-related homicides weren't the highest priority of the police. Beatriz shared the cocaine with the driver, who brought them to Ferry Point Park, a secluded spot beneath the Whitestone Bridge. There, in the shadows, Taz, George's hit man, sat waiting. The plan was for Dean to get out of the car—ostensibly to go to the bathroom—and to somehow get Beatriz out of the car, too. So Dean shamed her for snorting in front of the driver: "Respect yourself. Stop sniffing in front of the man so much." As Beatriz stepped out to join Dean, Taz approached and shot her twice from behind. Immediately her body went into spasms; Taz moved forward, grabbed her shoulder to steady her, and shot her again, then again. The gun jammed. Taz and Dean ran for their cars. Beatriz fell to her knees, screaming, "Dean, help me. Please don't leave me, please." Later that night, George sent a man named Moby back to the park to make sure that she was dead.

Jessica was so distraught that Danny called George in a panic—Danny was afraid that Jessica was going to hurt herself. George instructed Danny to try to calm her down. George visited Jessica but got irritated by her hysterics and left. Danny, however, felt for Jessica; by this point he was spending more time with George's girlfriend than George was. Danny tried to comfort her. They began an affair that night. Shortly afterward, Jessica was questioned by homicide detectives, but nothing came of it.

Years later, during his testimony at Taz's trial, Rascal remembered the escalation of fear within the Obsession organization that followed Beatriz's murder. George reminded workers that if they came up short, or slacked off, "a Taz special" could be easily arranged. Nearly everyone was subjected to these threats, Rascal said, but "Jessica in particular."

CHAPTER SIX

That December, Lourdes was facing eviction from her apartment on Tremont. She owed rent and the super claimed she ran a den of drug activity. Robert was no longer there; he had moved to Florida and become a Jehovah's Witness. "There was no way I was going to have a criminal record, guilty by association," Robert later said. Elaine and Angel moved in with Angel's mother, who lived around the corner. To help out, George agreed to float Angel a brick of heroin on consignment. But impatience got the best of the family business team. Instead of diluting the dope and bagging it for a 120 percent profit, they immediately unloaded the brick for $30,000 and the family went on a spending spree. Lourdes celebrated her thirty-eighth birthday with two gold wedding bands: she married Que-Que legally, and the newlyweds abandoned the apartment on Tremont for a new start in another run-down tenement on a street named Vyse. The relocation wasn't much of an improvement, although Lourdes hooked up a telephone and some of the rooms had rugs. But just having the means to move boosted Lourdes's spirits. She threw herself a wedding reception to celebrate—a weeklong party that spent down what remained of the cash, much of it on coke.

George blamed himself for the fiasco and claimed that he would have killed them all for disrespect if they had not been Jessica's family. Lourdes had proven herself to be a straight-out fiend, he said, and had only Jessica to thank for her life. From then on, he avoided Lourdes's apartment; if Lourdes was that heedless of her daughter's safety, she wouldn't think twice about setting him up. Lourdes said, "I didn't even know where my daughter lived." George also wanted Jessica to stay clear of Vyse. Sometimes, when he left the apartment on Henwood, he locked Jessica in from the outside. He tolerated Jessica's occasional visits to Serena but didn't want the child underfoot. Children were unwitting messengers, and Serena was three—old enough to answer nosy questions but too young to hold to a lie.

Jessica did, however, trust Cesar with her address. The basement apartment sat on a dead-end street, not far from Tremont. Jessica generally shied away from Vyse after George's beatings, but one day, Cesar surprised her. He inquired about the bruises. Jessica assured him, "Me and George just had a little fight." She didn't want Cesar to get involved; she knew that her brother was crazy enough to try to set things right. Cesar had his own code of chivalry: he'd always defended her reputation on the street regardless, whether or not the gossip was true.

Cesar's own reputation might still have been small-town to Boy George's big-city standard, but Cesar was recognized and avoided on East Tremont. That winter, he'd reunited with Rocco, and together with two other boys, they'd formed their own little crew. The boys called their street family FMP—Four Man Posse. Besides Cesar and Rocco, there was a short, quiet boy named Mighty, and a worrier named Tito. Each boy, in his own way, came from Tremont—Rocco still lived next to Cesar's old building; Mighty lived around the corner, on Echo Place; Tito lived across the street. "That was a nice little rugged corner of the Bronx that breeded a lot of jailbirds," Cesar said. The boys knew every corner where the ghosts of notorious local crimes still hovered, legendary acts committed by boys who were now locked-up men. If place was identity, years of scaling rooftops, dangling from fire escapes, and riding bicycles through the narrow alleys had made Tremont theirs. Tremont raised them up.

The boys played Manhunt and Knock-Out. Knock-Out was their favorite. One boy would pick an unsuspecting male passerby and the other boy had to knock him down. Whichever boy succeeded, won—*Mike Tyson*, they would shout, *crowned!* They robbed a bicycle store and armed themselves. They bought an M1, a .45, and a shotgun and set about committing robberies. They added two .357s, a .38, a .45, an M1, and a Tech 9 to their arsenal. They stashed the guns under Cesar's bed and above an awning near his old elementary school. Jessica worried about Cesar and asked Boy George to talk some sense to him. One night, Boy George invited Cesar up to Grande Billiards to play pool.

The bouncers waved the boys through the first security check at the downstairs entrance, past the other customers waiting to be frisked. Clearance at the second security checkpoint went just as smoothly. The pool players saw Boy George approaching and surrendered the coveted center-floor table. Cesar felt that standing with Boy George was like being in the gangster movies he loved.

George played the part. He counted out $1,000 and placed the bills on the table. He said, "Cesar Augustus. I'm going to tell you what. You win, it's yours." George was the only one who ever addressed Cesar formally. Cesar won the game. He won the $2,000 game after that. He won until the pot reached $49,000, after which George said, "One more game for everything."

"Everything but a thousand," Cesar said knowingly. George was testing him. As expected, George won the final round. Cesar asked George to give him work.

George discouraged Cesar: "If something happens to you, I don't want your mother blaming me."

Now and then, when George would spot Cesar on the street and give him a lift, Cesar would still try to convince him: "Man, let me work for you!"

Without glancing at the bouncing beanstalk in the leather passenger seat beside him, Boy George would answer, "You're not a stupid kid, Augustus. Go to school, go to school, *go to school!*"

Some days, Coco headed for Cesar instead of classes. If she couldn't find Cesar around the bodega at Andrews Avenue, she boarded the 36 bus and headed east. She shied away from self-assertion, but when it came to hunting down Cesar, she was dogged in her pursuit. "I would just pop up," she said. Usually, Cesar wasn't home. He was courting trouble, or ducking out from the consequences of trouble he'd caused, or, unknown to Coco, flirting with other girls on nearby streets. Coco sometimes arrived in the afternoon and found Lourdes sleeping. If Lourdes woke in a dark mood, both Little Star and Coco knew not to ask for anything, not even a glass of water.

If Lourdes was feeling energized after an argument with her husband, she would enlist Coco to help her clean. They'd turn the radio to Lourdes's favorite Spanish station—93.7 WADO. She would lean on the broom and introduce Coco to the mop. Coco would fill a bucket with hot water in the bathtub, then pour in the King Pine cleaner that Lourdes kept beneath the sink. She'd lug the bucket to Lourdes, who would be singing and sweeping and cursing up a dusty storm.

Coco would mop while Lourdes lifted furniture and ashtrays and children, placing them wherever they wouldn't topple—on the kitchen table, on the beds, on the couch. After mopping came laundry. Lourdes did not like to go anywhere, even to the Laundromat, alone. Coco accompanied her. Back home, they'd string a clothesline along the hall to dry the leggings and baby T-shirts and baby socks, and the damp-clothes smell would blend with the King Pine, scenting the apartment. But even with dinner done and the laundry hanging, with Jessica's three girls bathed and changed, their hair done, Lourdes's anger was not necessarily used through.

The best days were when Coco found Lourdes cooking. Lourdes's beauty shone in the kitchen, and Coco loved to see her bustling among her steaming pots. With one hand stirring *arroz con pollo* and the other holding a Newport, Lourdes did dance moves in her slippers, belting out lyrics, clamoring for Coco to pass her the shrimps or to *Stay out of the way, baby, this pot is hot!* Ordinarily snooty neighbors would knock on the door, rendered shameless by the enticing smells. "The people from the building come to my house to eat my food," Lourdes said. When there was money, Lourdes was proud that she could provide so well for so many hungry mouths. When she didn't have money, neighbors pooled change for the ingredients, as if it were Sunday night and people were collecting for a bag of weed.

Never would Lourdes stoop to cooking with the store-bought jars of Goya or packets of Sazón that her lazy daughters used. *Sofrito* had to be homemade. She valued her *pilón*—her mortar and pestle—even more than her statue of Saint Lazarus and her Irish friendship wedding ring. "When I move, it's the first thing I pack," she said. Food made any apartment feel like a home—even Vyse, which to everyone's distress was infested with rats. Her mother had given Lourdes the *pilón* as a gift when she was fifteen years old; Lourdes had been cooking for nine years by then.

Coco loved rainy days because bad weather temporarily released the grip of the streets: Cesar stayed indoors and his friends stayed home. Coco would show up and, without a word, start taking her clothes off. "Wait," Cesar would say, "I'm not even awake." They spent whole mornings and afternoons in bed, having sex and playing Nintendo. Cesar had a fancy bed with a mirrored headboard. Coco, at those times, felt as if all life were happening there. Sometimes, if Cesar wasn't in the mood to make love, Coco could convince him.

"She would just take the sex from me," Cesar said. At first, it unnerved him, but he grew to like it. Coco was provocative without being nasty. They talked, too. Cesar asked her things:

"Do you love me?"

"Yeah," Coco answered.

"But why? What you love about me?"

"Everything about you."

"You are not telling me what I want to hear."

Direct questions made Coco nervous. They reminded her of her stepfather, Richie, and that she never did well on tests. Mercifully, such moments were usually interrupted because something was always going on at Lourdes's house, and Cesar's friends never stayed away for long.

*   *   *

In some ways, Four Man Posse was better than blood family. Family always brought with it inherited problems and allegiances, whereas FMP created beefs that they stood a chance of fixing and set their own rules. Loyalty was paramount. Nothing was to come between them—not other guys or crews, and never girls. Sisters were off-limits. All moms automatically got respect. The steps of Rocco's building on Tremont served as the official meeting place. The boys pledged to take bullets for each other, never ask questions if asked for backup, and never rat each other out. Girls could be shared, but if you took another guy's girl, you had to tell the boy face-to-face. If a member really liked a girl, the other FMP members could try to kick it to her, but if she remained true, the other boys had to leave her alone for good. If an FMP member ever fell in love, FMP still came first. "Your friend is going to last forever," Cesar said. "Your girl ain't. If you shoot somebody for your girl and you get twenty-five-to-life, she won't last. You do it for a friend, he will."

Live by the gun, die by the gun was their motto, *Scarface* their favorite movie. Cesar's favorite scene was of Al Pacino lecturing the patrons of a fine restaurant. The diners stared at Pacino and his entourage, frightened but mesmerized. By being scapegoats for all that was bad, Pacino told them, criminals fulfilled people's need to believe they were purely good. Cesar liked talking about the bond between Pacino and his partners. He felt that way toward Rocco and Tito and Mighty—his homeboys, his crimeys, his family, his crew. Everyone swore by FMP's rules, which weren't so different from those of previous generations of Tremont kids. Only Cesar and Mighty, however, took the vows to heart.

Since winter, George had been dating a shy, chubby girl named Gladys who had straight silky hair like Jessica's. Gladys lived with her Catholic parents in a single-family home in a working-class neighborhood in the Bronx. "From a straight-up *Little House on the Prairie* neighborhood," said George, both pleased and charmed. He was proud of Gladys. He needled Jessica by saying how much he preferred Gladys's ladylike company. Gladys worked as a teller in a Manhattan bank. He drove her downtown some mornings, on his way to Gleason's Gym. Gladys believed George's money came from his father, who "worked in construction." George had promised to take Jessica to Hawaii, but he took Gladys instead.

George didn't bother to hide the photographs of the vacation: Gladys leaning lazily on George's shoulder; Gladys smiling beneath palm trees; Gladys's thick fingers clutching fancy neon drinks. It was Gladys he jetted to San Francisco on a day trip to fetch a pair of Nikes that weren't in stock in New York. It was Gladys he took to restaurants. But when he invited her to the black-tie company party he'd planned for Christmas Eve, Jessica had reached her limit: Vada could have him in Puerto Rico and Gladys could take the best of him, but on that special night, Jessica was determined to be the girl on George's arm. He didn't put up a fight.

Jessica shopped along Fifth Avenue and found the perfect dress—an off-the-shoulder white satin gown. She treated herself to a manicure and a pedicure. The day of the gala, she spent the afternoon in a hair salon. She took so long getting ready that George threatened to leave without her. She teetered after him in her satin white high heels and finished putting on her makeup in the car. Then she slid her hands into the white satin gloves that matched her dress.

Meanwhile, at the World Yacht dock in Manhattan, Obsession employees and their dates waited and waited for their host. The 121 guests had arrived by the modes of transportation proper to their caste: by BMW and Mercedes, by rented limousine, by livery cab. Gladys and a girlfriend milled about in the anxious crowd. Finally, the car pulled up, the valet opened the door, and Boy George stepped out in his Bally shoes. The crowd cheered and clapped. He strode up the ramp of the *Riveranda* yacht in his silk tuxedo and waved to his people. Jessica hung on his other arm. The DJ announced, "Mr. and Mrs. Boy George!"

Jessica relished Gladys's reaction. "You shoulda seen that girl's neck snap," she recalled. "She had pretty hair, I'll give her that. But she wasn't as pretty as me. I looked like Cinderella, with the prince right next to me."

Before dinner, George gave a short speech that one manager remembers as characteristically succinct: "Let's go out there and make some money. Thank you for coming." The menu included steak tartare, skewered lamb, prime rib, and $12,000 worth of Moët. Loose Touch and the Jungle Brothers performed. George paid Big Daddy Kane $12,000 for a fifteen-minute rap. Safire never sang a note, but she supposedly pocketed $3,000 (without a private dressing room, she claimed, she couldn't be expected to perform).

10-4 had ordered printed raffle tickets listing prizes for the Boy George Christmas Give Away ("winners to be announced by the host"). First prize was a loaded Mitsubishi Galant; second, $10,000; third, a Hawaiian trip for two; fourth place, Disney World. Door prizes included a home entertainment center, a Macy's gift certificate, a "nite on the town," and $100 bills that the captain of the ship noted none of the guests bothered to claim. 10-4 received a gold Rolex and $50,000; George gave Snuff a brand-new BMW 750. To four of his top men, George presented diamond-studded gold belt buckles, appraised at $7,500 each. Jessica didn't win anything, but she wasn't thinking about material things. "What I need a prize for? I had him," she said.

The seating was organized by drug spot; managers sat among the pitchers and dealers who worked for them. One had all his boys wearing fedoras, which they called Godfather hats; another table sported red cummerbunds. Plenty of guests mugged for the roaming photographer. He snapped lots of pictures—of guys leaning forward, toasting, their eyes bloodshot, grinning above abundant tables, of the girls beside them in slinky satin and taffeta swirls. It was like prom night, but with an open bar and no chaperons. Boy George paid for everything—in cash. The bill from World Yacht alone ran to more than $30,000.

Fights erupted as the night wore on. One guest challenged a drunken dealer, who had perched on the tip of the ship's bow, to swim ashore. Another guest was dragged to the deck, stripped to his underwear, and beaten brutally for trying to steal a diamond pendant from a female guest. Jessica fantasized about inviting Gladys to the deck and tossing her overboard. "I was around him so much that I started thinking like him," Jessica later said. But she was having too much fun dancing to start a fight.

For George, of course, the party had a purpose: pleasure reinforced loyalty, and loyalty was essential to his business. He said, "It's good to bring them together, so they know, 'Listen, man, you have a family here. If anything ever goes wrong, this is the type of force that's coming behind you.'" That force would soon be tested. The professional photographs of each table, so meticulously arranged by drug location, would prove invaluable in identifying the players in the Obsession hierarchy.

After New Year's, Boy George's best heroin source once again dried up. George called Lourdes's, looking for Jessica. She had been staying at Vyse, following another beating. Cesar answered the phone.

"Whassup, homie?" George asked.

Cesar answered, "I signed up for school."

"Meet me at Tremont," George said.

Cesar had just spent a week at Spofford Hall, a juvenile detention center in the South Bronx, for a robbery he hadn't committed. (He'd instructed Coco to bring his Nintendo to her sister Iris for safekeeping, so it wouldn't get hocked while he was gone.) One of the terms of Cesar's probation was that he return to school. George pulled up to the corner of Tremont in a white BMW. Cesar was still hoping that George was going to offer him a job. Instead he said, "Want to go to the Poconos?"

"I'm just a little kid. I can't go to the Poconos," Cesar replied. His ex-stepfather, Big Daddy, had taken his mother there.

"We're going to the Poconos," George said. Signing up for school merited encouragement. George might also have felt the need to smooth things over with Jessica, who had been in exile at Lourdes's for almost a month. George added, "There's got to be some pussy involved in the trip. Get a girl."

Cesar called Coco. Coco had only been outside of the city twice— once, on a family trip to Disney World, when her father was alive, and to Binghamton, New York, where she'd once gone as a camper with the Fresh Air Fund. Coco told Foxy that she was going away with Cesar's older sister. Foxy called Lourdes to double-check. Lourdes covered for Coco, but Foxy hesitated until Jessica called and warmly assured her that Coco would be fine—a girls-only trip.

Off the foursome drove in a white stretch limousine. The car even had a name—Excalibur. The white lights on the roof looked like crystals. The winter day was clear. Coco and Cesar sat beside each other in red leather seats. The leather reminded Coco of the jacket Cesar had worn when they'd first met. Jessica and Boy George sat across from them, but they seemed very far away.

The chauffeur drove right over the potholes. Coco wished they could loop around her block so she could show the car off to her friends. The limousine joined traffic on the Major Deegan, then crossed over the majesty of the George Washington Bridge. They were now in another state.

To celebrate Cesar's return to school, Boy George opened the cooler and pulled out a bottle of Moët. He wanted everyone to drink. He himself wouldn't, because alcohol disrupted his training regimen. Coco wouldn't, because alcohol made her queasy. Jessica wouldn't, because she wasn't a drinker and wasn't in a partying mood just yet.

"Whoever doesn't drink has to walk—I'm leaving you on the side of the road," Boy George told them.

"He means it," Jessica whispered. "Listen to him cuz he say he'll leave you and he will, he did it to me." During one excursion to Atlantic City, he'd abandoned Jessica beside the highway. Another time, he'd left his spot managers at Great Adventure as a practical joke.

Coco could tell from the funny face Cesar made that the champagne nauseated him, "so I drank mine and I drank his." Jessica had to drink until the champagne ran out. George told the chauffeur to pull over to the breakdown lane. Jessica stuck her head out of the power window and vomited, clasping her hair at the nape of her chain-draped neck.

Excalibur had its own VCR. They watched a videotape of Andrew Dice Clay, George's favorite comedian. George had a big, echoing laugh. Cesar remembers thinking, "This is some rich shit going on." He was surprised at how friendly George was. "I didn't think he'd be talking to me, you know, cuz he was rich." Coco thought that Boy George's laughter sounded fake.

The Mount Airy Lodge appeared ahead, a palace tucked in the snow. It was the largest resort in the Poconos. The limousine pulled up to the entrance and Coco stepped out onto a red carpet. Through the lobby's smoky windows, she could see a chandelier. As George registered, Coco and Cesar and Jessica stood in the lobby and watched the guests pass. People chatted, skis balanced on their shoulders, and strolled nonchalantly in boots, as though the Mount Airy Lodge were something that happened every day. Boy George handed Cesar his own set of keys. Like the limo, the room had a name—the Crystal Palace Suite.

Everything was color-coordinated in gold and powder blue. There was a TV, a stereo, a fireplace with a log that never stopped burning. The red Jacuzzi in the huge bathroom was shaped like a heart. The bed was round and there were mirrors on the ceiling and the walls. The living room opened onto a miniature swimming pool. The room was so interesting, Coco thought, that you'd never need the street. And even if they did go outside, no one was looking to fight.

George equipped the group with skis, boots, and poles, and then he and Cesar deposited the girls on the bunny slope and took off. Coco was nervous with excitement; this was the first time she and Jessica had been able to hang out. Jessica was warm and open, and she didn't mind looking dumb. A T-bar dragged them up through swarming crowds of little kids. Neither girl could ski more than three feet without falling down. Their legs split. Their knees caved in. They laughed so hard they could not stand up. Coco understood why Cesar was so attached to his sister.

As the girls waited in line for the T-bar, they spotted George and Cesar swooping down an advanced trail. Cesar had never skied before, but he was athletically gifted. The girls screamed and waved frantically, but the boys didn't even turn to look. Boy George admired Cesar's guts; the kid was willing to try everything. And he was bold with Boy George as well:

at one point, Cesar told George, "If you gonna be with my sister, you got to accept her kids."

"What's between me and your sister is between me and your sister," George answered, but he gave the kid credit for having heart. Jessica and Coco, soaked and cold, waited for the boys indoors.

Coco would remember this afternoon as one of her happiest: the breeziness of the families in their bright jackets with matching hats and gloves; the confident little boy who actually hovered over them after they'd fallen and politely offered help; the trail of blue blotches that Jessica's new jeans left in the snow.

That night, the boys wandered off again. They said they were going to the casino, but Jessica knew they were cruising for girls. She didn't mind. She and Coco were having their own good time, dipping their legs in the heated swimming pool. Suddenly, the lights went out, and the girls sat in near darkness. Only the underwater spotlights in the pool glowed. A croaky voice broke the silence. It was George pretending to be Jason from the movie *Friday the 13th.* "We were so scared," Jessica remembers. "That was when there were things that could scare me." Boy George tossed Jessica in the water, fully clothed.

Back in their own Crystal Palace Suite, Coco and Cesar pretended they were on their honeymoon. They made love on the round bed and ordered food and watched TV and made love again in the heart-shaped Jacuzzi and laughed and playfought and never went to sleep. "We broke night," Coco said. From their bed, they watched the morning brighten.

Sometimes, in the Bronx, Coco broke night in her bedroom, watching the police conducting surveillance on the roof of the building across the way. Three Cuban brothers ran their drug operation from several of the apartments, and there was always activity. Countless times, Cesar and Rocco broke night on the street. But daybreak in the Poconos was different. They weren't facing time to kill, or feeling left behind, or stuck. There was nobody out to hurt them, no sad mothers or brothers or sisters to worry about. The Poconos held promises beyond the reach of the usual; they could ski again, or play basketball, or go ice-skating, or ride a snowmobile.

But the peace was what Cesar cherished most, the respite from acting tough. He later said, "That's enough to hold a memory in." That weekend in the Poconos was the only honeymoon Cesar and Coco would ever have, although they would remain in love for many years. They were both fourteen.

CHAPTER SEVEN

In the early spring of 1989, George installed Jessica in his mother's old apartment on Morris Avenue. His brother, Enrique, lived there still. That George let Jessica join his family mattered a lot to her. Not long before, she had ordered Milagros to bring her the twins. Now she finally had a home; she even had a brother-in-law, if not quite a husband. She was ready to act like a mother and a wife.

Milagros was distressed about losing the twins; she had taken care of Brittany and Stephanie for the last two years. The sudden nature of the separation was especially brutal: a friend of Jessica's had greeted Milagros on the street with a machete, ushered the girls inside the building, and warned Milagros never to visit again. Jessica had refused to come out. Milagros worried that Brittany and Stephanie would feel bewildered and hurt, and that they might not be safe in George's household, but she saw nowhere to turn for help. She didn't want to risk angering George. Milagros comforted herself with the thought that the arrangement would never last. In the meantime, she inherited Kevin, the little boy she and her mother used to watch. Kevin's own mother had been arrested, and BCW, the Bureau of Child Welfare, had come for him; he was headed for foster care unless Milagros took him in.

George didn't spend much time in the apartment at Morris, but Jessica and George's brother hung out. Enrique was working at Fordham University as a security guard. On his way home, he'd call in to see what Jessica needed. She always needed — rice, Burger King for the girls, something to unclog the bathtub.

"What am I? A home-delivery man?" he would joke.

Enrique liked Jessica. They laughed over the stupidest things. He wasn't much of a ladies' man, so she introduced him to her friends. He also saw how hard she tried to please his brother. George would call and tell Jessica to prepare dinner, then not show up. He mocked the love notes that she sprayed with perfume and left on top of their satin sheets. He called her *stupid* and *ugly* and *fat, fat cow, fat bitch, fat fucking dumbo bitch*, and *ho*.

When George was mean to Jessica, she would sometimes turn her rage and frustration on her little girls, calling them *stupid* and *crackheads*, then mocking their tears. "Stupid bitch, what the fuck is your problem," she would snap. "Turn on the TV!" George berated her for being a rotten mother, but he had even less tolerance for children than she did. Even his jovial paternal moods were mixed with cruelty. He pitted the twins against one another to playfight, which was common—families routinely toughened up their kids this way—but George always crossed the line. He'd force the twins to fight even after they cried—not the early cries of hurt that everyone seemed to ignore, but deep sobs of distress. Once, he tossed Brittany into the bathtub; another time, he folded Stephanie up in the pullout couch.

Playfights with Jessica soured just as inexplicably. One time, he hit her so hard during a mock wrestle that his hand swelled. "I ain't gonna wreck myself over this," he muttered, and swung at her with a stick instead. When Jessica laughed, George went berserk. "Ever since I was little, whenever somebody starts hitting me, I start laughing," Jessica later said. "And if I laugh, he thinks I'm laughing on him, and he just keeps beating me."

George taunted Jessica: she had no place to go, her own family didn't want her, people hung out with her only because of his money, her mother was a fiend, she'd abandoned her own kids. Jessica comforted herself by taking inventory of what she had: her old hooky partner, Lillian, for one, had been her friend long before Boy George. "I have Lillian," Jessica repeated to herself like a mantra, as though the assertion of sisterhood defended her against what she feared was true.

One weekend, unknown to Jessica, George took Lillian to Atlantic City. Then he asked Jessica why she had not spent time with her friend.

"Lillian was away," Jessica said.

"Do you wonder where she was? Your friend?" George grinned. "I just fucked her. Call her up."

Lillian denied that she had been with George, until George got on the line and described what she had been wearing when he'd deposited her in front of her mother's building, just an hour earlier. Lillian hung up. Jessica rushed to Lillian's, but Lillian had fled. Jessica told Lillian's boyfriend what had happened, then seduced him, after which she smugly reported her conquest back to George. Predictably, George beat her up, but that time, he did not kick her out. That month at the Morris Avenue apartment was her longest continuous stretch of living with George, which was to Jessica a significant accomplishment. She'd never made it that long with any man. Unfortunately, that April was the same month a federal judge approved a warrant for the FBI to install a wiretap.

*   *   *

The wiretaps largely documented Jessica's conversations; George was usually out and about while she spent the better part of her days on the phone, shifting between people on call-waiting. She paged beepers obsessively. She pined for Serena, whom she often didn't see for weeks, even though she couldn't handle Serena when she had her for any length of time. Jessica was bored and depressed. Only in those conversations about intrigues and plans, or during the terrified calls placed to girlfriends after George's beatings, did she sound energized.

She continued to harass Gladys, the bank teller, with crank calls. She moaned over a girl named Erica whom George had met in Hawaii, a Millie from Puerto Rico, and a local drug-dealing girl named Razor, who drove a Rolls-Royce. But being neglected had some advantages: Jessica kept up with a busy love life of her own. She continued to meet George's associate Danny. She called Puma, sometimes to see him, but as often to complain about the neglect she suffered from George.

"Trinket there?" she'd ask.

"Yeah," Puma would say. Once he pretended to arrange a drug deal as a cover for their next rendezvous.

Jessica would pretend that she was sneaking out to see Serena, and Enrique would baby-sit Brittany and Stephanie, unknowingly covering one layer of Jessica's double lies. Sometimes Jessica didn't feel like going out, but Enrique insisted; he was extremely attached to the twins.

Other prospects absorbed George. His heroin supply had returned and Obsession continued to sell well, which made laundering money a priority. He worked with a stockbroker who converted sneaker boxes full of tens and twenties into bonds. George had hired a financial consultant to diversify his business interests, and now he owned shares in a water filtration company and was considering building a strip mall and franchising a fast-food chicken chain. He backed several promising young boxers.

While 10-4 managed most of the daily business, George attempted to launch several new heroin spots in Manhattan. He set up stores on Fifth Avenue and 105th Street, First Avenue at 115th, and 132nd Street between Madison and Park. None took off. He launched a second brand name, Sledgehammer, but needed another mill so as not to cut into Obsession's production. "What are you trying to be," 10-4 asked him, "McDonald's *and* Burger King?" George bought cars and shipped some to Puerto Rico. He flew Rascal and Danny and 10-4 to San Juan with suitcases full of cash. He also kept in close touch with Vada, who was in the midst of renovating their country house.

George had bought the place the year before, for $140,000 in cash. Landscapers dug and raked and planted. Laborers mixed tar for a basketball court. The brass bathroom fixtures were ripped out and replaced with gold plate. George installed a swimming pool with the tiles arranged in his initials above a replica of the Obsession crown. When Fried Rice visited, he was struck by the discrepancy between the opulence of the house and its dirt-poor surroundings: "The inside didn't match the outside," he said. "It was like wearing a twenty-dollar dress with a three-hundred-dollar bra."

Jessica envied Vada's position, but Vada rarely came to the Bronx and their interactions were limited to the telephone. Vada would say, "Little Miss Wicked Witch of the East, put my husband on." Jessica had to show Vada respect, but she managed to get her digs in. She'd hold out the receiver as though it were infected and coo, "Your *girl*, honey," and delicately pass the phone to George. She denied Vada the honor of calling her his wife.

George finally proposed to Jessica that spring, in part to make up for taking another girl to Hawaii on Jessica's birthday; he gave her money to buy a diamond ring and encouraged her to take a formal portrait, which she did. She wore a corsage, and the photographer superimposed her image inside an enlargement of the ring.

In late April, Boy George was making arrangements for another shipment of heroin. Rascal called; George was out; Rascal told Jessica to page George's supplier to relay a new meeting place. Jessica took down the necessary information, but she was less focused on George's business than his love life. The engagement had done little to allay her fears about the competition:

Jessica: "No girls are with you, right?"
Rascal: "Huh?"
Jessica: "He ain't with no girl?"
Rascal: "What?"
Jessica: "You'se are not with no girls, right?"
Rascal (sarcastically): "Yeah, with four girls."

But Jessica's brief call to Fried Rice would make her a coconspirator in George's business. Conspiracy law cast a wide net: technically, a coconspirator could be held liable for the cumulative amount of drugs that passed through a criminal enterprise. Harsh drug laws determined prison sentences by drug weight; unfortunately for Jessica, George was about to make the biggest deal of his life. Five days after the phone call, George and another dealer went in on a deal for thirty-two bricks of premium China white heroin; they paid $1.1 million, cash. Each brick was worth at least $175,000 on the street. The exchange took place at the Whitestone Lanes in Queens. Jessica's relaying of the message was tape-recorded on the wiretaps.

10-4 stored fifteen bricks of George's seventeen-brick share at a stash house and brought two to the new mill at 740 243rd Street for processing. The workers had already assembled. George did the honors of the first cut; the potency of the dope made George and 10-4 ill. They'd just opened the mill, and there was no furniture besides the table and chairs. The two men retreated to a back bedroom and lay down on the carpeting, where they slept until 9:00 the next morning. George took food orders for the table and went to the store. While he was gone, Rascal and Danny arrived to make the day's first batch of deliveries. They were supposed to feed the spots directly, but they'd secretly farmed out the task to Moby. Usually, Moby paged Rascal to confirm the drop-off, but that morning he didn't. Rascal called Moby's mother, suspecting something had gone wrong, and it had: Moby had been arrested. Rascal called 10-4, who instructed him to return to the mill.

By then, the next batch of work was ready. 10-4 told Rascal and Danny to deliver it while he delivered Moby's bad news to George. Rascal and Danny took a cab. Rascal was so worried about George's reaction that he didn't immediately notice the DEA agents who'd just cut them off in a white BMW. There was no time to discard the heroin in the I ♥ NY bag at his feet.

10-4 remained unaware of the extent of the growing crisis until early the following morning, after he dropped his son off at school. Still in his pajamas, 10-4 called Rascal's mother from a pay phone: Rascal and Danny had been arrested with over ten thousand Obsession glassines. None of the stores were open for business. 10-4 paged the managers, and none returned his calls. He paged them again. The managers had been arrested, and the pagers had been confiscated and were flashing his code on the desks of the detectives who'd worked the Obsession case for years.

At 8:36 A.M., 10-4 dialed the Morris Avenue apartment. George was sleeping with Jessica in the bed that his mother had left behind. DEA agents posing as Con Edison repairmen waited in a parked Con Ed truck. Others waited in unmarked cars, eyeing the entrance of the building through binoculars. All wore bullet-proof vests. The government agents monitoring the wiretap heard 10-4 tell George to meet him beneath a nearby streetlight, bring plenty of money, and be prepared to break out, to "do a Jimmy James Brown." The two bricks of heroin that had been milled the night before had disappeared.

Boy George hurriedly dressed and told Jessica, "I gotta go."

"Where you going?" she asked sleepily.

"Don't worry. I gotta go, I'll call you from where I am and maybe you can visit me." He grabbed $7,500 and instructed Jessica to burn his photographs: the blown-up picture of him in Hawaii, his arms covered in parakeets; shots from the Christmas party; the picture of him posing like Rambo, strapped with guns. In one etching, Boy George stood shoulder to shoulder with his Mafia heroes—Fat Tony, John Gotti, and Carmine Persico. These precautions were unnecessary, however; the agents nabbed George as soon as he hit the street.

The feds drove Boy George through Central Park on their way to central booking. As he looked out the window of the white Lincoln Mark IV, one of the agents pointed to a seedling: "See that plant? It's gonna be a tree when you get out."

The police detained Jessica and Enrique while they searched the apartment, then arrested them. George assured the investigators that they weren't involved. Jessica and Enrique were interrogated and eventually released. Jessica scribbled a notation in her pocket calendar: "Bad day (went to jail.)"

CHAPTER EIGHT

After questioning George at DEA headquarters, agents brought him to the Metropolitan Correctional Center, in lower Manhattan, where he joined 10-4 and other members of the Obsession crew. 10-4 flipped in less than a week. Outside, agents confiscated money and property under the federal forfeiture laws. They'd already found one of George's Porsches and a Mercedes that had just received $50,000 worth of custom bodywork. Meanwhile, as word of 10-4's defection spread, the loyalist ranks continued to dwindle. Boy George would glare around the bullpen and say, "Who's next?"

Vada was next, although she never snitched. It was rumored that she had run off with the man who'd tried to sell George shares in the fast-food chicken chain. By the time the DEA got to George's house in Puerto Rico, nothing much was left to take: no cars, no cash, no jewelry. They found leftover food and a bottle of Calvin Klein's Obsession perfume. Pair after pair of sneakers remained neatly lined up in a walk-in closet. The agents drained the built-in swimming pool so they could take snapshots of the incriminating tile work. George never heard from Vada or their son again.

It took prison to make George realize what Jessica had believed since they'd met—that she was the right one to be his wife. The morning of the Obsession roundup, when she called George's mother to relay his instructions about destroying evidence, the wiretap recorded Jessica's prescient concern: "You know what makes me laugh?" Jessica told her. "The same people that talk are telling him how he can't trust me because I'm gonna squeal on him." She collected her three daughters and moved to his mother's. George doubted Jessica would betray him, but he still wanted Rita to keep a close watch on her. Jessica's day calendar, however, showed a woman who took her duties seriously:

> Went to court.
> Serena's birthday.
> Went to see Honey.
> Run Errands!
> Go with Grandma to doctors.

Went to see George.
Go see George.

Jessica learned that it was smart to arrive at the Metropolitan Correctional Center no later than eleven-fifteen for the noontime visit, which sometimes didn't start until one o'clock. Prison visiting—like going to the emergency room, or to welfare—subjected people to lengthy, arbitrary delays. Jessica had to wait for a guard to give her a form, longer for the guard to collect it. There was almost always a line. Veteran visitors brought their own pens and change for the locker and the vending machines. They knew to stay close to the door to hear their name called. Guards summoned women by the last name of the inmate they were visiting. To step up for the notorious George Rivera was for Jessica a point of pride.

It could take another hour to complete the processing: coats and bags lurched along the conveyor beneath the X ray. Jessica dropped her jewelry and beepers into a grungy plastic tray. Boy George had given her his favorite charm for safekeeping—two tiny gold boxing gloves, which symbolized the Golden Gloves boxing competition he still planned to win. She wore the delicate charm on a slender gold chain around her neck. "Because I'm his champ," she said.

Once she cleared the metal detector, she had her hand stamped, was buzzed into the interior lobby, lined up again, and signed the visitors' log. She exchanged her ID for a locker key. Visitors had to store most of their belongings in a locker. When George's unit—5-South—was called, she was buzzed into yet another interior hallway. She placed her hand beneath an ultraviolet light. A guard checked her hand for the stamp, and another guard rode with her in the elevator to the fifth floor. There, in the hallway, she waited again. A guard unlocked a door that granted access to yet another short hall, where visitors could buy snacks. George refused junk food, though, so Jessica usually bought only a diet soda for herself. The hall ran between two oval visiting rooms, visible through thick glass. Smudged plastic chairs lined the walls of each room, facing inward, as if recently vacated by an encounter group. Jessica was assigned a chair. She sat. She waited. At some point, the inmate was "produced." Visits usually lasted an hour, unless your inmate had pull with the guard. George did.

Jessica briefed George about what she'd heard on the street: who planned to plead guilty, who else might rat. At one point, rumors were circulating that his mother might cooperate with the police. Jessica's attempt to live with Rita didn't work out: the two women argued over money and George's left-behind things. Jessica complained to George that his mother had no patience with children; she claimed that Rita used George's rottweiler to terrorize the girls. Rita charged Jessica with laziness and disrespect. By summertime, Jessica had brought the girls back to her mother's house. Lourdes was still living with Que-Que and Cesar in the dismal apartment on Vyse.

Jessica didn't make much time for her daughters, but she dressed them well and documented their good-looking life in photographs. She bought sailor suits, socks and panties, barrettes and bracelets, headbands and adorable hats. She surprised them with a Barbie playhouse and equipped a play kitchen with miniature dishes and pots and pans. She stuffed the play refrigerator with play food and stocked the miniature shelves. It felt good to provide her girls with the things that she'd wanted herself as a child. Cesar inherited several of Boy George's name-brand sweat suits and pairs of his unused sneakers. Jessica added to her collection of leather coats. She had more than forty: full-length and waist-length, car coats and jackets, one lined in mink.

At first, Jessica visited George every day. In their long, undistracted hours together, Boy George opened up to Jessica. Despite the cool front he projected, his situation was extremely grim. If convicted under the conspiracy law, he faced a possible life sentence. Rascal and 10-4 were cell mates: by June, Rascal joined the government, followed by Danny. Throughout the betrayals, Jessica remained a stalwart friend. "He just came close to me, and this, while he was in jail. We shared a lot of things together," she said.

Jessica mentioned the upcoming birthday of one of her girlfriends, and George told Jessica to take a thousand dollars and do the birthday right. He booked a Mercedes-Benz limousine to deliver her and her friends to Victor's Café. They ate an enormous meal. He called Victor's Café on the pay phone that night to send his good wishes. Placing direct calls to unauthorized numbers from prison required some maneuvering. Jessica and her friends got drunk on champagne. They snapped pictures of themselves eating cherries, slicing knives into steak. The *plátano* had candles. The handsome waiters sang.

The celebration was a vast improvement over Jessica's own birthday, when George had been in Hawaii with that other girl. He'd bawled Jessica out when she'd tracked him down in the honeymoon suite to ask why he hadn't called. Now George called several times a day. He dedicated a song to her—Paula Abdul's "Forever Your Girl." He marveled at her apparent loyalty. Had Jessica been the one locked up, George said, "probably the same day I woulda been fucking somebody else."

Publicly, George treated his detainment as a temporary setback, but the other drug dealers regarded the collapse of Obsession the same way he'd regarded the downfall of the Torres brothers' operation years before. One person's misfortune was another's opportunity. There were always customers to satisfy. A crew revived the Blue Thunder brand name. Jessica's street currency was also renewed. Dealers were interested in getting to know Boy George's girl. And she was interested in getting to know them—maybe because she was George's girl, or maybe just because she was Jessica.

Inside, George languished in the MCC, obsessing about his business, his future, and Jessica's whereabouts. She brought him pornography and his favorite, *Yachting Magazine*. He'd redesign the two-hundred-footers, adding Jacuzzis to their decks. "I get a scrap paper," he said, "and I draw."

Outside, Jessica was enjoying his money. She crammed as many girl-friends as would fit into limousines and treated everyone to dinner and dancing. "With the money, Jessica began to change—like I thought she would," said Lourdes. "She would spend a thousand at a club—not that I want any for myself, I didn't—but you take away something from my grandchildrens." Jessica sarcastically prompted Lourdes's faulty short-term memory: "Ma, ain't you forgetting that you get the girls' welfare checks?" But Jessica did buy Lourdes a washing machine and give her money for the rent and the light.

Soon, Jessica and her little cousin Daisy were going out dancing almost every night. Short and tall, experienced and trusting, Jessica and Daisy made an excellent team: Jessica dated drug dealers, and the dealers had friends who went with Daisy. Jessica introduced her little cousin to the night world. It was a summer of cocaine, clubs, and hotel rooms, and thick, airless visits to the MCC. One boy let Jessica drive his red Corvette.

Jessica inherited the lease to a project apartment from her maternal grandmother, who had moved to Florida. Jessica could not imagine living in the one-bedroom high-rise alone, on 54th Street and Tenth Avenue in Manhattan, but it was a safe place for her to store valuables—too many people passed through Lourdes's apartment on Vyse. On those nights Jessica and Daisy went clubbing in the city, the apartment served as a convenient place to crash. They also occasionally entertained boys there, but Jessica still preferred to sleep at her mother's.

From time to time, Jessica ran into Coco there. Coco loved hearing about the adventures of her wild sister-in-law: Jessica once dragged Daisy beneath a car during a shoot-out; another time, she and Daisy went to a hotel with two brothers, and Jessica paid the tab. Jessica had the same way with men that Cesar had with girls. She'd go to Grande Billiards and pretend she couldn't play pool. She liked to wear white leggings and a low-cut top. With her beeper tucked into the V of her cleavage, she'd ask a handsome boy to help her take a shot. The boy usually would. He'd place his arms around Jessica from the back and she would bend over the table to aim, pressing her butt into his crotch. It was a simple gesture, and it always worked.

Jessica lived the fast life. She took cabs everywhere. "I guess George got me used to that, constantly moving around," she said. That summer, Little Star traveled by car so often that she balked when Coco put her on a bus to take her to Foxy's block.

A formidable grapevine connected prison and the street, and news of Jessica's booming social life soon reached George. He confronted her; she denied the allegations. He yelled at Jessica and complained to his mother, who encouraged him to give Jessica room. To prove her devotion, Jessica agreed to get a tattoo. "If you love me, you'll do it," George said. He demanded high quality, not some crude ghetto tattoo drawn by an ex-con with only two colors and crayon lines. He researched the trade magazines until he discovered a tattoo artist in Elizabeth, New Jersey, who'd been rated one of the nation's best.

The first tattoo, a heart with a rose high on her right thigh, was elegant. *George*. She opened the slit on her skirt to show George on her next visit to the MCC. "You stupid bitch!" he said with appreciative incredulity. On the elevator ride back down to the exit, one of the other inmates' girlfriends expressed her exasperation with Jessica: now her boyfriend wanted her to get one, too. Jessica's next read *Jess loves George*, with an arrow over her actual heart. He promised to get the same one with the names reversed.

In August, four months after he was arrested, the authorities transferred George to Otisville, a holding facility upstate, where he would wait over a year for his trial to begin. With the distance, Jessica's calendar entries dwindled; their monthly anniversary became the only notation concerning George. By October, the commemorative *George and Jessica's* anniversary had inverted to *Jessica and George's* anniversary. On the back page of her little black book she asked hard questions of herself:

1. Is this a punishment from God for me not to be happy
2. Do I really Love this person
3. Do I really wanna be Happy with
4. Could I really wait for George
5. How can I help myself besides him
6. Will I ever be happy
7. Does he really Love me.
8. Do I need companion from another man
9. What will I really do for this person? What are my limits?
10. When I say that I promise I'm promise the opposite or I'm I lieing just a little bit, or do my promises mean nothing.

Yet she continued with her more public testaments of loyalty. Altogether, she got six tattoos in his honor, including a banner reading *Property of George* across her buttocks and a poem, written on a scroll, which unrolled just above her shoulder blade:

> *George*
> *No matter where I am*
> *or what I'm doing*
> *You're always there*
> *Always on my mind*
> *and in my heart*

It was as if Jessica was trying to convince herself of love from the outside in.

Circumstances forced George to adjust to Jessica's escapades. Still, he was shocked when he finally listened to the wiretaps. He'd been given copies of the tapes in preparation for his trial; they filled a large box. Jessica received the first blast of his reaction in the middle of the night. She was at Lourdes's. "What time is it?" she asked.

"Bitch, listen to this." George played a cassette into the receiver.

"How'd you get to use the phone?" Jessica stalled.

"Don't mind how I got to use the phone, you fucking bitch, listen to this." And so it went. The DEA's wiretaps had recorded the calls she'd made from the Morris Avenue apartment she'd shared with George—her intimate exchanges with Danny and Puma; uncensored conversations with girlfriends about sex and life with George. The wiretaps also explained a mysterious visit earlier that spring by the New York City Police that had continued to baffle George. An officer had appeared in response to an anonymous report of domestic violence. It was true that George had hurt the twins, who were with Jessica at the time. But George had doubted that his neighbors would have dared to call the cops on him. In fact, a DEA agent had called the local police after overhearing Jessica's panicked call to a friend.

Jessica claimed the government had framed her: "It's some white girl's voice." She reminded George how she'd stood by him in the most important way—she had refused to snitch on him. She remained one of his only friends. But that type of loyalty wasn't enough to appease George's anger. Tombstones, he would say, were going like hotcakes. He fantasized openly about delivering her to Lourdes in separate body parts.

Night after night, in his cell, Boy George played and replayed the cassettes. Jessica's voice surrounded him. In real time, she was rarely home—or was ignoring his phone calls. He obsessively tried to reach her at the Manhattan apartment, where he caught only her breathy recording for the answering machine, which she'd tailored in anticipation of his prison calls: "Hello, yes, I accept a collect call . . ." Boy George was finally listening to Jessica, just as she was moving out of range.

CHAPTER NINE

Cesar had gone from acting like a hoodlum to being one; his tough posture had calcified and become part of his identity. He called himself a stickup kid. As he remembers it, he went from playing tag to hiding drugs in his pocket to carrying guns. "That part where you and your boys go to the movies? I passed right by that," he said. His friend Tito still dreamed of becoming a professional baseball player. Mighty never spoke much about the future, but then Mighty never spoke much. Rocco was more interested in the gangster lifestyle; when asked his age, he would jokingly reply, "Twenty-five to life." But Cesar liked being a gangster. Like George, he did not equivocate: he took action. He had become FMP's acknowledged leader.

FMP's crimes had become more serious. Cesar and Mighty were the boldest, with Rocco and Tito following their increasingly reckless leads. They would listen to Public Enemy to get pumped. They did a daylight robbery on Fordham with a Dillinger two-shot. They hunted for victims on the subway. Mighty often got carried away. Said Rocco, "He had that Napoléon complex, because he was short." One time, while Cesar cleaned out a guy's pockets, Mighty pulled off his shoes. Rocco, who had his eye on the man's white jacket, warned Mighty, "No blood," but Mighty punched him in the nose anyway, ruining the jacket. Another time, they were riding around in Rocco's car when they spotted a man with a Walkman and a car radio, looking for a livery cab. With its tinted windows, Rocco's Caprice Classic passed as one. Rocco dropped off Cesar and Mighty, looped around the block, and the man got in. Rocco sped ahead, collected his friends, and ordered the terrified man to give them everything. "I'm Puerto Rican," the man begged as Cesar ransacked his pockets. Rocco replied, "We're not robbing you for your nationality." When the man shit on himself, Mighty went crazy and started beating him over the head with The Club. "Mighty, don't make him bleed! Don't bleed in the car!" Rocco yelled. It was all they could do to throw the guy out on the street before Mighty finished him off. Later, they used Lourdes's Ajax to clean up the mess.

✳   ✳   ✳

Jessica cautioned Cesar. He ignored her. She appealed to George. George wrote Cesar a long letter from prison, addressing him as "my dearest brother in law." He reminisced about the Poconos. He told Cesar that his staying out all night worried his family. He told him doing real time was no joke: "Remember the white man doesn't give a fuck about you o.k. . . . he's going home to a soft bed while your in jail suffering." George described the loneliness of prison and the feeling of being abandoned by friends. He told Cesar that he loved him and how he hoped they'd cross paths again, "but not in here." He wanted Cesar to benefit from his predicament. The postscript read: "Take care of your family leave the streets alone. Because all your going to do is die or being in jail—another memory like BOY GEORGE."

Boy George's warning didn't temper Cesar. He was hardheaded and young and beautiful, bursting with angry energy, all of which probably contributed to his lopsided puritanism. He understood that his actions had consequences, but in this world, the consequences seemed less determined by desire or intention than by the luck of the draw.

One afternoon that fall, Coco stopped by Lourdes's. She'd just come from the health clinic on Burnside Avenue. She waited for Cesar. He came home, and she followed him into his room. He stretched out on the bed. She leaned against the windowsill. Nervously, she told him what she hoped he'd feel was good news.

They'd wanted a baby. They'd never used contraception and they'd been making love—a lot—for over a year. They'd finally gotten lucky.

"Come here," he said. His seriousness worried her. He placed his ear against her stomach. Then he leaned back against the headboard and pulled her onto him. She rested her head against his chest. She remembers hearing his heart beating and how he'd brushed hair from her eyes. He loved it when Coco blew-dry her hair and wore it loose and straight, like Jessica's. Coco tried to believe he was happy about their baby, but "I have a headache" was all he said.

They fell asleep and woke up and made love. Rocco stopped by. Cesar showered. He and Rocco left. Coco washed the dishes and swept the floor and mopped. She showered quickly; she hated standing beneath the hole in the ceiling above the tub, where there were rats. She slipped into a favorite sleeveless blue dress. She liked the way the material swished around her ankles. She strapped on brown sandals. She dabbed her neck and wrists with Lourdes's perfume.

"I'ma see you later," Coco said.

"See you later, Mami," Lourdes said.

Coco swept down to the street; the air felt good between her toes. She settled into a window seat on the bus. As it climbed Tremont, she spotted Rocco and Cesar on the sidewalk by the Concourse. She peered at Cesar from a distance, without his knowing, just the way she had when she'd eyed him on University before they'd met. Her heart sank—he had his arms around another girl. "I died," Coco said. At that moment, a small part of her did.

Back at her mother's, Coco dressed to fight. She doubled up on T-shirts to avoid giving the street a free show. She tucked razor blades in her ponytail and rubbed her face with her trusty Vaseline. By the time she returned to Tremont, the girl had disappeared. Coco and Cesar had a shouting match in the lobby of Felix's building on Mount Hope; Cesar reprimanded her for daring to think about brawling with a belly. Within weeks, however, Cesar's betrayal was eclipsed by his arrest.

There had been a shoot-out. The police hauled in Cesar, Mighty, and Rocco and questioned them separately. They were all responsible, but Cesar lied to protect his friends, knowing that he'd receive less time as a juvenile. Mighty also tried to take the rap. Rocco didn't answer any questions; he had a private attorney. Rocco and Mighty got shipped to Rikers and Cesar landed back at Spofford Hall.

When Lourdes and Coco visited Cesar at Spofford, Coco recognized the girl Cesar had been hugging on Tremont. The girl had tie-dyed *Casper*, Cesar's graffiti tag, in Clorox along her impressive thigh. How did she know Cesar was at Spofford? How many times had she visited? "This bitch is not going before me," Coco remembered thinking. Coco wasn't ordinarily assertive, certainly not with officials, but she turned to the guard. "When we going in?" Coco might have to share Cesar with other girls, but at least she was pregnant. She hoped to give him a son; regardless, she'd give him his first and therefore always be up front.

Coco had hopes that Cesar wouldn't stay in prison too long; boys from her neighborhood were always drifting in and out: Hype, Cesar's old friend from West Tremont, was at Spofford, and so was Coco's childhood boyfriend, Wishman, along with another boy Coco knew. She dispensed her optimism in the bottled message of her Christmas cards. They read, "From Cesar, Coco & our new year baby thats coming soon!" All fall, Coco had been cutting school; that January 1990, right after Cesar was sentenced, she officially withdrew.

*   *   *

Coco was the only one to attend Cesar's sentencing. She was six months pregnant. Lourdes had intended to go, but she'd been admitted to the hospital after having two seizures; Jessica had promised to be there, but she didn't show up. Jessica had been hanging around with Papito, a colleague of George's who was trying to market some of his unconfiscated heroin for him. One night, while Jessica waited in Papito's car with one of the twins and Papito's girlfriend, police surrounded them. In addition to 109 heroin glassines, the police found an annotated copy of George's indictment in Papito's pocket. Scribbled instructions—"Quiet their mouths"— headed a list that included the codefendants, the U.S. attorneys handling the case, and the judge. The police arrested Papito and detained Jessica for hours before letting her go. Now she was lying low.

Coco brought sunflower seeds to slip to Cesar at his sentencing, but all she could do was wave. Cesar and Mighty drew indeterminate sentences of two to six years for the shooting. Mighty was sixteen and sentenced as an adult; at fifteen, Cesar still qualified as a juvenile and was sent to the Division for Youth, known on the streets as DFY. Rocco received five years probation. Coco joined another unpopular sorority: not only was she a pregnant teenager, now she was a jailbird's wife.

To Coco, the biggest difference between Cesar jailed and Cesar free was attention. "He pay more attention to me when he in," she said. "When he out, he be hanging with his friends." But Coco, unlike Jessica, found being in the spotlight uncomfortable. She'd felt more at ease waiting in the wings—monitoring Cesar's movements through what she'd glean from Lourdes, stringing together hints like a sleuth. Now the relationship was less of a game. Face-to-face in the visiting room with full hours stretched out before them, Coco and Cesar had to figure out new ways to communicate; they weren't even supposed to kiss. She smuggled in contraband—cherry Now and Laters, Mike and Ikes, sunflower seeds.

Sometimes Cesar wrote Coco every day—love letters, angry letters, letters brimming with baby instructions and fathering commands. Increasingly neat and intricate penmanship filled pages upon pages. Cesar was attending classes for his high school equivalency diploma, and he began to think about the future, largely in terms of avoiding the past:

Dear Coco
    What's up Baby! How are you doing fine I hope. As for me I'm okay, listen Coco what are you planning to do with your life, where

are you going to bring up my Kid, Is it going to be safe for my kid, are
you going to take care of it or your family is, Coco Im going to let you
know ahead of time I dont want nobody hitting my kid unless he or
she does something Bad, but if somebodies going to it's going to be
you or me, Not my mother or your mother or anybody else in our fam-
ilies Don't Let me see my kid all dirty or always shitty, when the baby
need's his or her pamper changed you or another girl change it, Im
talking about somebody in your family or my family, not none of your
dirty ass friends, Coco the reason why Im telling you all this is
because I don't want anything to happen to my kid, Or better yet our
kid we both made it, not only me and not only you . . .

If love was a race, Coco had to catch up. Hope and need bumped into the emphatic threats if Coco did not write often or wasn't home to get his call. Cesar calculated Coco's value in terms of her ability to protect the baby and her sexual loyalty to him:

Coco take care of our baby because if any thing happens to it I'm
going to murder you I know I always tell you that for little stupid
things, but this time I mean it. I better not find out that you had a
boyfriend or even attempt to kiss anybody even close to the lips Im
going to beat the shit out you, the reason I say this is because I love
you a lot . . . if I didn't love you I wouldn't give a fuck . . .

The only future that Cesar saw was the baby; their only joy as a couple had occurred in the past:

Do you remember in the Poconos when we made love in the
jacuzi, in the shower, on the sofa, in the round bed, in the pool, that
shit was no joke, I alway remeber that shit, remember the Jacuzzi with
all them bubbles coming up in to the water from the bottom, remem-
ber when we use to argue and then make love after that, that shit was
so good I loved all that shit, but most of all I loved you and still do.

Maintaining his life on the outside was now hers to do: visiting, deliver-ing messages to friends, supplying sneakers, sending him letters and mailing photographs, which he called flicks.

In prison, photographs were currency, like food or money. Flicks proved that you existed and that you were still connected to the world out-side. As her pregnancy began to show, he demanded belly, but only

Polaroids: "I don't want you to take them with a regular camera because when they develop the film they look at the pictures, So I dont want anybody seeing your body except me, that body is for my eye's only." Yet the pictures could not be so explicit they would constitute a violation of the prison's discretionary rules. Coco could not figure out the official line between acceptable and sexy. How much belly was too much? The boundaries she observed came from the street. Prisons were different. She already knew she could not send pictures in bathing suits, because the prison had sent some back.

Cesar's requests became elaborate. He wanted sexy letters—"Tell me what your going to do to me but I want you to talk to me even more dirty than you do now, ok"—and he wanted the sexy letters long: "I hate when you write to me and only write three little sentences about us making love. I hope the next letter you write has like two pages of sex talk only. Do you think you could make me cum in a letter?"

Cesar rarely confessed his fears in person, but he did on paper. The nights were the most painful. You could not break them, as he had by staying up all night in the street. Nightmares visited:

> . . . Last night I had a dream that when I got out you were pregnant and the father of that kid was Kodak. And in my dream I saw you fucking him, and that you were fucking for a long time before I came out. I hope that dream don't come true, because yo Coco Im going to kill you and him and take my kid.

In fact, Coco had been seeing Kodak. It was impossible not to: he still lived across the street. Every day, all day, Kodak stood in front of his mother's building dealing drugs. Coco had no excuse not to talk. After all, words weren't dangerous. Coco didn't want to disrespect Kodak; he was her first. Besides, he looked too good.

Cesar had already heard about their conversations by the time they kissed. Coco had been walking across the abandoned lot near her mother's building toward Andrews. She remembered it vividly both because of what happened, and because it was the only time she recalled having ever been alone. Her house was never empty, and she never ventured to the store without her little brother or a cousin or a friend. Kodak saw his chance. He approached her and said, "Coco, you look good." Then he kissed her—a nighttime kiss in the public light of day. Coco felt uncomfortable, embarrassed, and thrilled.

She lied to Cesar on their next visit. She told Cesar it was a kiss she didn't want; she said she hadn't kissed Kodak back. Cesar went crazy. She stood up to leave. He shouted, "Sit the fuck down." She sat. Cesar berated her throughout that visit, and continued in the mail:

> . . . *I know your going to fuck somebody so I don't put my mind to it. the only thing I realy care about is my kid. . . . you know why I didn't want a girl that wasn't a virgin. . . . But that's okay because your going to regret that believe me Im going to make you pay for what you put me threw and it's not by hitting you so don't worry about that. So that's all I have to say to your dum ass. You better write back every single day to let me know how's your belly. Alright you dont have to say anything about you because I don't CARE BECAUSE YOU FUCKED WITH MY HEAD LONG ENOUGH. REMEMBER DO WHATEVER YOU WANT AFTER YOU HAVE THE BABY BECAUSE THAT'S ALL I CARE ABOUT IS MY KID*

The unborn baby helped smooth things over. "Yo when are you going to give birth," Cesar wrote, more tenderly. He despaired the restricted access he would have in jail. He hated being an absent father, like his own father, who'd moved out when Cesar was just two. "For the next four years I'm going to have to handle it," Cesar wrote. "But any way at least I have something that's mine and will never stop loving me. MY KID."

In April, a healthy, full-term baby girl arrived:

Dear: Coco
> . . . *Take care of her dont let nobody I mean nobody kiss her face or lips ok. Not even when she get's older . . . Coco I filled out the Babybook. She wiegh's 6 pounds 13 ounces and 1/2 she is 18 inches long has brown hair and blue and light brown eye's right. Her name is Mercedes Antonia Santos.*

Fatherhood further escalated his demands. Since the baby might get sick in cold weather, Coco was to visit only on warm days. He wanted Coco to document each day he was missing with photographs. Coco loved the assignment; she'd always been a shutterbug, and as long as she didn't take pictures of the baby sleeping, no picture of a baby could be wrong. (Sleeping-baby pictures were bad luck because the babies looked as though they were dead.) Cesar still made his usual requests, but the questions about Mercedes now came first: Does she still have that rash?

That bump on her chest? He built her a toy chest in his woodworking class, which he inscribed: *To Mercedes from Daddy.* Now he signed off his letters, *Father Cesar, Daughter Mercedes, Mother Coco.* Fatherhood reorganized the rankings in his heart. Coco had been demoted, but her standing plummeted still further when Cesar learned that Sunny, her ex-boyfriend Wishman's mother, had attended Mercedes's birth.

For a full page, Cesar capitalized his ranting: "YO COCO WHAT THE FUCK WAS THAT BITCH SUNNY DOING IN THE HOSPITAL. YO COCO IF I FIND OUT MY KID GOES TO SUNNY'S HOUSE IM GOING TO BREAK YOUR FUCKING FACE." Then he abruptly retreated to lowercase. It was as if he had suddenly realized there had been a power shift:

> But Coco dont take the Baby from me no matter what happen's
> dont take my heart. Because then Im going to take yours out through
> your mouth. So just keep that shit in mind ok. Take good care of my
> princes alright. Bye, Bye CASPER ROCK and HIS PRINCES
> Mercedes Antonia Santos

The more possessive Cesar became, the more Coco avoided him. It may have been the spring weather, too, and Coco's feeling free of her belly's weight. Coco would dress Mercedes, and they would hit the streets. Cesar called and Foxy reluctantly covered for her daughter, using the excuses women always used:

She took the baby to the clinic.
She went to get the baby's WIC.
She went to buy the baby an outfit.
Oh, but Cesar, she went to the store.

Foxy didn't want to admit that Coco was hanging out again. Coco would leave Mercedes with Foxy and go dancing, or dipping into night pool—hopping the fence to swim after hours at Roberto Clemente State Park. Coco continued to flirt with Kodak. He flirted back. But Foxy resented having to lie to Cesar. She also resented being saddled with another grandchild, and more were on the way—her oldest son Manuel's girlfriend was pregnant, and Iris was pregnant with her second child. Iris sometimes left her oldest boy at Foxy's. Luckily, Richie helped; he fed and changed him; he took the child outside with his little plastic car when he went to cop his heroin. Foxy loved her grandchildren, but she had been raising children since she was fourteen and she wanted a break.

Other grandmothers in the neighborhood would have sympathized.

They certainly made their crisp comments, which the hardheaded young girls ignored:

You made your bed, now you're gonna fall on it.

You had fun making it.

I'm the grandmother, not the mother.

You're a woman, not a girl.

Coco eventually heeded Foxy's complaints and dropped Mercedes off at Lourdes's, where she ran into Jessica. Jessica was running around that summer, doing research for Boy George's upcoming case. Coco got to know Jessica better, and Little Star kept Mercedes company.

CHAPTER TEN

George had returned to the MCC by August 1990, when jury selection began for his trial. He needed a girl Friday and an ally. Jessica visited. He helped her bypass the tedious processing procedure with a phony paralegal pass procured by a private investigator. The paralegal pass granted Jessica legal access, which meant no restrictions on visiting hours. Jessica dressed professionally for the ruse. "George likes me to represent myself as a young sophisticated lady," she said. "I love it. I love to dress up. I like to look important, I like to look sexy." She wore blazers with tight, short skirts and sheer stockings to show off her legs. Once, she ran into John Gotti. She lugged briefcases stuffed with contraband food. They devised a code for his requests. George would ask, "What are you cooking for the girls?" and he'd amend the menu. "Don't they want *rabo guisado*?" he'd say, or, "I thought you were making *tostónes*." She packed weed in the cylinders of Hi-Liters, and he brought his empty ones, and they traded. They enjoyed the privacy of a cinder-block attorney-client room. George shadowboxed; Jessica performed little dances; they had sex; they talked. George sometimes kept her there all day. Jessica later said of her paralegal duties, "Nothing *legal* went on in there!"

Jessica also ran errands. She flew to Florida on "confidential business" and trekked up and down Fifth Avenue shopping for his outfits for court. George's sartorial demands were exacting. He wanted only patterned pullover sweaters. The slacks had to have cuffs. The socks had to match the slacks. Jessica carted dirty clothes to the dry cleaner's and clean ones back to the MCC. She carted sneaker boxes of cash to his broker on Wall Street, who briefly hired her as a receptionist. "George would call. 'How's the stock doing?' And I'd be like, 'Reebok's going up!' "

Her grandmother's Manhattan apartment turned out to be a convenient place for Jessica to stay on trial days. George expected her in the courtroom. Jessica said it was because he loved her; George said her presence in the courtroom reduced the risk of her being subpoenaed to testify.

George also expected her to continue visiting him at the MCC. One night, on her way home, some boys robbed her on the platform of the Fifty-ninth Street station and took her engagement ring. She was glad she had taken that portrait: What Jessica valued, perhaps more than the relationship, was the evidence of it.

At Harlem Valley, a juvenile detention center in Wingdale, New York, the boys divided themselves by block and neighborhood, just as they did at home. Cesar's connection to Boy George preceded him. Cesar said, "When I got there, they be like, 'Yo, that's Boy George's brother-in-law,' and guys be coming up and saying, 'Yo, I knew Boy George.'" But Cesar chose not to exploit the association.

Harlem Valley had the best conditions Cesar would experience during his prison years. At the time, juveniles were still treated like teenagers. George could place only collect calls; Cesar could receive calls and dial outgoing calls directly. George had to ask Jessica to send in photographs. Cesar shot his own rolls of film with a camera the staff let the teenagers use. He mailed Coco pictures of him sitting in his cinder-block room, on his Ninja Turtle sheets. George's Walkman had only an AM radio; all cassettes had to be mailed directly from the distributor. Coco sent Cesar homemade mix tapes, her selections encoding private memories. George bribed guards to bring in food from Little Italy and Chinatown. Cesar ate the home-cooked food that Lourdes brought in Tupperware.

At first, Lourdes visited often. Her home cooking reminded Cesar of the happiest periods of his childhood, when life was the way he liked it—predictable and strict. He still remembered those first months in the Bronx with fondness: Lourdes had continued working off-the-books at a factory that made costume jewelry. In the morning, she prepared oatmeal for everyone—her special kind. After school, they waited for her in a pizza parlor near the factory. There was a bedtime. You even had to ask for water. "Without the men, we lived a structured, disciplined life," Cesar said.

Harlem Valley was strict. The guards inquired about Lourdes's packages. They sniffed them and tested her dishes. They phoned her in the Bronx and said, "Mrs. Morales, you coming up?" They placed orders; the extra cash helped. If Cesar managed to reach his mother before she visited, she told him about the menu.

"You want that, Papi?" she asked.

"I guess that's all right," Cesar said. He liked everything she cooked.

Lourdes hoped prison might teach Cesar lessons she had not been able to. She wasn't optimistic but didn't see a choice. At least Cesar was safer at Harlem Valley; none of the kids had guns. Two bigger boys had already jumped him and stolen his sneakers. Rocco saw the bruises during a visit and snapped a Polaroid for evidence. But Cesar refused to press charges—he'd handle it privately; making a reputation was the only way to ensure that other boys didn't mess with him. Rocco eventually passed along the disturbing photograph to Coco, who placed it facedown in an album. Sometimes she slipped it out of the plastic sheets, kissed the black-and-blue marks on his swollen face, and tenderly put it back again.

Lourdes willed herself to believe Cesar could protect himself in juvenile. She knew machismo often wilted under pressure, but he'd owned up to the consequences of his bad actions, and Cesar was a fighter. She said, "A ratter will never become a man. He will become an insect." They could say what they wanted about her, but when it came to her baby, she could hold her head high on the street.

Of the thirty-three defendants originally charged in the Obsession case, only George and five codefendants rose for the entrance of Judge Shirley Wohl Kram on the opening day of the first trial. One of them was Miranda, who, at the time of her arrest, had been out of George's life and the drug business for two years and refused to plead guilty. Her sister also went to trial; she was a bank teller who'd only briefly worked at one of George's mills. Most of the other lower-level workers accepted guilty pleas; they had little useful information to trade. 10-4, Rascal, and Danny were facing thirty- and forty-year sentences, and hoping their cooperation would cut down their jail time. In exchange for 10-4's testimony, the U.S. attorneys agreed not to prosecute his son.

10-4's days of testimony, in which he matter-of-factly explained the drug business in punishing detail, set the pedestrian tone for a story that the lawyers alternately tried to dramatize or dismiss over the next three long months. Being stuck in the courtroom was not so dissimilar to the insularity of a block in the ghetto; other people's humiliations became a source of entertainment, and the seriousness of what was at stake got lost in the heightened significance of petty things.

Scores of agents and officers and experts would testify, including a quivering car salesman who had sold George several cars. The prosecutors would display the piles of weapons, the flamboyant jewelry, and the boxes of empty glassines with the red Obsession crown. At one point, they would theatrically introduce a "real" king's crown—a rhinestone costume crown someone had given George as a joke. There were other silly moments, such as when a pig latin specialist soberly deconstructed Boy George's attempts to speak in code. Just three weeks before his arrest, George had said over the phone to a friend, "I gotta write my shit down somewhere secret and shit. I gotta code it up." In the following conversation, which was played for the jurors, George was bemoaning a dry spell to his friend Snuff. George was considering temporarily opening crack spots—"ackie-jays"—to keep money—"paper"—coming in, and also to keep Obsession workers from defecting to other jobs:

Snuff: I got plenty aper-pay, though.

George: Oh, I got plenty, but still I just don't wanna fuck around and one day starve and shit, that's not the thing about the aper-pay . . .

Snuff: Yeah.

George: That's all I worry about cause them niggers there man if I catch them niggers making aper-pay somewhere else, ah man, we're going to have a crucifixion out here.

Snuff: Well! . . . I know what you mean, what if they elly-say aggies-bay in the otty-spay?

George: Yep, you know what I'm a do, too. I'm a open up ackie-jays man.

Snuff: Ackie-jays for what?

George: Just for fucking emergency purposes, brother, you crazy? Right now, it would've been cleaning up.

During the interminable court breaks, George's codefendants would sometimes play Nerf football in the hall, but Boy George focused on the larger game, as he so often had. Each morning, he'd hand his lawyer a list of questions and concerns he'd devised from mulling over the testimony given the day before. He studied shorthand in an attempt to keep his note-taking of the court proceedings up to speed. At night, he combed the Bible for strategy. "I can take arguments out of there," he said. He scorned the chumminess developing among the courtroom regulars. One day, when Miranda amicably chatted with a case agent, George hissed: "What the *fuck* are you talking to him for? He's trying to put you away for the rest of your natural life!"

For years, the Obsession case would continue, in large part because of 10-4's record-keeping and help: the police would arrest the company hit man, Taz, that December; not long afterward, Snuff and two of the Chinese suppliers would be apprehended and successfully tried. Papito—the man who'd been arrested with heroin glassines and the annotated copy of George's indictment—would end up dead, and the bound and brutalized corpse of Joey Navedo, George's old mentor and informant, would be found in Florida, in the trunk of a car. But the morning of opening arguments, George was hopeful, respectful, and appropriately dressed: his lawyer cast him as a flashy jewelry dealer with bad luck in bookkeepers and poor taste in friends.

That same September, Jessica ran into Felix, the older man from Tremont she'd known from girlhood. Felix still hung around the same bodega near his apartment on Mount Hope Place. He still parceled out dollar bills to little kids as he had with Jessica. And he still maintained his soft spot for her. Jessica told him that Lourdes and Little Star were about to be evicted from Vyse, and Felix invited them to stay with him. He told Jessica that he was planning to move to Florida; his son had committed suicide, and Felix wanted to get away. Shortly after that lucky meeting, Lourdes, Que-Que, Jessica, and Little Star moved to Mount Hope. But the commotion and the financial strains of the household drove Felix out.

Lourdes's new block of Mount Hope ran parallel to her old stretch of Tremont: if she peered out of the security gates from the living room window, she could see her old apartment. But the new place was more spacious than either Tremont or Vyse. Felix's building retained a trace of grandeur. The front door was ornate, with wrought-iron patterning, even though the glass was often broken. The floors were marble, and the building had an intercom, even though it never functioned (guests pushed their hands past shards of glass to let themselves in). The lobby had a fireplace, its flue plugged with cement, like a pacifier. Sometimes the elevator worked. Lourdes already knew lots of the neighbors; for all the shuffling around between apartments, few people left the neighborhood. Tito, Cesar's old friend from FMP, was working one corner of Mount Hope; the recognition afforded Lourdes respect, and a certain measure of protection.

The apartment itself was like lots of the apartments that Lourdes had lived in: dusky bedrooms; a cramped, patched bathroom; a narrow, sloping hall. Plaster crumbled off the walls in the kitchen; the colors in the stairwell were the familiar slumlord favorites—harsh mustard, reddish brown. The old windows gave too little air in summer, too much in winter, and never enough natural light. But, as she had countless times before, Lourdes dug in to work. She put a table in a dining nook, beneath an alcove, where she carefully placed Saint Lazarus and meticulously arranged his shrine. She scrubbed the floors on her hands and knees. She washed down the walls, then tackled the kitchen, unpacked her mortar and pestle, and nailed her lucky horseshoe above her door. Little Star, who had just turned five, stayed close to her grandmother. Jessica came and went.

One day, as Jessica and Daisy strolled down Mount Hope toward the corner store, Jessica spotted Tito standing beside the phone.

"Tito man," she remembered saying. "You blossomed! You done blossomed up!" Back at Lourdes's apartment, Jessica called the pay phone. Tito answered; he treated it as his private business line. In her sultry voice, she said, "Hello, handsome man."

"Who's this?" Tito asked.

"Who's this?" Jessica echoed back. She told him just how fine he looked. She described his outfit—beige-and-white Calvin Klein polo shirt, the beige jeans.

Tito became alarmed. Rival drug dealers sometimes sent girls as lures. Some of his and Rocco's most successful robberies had been possible because of tips they'd overheard from girls. The girls didn't necessarily leak information intentionally; dealers would show off their money and stashes to impress them, and the girls would naturally brag about what they'd seen. Jessica heard the fear in Tito's voice and revealed herself. Then she invited Tito to give her the ride she needed downtown.

Whether Tito remembered his vow to FMP—never go out with a homeboy's sister—he couldn't later recall. He'd had a crush on Jessica since he'd met Cesar. All FMP did. Tito had a wife, but suddenly there was Jessica in her grandmother's old apartment, sitting on the couch before him, lifting off her tank top in front of a window with a view of the George Washington Bridge, grinning her invitation with a question that had only one answer: "You mind if I take it off? It's hot!"

Coco saw more of Jessica after Lourdes moved to Mount Hope. She was too afraid to act like Jessica, but she learned a lot from Jessica's ways of handling things. Once, Coco accompanied Jessica to a restaurant with two drug dealers, one of whom Jessica was dating; the girls broke night talking and they watched pornography. Jessica knew all about handling locked-up men: she told Coco how guys "get more poetic, more romantic, they show that side of themselves they can't show on the street." She explained that you had to write boys about the things they wanted to hear while they were in prison, and that it was better to keep your problems and adventures to yourself. Coco unburdened her confusion about Cesar and Kodak to Jessica. Jessica listened without judgment; she loved both Tito and George.

Coco discovered Jessica wasn't the perfect girl she had imagined, though: "Sometimes she would be really fun, like, 'What are we gonna eat tonight?'—cuz we would order out—and other times she would be, like, 'Leave me the fuck alone.'" Sometimes Jessica deliberately antagonized George on the phone, and she could turn as abruptly on her children. When Jessica would head out to go dancing, she ignored Serena, who would claw at her legs, ripping her nylons, desperate for her not to leave. Lourdes attributed the up-and-down of her daughter's moods to her having been born in an elevator.

On the other hand, Jessica was generous to Coco. When Jessica flew to Puerto Rico, she gave Coco $100 to baby-sit, even though Coco would have done it for free. Coco spent part of the money on take-out food and sent the rest to Cesar. Coco and Jessica rarely went out together; instead, Coco stayed with the children and Jessica went out with Tito or one of her men. Coco welcomed the excuse to get away from her mother's, which was hectic. She styled the girls' hair. Coco said, "I used to spike their hair up." She slathered their tufts with Vaseline. They poured baby powder on the floor in the dining room and pretended to ice-skate. Serena liked to turn off the television and watch her reflection on the screen. She would sway back and forth, holding a hairbrush microphone.

Lourdes had once wanted to become a singer. She liked to tell whoever would listen that she was so talented as a girl that an agent invited her to join a touring singing group. Her mother had refused to let her go. The details of the story varied—sometimes her mother worked too hard and needed Lourdes to help with her siblings; sometimes Lourdes wanted to be a detective, a trucker, or an airline stewardess. But the theme remained—Lourdes yearning for freedom, her mother destroying her dreams. Her mother wanted her firstborn to be a son, and she used to joke with friends that she'd found Lourdes in a garbage can. Lourdes explained her lot largely as the result of spite: "If I couldn't be what I wanted, I wasn't gonna be nothing. And if I couldn't do what I wanted, I wasn't gonna do nothing."

Lourdes chided Jessica's ambitions and, like Lourdes, Jessica had resented it. George wasn't much better. When Jessica confessed she wanted to be an interior decorator, he scoffed, "Those people go to school." But when Serena confided to Jessica that she wanted to be a singer, Jessica protected her hope; she told Serena that she could do anything. The few minutes Jessica gave to Serena were Serena's entirely.

Every once in a while, Jessica brought Serena to court. Invisible to the reddening eyes of the judge and the jurors, Serena knelt on the floor, using the mahogany bench as a desk, quietly drawing pictures for Daddy George.

For a while after Cesar and Mighty went to prison, Rocco and Tito robbed drug dealers. George sent word to Rocco to attend the trial because each day's testimony was a master class: detectives outlined the latest surveillance techniques; the IRS representative explained tax laws; two solid years of state and federal investigation were presented in a clear, accessible language a jury could understand. "Sit here and listen to what these people say, because you're gonna need to know," George said. "Don't be stupid. Learn something. Learn the tax forms." But Rocco was losing the heart for crime. He'd fallen for a schoolgirl named Marlene. Then he also lost Tito, who had gone back to school and preferred to spend his free time playing baseball and hanging out with Jessica.

One girl did cull pointers to launch her own drug business, but most of the girlfriends of George's codefendants were eager for another sort of education; they relished learning what their boyfriends had been up to all the hours they'd been away from home. It came out that 10-4 had kept three girlfriends in three apartments that he'd cleverly furnished identically. One girl discovered that her boyfriend had moved her into a hotel not because of a gas leak, but because a rival dealer had threatened to murder her to punish him. Wives met the girlfriends they'd long known of, and girlfriends met other girlfriends they hadn't known about; some became cautious friends. Jessica lunched with Gladys, the bank teller George had dated. She also went clubbing with Isabel, the mother of his second son.

Jessica, Elaine, and Lourdes were all in the courtroom the day Mike Tyson appeared. Tyson had his own court date down the hall, but he stopped by to wish his old pal luck. Afterward, in the cafeteria, he asked Jessica on a date.

"I'll baby-sit," Lourdes offered. She held out her T-shirt for Tyson to autograph.

Jessica stared meaningfully at her mother. "Don't you have something to do tonight?"

"Then I'll baby-sit," Elaine piped up. Could he sign her napkin, too?

"Don't you have your own kids to baby-sit?" Jessica said curtly.

"You can bring your kids," Tyson suggested helpfully.

"My kids ain't supposed to be out late," Jessica said, confusing everyone.

This wasn't newfound independence. She was in love.

Tito let himself care about Jessica. She was six years older, and he knew she was a player, but he couldn't help himself. The sex was fantastic. They used to have competitions to see who could have the most orgasms. Tito was astonished at how much fun Jessica had in bed. After she came, she would laugh and laugh and he would say, "Jessica, what's wrong?" and she would say, "Nothing, stupid." Sometimes they snorted coke. She also mentored him about business. He said, "Jessica's a girl you could make money with."

Tito and Jessica managed to set up a part-time house at Jessica's apartment in Manhattan. FMP had effectively disbanded, but it provided the perfect cover for their affair. "Cesar's sister needs a ride," he'd say to his wife, or, if Jessica paged him, "It's Cesar's moms" or "Cesar's daughter's mother needs Pampers." Weekdays, Jessica attended George's trial and Tito went to school. At night, Jessica cooked while Tito did his homework. He still dabbled in robberies whenever Rocco popped up, but Rocco's schoolgirl was slowly pulling Rocco into the straight world. Jessica deftly managed both worlds: she nursed Tito back to health when a bullet grazed him in a shoot-out and surprised him with a cake when he made the tenth-grade honor roll.

One night, though, Tito made the mistake of answering the telephone.

"Hello," Tito said.

"Hello!" Boy George echoed. "Who the fuck is this?" Tito passed the receiver to Jessica.

"Hello," Jessica said.

"Who the *fuck* was that?"

"Please! My little brother's friend." She laughed richly and cooed to Tito, "He think you my man!"

Tito sometimes went to the Obsession trial to be close to Jessica. During one break in the testimony, Tito left the courtroom. He paged Jessica from the courthouse pay phone, an old-fashioned booth with brass fixtures and accordion doors. The code for *I LOVE YOU* flashed onto Jessica's beeper screen.

George saw Jessica stand. He gestured from the defense table. "Where are you going?" She pointed to her beeper.

"Sorry," Tito said, wrapping his arms around Jessica and pulling her into the booth. "I had to have a kiss."

"You crazy," Jessica said sleepily, and she gave him one.

George never found out about Jessica and Tito, but Cesar did, and he was furious. Tito was unstable—openly emotional. Cesar made it clear: "You can end it now, or when I get out, I'll end it." Tito ended the relationship. Jessica called Cesar crying, "You trying to ruin my life."

But Jessica continued to see Tito anyway. She would surprise him at his door in nothing but a leather trench coat and heels. Tito had to work to keep himself away from temptation. Like ex-cons who watched prison movies to keep straight, Tito watched home videos of himself having sex with Jessica. The tapes reminded him of what she was capable of doing with other men. Then Tito was arrested on a gun charge—for possession of a semiautomatic Tech 9. Jail terrified him. He posted bail and dutifully returned to his wife.

In mid-November 1990, the jury returned a partial verdict; they found George guilty of two of fourteen counts—tax evasion and conspiracy to run a continuing criminal enterprise. Four of George's codefendants, including Miranda, were also convicted; one lucky spot manager walked. George got sent back to Otisville and awaited sentencing.

Prisons, like hospitals, reduced relationships to essentials. George had Jessica, his mother, his brother, and Isabel, the mother of his second son. His friends had dropped away. George suggested that Jessica move in with Isabel. Jessica refused. George was running out of money. The trial had cost him over $200,000, and now he had to pay for an appeal. George's street contacts shrank with each new round of arrests. He believed his best chance at survival was to maintain an image of power, even as his power was diminishing. Maintaining leverage from the inside without money would be impossible. The holidays were approaching. Ostensibly, Jessica and George were still a couple, but by this time, she visited erratically, and the visits were often unpleasant.

Even after his conviction, George acted as though a successful appeal were guaranteed. He referred to the future with such vehemence that to suggest otherwise would have been almost embarrassing. George told his mother and brother not to come to the courtroom for his sentencing if they were going to show any emotion: "I don't want to see a teardrop fall. Because if you start with this teardrop shit and screaming, then you gonna mess me up. I wanna walk outta there with my head high, smilin', smiles, everyone! Smiles! This is just another card game we're playing here!" His father showed.

On March 13, 1991, paralegals and case agents packed the benches of the courtroom. There were so many spectators that people lined the walls. Extra federal marshals had been assigned to guard the doors and block the windows, should Boy George try to make a run for it, or try to hurt himself. Judge Kram told him that he was one of the most violent people ever to set foot in her courtroom. She said that in the long months of the proceedings, she had not seen any sign of remorse.

Boy George, in fact, had not been charged with any acts of violence. However, Judge Kram took the many violent accusations into account. Under the Federal Sentencing Guidelines, conduct that did not reach the evidentiary standards of a trial could affect sentencing. The contested evidence fell under the category of "relevant conduct," behavior that could be included if it related to the convictions or shed light on the circumstances of the crimes. Relevant conduct had only to satisfy a preponderance-of-the-evidence standard rather than the beyond-a-reasonable-doubt standard at trial.

In Boy George's case, the consequences of the relevant conduct were devastating. Behind the tax evasion and conspiracy convictions were charges of several Obsession organization murders. There were further death threats, including the one George had allegedly made against the prosecutors and the judge.

Boy George was twenty-three years old when he was sentenced. The judge committed him to federal prison for the term of his natural life. He had no option for parole. George laughed upon hearing the sentence — just as he'd planned — but the effect was more horrifying than defiant.

Jessica did not attend the proceeding. She tried unsuccessfully to comfort him on the telephone. George told her that he'd rather she were dead than free. Shortly afterward, the phone company shut off Lourdes's service.

CHAPTER ELEVEN

F oxy was the first to be furious about Coco's second pregnancy. The belly was Coco's, but Cesar's reaction was everyone's primary concern. "Why I gotta tell him you staying in, you make me look like a liar! I say you in, and you end up pregnant," Foxy yelled. Lourdes also showed little compassion for Coco, even though she'd been in the same unhappy place more than once herself—pregnant by a different boy from the father of her previous child.

Coco dialed Cesar's dormitory at Harlem Valley. She knew that if she didn't hurry, Lourdes or busybody Elaine would beat her to the news. "I got something to tell you," she remembered saying.

"What, you been doing on the street?"

"No, it's worse."

"Somebody came in you?"

"No, it's worse."

"What?"

"I'm pregnant."

Coco recalls hearing *ho* and *slut*, but not much after that: Cesar's fury made her stomach hurt. It didn't matter to Cesar that Kodak wasn't a stranger but the boy to whom she'd lost her virginity. It didn't even matter that Kodak was the only other boy besides Cesar with whom she'd ever had sex. "I went out with my girlfriends and ended up in his house" is how Coco could have explained it, but Cesar did not give her a chance.

His outrage assaulted her through the mail:

> *Coco I can't sleep at night because every time I close my eyes the picture of you having sex with him come clear in my mind. . . . If you would have never got pregnant it would've been much easier to handle. We could of still been friends. . . . I really really, really do hate you. And there is nothing that could change that feeling for you the way I hate you now is stronger than the way I use to love you. . . . I hate you more than I hate the people who I shot to get in here in the first place. I hate you more than I love my mother.*
>
> *. . . Coco this letter is only going to be seven pages long because we don't have anymore paper on the unit. But I don't think that a million*

*pieces of paper would be enough for me to really explain how much
I really do hate you.*

Coco reasoned that since the baby made her lose Cesar, the loss of the
baby might bring him back. She made an appointment for an abortion.
She went to the clinic but forgot her Medicaid card. She rescheduled and
missed the second appointment. She finally went for a third, but she'd lost
heart. Coco's sister, Iris, remembered Coco punching herself in the
stomach and throwing herself against the wall. "She did everything to try
and get rid of that baby," Iris said. But the baby survived all of it, so Coco
reckoned it was fate. All Cesar saw, however, was choice:

> *Coco the first thing I want to say is thanks a lot for ripping my
> heart a part the way you did. . . . Coco there's two girls out there that
> are virgins and are in love with me and I was dissing them just in
> order to try to make a family with you. But I fucked up because they
> might not be virgins anymore. So I lost both ways. I didn't only lose
> them but I lost you. Right now I need a real pretty girl that's a virgin
> and loves me so I don't have to worry about her first getting to her
> again.*

The usual rumors spread. Kodak denied the baby was his. Neighbors
gossiped. Jessica stood by Coco. She lobbied Cesar on Coco's behalf:
"Look at my life," she told her brother. "I have kids by different guys. People make mistakes. Why you gonna care about other people talking shit?"
Jessica knew Cesar was still in love with Coco.

In her bedroom at Foxy's, which she shared with Mercedes, Coco
made a shrine to the world's best ex-sister-in-law. Photographs of Jessica
covered the doors of her closet and one wall. Jessica didn't pose in front
of brick buildings with graffiti or kneel in dingy stairwells like other girls.
She sat in the front seat of a Batman-and-Robin car.

Kodak's mother was less supportive about the pregnancy. "That can't
be my son's," she told Coco, "because my son was locked up." But when
Nikki Victoria was born, in March of 1991, her birthmarks changed
Kodak's mother's mind: all her children had them. Jessica welcomed the
baby as her niece, and Lourdes welcomed Nikki as a granddaughter.
Cesar continued to berate Coco. Jessica advised Coco to be firm. "Don't
take pity on my brother. Leave him and he'll come back to you," she said.
Coco lacked the courage, but she appreciated Jessica's faith that she was
capable of taking a stand.

Cesar called Foxy's regularly to check on Mercedes—Coco would press the receiver to Mercedes's mouth to capture sounds—but Cesar's inquiries quickly turned into diatribes. If Foxy answered, the fighting started sooner. Cesar blamed Foxy for Coco's infidelity.

"See, I knew your daughter was with someone," Cesar said. "Your daughter's a fuckin' ho."

"You a fucking ho!" Foxy retorted.

"Ma, just hang up the phone," Coco pleaded.

"Fuck this motherfucker!" Foxy hollered. "Fuck this, this motherfucker gonna get me to shut up!"

"Oh, man, please stop, please stop," Coco begged, her words drowned by Foxy's shouts. "I didn't care what he was saying about me," Coco recalled later, "but I didn't want them arguing. I felt bad for my mother because she did know I was going dancing and everything, but she didn't know I was gonna come out pregnant. So I made her look like the liar." It was that eternal triangle that trapped so many of the girls and women Coco knew—the irresolvable conflict between blood and love and need, between you, your mother, and a man.

Coco tossed a big party for Mercedes's first birthday. First birthdays, like sweet sixteens, were a significant milestone; Mercedes had made a whole year, and Coco wanted to mark the accomplishment. Foxy knew a thing or two about throwing parties. For one Halloween celebration when Coco was younger, she and the kids had gathered leaves outside, then spread them around on the floor. Richie had made a scarecrow and Foxy had stuck a Philly blunt in its mouth. For Mercedes's birthday, Foxy charged $2 at the door. Jessica didn't have to pay—she was family. She wore the striped Gap polo shirt that Boy George had given her after their first date. She had a beeper in the left pocket of her jeans and another in her right. The bun on her head was covered with a green bandanna. Coco's ex-boyfriend Wishman's little brother Edwin watched Jessica dance.

Wishman and Edwin didn't get along. Wishman was the street type; Edwin was more of a mama's boy. That day, Edwin was baby-sitting his infant sister. He brought her into Coco's bedroom to change her diaper, and the next thing you know, there was Jessica, leaning against the bedroom door. He recognized her as the same girl in the collage on Coco's wall. Jessica was even prettier in person. "God, you're so gentle, that's so sweet, you're so gentle," Jessica said. "Someday you're gonna make a good father."

Later that night, the police raided the party, then unsuccessfully tried to convince Foxy to let them use her apartment for surveillance: they were still watching the Cuban drug dealers who were working out of the building across the street. Edwin and his friend Freddy gave Jessica and Daisy a ride to the apartment in Manhattan. Jessica invited the boys upstairs. "So what's the sleeping arrangements?" Jessica asked. Nobody said anything. Jessica had an idea. She called Daisy into the bedroom. The girls reemerged in only teddies. Freddy looked Daisy over and agreed to stay. He and Daisy took the living room.

Jessica realized that Edwin was nervous. She put on a bathrobe to help him relax. "I just need to do some stretches to unwind," she said. She touched her toes. She reached her arms up to the sky. She showed him her tattoos, and how she could almost do a split.

"Please," Edwin said. "Please stop doing that. Will you please stop doing that?"

"Yo, why?" she asked, mock innocently. She had the bathrobe on. He was fully clothed. "You're a good-looking boy."

"I'm not a boy."

"Well, you're a good-looking young man, you know."

"I'm not so young."

"Yeah, well, then, let's go to it."

"For real?" he asked.

Jessica laughed.

He said, "You sure?"

"He was sixteen at the time," Jessica said much later, still tender at the memory. She thought she would have to lead the way. "But," she added, "he proved me wrong."

Jessica started spending a lot of time at Sunny's with Edwin. Sunny liked having her around. Edwin later said that she was the only girlfriend of his that his mother ever liked, even though she was the type of girl that mothers warned boys about. Sunny still lived down the block from Coco, on Andrews Avenue. Jessica and Edwin shared a bottom bunk. Another of Edwin's brothers slept on top. Wishman had his own room because his fights with his brothers got too physical; Sunny, who also had a toddler and a baby, couldn't take the arguing. One time the boys got so rough with one another that she'd had to call the cops.

Sunny never had to wake Edwin twice for school. She and Jessica spent afternoons talking, sprawled across Sunny's big bed. Sunny remembered how hurt Jessica was about Lourdes, whom she described as self-absorbed and always into her men.

Sometimes Milagros brought the twins and Jessica kept them. Sunny didn't mind the additions to the crowded apartment: children played together, and the more there were, the easier it was to baby-sit. Serena sometimes stayed with Coco at Foxy's, or at Milagros's, but mostly she remained at Lourdes's.

George eventually tracked down Jessica at Sunny's. He wondered aloud what type of man dated freaks—like the freak Jessica would become if someone happened to toss acid in her pretty face. Was it true that she had AIDS? That her daughters were skinny and starving? "That's sad," he said scornfully. Sunny grabbed the receiver away from Jessica. George suggested that Sunny keep a close eye on her schoolboy son. Sunny called the phone company and requested a block on the phone to prevent incoming calls from jail. Soon after, her line went dead. Sunny went down to the pay phone and the phone company informed her that someone had called and requested that the service be shut off. Then a delivery boy appeared at Sunny's door, armed with a dozen white roses. The creepy bouquet included a card from George. He hoped she liked the roses; her son's funeral would be filled with flowers just like them.

Jessica still kept in touch with George. She said numbly, "If George wanted me dead, I'd have been dead by now." George's mother arranged conference calls: Jessica used a pay phone on the corner of 176th and Andrews, George called in from prison, and his mother hooked them up. The pay phone was the same one where Cesar used to hang out, with Coco watching from above.

From Sunny's living room, Jessica heard a cop-call. She was baby-sitting Sunny's daughters and her twins. The cop-call—*Po-Po*—was a neighborly warning sounded by whoever spotted the police, for anyone who might like to know; it was not a rare sound on Andrews. Jessica walked to the kitchen window to see if anything interesting was going on.

The street had been blocked. Cruisers had parked and others were pulling up. Then she heard, "Police! Open up! *Policía!*"

"I was like, 'How can all this be for me? Damn, I'm gonna have to pay for somebody else's mistakes and my tears are just coming out,'" Jessica later said. A police officer told her to find someone to collect the children. She called Coco, who ran the three blocks from Foxy's. Coco comforted the girls, who were hysterical, as an officer handcuffed Jessica and escorted her downstairs.

Since George's conviction, narcotics detectives had been driving his confiscated cars, and they were just as flashy as they'd been when

George cruised around in them. In the ongoing game between the police and the dealers, George's cars signaled that the government had won the latest round.

That day, waiting outside on Andrews Avenue, the cherubic Obsession case agent sat plumply in the driver's seat of one of the Mercedes. Jessica recognized him from her long days in court during George's trial. Another detective climbed in the back. Jessica recalled him leaning forward, his breath hot in her ear. "We hear you're a freak," he said.

"Your mother's a freak," Jessica said sweetly.

George's miniature TV sat silent in the dashboard. Jessica asked the case agent if she could make a call. She couldn't call Lourdes; Lourdes didn't have phone service; she wasn't even making her rent. Jessica unsuccessfully tried to reach Sunny to let her know that Coco had all the kids. The Bronx disappeared behind Jessica. In the passenger seat, she headed toward DEA headquarters in Manhattan, in the same Mercedes-Benz in which George had collected her on the night of their first date, three years earlier.

From the MCC, like George before her, Jessica called his mother collect. Rita told Jessica a time to call back the following day. At the prearranged time, George called in on a separate line and his mother hooked them up:

"Well, tell that bitch now she knows what it is to be in jail," Jessica could hear him shouting.

"Fuck him," she said.

"Fuck her," he said. Then they talked.

An NYPD case agent later said that there was no plan to arrest Jessica that spring. They had, in fact, been keeping tabs on her in the hope that she might lead them to Obsession money, or to workers still at large and further up the pyramid. But, for reasons that were never entirely clear, the strategy suddenly changed. George's lawyer believed that Jessica had been arrested in the hope that she would testify against the Obsession hit man, Taz, who had been arrested months earlier. According to the case agent, however, George put out a contract on Jessica. The plan for the hit was overheard on a prison wiretap: George would try to get Isabel to invite Jessica dancing, then have her pretend that she needed to make a phone call once they got to the club. She'd ask Jessica to accompany her outside, where Jessica would get shot. Her murder would be made to look like a botched robbery.

It took Jessica two months of working the telephone and writing letters on her own behalf to scrape together the $5,000 bail. Some of the money came from Elaine's father's sister-in-law, whom Jessica considered an aunt. Boy George reminded Jessica of what he used to say whenever she asked for money for Lourdes, or for one of the problems her family always had: "What the fuck do they do for you?"

"They my family."

"That's your *family*," he would say, mocking her. "That's your family, huh? My family do more for you than your family."

"It's true," conceded Jessica.

Jessica mailed Coco and Edwin visiting forms. Since they were both under eighteen, they had to get their mothers' signatures. That Mother's Day, Coco was the only one who remembered to mail Jessica a card.

During the time between Jessica's arrest and her sentencing, she and Coco became closer than they'd ever been before. Jessica wrote her niece from jail:

> To: My Baby Mercedes . . .
> Hi Mercedes how are you feeling? Well as for your titi jessica I'm chillin. I miss you so-so much. I can't wait to see you. I wonder if you forgot about me, or when you would go to sleep on my chest. I should be home for a little while then I'll have to go away for a long time. But I want you to remember one thing that your titi jessica loves you a whole Big Bunch. I know you can't read this now but when you get older you'll read it and see how much I love my little niece. Be a Good Girl and take care of your sister and Mommy. Love always your titi JESSICA.

Jessica told Coco in her letters that she was soon going to make bail. Her brother Robert and his girl, Shirley, had agreed to sign for her bail bond. Jessica had decided to plead guilty. "I was brought up that if you do something, you do it, and you don't stick the blame on somebody else," she said. Jessica's lawyer had made arrangements for her to turn herself in at the beginning of September, to give her time with her family. She already had her summer planned; Coco was flattered that her sister-in-law trusted her:

> Yo, if I'm not pregnant now, which I doubt, I'm sure gonna get pregnant for the two months I'm in Edwin's house, we're gonna have sex, for breakfast, brunch, lunch, dinner, dessert, non stop until

I drop, or he drops. . . . Coco I'm gonna finish this letter tomorrow
because I took my sleeping pills and their starting to take effect.

When Jessica finally got out, it was Coco whom she called to bring her
clothes—no way was she going to return to the Bronx in a prison uniform
in July, with everyone outside. Coco assembled what she could find: black
leggings, black sandals, and a lime green blouse. Jessica scooted into a
bathroom at the courthouse to change and put on her makeup. She and
Coco took the subway straight to Andrews, to Sunny's. Jessica's return was
like the first day out with a new baby:

Edwin, Jessica's here!

Hey, Jessica, I thought you was gone.

Jessica, you got fat!

Jessica saw Edwin's head pop out of Sunny's kitchen window, then disappear. The next thing she knew, she was in his arms. She stayed at
Sunny's until curfew, then borrowed money for a cab back to Lourdes's.
By the end of the week, she'd moved in with Sunny. Coco stopped by; she
and Wishman flirted, then disappeared in Wishman's room. Sunny
liked that Jessica and Coco were friends. The girls kept her sons indoors.
July in Morris Heights meant the streets were at their wildest.

That summer was a precious time. Some nights, Jessica and Edwin sat
on the fire escape for hours, suspended over Andrews, considering everything. "He even told me about his dreams and fears," she said. He was the
only boy she had loved besides Tito who didn't believe in hitting girls no
matter what they did. When Jessica smacked Edwin with a belt while he
was sleeping—some girl had called to say she was pregnant—Edwin
didn't get heated. He simply said, "Jessica, you crazy. Calm down."

In September 1991, the night before Jessica reported back to the MCC,
Sunny threw a party, and Coco met Milagros for the first time. Mercedes
and Nikki had fallen asleep, and Milagros, who was on her way to score
some coke, helped Coco carry them home. After leaving the girls at
Foxy's, they returned to the party. They tried not to laugh at Elaine, who'd
started crying while she toasted Jessica. Defiance was one thing in the face
of sadness, but people got uncomfortable with the softer side of unbearable things.

Jessica, Elaine, and Daisy decided to walk back to Lourdes's. On
Burnside Avenue, Jessica stopped and rapped on the window of a basement apartment where Tito was staying. He was still out on bail, and
they'd made plans to meet earlier that evening at a club on East

Tremont and Webster called the Devil's Nest. Neither went, but Tito was glad to catch a last glimpse of Jessica. "Click click click and she was gone," he said.

The girls broke night. The next morning, Lourdes refused to come out of her bedroom to say good-bye. Edwin, Elaine, and Daisy accompanied Jessica to the courthouse. She surprised them by suggesting the subway, even though they had enough money between them for a cab. "I was trying to drag it out, it was the hardest thing I ever had to do," she said. The guards made Jessica leave all her jewelry with her sister.

Later that evening, alone in the MCC, Jessica began to cry. She remembered thinking, "I can't believe I turned myself in. Why didn't I run away?"

CHAPTER TWELVE

Cesar arrived home unannounced weeks later, in October 1991. He stripped on the threshold of his mother's apartment; when she opened the door, his prison-issued clothes were puddled around his feet. Prison clothes brought a house bad luck. Lourdes ushered Cesar inside and peered down the hall conspiratorially. She thought he'd escaped. When Coco, who was visiting, heard Lourdes's happy shouting, she guessed that it was Cesar. She grabbed Nikki and hid.

Cesar had completed the minimum two years of his sentence. His release had been approved by the Division for Youth Board of Parole. The apartment to which he returned on Mount Hope Place was not much different from the one he'd left on Vyse, but the wear showed on his family. At forty, Lourdes had lost some of her resilience. Little Star, who was six, looked like a miniature mother, with dark circles under her eyes. Brittany and Stephanie were with Milagros, who had moved down the street from Coco's mother's, on Andrews Avenue. Robert had returned from Florida and now lived a regimented life in Brooklyn. He worked as a teller at a bank. Elaine lived with Angel and their two young sons in a tiny one-bedroom on Morrison. She was fighting to keep her house in order—her husband away from drugs and prison, and her two young sons away from their father's influence. Coco, with whom Cesar was still in love, had a baby that did not belong to him, and Jessica was stuck at the MCC.

Things had changed in Cesar's FMP family, too. His old compatriot Rocco was still with the ambitious schoolgirl, who seemed determined to change Rocco into a family man. Rocco was getting his GED and only robbing drug dealers part time. He encouraged Tito to stay in school and rob after class—Tito stood a chance to win a baseball scholarship—but Tito dropped out. Now he was dealing drugs and—unknown to Cesar—heavily using cocaine. Since Tito's affair with Jessica, the friendship with Cesar had cooled. Cesar later said that he had never entirely trusted Tito anyway. Tito had always struck Cesar as tentative, and a reluctance to act could be dangerous. Tito seemed even more paranoid than before. Only Mighty, who had gotten out of prison the day before Cesar, seemed familiar, like home.

But on Cesar's first day back, Lourdes nodded toward her bedroom, where Coco was hiding. Coco was so nervous that she couldn't hold her hands still enough to fix her hair, which she'd dyed blond.

"Hey, how you doing?" he asked, opening the bedroom door. His voice! She'd forgotten what it sounded like close in person, away from the echoing noise of a prison visiting room. Cesar looked more beautiful than ever to Coco, and he'd always been beautiful. His formerly thin arms had muscles. His stomach, which she saw because he rubbed it slowly as he spoke, had ripples. His presence made her head hurt—although the pain might have been caused by her habit of pulling the topknot of her pony-tail too tight. "Let me see your daughter?" he asked. Coco stared at his lips as he smiled at Nikki. It was impossible not to smile when you saw her—a grinning mocha baby with a splotch of birthmark on her chubby cheek. Her eyes had Kodak's long lashes, and like Coco's, they were bright. "She's beautiful, God bless her," Cesar said. That was all. He turned and left.

That same afternoon, Lourdes's husband, Que-Que, was arrested. "I'm glad you are taking him or I would have killed him myself!" Lourdes told the police. Their marriage had deteriorated since the move from Vyse to Mount Hope. Lourdes and Que-Que had been cocaine companions, but she said that he'd since pursued a private relationship with heroin, and that the challenge of getting the dope made him more sneaky and remote: he stole food stamps; pawned her jewelry, including her Irish friendship wedding ring; she couldn't trust him with the rent. "A pothead? Fine. Sniff a little coke? I understand. But oh no, not heroin," Lourdes said.

A condition of Cesar's parole was that he either get a job or return to school. He chose school, thinking it would be easier to skip. He enrolled in Bronx Community College. The BCC campus was on the west side, close to Foxy's. Cesar and Coco saw each other every day, and they imme-diately started sleeping together again. Coco stayed over at Lourdes's with Mercedes. Cesar walked Serena the half block to her school, then went to school himself. It wasn't always easy to rouse Little Star; she'd grown accustomed to Lourdes's schedule, breaking night and sleeping until early afternoon. But sometimes Coco woke to Serena's attempts to wake Cesar. "Tío," Little Star would say. "Tío, I gotta go to school. Wake up, Tío, wake up." She would already have fed and dressed herself.

"Take her, Coco," Cesar would mumble from beneath his pillow. Coco didn't mind. She'd grown fond of Serena, but she wondered how such an optimistic nickname had landed on a girl with such sad eyes. Lit-tle Star hardly seemed destined for brightness; she was more like an old lady. Her gravity spooked Coco; once, while she and Cesar were making

love, Coco spotted Little Star peeking through the wide gap underneath Cesar's door. She frequently asked Coco when Jessica was coming
home. "I don't know, Mami," Coco would say; then she would try to distract her with the offer of a game or a song. Coco preferred the sunny take
on things. Children should be rambunctious. Coco said, "Serena was too
grown for a six-year-old."

Sometimes Coco brought Serena back to Foxy's, where Coco lived with
Mercedes and Nikki in her bedroom. Serena was an easy child; she never
asked for anything or made a fuss. Nikki, on the other hand, had colic,
and Coco couldn't handle her. At night, Coco would pound on the wall
between her bedroom and her mother's room until Foxy or Richie came
and took Nikki away. Some afternoons, Coco left Nikki with Foxy—or
with Sheila, Nikki's godmother and Foxy's neighbor—and took Serena
and Mercedes to wait for Cesar to get out of class.

Bronx Community College sat on a hill above University Avenue,
which overlooked Aqueduct Park. Watching the students, Coco wished
she had never dropped out of school. Cesar shared whatever he was
learning—math, new words. She liked math best. He once teased her at
Lourdes's, in the shower, when she mispronounced *superb* "super-B."
Within a month, though, Cesar stopped attending college. The household needed money. He took a job overseeing crack sales just below the
college, in Aqueduct, and Coco and Mercedes waited for him there.

Privately, Cesar was loving; publicly, he referred to Coco only as his
daughter's mother. He brought other girls home, but they didn't stay the
night. Coco learned to wait out his company; she pretended that she
didn't mind the steady stream through his room. If he broke night, she and
Mercedes slept with Lourdes, or she retreated to Foxy's, or she and Mercedes relocated to Lourdes's couch.

But if Coco was resigned, Mercedes wasn't having it. Sometimes
Cesar would drive her around in Rocco's car. If he offered a girl a ride,
Mercedes refused to relinquish the passenger seat. She acted as though
the gray Ford Taurus were her private limousine. "My chair!" she'd say,
or, "Mommy's chair!" and the girl would have to sit in back.

Coco was hoping that her patience would restore Cesar's faith in her
loyalty. She briefly took a job at Youngland, a children's clothing store on
Fordham, but Lourdes, who had agreed to watch Mercedes, complained
about money, and Coco didn't earn enough to pay her more. Regardless,
Mercedes gave Coco a legitimate excuse for her constant visits to Mount
Hope:

Mercedes wants to see her father.
Mercy's crying for her father.
I swear, this girl, she is so attached!

Coco minded Cesar's other girls less as long as they kept changing, but then he started up with Lizette, and there were fewer other girls. Cesar knew Lizette from Vyse. By November, as far as Coco could tell, there was only herself, Lizette, and Lizette's best friend, Vicky. Cesar brought Vicky into his bedroom after Lizette went to school. Once, he called to Coco while Lizette showered. "Bring the baby," he said. But the thought of having sex with him right after he'd been with another girl made Coco uncomfortable.

"Let's go," he said.

"You just had sex with her but—"

"You don't like it, leave."

"I don't want to leave," Coco said.

"Then let's go."

Cesar still loved Coco, but he wanted to punish her for Nikki. He'd warned her when he was in Harlem Valley, "Coco, I am going to do everything in my power to make you suffer when I come out." Besides the other girls, he intentionally criticized Coco's appearance, twisting what made her happy and confident into a source of embarrassment. Instead of nudging her to stop her bad habit of picking her face, he acted disgusted. Instead of soothing Coco's self-consciousness about Nikki, he harped on her betrayal: "Every time I see his daughter I'm reminded of that."

Within weeks, Lizette was pregnant, and her mother dumped her at Lourdes's. Lizette remembered her saying to Lourdes, "I'm very ashamed of my daughter and what she did. You can keep her." At first, Lourdes was welcoming. While Cesar was out working the streets, she taught Lizette how to cook rice that didn't come out like a snowball, and how to season steak with pepper and vinegar. Lourdes also spent time with her friends in the bedroom, sniffing cocaine. She asked Lizette not to mention this to her son, and Lizette answered, "I don't know nothing," honoring a fundamental ghetto rule. Lizette later noted that at least Lourdes cared enough to hide her business; people in her house used to break night doing drugs right in front of her.

Lizette kept quiet about Lourdes's drugs, but Cesar would find out anyway, and Lourdes would think Lizette had snitched. The friendship between the older and younger woman soured; the arguments about cooking and housework began. Lourdes complained to Cesar that Lizette

was lazy; Lizette said Lourdes wanted her to do everything. Lizette told
Cesar that Lourdes was a hypocrite. Cesar agreed, but Lourdes was his
mother. Lizette thought Cesar acted less like Lourdes's son and more like
her man: he'd curse Lourdes out for her bad behavior and she would run
crying into the bedroom; he'd order her friends out of the apartment; he'd
decide whether she could go dancing and inspect the way she dressed.
One time, he frog-marched Lourdes back upstairs for wearing something
too revealing. In the meantime, Lizette and Little Star kept one another
company. "We grew a little bond," Lizette said. They watched TV and
colored. Little Star cried a lot. She told Lizette that she missed her
mother. Lizette missed her own mother, too.

For the most part, Coco had retreated to Foxy's. You could hate a rival
all you wanted to, but pregnancy merited respect. There were girls so hard
that they paid no mind to a belly, but Coco wasn't one of them. After
all, the unborn baby was innocent. If you cursed a pregnant girl and something bad happened to the baby, you could be cursed the rest of your natural life. Perhaps Lizette's baby might reestablish the balance that Nikki's
arrival had wrecked: Coco had Kodak's child, now Cesar would have
Lizette's; Coco and Cesar would be even. And Coco still continued to see
Cesar—every day—on the sly. Coco had convinced her little brother,
Hector, to trade bedrooms with her so that she would be near the fire
escape. That way, Coco could scramble down whenever Cesar pulled up
in Rocco's car and honked. "I forgave him," she said. "I forgave him
because I loved him and I didn't want to see the bad."

The badness, however, impressed and intimidated the men in Coco's
family. Cesar gave Richie money and once lent him his gun. Cesar let
Coco's older brother Manuel strut the gun around the block. But Cesar
had no tolerance for guys who were all talk. When it was discovered that
a cousin of Coco's was being regularly raped by her father, everyone
threatened to kill him, but it was Cesar who beat the guy up and ordered
him to leave the girl alone. Cesar bought Coco food if she hadn't eaten,
and whatever Mercedes needed. Coco's room was stocked. He also
bought things for Nikki, a gesture Coco interpreted hopefully. Even if he
saw Coco twice in an afternoon, he'd return to Foxy's every evening—
ostensibly to tuck in Mercedes. Coco would sneak out and leave the girls
in her room, asleep.

But at Lourdes's, Cesar ignored Coco completely. He passed her on his
way to the bathroom. Lizette followed. Coco could hear their laughter in
the shower. She and Cesar used to laugh like that. Cesar and Lizette
padded by again in towels, then reappeared, dressed, ready for the street.

On his way out, Cesar lifted Mercedes and nuzzled her neck with his nose. "Bye, Mercy, Daddy'll be back," he said. To Coco, he said, "Clean my sneakers. Do all them." She found a rag and the white shoe polish and opened the door to Cesar's bedroom. Photographs of Lizette and Cesar decorated the headboard of her old bed. Lizette had everything she thought Cesar wanted: an unmarked face, no height, no kids from other boys. Coco decided to be the best wife. Lizette cooked for him and did his laundry, but Coco wiped the scuff marks off pair after pair of his sneakers. She arranged them in his closet in neat lines. She ironed his T-shirts and his jeans. She said, "He never had to put a thing in the cleaners cuz I do the pleats."

Following his release from prison, Mighty spent a lot of time at Lourdes's; his mother and brother had moved away from Tremont, and he was dealing drugs in an abandoned house on Mount Hope. Mighty was family. When Lourdes cooked, she sent him down a plate; sometimes she traded the food for drugs. Mighty used Lourdes's bathroom. He wore Cesar's clothes. Lourdes felt that the boys' friendship fulfilled a lack of brother love. "Mighty had a brother the mother doted on. Robert never gave brother love to Cesar. What they were having, they were missing it— they put it together, the both of them," Lourdes said. The only thing Lourdes didn't like about Mighty was his drinking. Sober, he was beautiful—even shy—but alcohol made him mean.

Cesar trusted Mighty absolutely: "Mighty was an ultimate soldier. 'Whatever it is, I'm with it. Whatever it is, I'm there.' He was a field man. He felt comfortable in the action. He wasn't comfortable making decisions." That's what Cesar did. Mighty wasn't much of a talker, which gave his words more weight.

Mighty liked Lizette. He disliked Coco because she'd hurt Cesar. He eyed her coldly. "How you doing, slave girl? Slaving today?" he'd say. Alone with Coco, Mighty prodded her; why did she stay? Coco didn't know how to respond. His close attention made her feel awkward. She blamed herself for Cesar's mistreatment, and what business was it of Mighty's, anyway? "I used to tell him it don't bother me, which it did bother," she said.

Coco waged her counterattacks against Lizette—surreptitiously, while Lizette was in school. She tossed the stuffed animals Lizette gave Cesar in the incinerator. She carved *Coco and Cesar* inside his bedroom closet. She mauled their photographs, stabbing Lizette's image with a pen. She destroyed the picture of Cesar with his legs and arms wrapped from behind around Lizette, his hands cupping her bigger breasts. "I fucked them up so bad there was no way of making those pictures right," Coco said. She inscribed her name in the headboard, and a warning: *This bed belongs to Coco. Whoever sleeps in here is just a ho.*

Coco aimed the insults nearer Cesar, although she didn't challenge him directly: How could he stay in his room when Mercedes, his only child, longed to play with him? One day, Cesar walked past the living room without giving his baby girl a glance. Coco was watching TV with Mercedes and Lourdes and Little Star. "Don't disrespect my daughter like that," she finally snapped. He slammed the bedroom door.

That December 1991, Lizette was the one that Cesar brought to Jessica's sentencing. Coco accompanied Lourdes. The night before, Lizette slept in Cesar's room, and Coco spent the night with Mercedes on the couch.

Coco started crying as soon as she laid eyes on Jessica in the courtroom. Cesar hated crying and he hated courts. "Ma, I'm gonna go to my parole office now," he mumbled to Lourdes. Without saying good-bye to Jessica, he and Lizette left the sentencing. Cesar later admitted he could not bear to watch what was about to happen to his sister.

Had Jessica gone to trial, she would have faced a twenty-year mandatory minimum term. Instead, she pled guilty to one count of participating in a narcotics conspiracy. The judge asked Jessica if she had anything she wanted to say before he imposed his sentence. Jessica stood. She spoke softly. "Yes, Your Honor. I would just like to say that I'm sorry for the crime that I've committed, and all I hope for is to return to my family and to my mother."

Despite appearances, Jessica's sentence was not determined by the judge; federal mandatory minimums pretty much rendered judicial discretion moot. Drug quantity served as the main determinant of prison time. Freedom decreased by jumps of five, ten, and twenty years for each gram over a congressionally determined number. The judge said, "I do not, as a general proposition, make the type of statement that I am going to make now, but . . . I feel that this case is a case that really does not call for the mandatory minimum that exists here. I think you have to be punished and you should be punished, but I think a ten-year sentence in this case is unusually harsh, and I do not like imposing it, but I have an oath of office that I have to follow."

The proof of Jessica's actual involvement in the Obsession organization was limited: two entries in 10-4's ledger from her few days of working at the mill, and the brief message she'd passed on to George's supplier, recorded on the wiretap. However, to reduce the mandatory minimum term, Jessica would have had to cooperate, and she had refused. The only way to be granted immunity would be to confess every secret, but she was as loyal to George as Cesar had been to Rocco. She also had a family to protect, and Milagros, who was now going to have legal custody of the twins. Jessica wasn't sure that her children weren't better off without her. The judge continued, "And what I can make out of all this, you got yourself involved with this guy Rivera, and he certainly helped lead you astray. And you went there in the first place of your own free will. But what I would hope is that in prison you learn some kind of trade so that when you get out, you can stay out of trouble."

He granted Jessica a few extra minutes to say good-bye to her daughters. In the grandeur of the hushed courtroom, the children seemed especially small. Brittany and Stephanie, dressed in identical aqua sweat suits, hugged Jessica's legs. Serena clasped her waist desperately. Elaine had to peel them off. The marshal said it was time. Coco was too upset to touch Jessica; she clutched Mercedes instead. Lourdes slumped against the bench. Mercedes cried. Coco bounced her awkwardly. Mercedes cried louder.

"Did you bring her bottle? She's hungry, Mami, can't you tell, she's hungry," Lourdes said. "Where's Little Star?"

Serena had crept out into the hallway to try to catch one more look at her mother being taken away.

As it happened, two weeks earlier, Serena had lost the father she had never known. Puma had never made the comeback he'd hoped for in the entertainment world; instead, he'd continued dealing. His success didn't reach the scale of George's, but he'd done okay. He and his wife, Trinket, had moved to a residential neighborhood in Mount Vernon; Trinket wanted some distance from the Bronx and the inevitable fallout of Puma's work.

That same December, they'd attended a holiday party with their two sons. After the party, Puma had driven his family home and parked on the street in front of his house. He retrieved his baby son from the car seat and stepped onto the walk that led to his door. Trinket was trying to wake their older boy, who'd fallen asleep in the backseat, when two young men appeared from behind the shrubbery. Both were drug dealers who—until that moment—Puma had considered friends. Trinket covered her child's mouth with one hand and dragged him beneath the car. She heard Puma begging for the baby's life. She heard shots. Puma tossed the baby as the bullets hit him. The baby survived.

Just before Christmas, Cesar dropped in on Rocco. Rocco was shaving his head in the shower when one of his cohorts called in: there was a drug dealer to rob. "It's all in timing. 'Yo, it's on.' You gotta be there, or you'll miss it," Rocco said. But this time, Rocco wasn't moving fast enough. He said he still needed to dress, and his crime buddies wouldn't wait. He offered up Cesar as his replacement: "Let my boy go, he just got out, you can trust him."

Cesar came home with $25,000, intoxicated with the ease of the job. "Like snatching an old lady's purse," he said. He gave some to Rocco and tore through the rest. He bought himself a winter coat and clothes and sneakers and jewelry; he stocked the shelves with food and paid Lourdes's back rent and overdue electric bill; he bought gifts for Serena and a Christmas tree. He gave Lizette a nameplate necklace and some outfits. He didn't buy anything for Coco, but he did get Mercedes a black leather shearling. She was almost two. At first, the coat spooked her; she called it *kuko*—monster—and she cried, but Cesar coaxed her to put it on. Then she refused to take it off.

Early in January, Lizette lost the baby. Cesar was regaining interest in Coco and losing interest in Lizette, but even after the miscarriage, he still didn't have the heart to send Lizette back home; she had told him that her mother's boyfriend had made a pass at her. Lizette's miscarriage brought out Coco's boldness, though. One afternoon, she kicked open Cesar's bedroom door. "If you so much a woman, come out in this hall," she yelled to Lizette. "What is it, Cesar, you got another ho in there? Ho after ho after ho after ho! When you're done, why don't you come to your wife?"

Lourdes scurried to the kitchen and returned with a can opener. "Here," she said. "Hit her with this." It wasn't personal—Lourdes liked Lizette well enough—but a fight was a fight. Fights gave people some relief, some room to breathe, and added some entertainment to an otherwise gloomy day. The next time Coco got heated, Lourdes handed her a garlic press.

But even without the promise of a baby, Coco still envied Lizette. Lizette was closer to the center of things. "Cesar never went out with me, like holding hand in hand, or taking trains together, never. He went with her," Coco said.

*   *   *

Jessica had spent Christmas at the MCC, awaiting transfer to a permanent facility. She bided her time writing letters and waiting for her turn on the unit telephone. She wrote Trinket in care of Milagros and offered her condolences; she called Rocco, and they joked and had phone sex; she called Edwin. If Edwin wasn't home, she grilled his baby sisters about his whereabouts. She instructed the children to warn any rivals that Edwin already had a wife, who was dangerous and about to get out of jail. Jessica couldn't call Lourdes because her mother still didn't have a phone.

John Gotti was back at the MCC, and he sent food to the women on Jessica's unit, which the guards brought in for him from Little Italy. Jessica once ran into him on the inmate elevator, and Gotti recognized her from her paralegal days. "Mr. Dapper Don," she said, "it can happen to the best of us." They both laughed. Jessica later said, "He was so cute, with the hairstyle and everything. Now I was thinking, 'He's not so old.'"

Guards remembered Jessica, too. George and the Obsession case were already jailhouse legend: Jessica's six tattoos, her sex life, George's death threats, the exotic James Bond cars, the Christmas Eve party on the yacht. No one seemed surprised when Jessica got reprimanded for having sex with a male inmate named Jamal in an unmonitored room. Someone had snitched. Jamal was being represented by George's old attorney. "You'll always be Miss Rivera," a guard warned her. "If I was you, I wouldn't get involved with any man. The word's out."

But Jessica wasn't sure she wanted to be George's girl anymore; she liked Jamal. She told the captain, "I'm going to jail for ten years. I'm chasing this opportunity." Jamal arranged for his mother to deposit money in Jessica's meager commissary account and send Jessica sneakers before she got shipped away. The next stop was a holding facility in Georgia.

Meanwhile, Boy George, who was stationed in Lewisburg, made his own contributions to the prison rumor mill: Jessica heard that a beating was waiting for her in Georgia. But the women there who were allegedly so loyal to George's friends only fired insults. The authorities next shipped Jessica to Oklahoma, where she stayed for a month, and no one bothered to bother her. Finally, a prison bus delivered her, shackled and handcuffed, to her final destination—Florida. George had allegedly arranged for someone to greet Jessica with a beat-down. But that spring, just before her twenty-fourth birthday, she arrived at the maximum-security women's facility in Marianna and was processed in the same dreary, depressing way as everyone else.

A guard removed her leg irons and unlocked her handcuffs. She stripped and squatted and spread apart her buttocks. She coughed and coughed again—to dislodge potential contraband from body cavities. Then she stood. She ran her hands beneath her breasts, as she was ordered. She opened her mouth and raised her tongue. She lifted her arms and ran her fingers through her hair. She received a brown paper bag of hygienes—soap, toothpaste, deodorant—several changes of prison-issue clothes, an assignment to kitchen duty, and a cubicle.

CHAPTER THIRTEEN

That March 1992, Lizette returned to her mother's. Coco still lived with her two daughters at Foxy's, and Cesar continued to visit her there. He enjoyed the freedom of having no live-in girlfriend, but the fun soon ended. In May, the police picked him up on a parole violation: he'd been driving Rocco's car without a license. When he returned to his mother's, after a summer at Rikers, Serena had gone to Robert's, and her welfare benefits had gone with her. Lourdes hadn't paid the rent in months. She was using more than ever and had been spotted hanging out in the abandoned building on Mount Hope. Mighty gave Lourdes cocaine—to keep her business indoors, away from the gossip—but Cesar tried to calm her down by getting her interested in weed.

Cesar immediately reconnected with Coco, but he also met another girl named Roxanne. Roxanne had a swan's neck, almond-shaped eyes, and the posture of a dancer. She also had a welcome confidence with boys. She hung out with her friends on Tremont, in front of Kennedy Fried Chicken. All of Cesar's friends had tried to kick it to her—Rocco, Mighty, Tito—but Cesar, with his baby face, was the one she picked.

One afternoon, Coco passed by Mount Hope to show Cesar some photographs. Lourdes was hanging with her friends in front of the building.

"Cesar's not home" is how Lourdes greeted Coco. "Cesar's not home." Why did she say the same thing twice?

"Where's your son?" Coco asked.

"Oh, I don't know, Coco, he haven't came in from last night, he was hanging out with the guys."

"Okay, Ma, bye," Coco said. Lourdes underestimated her; she seemed to have forgotten that Coco was also a Sagittarius. Coco ducked inside the building, and when she heard the pounding music from the fifth floor, she knew immediately Cesar was upstairs.

He answered the door in just a towel. He refused to let her in. His hair was wet.

Roxanne, who lived a few blocks from Mount Hope, threw a party in the basement of her mother's building one night that fall. It was after 3 A.M. when Roxanne's cousin and Mighty decided to go get burgers. Mighty had been drinking. As they walked across the White Castle parking lot, Mighty exchanged words with a group of boys who were leaning against a car. The boys flashed their guns, but Mighty kept acting tough. He was also armed.

Roxanne's cousin knew Mighty well enough to worry, and she ran back to the party for Cesar. Cesar was about to get into a fight himself, but he broke away and ran to his friend's aid. By the time Cesar arrived, the boys were in the restaurant and Mighty was stewing in the parking lot. When Cesar failed to calm him, he accompanied him inside. The trouble exploded instantly. Guns blasting, Cesar and Mighty backed out the glass front doors.

Mighty had a habit of stepping in front of Cesar whenever they got into shoot-outs; he was shorter, and Cesar fired over his head. Cesar had repeatedly warned Mighty about this habit, but it was also a testament to the trust between them; Mighty would tease Cesar, saying that Cesar always had his back. But this time, Cesar slipped. He doesn't remember pulling the trigger, but he remembers his best friend going down, his chin lifting toward the sky as the bullet tore through the back of his head.

Rocco got word and ran down Tremont. By the time he reached White Castle, Cesar was gone, and Mighty had been rushed to Lincoln Hospital, where he died immediately. The police had already taped off the crime scene. Mighty's blood was everywhere.

Cesar ran to Roxanne's mother's, where Rocco later caught up with him. Rocco found Cesar muttering incoherently on Roxanne's twin bed and threatening to kill himself. Rocco managed to convince him to hand over his gun. The next day, Cesar and Roxanne went on the run. For several weeks the couple skulked from apartment to apartment, hotel to hotel, living on the McDonald's, sandwiches, and KFC that Roxanne retrieved for them.

Roxanne's mother had a boyfriend who supplied the fugitive couple with a steady stream of cash. As the weeks went on, Roxanne's mother and the boyfriend argued about the money. Roxanne's mother did not want her daughter doing time and gave Roxanne an earful whenever she came home and showered. Roxanne carted the frustration back to Cesar, who had started smoking cigarettes. He hated cigarettes. He battled with Roxanne, but anything was better than being alone with his thoughts. Their days consisted of sex and arguing—"Argue, fight, bed. Argue, fight, bed," Cesar said. Later he admitted, "I was stressing. I didn't handle it too good."

Coco was also overwhelmed by the gravity of what had happened, but she didn't know what to say, so she obsessed about Cesar being on the lam with another woman. She felt that Roxanne was not even pretty; she had to be at least part Dominican whether or not she admitted it, and she was slim, practically skinny. Coco wondered how Cesar could have sex with someone who had hair like a black girl's.

To raise some cash, Cesar made a few drug deliveries, riding the train to Bridgeport and New Haven. He kept in touch with Coco at Foxy's. He paged her. She called him back. "Coco, I gotta get out. Yo, Coco, I don't want to be here," he told her. Coco didn't know what "here" meant, because Cesar was everywhere. He'd been in a hotel by Van Cortlandt, in one in Yonkers near Rosedale, in his friend Luis's girl's apartment, just around the block from Lourdes's old apartment, on Anthony Avenue. Cesar stopped at Elaine's, and Milagros's, but both of them became so nervous that he had to move on. He crashed with a full-grown lady, the older sister of a friend, but he'd left when she pressured him for sex. He stayed in the basement of his old building on Tremont, where he and Coco made love on a weight-lifting bench. He even went to the Empire State Building with the super's son. Cesar had been to plenty of other places Coco never heard about, with people she didn't know, but Cesar told her things. He trusted Coco with his life even though he didn't trust her with other men. He told her he was scared, that he'd spent Christmas Eve in a cellar scribbling words on scraps of paper that didn't make sense. He said he realized that he hadn't done anything with his life. He still wanted to kill himself. They never spoke directly of Mighty; the subject was too painful. They did, however, speak about Roxanne.

Cesar knew Roxanne wasn't the cause of the anguish and tension, but he somehow still blamed her. She was pregnant. She couldn't decide what to do: One minute, she'd threaten to take out the baby. Then, if he agreed, she'd quip, "I'm keeping the baby. Think your ass gonna tell me what to do." Eventually, Roxanne did decide to keep the baby, stay with Cesar, but return to her mother's apartment. Cesar agreed to stay with Roxanne, sleep wherever he could, and see Coco on the side.

Unknown to both Coco and Roxanne, Cesar was also seeing another girl named Giselle, whom he paged whenever Roxanne or Coco couldn't be with him. Cesar could not sleep alone. Giselle was a neighborhood girl he knew from way back—even before he met Coco. One of Cesar's friends hid his stash at Giselle's mother's, and Cesar tagged along whenever he went to re-up. He hadn't seen Giselle for years. During that time, she had married, moved to Yonkers, had a son, and divorced. She'd recently returned to the neighborhood and was living with her mother. Her sister was dating Cesar's friend Luis.

Giselle and Cesar would meet up at her sister's place on Anthony. Giselle cooked for him. Cesar stayed up late with Luis and his friends, but Giselle wasn't a hang-out person; she usually left him to his company and climbed into her sister's bed with her baby son. After his guests left, Cesar would hide his 9mm Taurus with its two clips in a cigar box on top of a wall unit in the living room that blocked the window to the street. He would have preferred to keep his gun closer by, but Giselle's son was underfoot. Then he'd push the love seat into the couch, wake Giselle, and carry the baby back to bed.

It's unlikely that another girl would have changed Coco's devotion to Cesar. "To me," Coco said, "I was always with him. I knew we wasn't together, but to me, the way I looked at it, I was always with him. He didn't worry because I never was going toward anybody else. He knew that if he was with another girl, *Coco would take me back*. I would." Giselle, however, didn't accommodate the other girls so quickly. She made Cesar sleep alone the night after she spotted him on Mount Hope with Roxanne sitting on his lap.

In January 1993, Rambo, a Bronx homicide detective, changed out of his sweat suit and into a Con Ed employee uniform. Hulk's choice of a disguise was appropriate: gas leaks, like fires, were common in the neighborhood. That morning, a tip had come in, confirming where Cesar had spent the previous night. Hulk and the other undercovers drove to Anthony Avenue. They'd heard that Cesar didn't plan to surrender quietly.

Rambo, nicknamed for his pumped-up body, was known for solving cases. He'd transferred to the 46th in 1988, when the crack trade was exploding. Tremont, in its heyday, reliably gave him five shootings every week. Rambo was considered a fair cop by the neighborhood's tough guys because he didn't harass people unnecessarily. "He didn't set you up," said Cesar. "If you didn't have nothing on you, he wouldn't plant nothing on you. He'd say, 'I'm gonna get you, but I'm gonna get you fair and square.'" Rambo tracked down runaway daughters and retrieved stereos from ex-girlfriends; he brought Pampers on house calls and handed off twenties for milk. People confided in him; he never made someone who had too much time feel that he was in a rush. He respected the men, and if the women whistled, he was glad to remove his shirt and show off his chest.

During the four months he'd been trailing Cesar, Rambo and Lourdes had become cautious friends. He stopped by her apartment regularly and searched the place every time, but she didn't insult him, which he appreciated. "She was afraid," Rambo said. "She didn't want to rat on her own kid, but she knew if another cop or a rookie saw him, and he was armed, they were going to kill him, and she knew I wouldn't do that to the kid unless I had to." Rambo assured her that if Cesar surrendered, he'd take him in safely. Lourdes passed the word along to Cesar, as Rambo expected, but Cesar said again he wouldn't go without a fight. Rocco planted misleading rumors—that Cesar had fled to Puerto Rico, to Springfield, to Florida.

One afternoon, Cesar went to Big Joe's, in Mount Vernon, a tattoo shop. Cesar had never been tattooed before. He liked clean, untouched skin. He already had a burn mark on his shoulder from when Lourdes had dropped a pot of boiling water on him. But killing his best friend was a deeper cut, and this tattoo was to be his penance; it was a wound Cesar wanted the world to see.

Cesar boasted to the tattoo artist that the detective Rambo was chasing him.

"He's a friend of mine," the tattoo artist said. In fact, unbeknownst to Cesar, Rambo moonlighted for Big Joe as a body piercer.

Cesar added, "When you see him again, mention to him that Cesar was here." At first, Rambo thought the message was just another false lead. But then he learned that the tattoo, which was just above the boy's heart, read *Forgive me Mighty, R.I.P.*

Rambo rang the doorbell at Giselle's sister's. Police manned the fire escape, the alleyways, and the roof. When Giselle's sister opened the door, several police pushed in. Cesar was lying beside Giselle and her son in the living room, in their makeshift bed. Rambo handcuffed Cesar, then instructed Giselle to dress him. She passed her screaming son to her sister and guided Cesar's feet into a pair of sweats. Cesar told her to double up on his boxers and socks, so that he'd have a clean pair to wear in jail while he washed the others in the sink. She tied the laces of his Nikes and tucked twenty dollars in his pocket for deodorant and shampoo.

Rambo escorted Cesar to the 46th quietly. He let Lourdes bring in sandwiches and juice. Afterward, Cesar asked him, "So who called the cops on me?"

"You know what was your problem?" Rambo replied. "Too many girls."

*   *   *

Upon hearing the news, Coco cried, but after she heard that Cesar had been in bed with Giselle, she laughed. "That's just like him," she said. The police would have seen him naked. Roxanne had been dissed.

Coco was pregnant. She'd suspected the pregnancy but the first test had been negative. The second test was positive. Once again, she was carrying Cesar's baby, and once again he was locked up. "I bugged out for a minute. Then I got *happy*. I was like, 'All right, you know, *finally!*' I even thought I could write Cesar and give him good news." The good news was even better because it would upset Roxanne.

Cesar told Roxanne during a visit at Rikers Island, where he was being held. "That was the beginning of the end right there," he said. That May, in 1993, Roxanne gave birth to their daughter, whom she named Justine. Justine had Roxanne's eyes and Cesar's light complexion and wide grin. A friend of Cesar's named Ace hired a private attorney to represent Cesar, but then Ace was murdered. When the private attorney delivered the news, he suggested Cesar call Legal Aid or plead out. Cesar didn't trust Legal Aid: his last Legal Aid attorney had advised him to plead guilty to a robbery he hadn't even committed. The following month, Cesar pled guilty to one count of manslaughter. He was sentenced to an indeterminate term of nine years to life. He would serve at least the nine-year minimum. This time, however, the New York State Department of Corrections classified Cesar as an adult. He was nineteen.

Coxsackie Correctional Facility was the first of many maximum-security prisons among which Cesar would be shuttled over the coming years. Most of Coxsackie's inmates were young, so there was lots of fighting. Some inmates called it Gladiator Camp. Tito, his old friend from FMP, was there awaiting trial for the murder of his wife. Since he'd last seen Cesar, things had spun out of control: he'd continued robbing drug dealers and doing too much coke. Tito claimed that he had exchanged shots with an intruder, who'd shot his wife, then fired at him; the prosecutors would argue that Tito had killed his wife, then shot himself to cover it up.

Wherever the truth lay, Tito refused to plead guilty. Cesar tried to shake him out of it. Back when Tito only had a gun charge, he'd spent the night before his sentencing curled up at the foot of Rocco's bed. Cesar wasn't sure that Tito was hard enough to handle prison, but he knew that the fifteen years the district attorney had offered Tito was better than what he was bound to get if he went to court. Tito was determined to prove his innocence.

Cesar and Tito weren't on the same unit, but they hung out in the yard. They ragged on the other teams during handball games. They hollered, "East Tremont! East Tremont!" when they played basketball. They sat on the bleachers and talked. They never discussed Tito's relationship with Jessica, or what had happened to Mighty. They reminisced about better times. They spoke of all the other girls they'd known, or wished they'd known, and wondered who would answer the letters they floated into the world—Tito called them kites.

"The whole thing is about getting bitches to write to pass the time," Cesar said. Cesar cast a wide net. For starters, his correspondents included Coco, Roxanne, and Lizette. He wrote other girls in care of friends, because he only remembered the girls by nicknames or by their buildings or by their blocks. He told Tito, "We shoulda kept their addresses if this was the kind of life we was gonna lead."

Cesar's adult designation made him potentially eligible for conjugal visits called trailers. Trailers were named after actual trailers on the compound, where inmates could spend overnights with their families. To qualify for trailers, wives had to be legal wives. But trailers required a girl with resources—money for the food and traveling, persistence to assemble all the necessary documentation and fill out the required paperwork, and stamina to withstand the duration of her husband's bid.

Prison was the fulfillment of the empty promise of the ghetto: it positioned you even farther out on the margin of things. Cesar's ability to sustain vital relationships in the outside world could wither with each passing year. He didn't have the resources he had on the outside—spotless sneakers, brand-new clothes, his sexual prowess, different girls to impress and experience. Roxanne wasn't suited for the long haul; he'd yet to see their baby, and her explanations felt like excuses. All prison visitors needed ID, and Roxanne still hadn't gotten around to getting their daughter's birth certificate. Coco wanted to make the effort, but she was disorganized and easily distracted. Cesar wondered how long any girl would last without sex. "You try to fill your little black book," Cesar said. "You're gonna need a lot of spare tires throughout this ride."

Eight months later, a friend sent him Giselle's address.

CHAPTER FOURTEEN

The maximum-security prison in Marianna, Florida, where Jessica would spend the first two years of her incarceration, was the only high-security federal facility for women in the nation at that time. Although Jessica was a nonviolent offender with no previous record, she had to start her sentence in maximum detention because of the length of her term. The women who filled Marianna's antiseptic units were by and large minority and poor, with lives that in many ways were similar to Jessica's. The skyrocketing number of women in prison was the unintended consequence of a drug policy that snagged legions of small-timers in the attempt to bring the kingpins down. The perfunctory institutional attitude toward the women reflected their relative insignificance in the war on drugs: a high-tech fortress, Marianna operated more like a public hospital with extra rules than a prison containing violent criminals. The atmosphere was more depressing than punitive.

Jessica was popular at Marianna. She had lots of friends and suitors. She spoke up for the women whenever a guard gave them the runaround. She defended people who weren't even her friends. One time, when an unpopular guard confiscated photographs that revealed her cleavage, Jessica said, "I got implants and that's that."

"These are pictures for your family and friends. This isn't *Playboy*," said the guard.

"How do you know what *Playboy* looks like?" asked Jessica. The women got a kick out of that.

Prison was certainly less frightening and more boring than Jessica had imagined. She earned her GED. She landed a job with federal prison industries, UNICOR, where her inventive excuses earned her the name "The Idle Queen." During work, she'd claim she had diarrhea so she could go to her cell bathroom rather than the open one. "I turn on the soap opera, put on the sign 'Bathroom in Use,' and I just sit down, and when people walk by I make sounds," Jessica said. "I can drop sixteen minutes that way." She fantasized about getting a letter to Mike Tyson, who was also in prison: *Hey Mike, do you remember me? I'm George's girl.*

Jessica kept busy. She wrote to Coco and Edwin and Daisy and George. She wrote to Tito via Coco, and to Cesar, once their inmate-to-inmate correspondence was approved. She sent all the children in her family birthday and holiday cards. She conjured up aches and pains for the cute prison doctor in the hope that she'd get felt up. She fell for a volatile girl named Tamika and their arguments fought off whole afternoons and nights of the tedium. She signed up for every workshop the prison offered—about religion and parenting and HIV. "I tried to go in that battered women's group," she said, "but it was just too much for me. I'm in the sexual abuse group. I couldn't feel like I'm a battered wife."

Jessica was eager to share all that she was learning. She sent AIDS pamphlets to her daughters. Jessica's friends teased her, saying little girls weren't at risk for HIV. "No," Jessica said, "but I don't want them to be ignorant like me on the street." She wrote her little cousin Daisy, noting, "You should really get this," on a Xerox she'd included of her GED (not long afterward, Daisy did). Jessica mailed Mercedes a book to help her with her ABCs and tried to dissuade Coco from her eternal wish to gain weight. Jessica had started exercising in the yard. "Don't get fat," she wrote, "I have fat on top of fat on top of fat."

At first, Jessica welcomed her assignment to Florida because her maternal grandmother and several uncles lived there; before Jessica left, Lourdes had promised to move the girls down, so that she could keep in closer touch. The Florida contingent of Lourdes's family were working people, and whenever Lourdes visited, she straightened out: she'd return to the Bronx fatter, without circles beneath her eyes. Lourdes's feelings about Florida were nevertheless complicated. She was beholden to her siblings for flying her down there, and she sometimes felt used. She'd end up taking care of her mother, and doing the cooking and cleaning while everyone else went to work. That year, however, Lourdes never even left the city for a visit; things were so bad she rarely left the block.

Lourdes and Milagros had been hanging out and partying in the abandoned house on the corner; during the day, while they slept, Serena tried to keep her baby sisters quiet, in front of the TV. "She was good," Lourdes said. "She didn't touch anything." Elaine stopped by to check up on her nieces; she taught Serena how to heat up a can of SpaghettiOs. She warned her never to open the door, but Serena couldn't help it. Lourdes's friends came, and sometimes a neighbor offered to take Serena to the park. Hundreds of miles away, Jessica worried. She said, "The hanging out, the people coming in and out, my daughter didn't have no privacy."

Lourdes habitually responded to such accusations with righteous indignation. There was the time she said she'd found Que-Que's works inside his boot beneath the bed, within easy reach of the children—three bags of dope, a spoon, and a syringe. Serena had seen her backhand his skinny ass across the room! But Jessica knew the routine. She threatened her mother, "The friends you're hanging out with are going to lead you to me. Believe me, there is a bunk waiting for you."

With no one to walk her in the mornings, Serena missed more than two months of school and failed first grade. The Bureau of Child Welfare eventually paid a visit; Lourdes gave up custody. She said she was having a nervous breakdown and was afraid that she would end up hurting the girls. Jessica agreed to move Serena to Robert's more disciplined house in Brooklyn, where he lived near the Watchtower compound run by the Jehovah's Witnesses. He and Milagros were going to trade children on alternate weekends, to give one another a break. But the twins begged off the weekends at Robert's and Serena cried on Sundays when it was time to leave for Brooklyn. Robert later admitted that his house wasn't the most appealing place for a child. His marriage was rocky, and he was struggling with severe depression. After work, he headed straight for bed.

Jessica was the one in jail, but her family on the outside didn't seem to be doing much better. No one had enough money. Jessica needed commissary for snacks and stamps and hygienes. Lourdes had nothing to spare. Elaine was scraping by. Robert sent only his religious literature. Jessica called Milagros. Milagros said, "She don't know what it's like out here. I'm wearing clothes from two years ago. I buy things for the kids." Jessica's maternal grandmother sent money orders from time to time, and Coco, too, whenever she could afford $20 from her welfare check. Jessica's alienation from her family made it tougher for her to completely separate from George. "My mother won't send me twenty dollars, but when the electric bill wasn't paid or when they were going to be evicted, who got the money? I got the money. George paid," said Jessica.

George helped Jessica keep in touch with her daughters. His mother deposited money into Jessica's account (he'd attempted to wire money from his commissary into hers, but inmate-to-inmate transfers were not allowed). The money bought stamps and phone calls. Inmate access to telephones varied by facility. At the time, $4 to $5 was deducted from Jessica's commissary account for each call. The calls automatically disconnected after fifteen minutes. Each follow-up call required another $4 hookup fee. The only other option was to place the outgoing call collect, which was, for the impoverished families of inmates, a tremendous burden. Lourdes had lost her phone service long ago anyway. Milagros eventually placed a block against incoming collect calls; she couldn't cover the additional bill. Elaine, who also got collect calls from Cesar, limited Jessica to one call a month.

The situation frustrated Jessica. Her girls were too young to write. "By the time I talk to one, and she telling me what she did, and you know, that she loves me and misses me, just talks to me, those fifteen minutes are up. And I gotta call back anyway to talk to the other two, cuz they feel left out. So it's just before you know it, you have a dollar on your account."

The calls themselves were difficult. Stephanie would pick up the phone and say to Milagros, "Mommy, Jessica's on the phone." Serena stretched the cord all the way around Milagros's kitchen counter and curled into the receiver for privacy. She whispered "Yeah" and "No" to Jessica's inquiries. Jessica wondered how she was going to help her daughter deal with what happened to her when she was a little girl while she was just beginning to deal with what had happened to herself. "And I know there is so much more that she wants to say. And that I'm the only one she can say it to," Jessica said.

Milagros eventually retrieved Serena from Robert's; Robert said his wife envied the attention he lavished upon his niece. In addition to Jessica's three, Milagros still had Kevin, and baby-sat several more, including the younger of Puma and Trinket's two boys. Trinket had been crashing at Milagros's; she'd testified against the drug dealers who'd killed Puma, and threats had been made against her life. Serena shared a room with her sisters. She taped her photographs of Jessica above her bed. In one, perfect Shirley Temple curls spilled down her mother's arched back as she squinted in the sun. "To My Baby," read Jessica's curvy script. "Look at me, still trying to look pretty. Oh well so much for that! I love you, Jessica Jessica," as though her identity needed emphasis. Next to them were a few photos Jessica had forwarded from Daddy George.

George sometimes phoned the girls and reported the conversations back to Jessica. He sent them birthday cards. He remembered Jessica on Mother's Day. Lourdes didn't; George's mother did. Rita wrote, in part: "For a wonderful daughter-in-law. I bought another bird and I named it after you. . . . I am so sad about all that's going on. . . ."

The prison doctor placed Jessica on bed rest after Mother's Day because Serena's card had left Jessica distraught. "My daughter put on the picture 'I love you Jessica.' My family could've said, 'Serena, that's your mommy, not your Jessica. . . .' My face is so red, my eyes is all swolled up," she said. She couldn't hold down meals. "I think it's the stress. Everything

I eat, I throw up and the blood follows." She eagerly anticipated George's letters. "Nobody else loved me. Nobody else made me feel love."

Prisons limit inmate-to-inmate letters to family members or to codefendants for legal purposes. George and Jessica were allowed to correspond because they were both defendants in the Obsession case. Because of George's previous threats to Jessica, however, their letters were screened, but those parts most important to Jessica—his declarations of love—survived the monitoring. One letter he wrote with his blood. He further backed up his claims with hard evidence of his indifference to other girls: he forwarded photographs sent to him from Jessica's old rivals—Miranda, the green-eyed table manager from the mill, serving ten years at FCI Alderson, kneeling in the yard; Gladys, the bank teller, looking fat in flannel baby dolls. He sent Jessica lots of pictures of himself. In one, he stood somberly against a prison-drawn mural of the Manhattan skyline glittering with lights. On the back, he wrote, "Here I stand awaiting you. I will always love you Jessica. I have made myself your father figure, I can't turn my back on you, ever." On another, he asked, "Jessica Rivera when are you going to be ready for me, and a marriage?"

In the meantime, Jessica reclaimed Mrs. Rivera as her title and used it in her return address. She forwarded pictures of George to Coco and reported, "Me and my husband George are doing well." He promised to pay the girls' way to visit her. Coco showed the pictures to Mercedes and Nikki, but she did not grant George a spot on her wall. She didn't like George for Jessica. "He's too strict," Coco said.

During the second summer of Jessica's incarceration, George told his mother to bring Jessica's daughters to see her in Florida. Rita and George's stepfather agreed to take Serena for a few days because she was compliant, but the twins were too much of a handful. Once at the prison, Serena quickly made her place on Jessica's lap with her head burrowed into her mother's neck, her legs tightly wound around her waist. She asked Jessica to play with her in the children's room, but Jessica said, "Just a minute, sweetie, I'm going to talk to Grandma first." She was catching up on the news about George.

"You aren't going to spend time alone with me when you didn't see me for two years?" Serena asked.

"She's right," Jessica recalled thinking. "What am I doing? Sitting here with this woman, talking about George?"

Rita was forced to cool her heels with her husband as Jessica and Serena spent most of that first day's visit in the children's room. Serena was thrilled: she had the full attention of Jessica, who happily played game after game of Candy Land. They bought a bagel from the vending machine and heated it in a microwave. Slowly, Serena warmed to Jessica's questions. She told her mother that a trip to Coney Island had been planned for her eighth birthday, a few weeks away. Yes, she told Jessica, Títi Elaine and Títi Daisy wore her leather coats. Títi Coco's belly was getting big. Jessica asked about Lourdes. Serena said, "Grandma's taking the white medicine again."

Rita was not pleased about the way she had been treated; taking the backseat to a child apparently made her irritable. On the second day of the visit, she and Jessica argued, as they often did. "Come over here, we are leaving," Rita ordered Serena. Serena grabbed Jessica's leg and started screaming. A guard asked Rita to give the little girl time to say good-bye. Jessica watched Rita and her husband escort Serena away. She called after Rita's husband desperately, "Please, please take care of my baby girl. Please don't let her do anything to Serena!"

That night, Jessica begged the officer on duty to let her call the hotel. There was no answer. The guard said, "Don't worry, don't worry. You got as long as my shift." Jessica finally reached them. She said Rita had decided to cut the three-day visit short by a day; she'd already changed the airline reservations, and they were packed to go. Jessica asked if she could speak to Serena to say good-bye. Serena had spent the afternoon by the hotel swimming pool, and playing in the parking lot.

"Serena, what are you doing?" Jessica asked.

"I was outside watching the boys go around on the Big Wheel."

"Are you with anyone?"

"No."

"Are you sure?"

The truth was that Serena preferred to be outside.

Milagros had stood back as each girl spoke to Daddy George when he called, and she had brushed away their disappointment after he'd failed to deliver a promised pile of Christmas gifts. She'd tolerated his mockery about her love life, and his cruel insinuations about her need for a man. But Milagros reached the end of her patience when Rita deposited Serena in the lobby of the building following the Florida trip: according to Milagros, Rita had simply rung the buzzer and left Serena there. The building was dangerous. Junkies shot up in the stairwells and crackheads smoked in the halls. Serena was a child. Rita's behavior went beyond lack of courtesy; it threatened Serena's safety. Jessica could call herself

Mrs. Anyone, but for Milagros, the days of Daddy George had come to an end.

Serena returned to the summer camp Milagros had saved for. Police barricades barred traffic so that the children had room to play on the street. The counselors, two middle-aged women from Milagros's building, smoked and chatted the day down on chairs near a dripping hydrant, beside a cooler full of soda that the children weren't allowed to touch. Children crawled in and out of an abandoned car. Serena didn't say much about her visit to Jessica, but she did tell her friends and cousins about the swimming pool and the Big Wheel and the toys in the children's room.

Back in Florida, Jessica mulled over the visit, trying to remember every detail. At one point, Serena had whispered, "Mommy, can I axe you a question?" But then she'd retreated. Just before she'd said good-bye, Serena had tried again. "Are you okay?" she asked her mother. "Do they do bad things to you in here?"

"That's jail on television," Jessica assured her.

From now on, Jessica would be careful to mail Serena photographs that made prison look like a place of friends and fun. She sent one along in which she cuddled a fluffy puppy. In another, she posed by a stretch of sand out of view of the security fence. Prison looked more inviting than the street.

Jessica called Serena to wish her a happy eighth birthday. "Is that a beach where you take the pictures?" Serena asked.

"It's a beach and it's a pretty beach and there is a pool and I have fun here," Jessica lied.

"If you having so much fun," Serena asked, "why don't you come here instead?" Serena asked.

PART II

Lockdown

B ack in the Bronx, in their frilly bedroom at Milagros's, the twin girls sat on their beds excitedly. The beds were rafts. The girls' thoughts floated, bound for Coney Island, where they were going to celebrate Serena's birthday at the beach. It was the first year all the girls had lived together and shared a bedroom without worrying that their big sister had to stay behind, or leave. Below them, on the linoleum floor, were their purple summer clogs from Payless, capsized shoe-boats, decorated with turquoise and yellow hippie flowers.

Brittany and Stephanie were six, still twiggy, with prominent brows on moony faces that tapered upward to wispy topknots, giving their heads the shape of tulip bulbs. Milagros had given them home-style bangs that accented the mournful expression of their heavy-lidded eyes. But the twins were actually lighthearted and agile, squealing as they chased one another. Serena shared none of their breeziness. She was only slightly bigger, but her bearing seemed much heavier. The morning of her eighth birthday, she slept late; Brittany and Stephanie wished she'd wake up. They sat on the side of their bed, watching her, their four skinny legs swinging impatiently.

Serena rolled over, her legs spread across the sheet's flat faces of Beauty and the Beast. Her long hair fell in tangles. She didn't usually sleep well. The street noises scared her. The music, the sirens, the hollering and shooting from the after-hours club on University, sounds on top of sounds. Serena blinked, then slowly pushed herself up. She rubbed her eyes.

Serena's half-brother Lucas, Trinket and Puma's two-year-old, made a brief appearance in the doorway. He was the child in Puma's arms the night he was gunned down. Serena glanced at Lucas dispassionately. Strapped to his stroller, he'd propelled himself forward by violent jerks. Milagros's fat arm swept him away.

"Happy birthday, Serena!" Stephanie said.

"Yeah, happy birthday!" Brittany added.

Serena swatted away their attention as she yawned. She inspected a stick-on tattoo heart on her arm. Milagros boomed, "Brittany-StephanieSerena! Come eat!" Serena dropped off the bed. "Come on," she instructed her sisters, leading them into the hall.

"You didn't say happy birthday to Serena," Brittany reminded Trinket, who was clicking around the apartment hurriedly in her high heels, late for work. Trinket came to a dead stop, placed her hands on Serena's shoulders, and backed her into the bedroom. "Happy Birthday" wafted out. Serena emerged with a shy smile and, on her cheek, a lipstick kiss. Except for the beds, and a few chairs, Milagros had no furniture. The children squeezed into tiny plastic chairs at a pint-size table that they had already outgrown. Serena served her siblings the pancakes Milagros had prepared.

Elaine bustled in with her two spotless sons and recalcitrant husband, Angel, in tow. Angel had stopped using drugs, but Elaine hadn't forgiven him. Just that morning she had been reminded of the camera that could have taken Serena's birthday pictures if it hadn't been hawked for dope. Once, he had sold off all her furniture; luckily, Jessica had given them a bedroom set from one of George's apartments, following his arrest. Elaine had needed money so badly that year that she'd even milled some of George's drugs under his guidance from the MCC.

Angel parked the cooler in Milagros's kitchen and joined Kevin on the floor; Kevin, who was ten, was watching a bootleg video of the gang movie *Blood In, Blood Out*. Lourdes had promised she was coming, but only Serena actually expected her. Coco surprised everyone by arriving on time.

"Títi, look," Serena said, leading Coco into her room. She handed her aunt a school notebook opened to a page where the words *I wish* were followed by a blank, in which she'd written, "I wish there were no drug in the world, that would be nice."

"Thass good," Coco said, but she preferred to keep the day upbeat. Birthdays should be happy; they were the biggest events of the year. "Now, why don't ya'll sing me a song? Mercy, show your cousins the song I taught you. I sang it when I was your age, 'Kind Kind Mother.'"

The twins started, and Mercedes and Serena and Nikki joined in; Nikki's eagerness transformed her unintelligible words into a respectable gurgling sound. Coco clapped and nodded with each syllable of every plodding verse. It was a song that Foxy's older sister, Aida, had learned while she was in the youth house and had sung to Foxy, which Foxy had taught her daughter, in turn:

> I had a kind kind mother
> She was so kind to me
> And when I got in trouble

She held me on her knee
That night when I was sleeping
Upon my mother's bed
An angel came down from heaven
And told me she was dead
That morning when I woke up
I found my dream come true
Now she's up in heaven
That's why the skies are blue
Now children obey they mother
Especially when they small
Cuz if you shall lose your mother
You lose the best of all!

Finally, the adults were ready. The children assembled in the hall. "Did Mommy close the window?" Serena asked Kevin, pushing the button to the elevator.

"I dunno," he said. The elevator door clunked open. Stephanie hopped over a puddle of urine. There were puddles in the lobby, too, but these were pungent with King Pine. The super was hosing down the walls for his morning mop-up. "Hello!" he called out to the train of children.

"Hello!" each one shouted, ducking through the missing panel at the base of the security entryway.

"*Dios bendiga tu barriga,*" he said to Coco. God bless your belly.

"Thank you," Coco said. She didn't speak Spanish, but she understood common phrases. The super wiped over a tattered copy of "Respect Thy Neighbor Commandments" stuck on the wall. "Help Thy Neighbor" and "Get to Know Thy Neighbor" were the only commandments not too pen-stabbed to be illegible. Outside, the sidewalk warmed. Angel pushed the cooler, which he'd strapped to a shopping cart, as far as the subway and said good-bye to the women and children.

At Coney Island, the wind made it too cold to swim, but the children ran in the sand and splashed their feet in the waves. The group trooped up to the boardwalk for lunch. On a picnic table outside the boarded-up Freak Show, everyone except Elaine's sons munched on Elaine's chicken and rice and beans. Her boys weren't hungry because Elaine had earlier spirited them away and treated them to McDonald's, on the sly.

Damp clothes made the children shiver. Their lips were blue. With the gusts of wind, it was impossible to light the candles on Serena's birthday cake, which was soon dusted with sand and ripped apart for a cake fight; Milagros tossed the remains in a garbage can. Serena spent the rest of her birthday lifting her sisters and cousins in and out of the seats of baby rides. For the long trip back to the Bronx, Serena, exhausted, sank into the subway seat next to Coco. Brooklyn passed in a rush. Serena watched the rooftops of the houses. "I want to live in a house," she said.

"Me, too, Mami," said Coco. "When I get my apartment, I want to get it big enough for Mommy Jessica to come and live."

Serena pointed out a fence. "A pregnant lady couldn't get over that fence," she observed. She distractedly brushed the sand from the soles of her sneakers. "My best birthday was my sixth birthday."

That was the summer before her mother went away. Jessica had rented a community center in the projects and threw Serena a big party. All of Serena's friends and family came for the celebration, said Serena, "even people from Florida." Streamers and balloons draped the tables and bags were stuffed with candy. Jessica had hired a DJ, and a clown who painted the children's faces. Even Lourdes showed. Serena still had the pictures of herself and her grandmother, cheeks pressed together, beside her layered Minnie Mouse birthday cake.

Two years later, Serena sat on the subway, contemplative and sticky with sand. Nikki sucked her thumb and leaned cautiously against Coco's big belly. Mercedes confidently plopped her head in what remained of Coco's lap.

"Old people should think like children," Serena whispered cryptically. Coco nodded. It was advice that, at nineteen, she easily took to heart. Coco covered Mercedes's shoulders with a towel and tightened her grip. The F train turned northward and jerked underground toward the Bronx.

Coco was having a difficult year. First, Cesar had gone away for Mighty's death. A few months later, Coco's mother, Foxy, had a nervous breakdown and spent three weeks as an inpatient at a public psychiatric hospital. When Foxy was given a day-release pass, she came home, but after less than an hour, she called a cab to take her back. Home completely overwhelmed her. On the psychiatric ward, she rested. A new beau named Hernan had been visiting; they'd talk for hours and make out on her bed until the nurse would interrupt them and tell him he'd have to leave.

After Foxy was discharged, she'd spend the days with Hernan and his friends in a nearby park, or in front of the Oval Pharmacy, where she had her new antianxiety and antidepressant prescriptions filled. She would tell her family that she'd been at an appointment at the hospital. Foxy said, "I did not want to go back home." But Coco didn't like living there without her mother; the ordinarily chaotic house felt sad and bleak. Iris and Manuel had moved out, and her stepfather, Richie, seemed desperate. Coco's little brother, Hector, had been expelled from junior high for shooting a gun into the air near his school. When Foxy returned at night, Richie and Foxy would start fighting, and Hector would inevitably get involved. Sometimes Coco took the girls down the block and went to Milagros's. But more often than not, Coco found Milagros's boring—or, if Milagros was high, uncomfortable. Then Foxy and Milagros started hanging out and partying: Coco complained, but they paid her no mind. Coco couldn't escape to Lourdes's. Lourdes had been evicted again and was living with a Dominican drug dealer, who scared Coco, and worse yet, sometimes provided Foxy and Milagros with their drugs.

That June 1993, when Coco was five months pregnant, she decided to "go homeless." Going homeless meant entering the city shelter system to begin the long process of acquiring an apartment you could call your own. By entering a shelter, Coco could qualify for New York City public housing and get her name on the lengthy waiting list. Twice Foxy had personally escorted Coco to the shelter, and twice Coco had followed her mother right back home. The shelters scared Coco, especially the coed one. After her last attempt, Coco had said, "I'ma live here with my mother till I grow gray hair." But Foxy encouraged her youngest daughter's faltering steps toward independence. Coco's older brother and sister and their families had gone homeless successfully. This time, as a pregnant mother of two, Coco qualified for emergency placement. She finally made up her mind to try again with a friend, whose uncle offered the girls a ride. Foxy was out, so Coco avoided the good-bye. She had no money, which turned out to be lucky, because Coco later said that if she had, she would have returned home by cab.

Her girlfriend helped her through the processing—waiting and soothing the children, who became hungry, then cranky. They complained and cried until they fell asleep on the floor as the night cracked open into day. Coco got sent to Thorpe House, a transitional residence for women and children on Crotona Avenue. The refurbished building was just a block from the hooky house where Serena had been conceived.

Thorpe House had been renovated by the Dominican Congregation of Our Lady of the Rosary. The four-story tawny brick building sheltered sixteen families. A wrought-iron fence topped with barbed wire separated the back of the house from the courtyard of a fourteen-story project that towered over Thorpe from behind. On sunny days, the smashed glass on the sidewalk sparkled; gnarls of cassette tape, looped along the barbed wire, glistened. There was a brightness to the place.

Across the street, trees shaded a tiny park with benches, their branches decorated with empty plastic bags. On one trunk hung a wooden cross with plastic flowers and fraying ribbons, in memory of the victims of a triple murder that had taken place just before Coco moved in.

The nuns assigned Coco an apartment on the first floor. Her door stood just past the security guard's cubbyhole, at the end of a short hall. The door opened directly into her living room; a kitchen, situated in the far right corner, sat opposite two bedrooms. Coco smothered the living room walls with photographs, re-creating the bedroom she'd left behind. One of the first things she did was to take her girls to get their portraits taken at Sears on Fordham. She placed eight-by-eleven-inch pictures in the window, facing outward. She'd spotted one of Cesar's old girlfriends on a nearby corner—the one she'd seen him hugging on Tremont. The portraits showed off Coco's beautiful daughters just in case the girl passed by her street.

Coco and the girls used only one of the bedrooms; in the other, Coco piled up the donated furniture she didn't like. She and Mercedes shared a twin bed; Nikki used the mattress below, which pulled out like a trundle bed. The room's window overlooked an abandoned lot and a barricaded single-family home. Coco blocked the window with a bureau to protect her girls from the gunfire she sometimes heard at night. On top of the bureau stood a statue of the Virgin Mary and a ceramic bassinet. Beside them she placed a porcelain unicorn she was safekeeping for Lourdes until Lourdes found a more reliable home. Squeezed next to the bureau was a small desk where Coco wrote to Cesar after the girls fell asleep. She hated to be alone—even steps away from her daughters in the living room. Sometimes she woke Mercedes up to keep her company at night.

Whenever Coco had change for the pay phone, she called her mother's. Foxy wasn't often home; she was usually with Hernan. Coco bristled at the very idea of her mother having a new boyfriend and harangued Foxy about Hernan every chance she could. Hernan was a short Vietnam veteran with thick black hair and dark skin. Coco thought he looked like a rapist, and that Foxy, whose complexion was light and flawless, was too good for him. Foxy was still seeing Coco's stepfather, Richie, expecting her eighth grandchild, and yet here she was, acting like a kid. Coco urged whoever was at her mother's to come visit. People promised to come by but rarely did.

The Thorpe House staff aimed to equip the mothers with independent living skills, to reroute their formidable streetwise savvy toward the less tumultuous routines of the conventional world. But the two sets of skills didn't add up: one was geared for hilly terrain, like four-wheel drive; the other assumed the roads were level and paved. Like some of the other residents, Coco intuited the limitations of the optimism, yet she was more willing than many of her Thorpe House peers to hear out the nuns. Coco had survived extreme hardship without becoming hard. She was eager to devise a plan for her future and was open to the help Thorpe offered, even though it was often unclear how it applied to her life. Her caseworker, a gray-haired Irish nun named Sister Christine, quickly developed a fondness for her.

Coco responded most enthusiastically to the workshops on money and budgeting. Every two weeks, she received $125 from welfare, by which time she was often $110 in debt. Thorpe covered utilities and rent. Coco hoped the budgeting workshops would teach her how to stop having to struggle—a problem for which she blamed herself. The day checks arrived was pickup day. After she picked up, Coco immediately counted for one top priority: *People I Owe Money To.* She always owed someone something—$8 to Thorpe for change for washing, $6 to a neighbor for food, $15 to Dayland, a drug dealer from around her mother's way, who had lent her $200 the previous Christmas when she had had no money for gifts. Coco earmarked the cash by writing the names—"Dayland's," "Sheila's"—on the actual bills. She also deducted for tokens for appointments and put money aside for a cab in case of emergency. It wasn't unusual for her to have $5 left, which she had to stretch for the next two weeks.

She usually owed someone food stamps. Luckily, Coco's girls were under five and still qualified for WIC—Women, Infants, and Children, a supplemental food program. Through WIC, she received dated vouchers and exchanged them for specified items—eggs, cereal, and most preciously, milk. What remained of the money went to clothes for the girls and necessary toiletries. Children's looks reflected the quality of mothering; sloppiness and dirt were physical evidence of failure, of poverty winning its battle against you. Coco would keep the girls indoors rather than let them look busted-up outside. She spent hours on their hair, twisting and tugging, braiding and curling, liberally applying Vaseline. When she was done, she'd briskly rub her palms together and wipe a hand down each daughter's face; Vaseline also kept their skin from getting patchy. "I want them to be perfect. They are so beautiful," Coco said. It irritated her that she'd send Mercedes off to preschool looking brand-new, and they'd return her with a top splotched with finger paint. Weeks ahead of time, Coco estimated the price of the clothes she wanted, including tax. As soon as she possibly could, she made a deposit and put them on layaway.

But budgeting didn't mitigate one of Coco's greatest problems— everyone around her also needed, and Coco didn't know how to refuse. Sometimes Coco spent down her money just so she could be the one to use it, which allowed her to maintain her integrity. "This way if the girls in my house come to ask me for money, I tell them *no*, and I ain't lying," Coco said. Drinking men were employing a similar logic when they bought beer, bottle by bottle, at the corner store: better that way than a six-pack, even though the single bottles cost more. Otherwise, you either shared your beer or got the reputation of being greedy for refusing your friends; the trips to the store also broke up the boredom and gave folks something to do.

Coco's sister, Iris, however, knew how to take care of business. Her method was a stern personality. Hardness kept at bay all kinds of problems, and Iris could ward off potential borrowers with one stony look. Coco was too open; even if she avoided being a bank for near strangers, she ended up as the neighborhood grocery store: "They be knocking at all hours of the day and night, 'Coco, you got this? Coco, you got that?' " Cash had to stretch further with Cesar jailed. He needed winter boots, a coat, socks, towels and sheets, and commissary money for his hygienes and stamps. Then he asked for extra things—such as a door-size reproduction of his favorite photograph of Mercedes with her hair in Shirley Temple curls. Coco didn't know how to tell him no. "The welfare money, that's the girls'. It belongs to the girls, not him," she would say, but only to herself. The one time she explained to him she had no money, he told her to borrow it. Delilah, the loan shark from her mother's block, charged a 100 percent markup for whatever amount she lent and doubled the bill every week. Coco's $20 loans routinely cost her $60, so she did with him what she'd done with the nuns—sweetly demurred until avoiding became impossible, then made promises she couldn't deliver, then apologized and blamed herself.

One day, Coco and Iris went shopping. Although Coco had figured out her budget, she deferred to Iris, whom she considered a financial whiz. Iris was the only person Coco knew who actually survived on her welfare benefits. "I'm gonna give you my list of people I owe and you have to divide it up," Coco said to Iris. Iris brought her to Big R Food Warehouse and suggested Coco buy the enormous packets of chicken and pork chops. Iris divided them into smaller portions and froze them separately; Coco often forgot to defrost meat in enough time for dinner. Iris had her children's school clothes pressed and laid on a chair the night before; Coco was constantly rummaging around for the hairbrush or a matching sock. Coco knew she couldn't replicate Iris's strict adherence to order, but she longed for her girls to sleep in rooms like Iris's rooms. "They for beautiful people," said Coco. In her niece's bedroom, everything matched—curtains and bedspreads and sheets.

But Coco's pride in her sister's way was mixed with concern. The rigidity of Iris's approach to her predicament generated its own problems. Iris lived in a housing project, and it was dangerous to take the elevators early in the morning, or late at night, alone. She rarely ventured anywhere without her husband, Armando—even to visit family. The toll of this vigilance was apparent in Armando's anxious eyes and the grim set of Iris's jaw. Mainly, though, it was Iris's unhappiness that upset Coco. The family anxiety projected an unspoken, unappealing truth: that even living right—which is what Coco called it—was just another precarious hold. Poverty pulled everybody down. Coco loosened her body to minimize the impact of the fall; Iris and Armando froze, and the chill stiffened their kids, as well. Even indoors, when Armando planted himself in his favorite chair he gripped the arms.

Babyland, Kiddieworld, Youngland—these were Coco's favorite stores. Strollers hung from the ceilings. High chairs and rockers and swings lined row after row; the circular racks were choked with brightly colored clothes. Whole departments were devoted to each passing phase of a baby's life. At Youngland, Iris exchanged the $12.99 jeans Coco had put on layaway for a similar style Iris had found for half the price; Coco would never have had the defiance to ignore the clerk's snooty look. She and Iris waited in line. The counter loomed above them like a police precinct desk. Coco counted twenty-three kinds of hair bands. "My girls have all the hair bands except for the whistles," she said. This omission bothered her. "It's better to have girls, because you can let them wear things as long as they look pretty," Coco said. Boys required name brands. Coco and Iris chuckled over the realization that they rarely shopped for themselves. "My panties have *holes*," Coco said to Iris elatedly. Outside, she gave $3 to a homeless man.

Coco's Thorpe House caseworker, Sister Christine, worried about Coco's generosity. When you were poor, you had to have luck and do nearly everything absolutely right. In a life as vulnerable to outside forces as Coco's and her two little girls', the consequences of even the most mundane act of kindness could be severe. The $10 loan to a neighbor might mean no bus fare, which might mean a missed appointment, which might lead to a two-week loss of WIC. Hungry children increased the tension of a stressed household. If the resolution was going to a loan shark, the $10 cost $40 or $50, effectively pushing Coco back a month. But to Coco, nothing was more important than family, and family included Cesar and Lourdes and friends, both new and old. Coco gave Foxy some of her food stamps, in addition to WIC tickets, because Foxy was feeding seven people on her youngest son's SSI and paying all the bills.

Sister Christine wanted to tell Coco, *Get away from your family.* But she couldn't. Not everyone could clamber onto a lifeboat from a sinking raft. You either made your way by hardening up, like Iris, or you stayed stuck. Coco didn't see a choice. She admired Iris's accomplishments, but she couldn't live like that. Nor could she be like her older brother, Manuel, who dressed himself better than his children. Coco couldn't ignore the people she cared for, which is why Foxy and her little brother Hector turned to her first for help. The word that came to Sister Christine's mind whenever she thought of Coco was *enmeshed.* Coco would have said that she had heart.

CHAPTER SIXTEEN

Months after Coco had moved to Thorpe House, she was still visiting Foxy's five or six times a week. The returning gave her a sense of purpose. However, sustaining the connection cost her—she missed appointments, her housing-application case lost momentum, not to mention the money she spent on bus fare. Still, she clung to her mother's block and treated Thorpe as a satellite. There were dollar stores near Thorpe, but Coco bought her shampoo and soap at Bank of Bargains on University. There was a C-Town in her new neighborhood, but Coco preferred the one nearest home, where she could sometimes convince Foxy to shop with her. This devotion required Coco to pay a cab to take her, the girls, and the month's twenty-three bags of groceries back along Tremont to Thorpe. At Foxy's, Hector had taken over Coco's old bedroom, but he let Coco keep her closet as an archive of cherished things: the black leather shearling coat Cesar had bought for Mercedes; two white fake-fur coats the girls had worn the previous Easter; Mercedes's handmade pink satin birthday-party dress.

Coco's new life was deeply entrenched with bureaucracies. The wide net of her institutional contacts with city, state, and federal agencies didn't make her small world any bigger, however: the same girls and women traveled to the same offices with similar needs and waited for verdicts that seemed to be issued arbitrarily. The meetings themselves were usually pointless and brief—often just minutes—but the waits were sometimes whole mornings or afternoons. Coco's days were a string of appointments—planned and unplanned visits to the clinic, recertification at welfare, screenings for public housing, the twice-monthly sign-in to collect her WIC. She reported weekly to the nuns who ran the shelter—for apartment checks (for cleanliness), refrigerator checks (for cleanliness and food), and for lectures about parenting and health. If Coco wasn't getting the girls ready for an appointment, on the way to an appointment, or on the bus ride home from one, she was in a room crowded with women and children in the long yawn of waiting to be seen.

Even so, Coco was always glad to escape the shelter, where she felt constrained by its rules. "It's so boring," she said of Thorpe. Anything was better than being stuck indoors with her two restless girls, no money, no

149

telephone, her looming belly, and a nun at the door reminding her of some failed responsibility. Coco liked the nuns themselves, but didn't like how "they all into my business." There was a curfew, and you had to request a pass for an overnight guest. When, in recreation, Coco carved a clutch of balloons on a wooden plaque and inscribed Cesar's name inside one balloon, in glitter, a staff person asked, "Why you always putting that guy's name?" No one commented on the balloons inscribed with "Mercedes," "Nikki," and "Unborn Baby"; Cesar was part of Coco, too!

Coco signed out of Thorpe to conduct her business. Under "Destination," if she didn't write "welfare" or "the clinic," she scribbled "mother's" or "mother-in-law's." She caught the 36 bus on the corner of Crotona Avenue and disembarked on Tremont, near the Concourse. Lourdes brought her up-to-date on gossip, especially about Roxanne. Roxanne and her baby also passed by Lourdes's frequently, and the possibility of a chance encounter gave the otherwise repetitive days a charge. Roxanne had said that if she saw Coco, she'd kick her in the stomach—at least, that's what Roxanne's sister had told Lourdes and Lourdes had told Elaine and Elaine had told Coco.

Otherwise, Coco went to Foxy's, but she didn't get much attention there. Sometimes she stopped by Sheila's, Foxy's neighbor, or she passed by Milagros's. Milagros still lived on Andrews, a few blocks from Foxy's, with Kevin, and Jessica's three girls. Sometimes Milagros would baby-sit so that Coco could go clubbing, but the frequent fights and shoot-outs at the clubs dampened her enjoyment, now that she had children: "I would be there dancing, and all I be doing is thinking of them. What if something happened to me and they waiting for their mother and I never come home?" Sometimes Coco would baby-sit, and Milagros would go get high, what Coco called "do her thing." Lots of afternoons, they talked, and Coco would amicably reject Milagros's advice about Cesar. Sometimes they let other people's problems talk: One day, on a talk show called *Shirley*, the topic was marriage without sex. On the *Shirley* set, dumpy women with bad posture sat in an uneven row, jiggling their feet in too-short skirts. Subtitles ran beneath their double chins: *Didn't have sex in her ten-year marriage* or *Hasn't had sex in six years.*

"I could never go more than two months. You going to go nine years. You gonna be able to do it?" Milagros asked.

"I know this, I ain't never going to look like that, all fat and ugly looking," said Coco, scoffing. "That's why I want to get married. I can only do it if I can be married." If Cesar chose Roxanne to be his legal wife, Coco planned to remain alone. Cesar vacillated about his marriage plans. He said Coco needed to prove her loyalty. Milagros told Coco she was only setting herself up to be hurt. Coco suspected that Cesar was waiting to see if she gave him a son.

While Coco and Milagros watched television, the children played in one bedroom. Serena organized a game called Moving. The play baby stroller had already been packed with baby powder, the dolls strapped with knapsacks, ready to go. Brittany was scrunched up on the windowsill, painting her toenails, knees to her ears, leaning against the window guard. Stephanie applied fake makeup to Mercedes's upturned face. Serena balanced a tray toppling with the fake food bought years earlier by Jessica.

"We're moving," she announced. They had no destination. She added, "We gotta bring this food. We just need to take our things."

Milagros, in fact, had been talking a lot about moving. In the last year, she'd lost her closest friends to prison and death: Jessica was locked up; Puma had been gunned down. Milagros wanted to get away from the partying; she'd been using too much coke. She also wanted to put some distance between herself and Kevin's mother, who was due out of jail and making noises about taking Kevin back. And the Bronx had nothing for the children. The only play area was a concrete space between two buildings. Kevin was eleven and regularly getting into trouble at his school. "When he asks me if he can carry a knife, I think it's time to do something," Milagros said. He had already been mugged, and recently, there'd been another stabbing at his junior high, the same one Coco had attended. Twice a day, Milagros had to walk to the school to escort Kevin to the bathroom because he was too afraid to go alone.

Milagros's older brother, who was married to one of Puma's sisters, had recently joined a growing number of Bronx friends and neighbors who had moved upstate, and the news that drifted back to Milagros was all good. Apartments were spacious. Children could play outdoors safely. Schools were strict about classwork and attendance. Mothers didn't have to break night waiting in the emergency room. There were jobs. Willy, the twins' father, already lived there, as did his mother and several sisters. Milagros thought it would be good for the twins to be near him, and the family could help take care of the children so that she could return to work.

Milagros suggested to Coco that she join her; they could go through the shelter together and help one another with the kids.

"I can't be that far from my mother," Coco said.

"Coco, you is a mama's girl," Milagros said affectionately. But she'd started Coco thinking.

*   *   *

Coco appeared content during those spells she stayed put at Thorpe, almost in spite of herself. She loved the games during parent-child recreation. She excelled at apartment inspection. She was exuberant after meeting with Sister Christine and filling out the housing-application forms. She threw herself into the role-plays in drama, playing a pregnant girl jealous of an unpregnant friend working toward her GED. She had meat thawing under a stream of hot water in the kitchen sink by the time she fetched Mercedes from preschool and Nikki from day care. Day care, in Nikki's case, meant mornings spent with an anxious lady in a dark apartment in front of the TV; the lady's husband walked around the house in his undershirt and dress slacks. Coco didn't like the situation, but she thought it was unfair to send Mercedes to school and keep Nikki home, and it was hard to complete anything with both of them underfoot.

In sunny weather, Coco brought the girls across the street. Mercedes rode her tricycle in the little park. Coco would borrow Sister Christine's camera if she had money for film. Taking pictures was one of Coco's greatest pleasures; Nikki loved posing almost as much. She'd jut out her hip, tuck her chin in, and beam. Mercedes preferred the gangsta style she saw in the Polaroids of her father and his friends—hands on bent knees, with a menacing look of having been interrupted, or standing, arms folded across her chest, her expression intently grim. Nikki loved girlish clothes, but if Coco dressed Mercedes sexy—cropped tops that showed off her belly—Mercedes got anxious. A few times, when she was younger, she'd wet herself. Like Serena, Mercedes was shy about showing off her body. So Coco gave Mercedes a sporty style instead.

At dusk, Coco would settle the girls in the tub while she started dinner, which the girls ate from plastic bowls on their laps in front of the TV. *Cops* was Mercedes's favorite show. Coco prepared rice and beans and fried chicken, or rice and beans and fried pork chops, or rice and beans and Spam, or—if it was the end of the month—rice and beans. It was always a battle to get Nikki to eat and to get Mercedes in bed. Coco easily won with Nikki, but often surrendered to Mercedes, then—in an attempt to be fair—let Nikki stay up, too. After Coco carried the sleeping girls into the bedroom, she always turned on the radio. Like her, Mercedes and Nikki couldn't rest in silence. Then Coco cleaned, or visited with Jezel and Maritza, the other Puerto Rican girls at Thorpe.

A group of the mothers stayed up late one night talking in Jezel's apartment. Coco told them about Cesar—their first meeting, his other girls, how they planned to marry if he decided on her.

"I'd have binned him if he did all that to me," one girl said.

"You won't know until you stand in my shoes what my love is," Coco said, her eyes filling with tears. "I am in love."

"I bet you in love. But all he ever done for you is got you pregnant," the girl said.

Coco socialized less after that. She rearranged her living room furniture a lot, as many as three times a week; Mercedes and Nikki came home to a new house every day. She longed for visitors. Foxy was "always making excuses." Lourdes was "all into her business." Iris needed her husband's permission to visit, although she did manage to pass by, said Coco, "once in a blue." At least Cesar kept her company.

Whenever Coco returned to Thorpe, she beelined for the mailbox. No load of groceries, no weight of a sleeping child, kept her from the silver boxes first. She got letters from her old boyfriend Wishman, who was in prison on attempted murder charges in Baltimore, but Cesar's letters were the ones Coco craved. "When he don't write, I get depressed," Coco said. Envelopes addressed with his surname, to *Coco Santos*, promised good news; *Coco Rodriguez* letters, addressed to her own name, were ominous. If *Santos* had been crossed out and replaced with *Rodriguez*, she tried to open the letters in private, to avoid crying in front of the girls—then they'd cry, too—but she rarely had the patience to wait.

Coco composed long letters in reply. She also copied by hand letters Cesar sent her to forward to his incarcerated friends. They wrote in a secret code, which Coco tried to decipher. His friends may have been in prison, but through their letters she learned some of the juiciest gossip on the street. A few times she took the liberty of introducing herself: "By the way, this is Cesar's wife, Coco, the one that had his first child and now his last," she once added. These communications suited her indirect style.

Cesar complained about prison, but it sometimes seemed easier and more fun than Coco's life. Cesar had no children to feed and bathe and dress; he had no worries about basic necessities; he lived in a dorm with his friends. Hype, the boy who had introduced Cesar to West Tremont, was also at Harlem Valley. They had towel fights after showers and played basketball for whole afternoons. Cesar was studying for his GED; he already had better penmanship and a larger vocabulary. Coco's limitations were her failures; but Cesar's immobility was the prison's fault. And Cesar still dictated the terms of the relationship—to choose her or to cast her aside. She wrote him and asked if it was okay if she gave birth to a girl. "Coco," he wrote back. "I hope if it's a girl you don't start that bullshit about (I hope you love her) because you know that no matter what it is I'll love her or him. As long as it's mine I don't give a fuck if it's gay I'll still love it the same so don't sweat it alright!"

Coco felt anxious because Cesar was always after her to visit and the visits were costly, and hard to manage with two kids. She had been trying to save the $60 to take the bus upstate. One afternoon, she got lucky—Cesar was transferred down to New York City, so she didn't have to travel. Then she got luckier still—he called.

"Good news!" Coco shouted as she hung up the receiver of the pay phone in the Thorpe House hallway. "Cesar is in Rikers!" She popped her head into her neighbor's door. Jezel sat at her small kitchen table, breathing out a long, strong stream of Newport smoke.

"I can go, girl, I can go," Jezel said. Jezel had been dating Tito by telephone. Tito had asked Coco to hook him up. Coco, remembering how much Tito loved Jessica, deduced that Tito liked women with big butts and breasts, but the qualifying credential was Jezel's toughness; Coco had also pieced together that Tito was locked up for killing his wife.

Jezel distracted Tito from the boredom of prison, and Tito distracted Jezel from the boredom of the shelter. Jezel returned Coco's favor by introducing Coco to a nephew who was serving time as well. Jezel's nephew mailed Coco intricate cartoon drawings, shaded neatly in colored pencil. Cesar didn't send drawings. The nephew also complimented Coco and asked her questions about her life. Coco was curious what crime the nephew had committed, but, she said, "Unless they tell you, don't ask."

Coco hopped down the stairs and into her apartment and turned up the radio. "Daddy is in Rikers, Mercy," she sang.

"Daddy is in Rikers!" Mercedes repeated. She bobbed her chin in time to the music, trying to imitate her mother, who was now doing a Jamaican dance she'd learned from a neighbor the night before. Mercedes thrust her hips as if she were Hula-Hooping and reached her chubby arms up through the air. "I want to go see Daddy!" she chirped. "Daddy is in Rikers!" Coco touched her girls less now that they'd grown older, but she was so elated that she held Mercedes's hands.

Coco's physicality with her children tended to have a purpose—adornment or punishment. She roughly dried them after their baths, stilled them to pull on their clothes, and tugged their heads back as she brushed and braided and twisted and tightened their hair. Even her tenderness was often gruff. The night before they were to visit Rikers, Coco settled in to work on Cesar's favorite hairstyle on Mercedes—Shirley Temple curls. Mercedes bristled. "Hold still, Mami," Coco said. "Don't you want to look pretty for Daddy?" Getting pretty took well over an hour. Coco decided on the outfits ahead of time: theirs (striped-purple zip sweatshirts with black baggy jeans), and hers (a light blue-green sweat suit with a hair clip to match). The girls splashed in the tub while Coco ironed. She cleaned their already-cleaned ears again, because sometimes Cesar inspected them. Before they went to bed, she painted their toes and the little moons of their fingernails.

She felt excited about seeing Cesar, but she felt some reluctance, too. The trouble was the red spots; she had been picking her face. It was a habit her great-grandmother had had. Tiny circles flecked her skin and spilled off her button nose. Coco tried hard not to pick, but at night when her girls fell asleep, if she couldn't sleep herself, she picked. She stood before the bathroom mirror and leaned over the sink. She started by inspecting. Even then, she told herself, "Don't pick, don't pick, don't pick!" She was not dissatisfied with her reflection; in fact, Coco usually liked her looks. The culprits were the quiet and the darkness. The next thing she knew she was pressing into her cheeks with her fingernails— which, in an attempt to curb this urge, she'd clipped. She dug deeply enough to make her face bleed.

The marks worried her less when Cesar was upstate. Upstate visits required advance planning and gave her splotches time to fade. Cocoa butter helped to erase them, but now her face was covered. She could already hear him yelling tomorrow at Rikers—*You keep fucking with your face like that ain't nobody gonna love you. Stop messing with your face!* His letters always had a line or two about the marks. The spots mapped her self-inflicted failures. At the same time, Coco interpreted Cesar's haranguing as a sign of love. Cesar wanted his girls and children to look good in the visiting room. A good-looking girl enhanced his stature, much as she would on the street.

The following day, on Rikers Island, handwritten signs greeted Coco. Visitors were invited to drop contraband in a forgiveness box: *Women's jail on the Island with lots of rooms for a short/long stay too/So don't be the one.* Another sign said, *Check your self be for i do.* That day, a heavyset woman was caught trying to smuggle in heroin. Afterward, a guard hollered over the long line of women and grandmothers and little boys and girls waiting to be searched: "You better not be bring drugs in here. I may not be no gynecologist, but I know how to do the job!" No one came forward. Another line snaked toward the final metal detector. Everyone had to remove their socks and shoes.

"Things are getting outrageous in here," whispered a woman behind

Coco. Another said, "Are you shitting me?" "I got my man," joked another, "ain't no woman but a gynecologist going to look up my part." A tall woman hiked up her skirt. "They can kiss my ass," she said, a defiant cowgirl striding away in her muscular bare feet.

Mercedes stared at the woman who'd been caught: she was crying softly as her youngest child dug into her belly, sobbing. The woman's older boy sipped nonchalantly from a can of 7UP a guard had given him, but he hadn't yet mastered coolness; when another officer handcuffed his mother, the boy's petrified eyes locked on her, giving him away.

It took another hour for Coco and the girls to reach the visiting area. The girls spotted Cesar across the vast dim space and darted over to him. He kissed Coco distractedly and took his assigned seat. His bright orange jumpsuit puffed out like a parachute. As the girls clambered on his lap, he craned his neck and scanned the room. Visits gave inmates a chance to see friends in other units and gather intelligence. Three tables away, he spotted Rocco talking to his mother. Rocco's baby brother had curled into the plastic seat like a prawn. Cesar wanted Rocco to visit his unit. Coco wanted Cesar's attention, although her face betrayed no sign of impatience or need.

Cesar mouthed to Rocco, "Come over to my side. You gotta come over to my side, man." Rocco had been brought down from his upstate prison as a codefendant in Cesar's pending case. Cesar's transfer to Rikers resulted from a new warrant. He and Rocco, who was finishing his time for a drug conviction, were being charged with a Manhattan robbery. Cesar couldn't remember every mugging, but he was certain that he wasn't guilty of this one; they'd only robbed people in the Bronx.

Finally, Cesar turned to Coco. "I saw my dad, I saw him today," he said. Cesar glanced around, as though the announcement were insignificant, but his eyes showed that he was pleased. Cesar had not seen his father for years; now he was also at Rikers, serving time on a drug charge. Cesar was waiting in the chow line and recognized his father, who was pushing a mess hall cart.

Cesar snatched the bottle cap the girls were tossing—the claim ticket for the clothes Coco had left for him in the property room—and tried to get Mercedes to play with him. He threw fake punches. She jerked her chin back and looked at her mother. He brushed her pouting lips with a slow jab. She retreated. "Oops! Here's Nikki! I don't love you no more!" he said, and he scooped Nikki onto his lap. Mercedes burrowed into Coco's armpit. Coco later said she sympathized with her daughter's hurt reaction; Cesar leveraged his affection for other girls against her all the time.

"Do you love me?" Nikki asked Cesar.

"I love you," he said flatly.

"You my daddy?" she persisted.

"Yep," he said, looking away. Coco and Cesar sat awkwardly. She struggled to engage him in conversation. She complimented the cleanliness of the unit, which was relatively new. "You get my letter about the baby's—" she tried softly. She had written him her idea for a name for a girl. Originally, Cesar had wanted Giselle. Now he preferred Whitney, the same name he'd wanted for Mercedes. Coco suspected—as it turned out, rightly—that Whitney was one of Cesar's girls.

"Nautica," Cesar said, interrupting Coco. His voice turned hard. "*Nautica*—what the fuck kinda name is *that*?" Coco bit her lip. A couple kissed one row over. The man's hands moved inside the girl's untucked shirt. She straddled the small table intended to keep a distance between them, his knees pressed in prayer between her legs. The airplanes from La Guardia sounded as if they were about to land on the roof.

The girls were also exploring the acceptable limits of visitation. They trekked over to Rocco and Rocco's mother. "Next time you come, pull my father down so Mercy can meet her grandfather," Cesar mumbled to Coco. There were just minutes left. "What's this about you and Roxanne?" he asked.

"She won't let me see the baby," said Coco. "Mercedes wants to see her sister."

"I don't want you fighting," he said. He kissed only the girls good-bye. The visitors collected beside the gate at the first of several exits. Nikki watched her mother watching Cesar.

"Bye, Daddy," Nikki said softly. Cesar and Rocco talked animatedly as they waited to be searched. Coco peered at Cesar.

"Bye, Daddy," Nikki tried again, louder.

"That's not your daddy," Coco reminded her.

"No!" Nikki chastised herself. "Cesar!"

The severity of Nikki's voice caught Coco's attention, and she tried to reassure her daughter. "Your daddy look like *you*," Coco said to Nikki tenderly.

Not too long after her visit to Rikers, Coco, still in her coat after collecting Mercedes from preschool, sat in her apartment, Cesar's latest letter balanced on her belly. Tears dampened the paper. Mercedes clutched the chair. Nikki, sitting cross-legged in the corner of the kitchen, rocked herself to a private song near the overflowing garbage can. The letter, which had been addressed to Coco Santos, began promisingly:

> *Ever since I was little I always wanted to have kids and be a father to them because I never really had a father. But I fucked up and I still have another chance, and I promise myself that I am going to do the right thing this time, if not for me for my children. I'm going to tell you something that nobody knows about except Mighty may he rest in peace.*
>
> *Coco, if it's not a boy and I want to have another one from you would you let me? Because I ain't going to stop having kids until I have a son. I don't care if I end up with 15 daughters, I'm still going to keep on. I think you're carrying a girl, I don't know why but that's just how I feel. I want a son so bad that I think I ain't never going to have a little boy. . . . If you don't give me my kids I'll have them from someone else. See Roxanne she said she'll never have another child from me that stupid bitch. I don't need her. She's not the only girl who can have kids.*

The mugging charge was dismissed and Cesar had been returned to Coxsackie. The bad part of the letter involved Cesar's discovery that another girl had a daughter of his. Cesar wanted Coco to track down his baby's mother. The only clues were her name, Whitney, and an approximate address, a building near Burnside on Davidson. The child was said to look just like Mercedes.

The actual Mercedes was clamoring for Coco's attention. She had learned a new song in preschool. "Put the letter down, Mommy, and hear me sing," she urged. Cesar instructed Coco to pretend that she was his sister, searching for a long-lost niece. "Tell the bitch I want the baby to have my name," Cesar wrote. The theme song from *Cops* wafted out of the bedroom—"Bad boys, bad boys, whatcha gonna do? Whatcha gonna do when they come for you?"

Coco said, "Oh! Mercedes! Go watch it, *Cops* in the bedroom!" and pointed Mercedes toward the siren sound. Mercedes drifted toward it, humming the song in an eerie monotone. Nikki padded after her big sister. Coco wept.

CHAPTER SEVENTEEN

Lourdes was dressed like a schoolgirl the cold September morning in 1993 when she went to see her youngest son. She wore a green-and-cranberry-striped hoodie and matching green leggings. She sported canvas shoes. A gold scrunchie cinched her waist-length hair into a bun. Slender gold hoops dangled from her ears. She'd painted her lips summer pink. But by the time Lourdes laid eyes on the tree-lined drive of Coxsackie Correctional Facility, she looked as though she'd imploded. She hated prisons. "Because I feel the pain of the whole room, of the whole people in jail, and I can't take it," she said. She dragged behind Mercedes, who hopped toward the front gate, which was topped by tall loops of razor wire. Cows grazed in a nearby pasture. Lourdes kept her head down during the lengthy processing. When the guard asked her, "What's your relationship to the inmate?" Lourdes whispered, "Mother"—a word she usually proclaimed.

Across her belly, one arm rested in a sling. The stories of how she came to have a cast were lively and various: she preferred the tale about a trip she took with her man, Domingo, to buy chickens, his admirable intervention in someone else's domestic trouble, and her diving in front of him to block the bullet that the enraged husband had sent his way. For the prison visit, Lourdes had done her best to look buoyant, perhaps to minimize the wrath she anticipated from her son.

The guard assigned to the visiting room at Coxsackie was immersed in a book of word games. Lourdes, Coco, and Mercedes waited beside him to be acknowledged. Finally, pushing his chin in the general direction of their seat assignments, he said, "Sit second table, by the window," without lifting his head. Coco and Lourdes hesitated. They searched the room, perplexed. "Over there," he said impatiently, without offering further direction. They tiptoed uncertainly down several steps and to the center of the room. "See that black girl sitting with that white guy? NEAR HER!" the guard screamed.

Lourdes slid into a seat covered in greasy dirt so thick that other visitors had marked their presence in it with initials and hearts. The chair wobbled. "Can I switch chairs? Where do he come from?" she asked.

Mercedes pointed to a door. "*Abuela*, Daddy come out from there," she said. Lourdes tapped her left leg compulsively. When Cesar finally stepped through the inmate entrance, Mercedes bolted across the room; a guard removed his handcuffs just in time for him to catch her as she leaped into his arms. Cesar carried her to the desk guard, who took his ID number down, and he bounced Mercedes joyfully as he approached Lourdes and Coco. Lourdes stood. Cesar placed Mercedes down gently and hugged his mother, who sobbed. He kissed Coco's cheek softly. She was crying, too. "What are *you* crying for?" he asked. He smiled worriedly and regarded the women in his life, glancing back and forth—Coco with her belly and self-inflicted red spots; Lourdes, puffy-faced and sniffling; Mercedes peeking out happily beneath a head of perfect curls.

He dove straight into the heart of the trouble, staring directly into his mother's eyes: "So what's up with you? What's going on?" He knew most of it from Elaine, who believed that Domingo had beaten Lourdes for stealing his drugs. Elaine told Cesar about the resulting shoot-out between Domingo and her husband, Angel, how Domingo had threatened even Robert when he went to retrieve Lourdes's things. Elaine had called the police, and Domingo ended up in jail for carrying an unlicensed gun. Despite his family's posturing, Cesar knew the trouble—whatever it was—was his to fix. From prison, the business of fixing it was just that much harder. He'd already sent word to Rocco, who was back on the streets.

What Cesar didn't know was that, while Robert was making arrangements to get his mother to Florida, Lourdes had bailed Domingo out and returned to him. As Lourdes launched into her version of the story, Cesar's expression flattened. His body became taut as Lourdes went on about how Elaine just cared for herself, how Elaine's husband was a liar, how although Robert had invited Lourdes to stay with him and his wife, she couldn't stay as far away as Brooklyn, let alone survive their Jehovah's Witness rules.

Cesar turned to Coco, who sat quietly. He placed his large hand on her big belly. In one month, their baby was due. Cesar seemed steadied by his physical contact with the unborn baby. He asked his mother, "Where are you living?" She did not respond. He glanced at Coco. "Is she back with him?" he asked. Coco bit her lip and cast her eyes down. Lourdes relaunched an explanation that she'd gotten beaten up because of Angel, but Cesar's stare-down made her try another route. "Yes, I am back with my husband," she said. "We are back in the apartment—"

Cesar interrupted her. "He may give you food and he may give you clothes and he may give you shelter, but he did all that before without beating you and you gonna go back. And one day he's gonna beat you and you end up dead. What am I gonna do? Sit here?" Cesar crossed his legs and placed his chin in his hand like *The Thinker*. "What kind of man is he? I'm a violent person and I don't hit my girlfriend. Look at all I done to Coco, but I ain't never hit her." He fixed his eyes on the distance to control his rising anger, then noticed Lourdes's quivering cheeks. His voice softened. "I couldn't do nothing when I was a kid, but I can do something now. It's no death. But I'm gonna get every bone broke. I know you love him and that's your business, but this is out of your hands. Let it be." He placed his arms around Coco and pressed his face into her breasts.

Conversation meandered; Coco listened while Cesar and Lourdes discussed Cesar's discovery of his other daughter. Mercedes padded over from across the room and presented Cesar with a car without a wheel. Hours passed. Cesar and Coco kissed; when Lourdes went to the bathroom, they necked. The food wrappers piled up. They caught up on family and friends. During a companionable lull, Cesar told Lourdes that he had recently tried heroin. He'd sniffed some with Tito, who was still at Coxsackie with him. Cesar didn't think he would use it again, although he admitted that the boredom of prison was killing him. "When somebody brings stuff in, and you get in prison and you be sitting here all day doing nothing, the programs—I hate that shit—and somebody says, 'You want to get high?' you get high," he said. Cesar instructed Coco to call Tito down the next time she came for a visit, so he could have visitors, too. She nodded, then excused herself, went into the bathroom, gripped the edge of the sink clogged with toilet paper and hair and cigarette butts, and cried. She never thought Cesar would try heroin. When he was out on the street, he had condemned every drug short of weed.

Meanwhile, Lourdes tucked stray strands of hair into her bun. "You'll fall in love again, it ain't the last man," Cesar assured his mother. Lourdes lifted her chin regally. A slat of afternoon sun pushed through the windows, which were so cloudy they looked as if they had been scrubbed with a giant Brillo pad.

"Time's up!" the droopy guard shouted. "Get out of here! Move it! Time to go!" Mercedes wanted more candy. There was no money, and only a Starburst left. "Can I have that?" she asked her father, who then popped it in his mouth. He exaggerated its deliciousness. "Bite it," he said, inviting her to sample the sticky gob on the tip of his tongue.

"Gim-*me*!" Mercedes cried. Cesar pulled out the gooey taffy and offered it to her, but just as she reached for it, he pulled it back. He teased her with the offer again, and just as she reached for it, he swallowed it and smacked his lips. He smothered her hurt feelings with hugs, making it into a game, drowning out her crying with laughter and kisses and silly smooching sounds. In the subtle tyranny of that moment beat the pulse of Cesar's neighborhood—the bid for attention, the undercurrent of hostility for so many small needs ignored and unmet, the pleasure of holding power, camouflaged in teasing, the rush of love. Then the moment passed, and Cesar's three-year-old daughter walked back out into the world and left him behind.

To Coco's relief, this time Mercedes didn't ask why Cesar wasn't coming home. Some parents lied to their children: they said the prison was a job or a hospital. Elaine used her brother as a lesson: she told her sons that Tío Cesar was paying the price for having done bad things. Coco thought it best to stay close to the truth while veering away from the harshness, so, whenever Mercedes asked, she assured her that Daddy would be home when he was done with being far away. When the guard ushered the visitors from the stuffy room, Coco did not turn back to Cesar. She said, "I get so much upset that I can't look back, then I miss him all the way home."

Coco and Mercedes searched for deer on the Thruway. Lourdes brooded, stoking her discontent: "George beat up Jessica with a two-by-four. Angel—am I right or am I wrong, Coco?—broke Elaine's jaw?" she exclaimed. In fact, it was George who broke Jessica's jaw. But there were so many fights and slights and brawls and arguments that it was hard to keep track of them. "Robert, now, he's a Jehovah's Witness and he is willing to let his younger brother get brought downstate and take care of this and get more time? He is a religious person, and that don't seem right to me. Did I tell them what to do when they get beaten up? Did I tell Jessica? Did I tell Elaine she had to leave Angel? Why do they get the right to tell me?" Coco and Mercedes fell asleep. Lourdes continued, "I told Cesar, 'Get out of that macho. Get out of that hoodlum! And get inside you the urge to freedom!'"

The anger gave way to sadness. Lourdes glanced over at a hill tapering up to a white colonial house. "One night in my life I want to sleep in a house like that, with a front porch, and all peace and quiet," she said. She rummaged through her purse for her cigarettes and searched for a Spanish station on the radio, which she finally found, over an hour later, after crossing the miraculous span of the Tappan Zee Bridge. She turned the volume up louder, then louder, the closer she got to the Bronx.

Cesar's friends and girlfriends appreciated his loyalty. If he considered you family, he stood by you, regardless. He was brutally honest and what he said could be hurtful, but it also made him trustworthy in a world with a high tolerance for obfuscation and ducking and lies. He was calculating about playing girls, but his flattery always had a foundation. With women, Cesar did not confuse staying true with fidelity. "I loved Coco with all of my heart and soul, yet I was never faithful to her," he said. Lizette gave him condoms whenever he went out. If Roxanne suspected him of cheating, he'd soothe her by saying, "Alright, but what girl could compete with you?" In prison, where business tended to be conducted through indirection, Cesar still presented his desires clearly and forcefully: he wanted a wife to help him through his sentence, a pretty enough stand-up girl who did her job—brought his children regularly to visits, offered companionship in trailers, put money in his commissary account. He hoped for a girl who would understand him and also check up on his mother, but he wasn't expecting that.

Coco wanted him to want her, though she was unsure of the terms of being chosen. To her mother, she hesitantly confided her conflicts about the marriage: "We rushing things. We trying to do things so fast, it's just coming out messed up." If they were married, she would have to support him, and there were so many other things she needed to do: get her own apartment, finish high school, get a good job, be an excellent mother and example to her girls. She wanted to earn her driver's license and save up for a convertible. She'd tool up to the front gates of the prison—with the girls in back—and swing open the passenger door the day Cesar was set free. Her boldest dream was to become a photographer. At the very least, she wanted to gain some weight in her butt and breasts and to stop picking her face.

Coco mostly kept her deepest doubts from Cesar, but not from herself. "My thoughts keep changing every day," she said. She had good reason for her confusion; Cesar sounded confused himself. He'd written that he loved her, but she remembered that he'd bragged about his ability to write letters just to gas her head. He had made that comment a long time ago, but now every time he wrote "I love you," she wondered, *Is he gassing my head now?* She felt almost certain that his promise to get a tattoo that read *Cesar loves Coco* was a lie. Boy George had promised the same to Jessica, but then he'd gotten only the outline of the heart and had never added Jessica's name.

Coco was glad that Cesar was honest about his other girls—most boys lied—but if she married Cesar, she didn't want other girls around. In fact, she didn't want other girls around right now. "I can't play you while I'm in here," he had protested, as though her worry was foolish, but

Coco knew that people got busy during visits. Once, Mercedes surprised a couple in a bathroom stall. Other couples managed to have sex in the open visiting room. Why else would otherwise stylish girls wear those ugly prairie skirts?

There were lots of things Coco didn't dare ask Cesar in her letters, but she wondered. How could he get in a fight if he was on lockdown? Was it really an accident that Tito had shot his wife? Why didn't Cesar rub his wrists after the guard removed the handcuffs? Didn't handcuffs hurt? With Cesar, though, she shared only the happier parts of her colliding thoughts: fantasies of the trailers; the sex she missed; Mercedes's latest escapades and accomplishments.

Coco didn't explain that she avoided visits when she didn't have enough money to buy him food from the vending machine, and that when she did visit, she felt too self-conscious to eat in front of him. She did not admit how hard it was for her to genuinely love Justine, the daughter he'd had with Roxanne. Justine was an innocent baby, but Coco felt jealous when he bragged about Justine's chubby arms. This failing shamed her. It also bothered her that Cesar's desire for a son seemed stronger than his love for his already born daughters. She wanted to be the one to give that to him, yet she also worried about losing a son, if she was lucky enough to have one. Coco already had concerns about the ways in which Mercedes acted like Cesar—and Mercedes was a girl. "That boy is gonna wanna be so much like his father, and I'm scared, God forbid, he end up just like him, behind bars, and I'm gonna have to go through what Lourdes's going through."

It was hard enough to be the girlfriend of a locked-up boy. Cesar's self-absorption was exhausting; he rarely asked questions of her: " 'Howse you, Mercedes, and our unborn child? Have the baby yet?' *Thass it.*" He tracked her visits as though he were a boss with a time card. He wanted sheets to match his towels, sweat suits coordinated with sneakers, nothing in black, gray, orange, or blue. If she came alone, he wanted the girls. If she brought the girls, they had to be dressed—stylishly. He constantly told her not to pay any mind to what other people said, but he also demanded that she look good for his friends. She could never be the perfect girl he wanted. And instead of assuring her that she was pretty, he shamed her for worrying. "Every letter you write to me now you're always saying, I got small breasts, and a medium ass, so what? If I ain't complaining, why should you?" He hated it when she broke down publicly. "I guess it's just that he don't want people to think that he made me cry," she said.

So she cried at home, in bed. "Nobody gonna see cuz it's in the night," she said. But her daughters did.

"Mommy, why you always crying?" Nikki would ask in her hoarse voice. Mercedes became angry with worry. She demanded that Coco stop, and her tough love sometimes helped.

Coco downplayed the hardship of raising her girls alone. She had whole conversations with Cesar's letters for days after they arrived. So he was sick of his girls having different mothers? "That's your business," she exclaimed to her bureau. What was she going to do about Nikki's father, who was about to get out of prison? "What I'm going to do? Put him in my pocket?" Coco asked the pay phone. Her Thorpe neighbors heard responses that never reached Cesar's ears: "He thinks I got nothing to do out here. He don't understand. I go to welfare. I take care of the girls. I got a life, too," she said, although she was not always certain she did. At the same time, Cesar's criticisms narrowed the impossible expectations of the larger world down to failures against which she could defend herself—what Cesar didn't understand, didn't say, couldn't see.

Before Cesar got shipped back to Coxsackie, Mercedes met her grandfather. Coco had taken her to Rikers with Lourdes, and had called down Cesar's father for a visit. Mercedes sat on his lap. Jessica heard about the visit and wrote Coco, chastising her for putting Mercedes at risk. Jessica revealed that Cesar's father had been the man who had abused her, and said that she didn't want her own daughters near him, "neither do I want my nieces sitting on his lap, because that is how it started with me. . . . I wouldn't want any of you to go through what I went through and is still going through." Coco sympathized with Jessica's feelings, but no man was going to do anything to a little girl with her mother sitting beside him. "I'm tired of my daughters having all these fake grandfathers!" Coco said in her own defense, albeit privately.

Coco soon told Cesar about Jessica's revelation. Fortunately, Cesar and his father were no longer incarcerated in the same prison by the time the dangerous news reached Cesar's ears.

Finally, toward the end of October, Coco's sister announced, "Coco's ready to push." Iris didn't meet Coco at the hospital, though; she'd already shown up for two false alarms. Neither did Coco's Thorpe House friend Jezel. Nikki's father had been released from prison, and she was staying with him and his wife in Baltimore. But Mercedes accompanied Coco to the hospital and waited in the hallway of the maternity ward while Coco was put in a delivery room.

The double doors at the end of the hallway banged open. Foxy bustled in wearing overalls and carrying apple Danish and hot chocolate, with Hernan in tow. She held up the bag of food like a torch. "He takes care of me," she said, gesturing rearward with her chin, plunking the bag on a chair. "Where's Coco?" Then she disappeared behind a door. Mercedes threw her arms around Hernan. Mercedes snubbed Hernan in Coco's presence, but that night Mercedes nuzzled him.

"Hello, Mercedes, how you doin'?" he asked deferentially.

"The cops took Mommy away," she said soberly. Hospital orderlies had escorted Coco to delivery from the emergency room. "We running from the cops. The cops took Mommy. We running from them to get her back."

Mercedes dragged herself up and down a hallway rail. She and Hernan wrestled. Mercedes asked Hernan for money, and he forfeited all his loose change. Coco peeked out into the hall and Mercedes approached her warily. She kissed her mother's belly, then her hand, like a troubadour. Coco gasped, then inched her way back into her room, and Mercedes returned to Hernan and said, with deep sadness, "I wanna lay down." He assembled a bed of chairs and lined it with their coats. She crawled on it and stared at the fluorescent lights on the ceiling. Restless, she clambered down. Then she dictated an imaginary letter to Cesar, updating him on the baby and the predicament of Jezel's son, whom Jezel had grounded at Thorpe. Mercedes held forth from the floor, where she lay on her side, making lazy arcs with her arm:

> *Dear Daddy,*
> *Mommy's having the baby now. ESJKLMNOP 1–2–3*
> *My mother's having the baby and I can't go over there because my mother said no. . . . He's in trouble cuz his mother no want him to go outside, that's why he's inside. . . . He's gonna stay inside for a week, then he's gonna come out for a second week. His mother hit him. She put him inside and her kick her butt.*
> *Goodbye Daddy*
> *I love him and he loves Mercedes. He hit me once for picking my face.*

Intermittently, Foxy ducked into the bathroom and smoked cigarettes. She fondly recalled Coco's birth, and her heavenly time in the psychiatric ward. "I wish I could go back to the hospital. I feel like it is the only time I can really get a rest," she said. Coco again stumbled out from her room and clutched the rail, groaning, "Mommy! Mommy! Mom-meeee!"

Foxy rushed to support her, and together they hobbled down the corridor. Mercedes joined them as they paused beside a poster about dilation, as if they were on a museum tour. Foxy pointed out the four-centimeter drawing—this was where Coco was right now.

"Oh my God! Oh my God!" Coco wheezed happily. Foxy assisted Coco back into her room. Mercedes looked lost.

"Childbirth, there's nothing like it," Hernan said nonchalantly, swinging his car radio between his knees.

Mercedes's brand-new sister, Nautica Cynthia Santos, had puffy eyelids and a red nose. A pink-and-white cotton cap topped her head. Mercedes had a different baby in mind—a boy—and she glanced over Nautica and eagerly searched the room. She landed her indictment on the midwife. "I thought it was supposed to be a brother," she said accusingly.

"You thought it was a boy, but look, it's a girl," the midwife said, invitingly. Mercedes stared at her baby sister. "Girl," she said, considering. She smiled shyly. She patted Nautica's head perfunctorily. "Where you get the baby, Mom?"

"Look what your mommy did," the midwife said.

"Your *father* did this," Foxy said slyly.

Nautica's tiny hands clenched in little fists. Coco beheld her new girl drowsily, murmuring, "She have her father's bubble lips."

Newborns—while they were new—had a way of mobilizing people. The following day, Hernan drove Foxy and Milagros to the hospital and collected Coco and Nautica and chauffeured them all back to Thorpe. He bought a big pizza and soda and juice and they celebrated in Coco's apartment. Foxy stayed the whole time, without coming up with an excuse to leave so she could go and get high. The next day, Foxy and Hernan delivered a crib. It had belonged to Iris's daughter, but Foxy had bought a new mattress. Iris promised to buy the baby a stroller, if a payment from her lawsuit came through; she'd had a miscarriage several years earlier, and Foxy had, without Iris's knowledge, filed a lawsuit under her name. The suit claimed that Iris's miscarriage had been caused by a tumble down defective stairs at Foxy's; Iris had reluctantly warmed to the idea. Relief sprouted from misfortune, but sometimes, as Foxy knew, you had to usher it along.

*   *   *

Thorpe House's management was built on clear expectations and consequences. Coco's pregnancy had granted her special status and a little slack; now she was just another mother again. But, to Sister Christine's dismay, Nautica's birth made Coco more restless. She became sassier— almost rowdy—as though Nautica's arrival had given Coco clearance to act street. She dyed her hair blond and blew it dry and straight, "dead like Jessica's." She got her nose pierced. She planned to go dancing. She dressed to go outdoors even when she was stuck inside. She bought three-inch fake-gold door-knocker earrings with the word LOVE suspended in the middle. She made announcements such as "I'm not going to go down just because I got three children," emphasizing her point with a shoulder roll. She rediscovered the fun of scrutinizing boys: "Now that I had the baby out, I'm ready to look!" Even her comments about Cesar were cheeky. "I don't have to listen to him, I ain't pregnant no more," she declared.

Mercedes didn't like this attitude in her mother, at least not when Coco directed it toward her father. "I love my daddy," Mercedes would say defensively. One afternoon, Mercedes pointed to a tire-repair shack on the way to Foxy's house. "What's that?" Mercedes asked.

Coco quipped, "Your father's house!" Mercedes usually laughed whenever Coco did, but she hesitated when Coco's comments about her father were sarcastic. Other times, mother and daughter bonded over their shared longing for the man they both adored. They belted out the song that reminded Coco of Cesar ("I Will Always Love You," by Whitney Houston). If Coco was lonely, Mercedes would somberly say, "I miss Daddy." If Coco mentioned her own curiosity about seeing the daughter Cesar had with Roxanne, Mercedes would suddenly claim to miss her sister.

If Coco's new attitude was hard on her daughter, it also robbed Coco of whatever pleasure she'd previously taken in her Thorpe House accomplishments. Before, other begrudging residents had clucked at Coco's enthusiasm, but now she put herself down. She dodged Sister Christine; she tore down the awards and certificates she had displayed and replaced them with photographs of Cesar. On the bottom of one diploma, her favorite staffer had written, "Wish you were here more." Coco barked, "I'm getting sick of these people, I don't need they stupid awards, what kind of award is that? Wish-you-were-here-more award?" She continued to travel—to Milagros's, to Lourdes's, to her mother's block—frequently missing curfew as a result. Coco also missed several house meetings and

Mercedes missed preschool. During apartment check, Coco had a point deducted for meat juice in the freezer, and two for a bathtub ring. She acted as though it didn't bother her, but it did. Taken alone, these violations weren't substantial, but the Thorpe House nuns knew that the viability of Coco and her family depended on her ability to maintain consistency in the little things.

CHAPTER EIGHTEEN

Coco's birthday, which fell on Thanksgiving that year, did not start out well. Her old neighborhood friends had promised to take her dancing. During the weeks before, whenever she ran into her girlfriends by her mother's, or at the clinic, or waiting for the bus, or in front of the pay phone by the store, they talked about the event. Coco had her outfit ironed and waiting three days before—a green-and-white hooded sweatshirt and a pair of baggy beige pants she'd borrowed from Hector. But that cold November night, her Thorpe friends went to Brooklyn and everyone else was broke. She briefly considered inviting out her brothers' girlfriends, but Manuel would never allow Yasmin to go, and Hector followed Manuel. Manuel expected Yasmin to stay stuck in Foxy's apartment even when he went to work.

But Coco stayed hopeful. Fortune could change suddenly. Nikki had returned from visiting her father, and Foxy had already agreed to baby-sit all three girls. No matter what, Coco had to go out. She borrowed her mother's coat and canvassed the neighborhood. She walked down the block to Milagros's, but Milagros had Thanksgiving dinner guests. Drunken couples slow-danced in the dim living room, beside a table piled with empty plates and crumbs. Coco felt uncomfortable and peeked into the girls' room, where a pile of children slept on the beds in the blue light of a TV screen. Serena, wide awake in the tangle, sat with her back pressed against the wall. Coco stood for a moment, and before leaving, gave Serena's worried face a kiss. Then she walked back down toward her mother's and visited her friend Angie. Angie had a black eye from a strict boyfriend. Angie's baby son squatted dully in a crib; his soiled mattress had no sheet. There was nothing else in the living room, other than a Mother's Day card that lay splayed on the floor.

Next, Coco went to see her friend Vanessa. Perhaps Vanessa could go out. Coco waded through the knee-high trash at Vanessa's mother's to get to the orderly oasis of Vanessa's room. It was crowded with girls, putting on makeup and talking about Vanessa's dilemma: she no longer wanted to be a virgin, but she was still in school. Her friends, most of whom had already dropped out, encouraged her to wait. Virginity and school were discussed as though they were inextricably linked; the loss of one seemed to guarantee the abandonment of the other. While Coco waited for Vanessa to figure out that she couldn't come dancing, she let Vanessa's niece play with her keys. Then Coco heard that her friend Terry had $9, and therefore might be willing to go out. Coco found Terry in the cavernous lobby of Angie's building, standing in a fog of somnolent girls, sipping beer from a Dixie cup. Coco's excitement almost felt like an intrusion. The girls silently shared one cigarette.

"Give me twenty minutes, Coco, so I can drink this and go upstairs and do what I gotta do," Terry said. What she had to do involved drugs. Coco didn't drink or smoke or do drugs. She had tried alcohol and weed when she was younger, but didn't like how either made her feel.

"I'll be back after I go visit my mother-in-law," Coco said. Lourdes would fuss over Coco—even on regular, boring days, when Coco visited, Lourdes made a scene.

In Lourdes's building on Mount Hope, someone had finally had it with the rickety elevator. Even when it worked, the buttons required slamming and improvisational rewiring. Now the button panel dangled. Coco pushed what remained of the fourth-floor button and the elevator jerked her up to the fifth. She hurried down to Lourdes's door. A cap covered the peephole—the top from one of Lourdes's favorite juice drinks, Sunny Delight.

Her new apartment was a tiny studio next to the building where she'd last lived. The super snuck the dark space in between the known apartments and didn't give the landlord the rent. The airless room was crammed to the ceiling with objects that suggested former or future promise: speakers, stereos, toolboxes, car radios, an exercise bicycle, TVs, VCRs. A Honda bumper nosed out of the wall; cameras hung, awaiting precious moments; even a Nikon was resting below the feet of Lourdes's statue of Saint Lazarus. The bed was center stage. The apartment door had to be closed to get into the refrigerator; a pair of handcuffs hooked the handle. There was a sink and a hot plate, no stove. Lourdes mourned the lack of a functioning kitchen. She couldn't even cook.

But the evening of Coco's birthday, the room had a festive air. The electricity, illegally wired through a neighbor's, had been cut off, and there were candles everywhere. Lourdes, holding forth from the bed, explained the predicament to Coco. The neighbor was a gay man with a crush on Domingo; a single visit to the gay man by her handsome husband would restore their light. But Domingo, she said mockingly, was frightened. When he left their apartment, he ducked beneath the peephole of the gay neighbor's door. "He's scared of a faggot!" she hacked.

Tucked into a space beside the refrigerator, an older man sipped from a bottle of beer wrapped in a paper bag. Beside him, Domingo leaned against the refrigerator, pretending to ignore Lourdes's taunts, which she hurled in English so that he couldn't understand. Domingo worked full-time at Hunts Point unloading vegetables from trailer trucks; he moonlighted dealing drugs. A recent immigrant from the Dominican Republic, he saw Mount Hope as a pit stop, and, it seemed, Lourdes as a lover-mother, who was becoming more burdensome than useful. But he didn't have any better place to go, nor did he want to lose the extra income from the dealing (Domingo later said Lourdes threatened to keep the business if he dared leave). His dream was to learn English and get his trucking license. Lourdes boasted that Domingo wanted her to give him his first child. She'd claim she was pregnant, then mourn the miscarriages that inevitably followed. When Jessica spoke to Elaine, she would say, "Howse Mommy? Pregnant again?"

Lourdes talked on, flapping her sling for emphasis. The flames from the candles flickered. She bragged about her long hair and her fine ass and her Puerto Rican power, how when she danced she didn't even need to flirt to get a man. Domingo raised his eyebrows mischievously at Lourdes, jingling the handcuffs hanging from the refrigerator handle like a prison guard. Lourdes scrambled off the bed and grabbed a wedding picture of her son Robert and his wife. She shook it like an angry fist. "You get married now, Mami," she said, nudging Coco with her bad arm. She claimed she'd filed a lawsuit. "When I get the money from this, I'm going to give you a fucking church wedding."

Coco burst into tears. "Why are you crying, Mami?" Lourdes asked, alarmed. She shot an accusing look at Domingo along with a blast of Spanish and demanded, "*Why is she crying?*" In what seemed like a single, fluid gesture, Lourdes then shooed Domingo away, ordered the old man off the only chair, sat Coco down, and knelt before her in the impossibly small space between the table and the wall of shelves.

"I don't know why, but I feel like I'm gonna cry, then I'm gonna laugh, then I'm gonna cry. I'm happy and upset. I don't know why I'm crying at the same time," Coco blurted out.

Lourdes understood the difficulty of birthdays. Milestones were unhappy times. Her forty-third birthday was only weeks away. She raised Coco's chin and placed her good hand firmly on Coco's wet cheek. In a throaty voice, she launched into a bluesy rendition of "Happy Birthday," putting her whole soul into the song. Then she broke into "Sixteen

Candles," refusing to let Coco's brown eyes wander, until she ended abruptly with her own applause. "Oh, I *love* that song!" Lourdes said. "*I love that song! Don't you love that song, Mami?*" Coco smiled shyly. "Happy birthday, Mami! Happy *birthday!*" Lourdes nearly shouted, pumping up her deflated hopefully-future-daughter-in-law. The decibel of the promises made up for what they lacked in conviction. Lourdes then announced in a normal tone of voice that Domingo would get Coco a winter coat. A guy he knew sold them from the back of a truck.

"I don't want to get my hopes up, because when my hopes get up, they always come down," Coco said, streaming down the stairs. She had not had a winter coat in years. Two little boys played soccer on a square of landing.

"Happy Thanksgiving," one said to her.

"Happy Thanksgiving!" she said back. She wrapped the windbreaker she'd borrowed from her mother around her and pushed out the heavy door. She scurried down Mount Hope Place, as she had so many times before, and into the light of Tremont Avenue.

Back at Foxy's, Coco checked in on the girls, then went back down to meet up with her friend Terry. It was so cold that only the drug dealers were out. Coco yelled to her little brother's bedroom window, "Hector! Throw down Mommy's scarf!" The scarf sailed down. Coco inhaled it as she wrapped it around her. "I smell just like my mother when she's smoking cigarettes and booter—ugghh!" she said. "I think I dressed too baggy tonight. I feel fat. I real skinny but I feel fat."

"You buggin', Coco," Terry said.

"Coco!" Hector yelled. He tossed down another missive from his room. To a matchbook he'd taped a free pass to a local club called The Fever. It stood on the corner of Webster and Tremont: Coco passed by the place whenever she took the 36 bus. Lourdes used to go dancing there when it was called the Devil's Nest. Now black streaks of lightning flashed across the sign: "The Fever—Catch It!" Coco hoped that she would run into Roxanne. Fights made things vivid. It was her birthday. Something had to happen. Something had to change.

The Fever occupied the basement of a decrepit building close to where Mighty had been shot. Bouncers haphazardly pat-frisked the customers. It cost an extra $5 to keep your coat, and a dollar to wear your hat. To parade in one's name brand must have been worth it, because most of the teenagers kept on their winter gear, even though the temperature climbed toward the tropical. Only the go-go girls were dressed to sweat, in leather hot pants and sequined bras.

Coco, in her topknot, looked vulnerable leading her friend Terry through the crowd. The girls danced without much enthusiasm. They whispered and danced some more. They stepped to the side of the floor and watched. Boys who could afford the $5 drinks clustered around the bar that surrounded the runway the go-go girls danced on. Bored, the girls flung their legs over the boys' hat-covered heads. Coco bought a drink that she still hadn't finished by the time they left, three hours later.

Back at Thorpe House, Coco realized that she'd forgotten to retrieve her keys from Vanessa's little niece. She was locked out, but she wanted to take advantage of her daughters' absence and clean. Although Coco would not admit it, she wanted to make a comeback on apartment check. She and Terry banged and body-slammed the front door of Thorpe for fifteen minutes and finally woke the security guard. He shuffled off in search of the master key. Coco slid down to the floor, while Terry perused a Thanksgiving bulletin board in the hall.

Terry scrutinized it closely. She needed glasses: her nose practically touched the paper turkeys stuck there. The nuns had prepared a photocopy that began, *I'm Thankful For . . .*

"She says *plane* instead of *place*, and she cannot even spell *God!*" Terry marveled at the errors of one essayist. She read Coco's aloud:

> *I'm Thankful For . . . My three pride and joy's Mercedes Nikki &*
> *Nautica. I thank god to have three beautiful girls. I'm thankful for*
> *having a great family that care for us a great deal. I'm glad to have*
> *a Mom thats there for me & understands me. I'm also greatful for*
> *the husband I have. He gives me headaches at times But we all go*
> *through that.*
>
> *Most of all I'm glad for finally being (living) on my own & being*
> *my self & finally I thank god for my girls to be one step ahead at a*
> *early age (school)*

Coco had drawn a smiley face with arrows pointed to the word *school*.

"I should go to jail," Coco said self-consciously. "Oh, they come outta prison smart. Cesar learned so much in there. You should see how much he knows." The Thorpe House guard must have fallen asleep downstairs, but Coco and Terry seemed neither to notice nor to care. They reminisced about their childhoods.

"I took my problems to the street," said Coco. "That's one thing, I never kepted them to myself. I guess it was because I wanted someone to talk to." She paused. Her mood seemed melancholy. Her habit of annotating her own life was another way to tuck in the wild strands. "I can't wait till my girls are old enough and I can talk to them about everything."

Finally, the security guard returned; he could not find the key. Back at Foxy's, the block was eerily still. Beside Foxy's building, on what had for years been abandoned lots, stood brand-new single-family homes: the city's latest attempt to improve the beleaguered neighborhood. The pastel units had outside light fixtures and driveways. The families parked their cars and checked the locks on their driveway gates, after which they slipped through barred doors and disappeared. In the middle of the neighborhood, the houses presented a surreal facade of cheer. They might have been intended to inspire, but the impossibility of acquiring something so close somehow had the opposite effect. The proximity made the failure pointed and personal.

It was five o'clock in the morning. Coco scanned her mother's windows. The apartment was dark. "My brother's asleep," she said. Terry wandered off toward her own mother's building. Coco collected the courage to go in. Her head pounded—she'd tied her ponytail knot too tight. "I feel so old," she said, hugging herself against whatever awaited her, on the cusp of her twentieth year.

Cesar didn't call Coco on her birthday. He'd been transferred upstate and was still waiting for phone privileges. But he'd written her a long letter that Coco read aloud to everyone who'd listen. The day she got it, she read it three times to herself. He wanted the relationship she wanted: "I told everybody up here that you had a girl and they were like, Damn, kid, you can't make a boy for shit. I told them me and you already planned on trying again. You already said Yes, don't change your mind."

He accepted Nikki: "I hate to admit it but it's also my fault that you got pregnant from Nikki. . . . I made you weak by always arguing with you and accusing you of things." He expanded her privileges: "Mamita, I'm giving you your freedom." He proclaimed her a woman. Prison had changed his ways: "The happier I make you, the more loyal you'll be. . . . Our relationship has no trust or understanding, it's only based on love and our children. I don't want it like that anymore. . . . I ain't never going to find another woman that will do 9 years with me or love me the way you do. I thought I had two women who cared, but they both with other men now. And that's Lizette and Roxanne. You are the only one who is still by my side."

He had only one request:

> *All I'm asking you is to leave your face ALONE. And don't cut your hair by yourself, and dress the way I like you to dress. Coco go to the beauty parlor every one or two months to get your hair cut. Dress like you care about yourself. Don't be wearing no dirty sneakers and stained clothes. Wash your sneakers and shoes. Do your hair, look pretty at all times. That's all I ask of you. I always dress nice, it ain't to impress no one else it's to impress myself and that's what you have to do impress yourself Coco.*

He called her "sweetheart." "I miss being with you. Talking kissing laughing joking arguing and making love."

The letter made her sad birthday the best yet.

"Ilovehimmysweetheart," Coco whispered back.

Foxy rarely told Coco what to do with her children. But ever since Nautica had been born, Foxy had made a point of urging her daughter to get Nautica's ears pierced; she wanted people to stop mistaking her granddaughter for a boy. Coco wanted to please her mother and stopped by Foxy's with the girls, hoping to borrow the $10 she needed to do it, but only her brother Manuel, and his girl, Yasmin, and Manuel's two children were home. Yasmin shuffled out of the bedroom in an oversize T-shirt and slippers, her long hair down.

"Can I have money for Nautica's earrings?" Coco asked Manuel.

"I'm not a bank," he said. Manuel was even harder than Iris. He was only twenty-three, but when it came to money, he acted like an old man. Yasmin modeled one of Coco's large door-knocker earrings. Manuel made a sour face. "You look too womanish with them. Stay like you are," he said.

Coco wanted much about her life to change. She wanted to marry and get her own apartment and go back to school. Sister Christine had told her about a high school program for young mothers, with on-site day care. Coco wanted to go. "You ain't going back to school?" she asked Yasmin encouragingly. Yasmin was fourteen.

"I want to," Yasmin said. "Everybody in school, they make me feel like they smart and I'm stupid."

"There's a school for girls like us. You're supposed to sign up now."

Coco told Yasmin that her Thorpe friend Jezel was taking training as a day-care aide. Day care didn't interest Jezel—she was impatient with children, especially her son—but it appealed to Coco because she loved kids.

"I want to go to school, but I need clothes. I won't go to school until I have clothes," Yasmin said. She also needed glasses.

"And when you get the clothes, what'll be the excuse after that?" asked Manuel, heading past her into the kitchen.

"There won't be no excuse because I want to go," Yasmin called after him, and rolled her eyes. She scooted close to Coco and whispered, "Coco, I think I'm pregnant!"

"Why don't you get it checked?" Coco asked.

"Because she's a derelict," Manuel said, returning to the couch.

"My brother's smoking crack," Coco teased.

Manuel crossed himself. "Thank God that I don't. Don't even joke about that." Nikki climbed onto her uncle's skinny lap. "You ain't supposed to go between a man's legs, Nikki!" Manuel said sharply. Nikki began to cry.

"Explain it to her better, look at her tears," Coco said.

"You ain't supposed to go between nobody's legs," Yasmin tried.

"Girl or boy," Manuel added.

"Especially a man," said Coco. She counted out four of her nine WIC tickets and tucked them in Foxy's sanitary napkin pack, where the boys wouldn't dare to look. Manuel surprised Coco by handing her $10 for Nautica's ears, and by giving Nikki a dollar for her shame.

At the jewelry store on Burnside Avenue, the ear-piercing lady straddled a tattered stool in her bullet-proof safety stall. She wore a gold suede jacket, and her black jeans had silver-fringed holes, strategically placed. Her clothes seemed like an attempt to keep her spirits up. The stereo blared. Gold chains and earrings stuffed the counter. She also had a card table piled high with toys—Barney knapsacks, knock-off Barbie dolls.

"I want this," Mercedes pleaded, pointing to everything.

"I don't got the money, Mercedes," Coco shouted. The music was so loud it was hard to hear.

"Take the baby's," Mercedes suggested practically.

"You don't want your sister to have earrings?" asked Coco.

"She look ugly in earrings," Mercedes said.

"So you and Nikki have earrings and your sister don't?"

"Yeah," Mercedes said. Nikki stood quietly.

Coco held Nautica's small head while the lady dotted each earlobe with a Magic Marker. Without warning, she punched the first pink rhinestone through. Nautica sucked in and screamed on the exhale. Tears streamed down Coco's face. The lady quickly stapled an earring into Nautica's other lobe.

Coco pushed the earring in. The post dug into Nautica's head. "They too big," she said, sniffling.

"I do lots of children," the lady said flatly.

"Oh," said Coco, working up her courage. The lady's tone ordinarily would have intimidated her, but Coco was speaking for a baby. "She's five weeks old, but—"

"I do *lots* of children just two weeks old," the lady said. End of chat.

Coco immediately returned to Foxy's to show her mother Nautica's earrings. In the elevator headed up, a neighbor glanced at the now unquestionably female Nautica. Her eyes then grazed over Mercedes, then Nikki, then she shook her head pityingly. "Coco, can't you do anything right? Three girls?" Coco smiled her crumpled smile and shrugged. The woman shuffled from the elevator and, without bothering to turn her head back, added wearily, "That's the only thing I done right. Had a son."

The pressure to buy things was always intense in the ghetto, but Christmas created a level of expectation that was unbearable, and the tension was further compounded by the blues that came with every holiday. Foxy didn't have any money to buy things for her grandkids, so she avoided her own children more than usual. Lourdes lost her sense of drama. Domingo said her battery was "down low." He urged Coco to bring by the children to recharge her spirits.

Christmas was even worse in prison. Jessica had crocheted hats and scarves for her girls and her nephews and nieces, but didn't have enough money for stamps to mail them out in time; she knocked herself out with prescription pills. Right before Christmas, Cesar got in a fight in the yard with a Muslim. Guards expected such outbursts around the holidays. Cesar spent Christmas Eve on keep-lock—room confinement—waiting to get shipped farther upstate to an isolation unit. He wrote to Coco, "I fucked up real bad this time."

Still, Coco always looked forward to Christmas. Unlike her vague plans for marriage and school and getting a job, Christmas was a piece of her future that she could actually envision, and she knew exactly how to make it a reality. She trimmed her door with blinking lights that played a Christmas medley. At the center, she placed a red wreath and pictures of her daughters. (Foxy trimmed her apartment door with tinsel and added a handwritten note among the miniature gift boxes: "If any-one steals anything from this door, Manuel and Hector live here and will fuck you up bad. Foxy.") While her bigger dreams prompted doubt and belittling remarks from others, nobody criticized a mother for doing right by her children at Christmas. That year, Thorpe House made the challenge easier: the children received lots of donated gifts, and the nuns provided the mothers with Christmas trees. Coco snapped pictures of Mercedes and Nikki sitting beside the tree, with Nautica sitting in Mercedes's lap.

But instead of taking advantage of the reprieve Thorpe House had given her, Coco bought gifts for everyone in her extended family—even though she hadn't paid off her debt to Dayland from the previous Christmas. It was another example of Coco's self-defeating generosity. But unlike so many of her efforts, which ended in disappointment, watching her family open their presents was truly gratifying.

Not long afterward, in a letter to Cesar, Coco confessed that her old puppy love, Wishman, had been writing her from prison. Cesar demanded that the correspondence stop. He suspected Wishman's intentions; Cesar, too, was writing other girls, and he was experiencing first-hand what could blossom from a prison correspondence.

For months, unknown to Coco, Cesar had been trading letters with Giselle, the girl he'd been with the morning of his arrest. At first, his notes had been a distraction to pass the time, another line tossed out to the outside world. A letter, even a boring one, improved a day. An excellent letter improved his spirit for weeks. To have your name shouted out at mail call proved you mattered. In the most depersonalized of institutions, an envelope conferred distinction: it was addressed, by name, only and directly to you. If you were a boy with a long term, letters reminded you of what was out there, what else was possible—which was why some lifers preferred no letters at all. Maintaining a correspondence also required imaginative leaps and concentration, skills that slowed the process of becoming institutionalized.

Correspondence could create a future within prison: letters might lead to visits, and visits were gifts. The vast majority of inmates receive no visits. Face-to-face contact gave a boy a better chance at kindling love. The next best thing might be someone on the other end of the phone line, a girl willing to accept your collect call; if she wasn't interested, maybe she'd introduce you to a sister or a cousin or an aunt. You had to read between the lines, which was a game—valuable for its fun and distraction even if the objective failed. Lots of boys asked girls for pictures, which were called flicks. Flicks were censored, but like so many of the rules in prison, inconsistency and luck played their parts, and plenty of the pictures got in. The girls dressed in lingerie and posed provocatively. Some girls sent flicks that were fiendish (one inventive woman put lipstick on her vagina for an exclusive print). Giselle was conservative. But during months of exchanging letters, something precious happened—Cesar and Giselle became friends.

It frustrated Cesar that the level of communication he had with Giselle did not seem possible with Coco or Roxanne. He confided his quandary to Giselle about whom to marry; she wouldn't tell him—it was his life—but the conversations calmed him down. Giselle remained on good terms with her ex-husband. They shared the raising of their little boy. Some guys in prison read *Cosmopolitan* to help them understand females, but Cesar mined Giselle's brain: he consulted her throughout the back-and-forth with Coco, the breakups and reunions and disappointments.

Giselle's looks reminded him of Jessica. She was short, dark-haired, and voluptuous. Her smile revealed the faintest trace of a scar from a childhood fight; her self-consciousness about the scar gave her the appealing impression of being shy. She took care of herself the way Cesar felt a real woman ought to: she had a standing Saturday appointment at the beauty parlor and kept her nails manicured.

Giselle urged Cesar to be patient with Coco. Coco was raising three girls alone, and Giselle found it hard raising one with help from her ex and her mother. She pointed out to Cesar that it wasn't easy to coordinate a prison visit with two small children and a baby. Still, Cesar privately wondered how Coco managed to write to Wishman if she was so pressed for time.

In Wishman's last letter to Coco, he'd reported that the federal charges against him had been dropped. Cesar figured Wishman was lining up Coco as one of his girls for his release. Wishman had requested photographs. Coco had sent them, although she didn't tell Cesar. Cesar understood Coco well enough to remain suspicious. He sometimes felt less like a husband-to-be than like the father of a wayward child.

Giselle gently reminded Cesar how fortunate Coco was to be able to stay home and raise his daughters. Giselle was so busy getting ahead that she rarely saw her son. Four nights a week, after full days of work, she attended classes at Bronx Community College, six until ten. Her son spent so much time with his grandmother that he called his grand-mother *Mommy* and Giselle by name.

Giselle's quiet and unexpected perspective expanded Cesar's own; her example offered him a different way of looking at familiar things. He looked forward to her letters. In a letter to Coco, perhaps drawing from Giselle's optimism, he dared to end his year on a hopeful note: "Happy New Years '94. 7 years and 10 months left, not 9 years no more."

CHAPTER NINETEEN

I t was a record-breaking winter. Snowstorm after snowstorm hit the city. One sluggish January afternoon at Thorpe House, Coco received a phone call. "Whassup, bitch?" said the caller.

"Who's *this*?" Coco asked.

"Who's *this*?" Jessica joked.

"Is this Jessica?" Coco squealed. The conversation had to be quick because Jessica's counselor had allowed Jessica to place the call directly— a rare privilege officially reserved for emergencies. Coco hurriedly told Jessica that Tito wanted more pictures; that Cesar had been shipped to Southport, a special prison farther upstate; that she planned to get a tattoo with Cesar's name. Coco also solicited Jessica's advice about what to do about a dream Mercedes had just had. Mercedes had awakened demanding to know where Cesar was. She seemed unable to separate the dream from life.

"Where's my daddy?" Mercedes asked.

"You be having a dream," Coco said.

"He be laying with me right here. Where he go?" Mercedes's intentness spooked Coco.

"You know where Daddy's at," Coco said sternly. Mercedes had started to cry.

Jessica instructed Coco to fill a glass half full of water and place it under the bed, directly below Mercedes's pillow. Jessica had learned the trick from Lourdes and swore it had once saved her life while she was living with George. She'd snuck out of the apartment without his knowledge, and during her absence, the apartment had been robbed. Jessica had paged George with the bad news and he'd calmly warned her that he was going to kill her when he returned home. Jessica had called Lourdes, panicked, and Lourdes instructed Jessica about the water glass. When George came back, he wasn't even angry.

Just the sound of Jessica's voice helped Coco feel better: "She made my day. She's the only one who could take me out of a bad mood."

When Coco got off the phone, Mercedes asked her mother to tell her again about the story of her dream about her father, a request she'd been repeating for weeks. Mercedes loved the idea of her daddy sleeping at her house. One of Mercedes's favorite stories about her father's short seven months of freedom was of those nights tucked snugly between her parents, at her grandmother's Mount Hope apartment, in her daddy's big bed.

Coco arranged to get her first tattoo the following week. Like so many things in her life, the tattoo was less a sign of conviction than an attempt to redeem herself. Jessica had been urging Coco to fight for Cesar—"If Roxanne sends one million pictures, you send two million"—and Cesar had even instructed her to buy their wedding rings. But wedding rings cost money and he also wanted the children to visit—which cost money—and he continued needing money for his commissary. Cesar had even pressured her into smuggling weed while he was at Rikers, and she'd felt that by saying yes that one time she'd permanently forfeited her right to refuse. "I don't want to end up like Jessica," Coco said. "God forbid I get caught, what's going to happen to my kids?" A tattoo was an easier way to prove her loyalty.

Manuel made the appointment for Coco at their mother's with a guy named Spider from whom he hoped to learn the craft. Manuel invited Coco to use his bedroom, which surprised Coco because Manuel didn't ordinarily allow people around his things. Coco was closer in spirit to Hector, a softhearted boy even when he tried acting hard.

Manuel's room was hooked up; he kept his bedroom locked against the rest of the family. He stored his own groceries there and also kept his own TV and stereo. His windows had curtains. Moët, Manuel's ferret, banged around her cage. Prayer cards from recent funerals of several of Manuel's friends leaned on a bureau, between neat rows of name-brand deodorant and aftershave. The room was stuffy, though; Foxy's apartment was either freezing or stifling; there was no middle ground.

Coco sat on the bed and opened one of the tattoo books. Hector's fourteen-year-old girlfriend, Iris, sat beside her. Coco's family sometimes referred to the brown-eyed beauty as Hector's Iris to distinguish her from Coco's older sister. Hector's Iris's mother was in prison, and although Hector's Iris technically lived with a sister, she spent most of her time at Foxy's house. Coco and Hector's Iris skimmed the tattoo sketchbooks like two girls flipping through fashion magazines. Iris was pregnant. Yasmin, Manuel's girl, was finally pregnant, too. Above them, a photograph of Jessica was tucked into the frame of a print entitled HOT STUFF, which depicted a sexy firewoman barely covered by an enormous hose. Coco and Iris scanned page after page, binder after binder, of dragons and Jesuses and Garfields and Tweety birds and unicorns. They admired an elaborately scripted *In Memory Of.* Coco said when she had money, she'd get one in her father's name.

"How much for three babies with their name and they birthdays?" Coco asked Spider.

"It depends," said Spider, pulling out his homemade drill. As Manuel went off in search of paper towels, Spider picked at the guitar strings he'd fashioned into needles. He cleaned one with Ajax. He labored intently beneath a headband he'd rolled down to the word *Marlboro*, as though the name brand were a literal thought. Spider's gray-hooded sweatshirt, which said nothing, was cut off at the waist. *Metallica* slashed across his hairy belly. Spider had learned his craft in prison. He'd first practiced on his forearm; his skills had improved significantly by the time he'd snaked his lessons around his neck. He snapped on latex gloves, over his skull-and-crossbones ring.

Meanwhile, Coco scanned more images. Any remotely female picture had titanic breasts; backs were arched. The illustrated women all seemed to be either threatened—chased by, say, a gorilla—or threatening— snorting guns, swallowing snakes. Coco liked the one of a big-breasted girl with flowing mermaid hair who held a gun in each hand and stood over the top of the world defiantly.

"That's pretty. That looks like Jessica," Coco said.

"That's cute, 'Eat Me!' " Iris said, pointing to a strawberry.

Coco spotted a reproduction of a photograph. "That woulda been nice, a picture of him," she murmured.

"I don't like to do those," Spider said.

Coco selected a heart laced with a flying banner, on which she wanted written *Coco Loves Cesar.* "But I want two ribbons," she added. Cesar wanted Coco's new tattoo placed over her heart, but she had a small scar there, which embarrassed her, and she decided instead on the thickest part of her right thigh. She lay across Manuel's bed on her stomach and shooed Mercedes and Nikki away. They backed up but hovered by the bedroom door.

"The one ribbon will wrap around and look like two," Spider promised.

"I wanted one ever since Jessica," Coco said. She gazed upward toward Jessica's photograph. Spider rubbed Mennen deodorant on her thigh. He pressed the ditto paper facedown and rubbed until the image appeared. Coco wanted purple, her favorite color, but Spider decided on blue, green, yellow, and red.

"My husband, Cesar, has a tattoo of his friend's name, on the left side of his chest, that says 'R.I.P.,' it's real nice," Coco said self-consciously. The room was silent except for the sound of a movie on the VCR. "I feel like I'm laying on the bed for my husband Cesar to come to me."

"You bugged," Iris said, and smiled. Spider measured the ink into a spoon. The needle drank it. He cut into Coco. She winced. She clasped a pillow to her chest. "I feel like I'm getting sliced. The way you peel an orange, that's how I feel my skin's coming out," she said. She dove beneath the pillow and covered her head.

"My mommy's crying," Mercedes said, alarmed. "My mommy's crying!" No one paid her any mind. Next, she tried exclaiming, "A rat!" Still, no response. She turned her back to everyone and crossed her arms. Nikki stood next to her sister, wearing an oversize T-shirt, which swallowed her arms and legs. It was an old favorite of Coco's that read 90% Bitch—10% Angel. Mercedes started bawling. Nikki tried a softer approach. "Mommy, why you getting a boo-boo?" she asked.

Richie, Coco's stepfather, peered in through the doorway. Richie was living at the Wards Island Men's Shelter, waiting for an apartment, but he was visiting Foxy's on a weekend pass. "Hey, gumba, whassup?" He looked down at Mercedes. "Why's Mercedes crying?" No one answered.

Foxy appeared behind him, wiping her hands on her apron. "I'd like a rose, I'll take it here," she said as she pounded hard above her breast. She dragged down the collar of her T-shirt and showed Spider a tattoo her brother had given her. It was supposed to be a rose, but the broad stem looked like a snap pea. "You want to continue that?" Foxy asked Spider sociably.

"Don't do anything, just let it heal. If you mess with it, it might get infected," said Spider.

"Coco, why the girls eating candy so close when I'm making dinner?" asked Foxy. Coco said nothing. She let the girls eat candy a lot of the time. Foxy and Richie went back into the kitchen. Mercedes's sobs had become softer and more rhythmic. Coco peeked from the pillow and smiled at her daughters. Mercedes pouted, then smiled back, relieved. Coco said, "I think that's what'll make me stronger, looking at my girls."

"Some people find this pleasurable. They get hooked on this, like addicted," Spider said. The temperature of the room rose. Sweat dripped from Spider's forehead onto Coco's leg. He sipped his Coke. The needle whined. He outlined the heart in blue. Coco limped down the hall and washed it with soap, the girls tagging close. Nikki babbled as she zigzagged down the hall, "Mommy, I lub you," her T-shirt dragging on the floor behind her.

Coco's uncle Benny, who'd botched Foxy's rose tattoo, cornered Coco near the bathroom. He practically lived at Foxy's. Prison and heroin had gotten the better of him, although he still had a spark. Foxy fondly called him "the man of a million and one lies." Benny still liked to hang out, but he'd calmed down some since discovering he'd tested positive for HIV. He warned Coco about unclean needles. "You don't want to hear a lecture, I know," he said, then delivered one, closing with "But you too old to hear a lecture."

Manuel admired the heart on Coco's leg. "That shit came out phat," he said, impressed.

Back in Manuel's bedroom, Nikki occupied herself on the floor with a coloring book. Spider still had a lot to fill in. Coco prepared for his next incision. She appealed to Jessica's photograph. She raised up her eyes, as if in prayer, and whispered, "Go, girl, go," bonding with Jessica through the suffering. "Thass one thing, Jessica know how to take pain," Coco boasted. She described the tattoo Jessica had over her bottom, *Property of George*. For her next tattoo, Coco wanted one like it, *Property of Cesar*, but with an arrow pointing down.

"Yo, what if you break up? What if you find another man?" Manuel asked sharply.

"They gotta accept it. It's who I am. It's a part of who I be."

"I wouldn't get no one's name but my children," Manuel said.

"He showed me things I never knew. If Cesar was ever to say 'I don't love you,' I'd of tored his face up."

"That's why you have to think twice about putting a man's name on your body. I'd only put my mother or my daughter," Manuel said.

Spider zigzagged the needle across the skin of Coco's drawn heart. He colored in the bare flesh. Nikki compared his drawing to hers and hopped around. "My mommy finished boo-boo! Boo-boo, my mommy happy," she said.

In the living room, Richie, Foxy, Benny, and some of Hector's friends played spades at the table, the music playing low. Mercedes clamored for Foxy's Malta drink. Spider packed up his drill, which Benny called "the AIDS machine," and headed out with Manuel and Yasmin, who were going to buy a Philly and weed for a blunt.

Coco still lounged on Manuel's bed, letting the wound dry. "I can't wait till summer," she said roguishly. She'd pass by Lourdes's way and make it her business to get seen. She relished the thought of strutting by all the Mount Hope girls Cesar had slept with, the jealousy she would arouse when she flashed her tattoo. Tattoos were almost as good as gold nameplate necklaces. Coco's daydream ended abruptly when a cockroach scurried across the bloody heart on her thigh.

Soon after he was transferred to Southport, Cesar broke up with Coco again. "The part that hurts is how he said he don't want to have no more kids with me. I want a boy. He knows that," she said. She blamed the breakup on her spotty face. In one of her countless letters of apology, Coco added a postscript: "I'm sorry for not being the girl you want me to be. I wish Pa, just for you, that I could be that perfect girl. But Im not." She still promised to send him money when she received her welfare check.

The next day, Cesar's homeboy Tito called in from Rikers to say hello. Tito called frequently because he manned one of the Rikers phone banks. For protection, he had joined the Latin Kings gang, and he extorted money for them from inmates who wanted to use the phone. "Your man broke up with me; it's because I pick my face and he won't let me have my baby boy," Coco informed him.

"Coco, leave your face alone and work shit out," Tito said. He tried to break it down for her: Cesar had been shipped to Southport for punishment for the fight he'd had with the Muslim. Southport was the facility where prison inmates went if the isolation units of their own prisons weren't punishment enough. Inmates at Southport endured twenty-four-hour lockdown in a single-man cell and severe restrictions on all outside contact and activity. Segregation made a guy go crazy, Tito explained. The box made a boy want to say "Fuck it" to everyone. Coco's duty as a wife was to make his time easier. Coco tested out Tito's theory on her sister, who was unconvinced. "Coco, it's like you in a box, because all you think of Cesar, Cesar, Cesar," Iris replied. Coco proffered her idea about her marked skin. "Your face is just an excuse," Iris said.

If reason played a part, its role kept changing. Coco and Cesar did soon get back together, then broke up again and reunited, for reasons Coco eventually lost track of. Coco's new GED tutor helped her with nouns, pronouns, adjectives. She showed him her tattoo. Coco was good at strong beginnings and lousy on follow-through. She missed several sessions. School-wise, she said, she started to "mess up." She wrote to Wishman and then to Cesar, to confess that she'd written Wishman. It was only February, and the snow seemed as though it would never stop. On the envelope of Cesar's last conciliatory letter was a reminder that suggested he knew, even if Coco didn't, the direction she was headed in: "Use your mind to control all your body parts." The next time her tutor came, they worked on social issues and verbs.

CHAPTER TWENTY

One night, Coco, Mercedes, and Nautica waited at Columbus Circle in Manhattan for the Prison Gap, a bus to Southport. Coco had left Nikki with Foxy; when things were rocky between him and Coco, Coco knew it was best to bring only his girls. A stable of old buses idled. Transportation companies like Operation Prison Gap, some managed by ex-convicts, hauled families and friends of prisoners upstate to visit loved ones. Without them, the visits would have been impossible; few people had cars. Prisons dotted the huge state, and inmates moved among them, seemingly arbitrarily. The bus riders were almost always women and children. Except for special charters on Mother's Day or Family Day, the buses serviced primarily men's facilities. Women inmates, like Jessica, had a much harder time seeing family. Passengers often recognized one another—from other routes, the long hours spent together waiting in processing, or the neighborhood; the majority of state prisoners came from the same parts of New York City. Some of the women became friends.

At Southport, Cesar was allowed only three hours of exercise a week. For this, he would be led, shackled, to a cage in a cube of walled-in yard, where he could do sit-ups, push-ups, squat thrusts, and jumping jacks. Showers were timed and also limited to three a week. Like Jessica, Cesar was obsessive about cleanliness and he found this especially difficult. He had no books. He had no photographs to look at. Radios were forbidden. He reflected upon his life. It surprised him that he didn't miss the girls and parties as much as being able to open the door of a refrigerator, or play peekaboo with Mercedes on the floor. He said, "The street is like a scapegoat. You get in a fight with your mother and you go out and you get blasted and you have a beef with someone on the street—but two minutes later you don't even remember what's the beef about." He did, however, remember a time he and Rocco broke into an apartment to steal drugs and discovered the dealer, and his baby son, at home. The dealer cried, "Hold up, not my kid!" and Cesar took the boy and moved him. Even though they only beat the guy and tied him up, Cesar started thinking about how horrible it must have been for the boy to see his father so scared.

The isolation of the box made him feel, at turns, morose and hyperactive. He'd started suffering anxiety attacks. In his letter to Coco, he'd sounded desperate. "I'm in a real state of depression," he'd written. Coco fretted because Cesar—for all he'd been through—had never expressed himself in this way in letters before.

The bus dispatcher greeted the passengers warmly. "Welcome, everybody," he said. "There are some rules for you to follow. We don't allow drugs on the bus. Please don't be getting drunk. Be considerate to others, have a good visit tomorrow. Take the same seat when you come out of the facility, and come back next week and bring a friend."

Coco gave Mercedes some candy and spread out Mercedes's old black shearling along the backseat to make a bed. She held Nautica until she dozed off, then gently placed her beside Mercedes, who had quickly fallen asleep. Veteran visitors had equipped themselves with rolls of quarters and crisp dollars for the vending machines, clear plastic bags for locker keys and change. Some brought along pretty outfits whose perfection they preserved in dry-cleaning bags. The cost of the trip used up most of Coco's money. Lourdes's boyfriend, Domingo, had given Coco $20 to deposit in Cesar's commissary, and Coco had budgeted an additional $20 for the vending machines, so Cesar and the girls could eat. She opened a sandwich she'd made for the ride and offered half to the woman seated next to her.

The woman declined, but offered Coco some of her springwater. As Coco sipped, the woman said, "This is such a good bus, quiet, the people nice, you just don't know." She recounted less savory trips—loud music, dueling girlfriends, wailing children, drunks. She showed Coco a picture of her son. The boy had just received a scholarship to private school from a local youth group.

"God bless him, he's beautiful," Coco murmured. She appreciated anybody's good news. Mercedes curled close to her baby sister, and Coco covered them both with the coat she'd borrowed from Foxy. The bright city disappeared and the bus drove on in the companionable dark. Some of the riders spaced out, their Walkmans singing in their ears. The women chattered; two girls played clapping games. An old woman made her way slowly down the aisle, balancing on her cane. Her lopsided belly dragged beneath drooping breasts, but her spirits were high. "I had me a stroke right there at Rikers, right there in the visiting room," she said. The man she'd been visiting had become her husband. Tomorrow, she bragged, he'd sign their first joint tax forms.

The night stretched on. Conversation quieted. Legs and arms dusted the aisle floor, children coughed, braids came undone. Coco looked out the window. She couldn't imagine moving upstate, as Milagros planned to do, living out in the country, away from her family. The old bus creaked and rolled.

Nautica woke first; she spit up and cried at dawn. Coco covered her hairy head with a cotton cap. "You going to see your daddy. I'm getting butterflies just thinking about seeing your daddy," Coco said. She raised Nautica up each time the bus bounced from a bump and smiled.

About a half hour from the prison, the bus pulled into a truck stop. The women gathered themselves and their dry cleaning and crowded into the cramped bathroom of the restaurant. There they tucked and scrutinized and tightened, sharing compliments and lipstick and complaints in the toasty bathroom air. They didn't want to dress in the bathroom at the prison, where they would lose precious minutes of their visits.

"I ain't never been to see my husband in nothing but a dress," said a young woman in a lime green sheath that showed her figure. An older woman gruffly forked her permed hair.

"Albany gave you the date?" one woman asked another. She was referring to the official approval to marry an inmate; the headquarters of the Department of Corrections was in Albany.

"My friend is going to make my wedding dress. I already have it all designed," answered the bride-to-be.

Coco leaned against the wall and listened and waited for the one bathroom stall to clear; she felt too self-conscious to undress in front of the others. She snuck a look in the mirror: to save money, she'd trimmed her own bangs. She'd slicked them down with Vaseline, which emphasized the jaggedness. A fresh spray of red spots flecked her cheeks.

"Here, I'll hold her," a lady offered, reaching for Nautica. Coco slipped into the stall and stepped into a conservative outfit Elaine had loaned her—a beige turtleneck and matching skirt, topped by an embroidered vest. She wore sheer stockings beneath the slitted skirt, so she could show Cesar her tattoo. Her own style was more sporty, but she wanted Cesar to see that she had matured.

In the prison processing area, Mercedes sat beside Coco, legs swinging, humming to herself. "You been here before?" a woman asked, sounding concerned. Her eye makeup was a rainbow. The woman positioned herself over Mercedes's head and mouthed, so Mercedes couldn't hear, "Expect bars—you can only touch his hands." Coco's eyes filled with tears.

All the visitors were allowed to the next stage of processing except Coco. Coco waited. Nautica dozed. Mercedes doodled. Coco showed her how to draw 👁❤U. "Your Títi Jessica taught me that," Coco said.

After fifteen minutes, Coco hesitantly approached the guard at the desk. She hadn't filled out the forms correctly, and he hadn't bothered to tell her. Already, she'd lost an hour. Mercedes rested her nose on the counter. "What's in your lunch box?" she asked the guard as Coco struggled to hold Nautica and to write at the same time.

The guard pointed to a kitchenette. "That's where I heat up my food," he said. A woman emerged from the ladies' room, transformed. The guard bent forward and whispered, "Who is the painted lady?"

"What's in your lunch box? Tell me!" Mercedes said.

"You sure talk a lot. I bet you are a little flirt."

The guard stamped Coco's hand with invisible ink, then stamped Mercedes's, and finally directed them to a door.

The doors led out to a short walkway that led into another building, where Coco and her daughters waited twelve minutes for two guards to finish a conversation, after which one yelled at Coco for setting off the metal detector because she'd forgotten to remove her watch. When she cleared the detector, they were allowed into the visiting room. Carrying Nautica, Coco slowly wound her way to her seat assignment at the end of the S-shaped rows. Mercedes paraded through, initially oblivious to the shackled men behind the wire mesh.

She caused a little stir; her blond curls bounced as she searched eagerly for her father. Coco slid onto a chair, which was bound to three others by chains. She pretended to be absorbed by Nautica, who wobbled on her thighs. Cesar stood in the interior cage, waiting for a guard to spring the gate. At last, Mercedes spotted him. He shuffled toward them, barely able to move. He was shackled with leg irons, and in handcuffs, both of which were attached to a chain around his waist. Mercedes looked terrified. "Come out! Over here," she said desperately.

"I can't," Cesar mumbled.

"Teasing ain't nice, come out!" Mercedes said.

"Can't you see I'm chained up? I can't move, Mercy," he said, lifting his wrists slightly.

"Take them off. Take them off," she demanded. "Take them off!"

"I can't."

"Play patty-cake!"

"Mercedes," Coco chided.

"I can't take them off, Mercedes," Cesar said.

Mercedes determinedly outlined the invisible ink the guard had stamped on her hand. Soon her gesture became vague. "Daddy, you have money at your house?" she asked quietly.

"No, Mercedes," he said sadly.

Then Mercedes brightened. It was as though she'd grasped that her father couldn't tolerate the view of himself that her panic reflected. "We are going to get bunk beds and Nikki is going to be on the bottom, and I am going to be on the top!" she chattered. "You can come over and sleep with me on the top, and we can take a bubble bath."

Cesar squinted, as though he had suddenly recognized her voice from far away.

"Wanna hear a song?" Mercedes asked. Then she sang. Her father was smitten by her performance until she said, "That's Nikki's daddy's song," puncturing the moment. He glanced over his shoulder stonily. "Look at Mommy's face," Mercedes urged. "Mommy been messing with her face."

Cesar hadn't teased Coco or complimented her dressy outfit. He'd said nothing about the tattoo, or the special Weeboks Nautica wore. When he had been in Harlem Valley and Mercedes had worn the cheaper, no-name-brand sneakers called skippies, he'd removed them and tossed them across the visiting room. Since then, Coco had made sure Mercedes wore name-brand sneakers for visits, but it didn't seem to matter—all because of her face. "I'm sick of it; if that's the way you want it, fine," Cesar said to Coco. For the next three hours, they did not speak.

Coco busied herself with Nautica. Nautica grabbed on to the mesh cage, which was covered in lipstick. Mercedes explored the visiting room and collected compliments.

"Oh, that girl, she yours?" Cesar's neighbor asked, watching Mercedes pass.

"That's her," said Cesar.

"She look like Shirley Temple."

"These are my two girls. I got two other kids with other wives, four kids altogether. I'm nineteen. I got started young, right?"

Again, Mercedes asked Cesar, "Daddy, you wanna hear a song?" She performed "Kind Kind Mother" and got stuck on a verse. She kept repeating the start of the verse until she reached her aborted end, then began from the beginning again. "I had a kind kind mother . . ." Cesar teased her, "What about your father, too?"

Around noon, Cesar finally spoke to Coco: "Get me something to eat." She bought three packages of chicken wings from the vending machine and waited beside the microwave. She tore open the packets of sauce and silently passed them beneath the slot. Cesar hunched over the styrofoam tray. He pushed the wings into his mouth. The handcuffs dug into his wrists.

After he'd finished, Coco cleared the trays. Cesar carefully wiped his hands. He looked to the side and reached through the slot and held what he could of Coco. Touch did what only touch could do.

Coco's words poured out. She told him about a new girl at Thorpe who knew all about the trailer visits. The girl had had a prison wedding. She had told Coco about all the right things to bring—satin sheets, and cream and strawberries. Coco had been learning new things, too, from watching pornography.

Cesar watched Coco soberly. He waited for her to finish, then said tenderly, "Sex ain't everything." The box had forced him to do some thinking. If they were going to marry, they needed to communicate. Coco bit her lip. His hope came across as a reprimand. "I want it to be you love me and I love you. Where happiness comes in is when I'm making you happy and you do things to make me happy," Cesar said.

Meanwhile, Mercedes stared at the couple beside them, a young, skinny black man with a full set of gold teeth, and a large, middle-aged white woman in a modest silk dress. He was angry; she looked tired. He beckoned her closer, and she pressed her substantial bosom against the mesh. She bowed her head to listen. He cursed. Then, methodically, he smashed his handcuffed hands into her chest. He continued speaking in low tones as he punched her, and she held her body taut to receive him. Only her head jerked back. Coco furtively watched.

"They been having trailers for years," Cesar said, without irony.

A guard climbed to the top of what looked like a lifeguard chair, a signal to Cesar that they had less than an hour of visiting left.

"I'm starting to think about going back to that cell, and it's got me real depressed," Cesar said. Besides letters, chess was the only activity that helped him pass the time in solitary. He'd made a chessboard out of paper, and his opponent shouted out his plays from down the hall. The pending good-bye wedged between them. "You better come next week or I'll punch you in the face, you got my hopes up," he said miserably.

By the end of the hour, the couple beside them had reconciled. The young man pressed one ear to the counter, penitent, as the woman braided his hair. The guard called time. Chairs scraped the linoleum. The men tried to stretch. Children's hands clasped the grating like small claws. One mother yelled to her husband, who was talking to the other men, "Look at your boy! Look at your boy!" The man to whom she called hopped, as if shaking off the visit. She shoved her son closer to the cage her man was in. "Say good-bye to your daddy. Look at your boy! Look at your boy!" She pressed the boy against what divided them. "Get your father! Get your father!" The boy's thin fingers gripped the wire. His father swatted a good-bye and turned back to the protection of his friends.

"Mom, he said good-bye! Dad said bye!" the boy exclaimed.

Coco noticed Cesar eyeing a teenage girl who'd joined the line. Nautica slept, heavy in Coco's arms.

Coco was relieved to breathe the fresh, cold air outside. She paused, watching Mercedes energetically climb the stairs into the bus. The idea of staying with Cesar and the reality of it were different; he was more demanding in person than he was in her fantasies. She couldn't possibly afford to visit again any time soon—the girls' birthdays were coming. Yet she couldn't tell him no. Coco was glad to be heading home, even though home was Thorpe.

Shortly afterward, Cesar wrote and told her to limit the girls' visits to Southport; he didn't want them to see him caged in any more than necessary.

Coco's trips to her mother's and Lourdes's were searching expeditions— she needed guidance, but Foxy and Lourdes were in no position to help; similar conflicts ruled their own lives. Still, Coco kept returning to the same places for answers again and again. Mercedes, who was almost four, was more direct; sometimes it was as though she voiced her mother's unspoken worries and doubts.

One day early that winter, Coco took the girls by Lourdes's. Lourdes was still denying that Domingo had anything to do with why her arm was in a cast. Lourdes was holding court in bed, her long hair loose, a blanket wrapped around her waist like the base of a Christmas tree. Two women sat on the bed beside her, while another scrubbed a blackened pot. Domingo sat at a half-open table, chopping cilantro. He placed fistfuls of the cut greens beside an impressive pile of garlic. A man stood beside him, sipping a beer. When Coco entered, all conversation stopped.

Lourdes beckoned her over. The ladies left. With her good arm, Lourdes whisked Nautica up. She held the whole of Nautica's head in her palm, infant face to Grandma. "Look at this fucking baby!" she shouted gleefully. "Mercy, give me her bottle." Mercedes removed the bottle from the side pocket of the brand-new baby bag and watched her grandmother nestle Nautica on her lap.

"Mami, braid my hair?" Lourdes asked Coco. Coco inched around the bed and began to separate Lourdes's hair into small clumps with her fingernails.

Mercedes stroked her grandmother's cast. "Who did that?"

"A boy," Lourdes said mischievously.

"Domingo did that," stated Mercedes.

"No, Mercy," said Lourdes, glancing at Domingo significantly. Only his eyes and eyebrows were visible through the bookshelf that divided the studio into a bedroom and kitchen. "Domingo did not do this," said Lourdes with emphasis. "He wouldn't do this to *Abuela*. Two *morenos* did this to me."

Domingo peeked around the shelving. "Do you like me?" he asked Mercedes playfully.

"He didn't do this to me," Lourdes repeated, trying to keep her audience. Mercedes appealed to her mother, but Coco concentrated on Lourdes's braid. Domingo was making a commotion rummaging in his pocket like a magician looking for his rabbit. Then he pulled out a dollar. Mercedes scrambled to the end of the bed to grab it. He pulled it away and laughed.

"What do you say, Mercedes?" Coco prompted.

"Thank you," Mercedes said. Domingo passed her the money. But Lourdes, to goad her boyfriend, returned to Mercedes's silenced questions about her injury at every opportunity: when Coco told her about the wedding rings she'd bought to marry Cesar, Lourdes said, "*Abuela* wouldn't lie to you, Mercy"; when Coco told her the latest news of Cesar, "Domingo wouldn't do this to *Abuela*," Lourdes replied. Finally, Coco brushed the top of Lourdes's long braid and then changed Nautica's diaper for the road.

"Candy candy candy," Domingo sang, helping Mercedes into her coat. He ushered her into the hall. "Candy candy candy," he continued, and led her into the elevator, then took her downstairs to Edward's grocery, a store across the street, where Cesar and Rocco used to play pool.

Coco waited outside with the baby. "Three enough for you, Coco?" asked a neighbor.

"For now. Me and my husband are going to try for another when he gets out, but that's nine years."

Coco wished that Lourdes would not expose Mercedes to so much of the confusion of her relationships. Whereas Nikki enjoyed playing with children, Mercedes preferred the company of adults, and Lourdes had a way of telling stories so the violent details beelined to the heart, barely pausing at the ear. Mercedes was a lot like Little Star had been, and although Coco had been the same way, she wanted Mercedes to be a child while she was a child.

Edward's Grocery had just reopened after being shut down following a drug raid. The new owner had revived it with a fresh coat of yellow paint. Mercedes and Domingo reappeared, a happy couple, Mercedes licking an icy and holding two lollipops in the hand that was free of his. Coco plucked one—the other was for Nikki—and stuck it in her ponytail.

That same winter, Coco finally received her preliminary acceptance for placement in housing. She should already have been settled in an apartment, but bureaucratic red tape and Coco's own disorganization kept delaying her move. Sister Christine worried: she didn't want Coco's holding pattern to serve as an ending point. "It's not that she was hard to reach," Sister Christine later said. "She was hard to keep on track."

Yet Coco was among the luckier tenants; plenty of the women had predicaments that were far worse—recent immigrants with violent husbands and no English; girls with violent tempers themselves; girls on drugs; girls with cancer and no family. Coco didn't spend coked-up weekends in hotels with friends of her boyfriend's, or ask someone to watch her kids so she could go to the store, then disappear for days. When the next-door neighbor covertly hosted an orgy, or the girls upstairs snuck out to smoke weed, Coco was the one who baby-sat. But these other women came and went, and Coco remained at Thorpe House, stuck between her future and her past.

Wishman's last letter had mentioned his release date. The attempted murder charges had been dropped. He was due out soon and wanted Coco to visit him at his mother's house. Coco no longer dressed as she had when they were in puppy love; all her money and effort went into her daughters. Yet she knew from the letters that Wishman was still attracted to her. She vowed that she wouldn't visit Wishman alone. She knew Wishman's sneaky ways, and she did not trust herself.

But the next thing she knew, there he was, at her Thorpe House apartment door, smiling, his blue-green eyes on her, handsome and interested, smelling of soap. She prepared a dinner. They flirted while she fed Nautica and put her to sleep. She settled Nikki and Mercedes in front of the TV in the living room. When she and Wishman stepped into the bedroom, Coco felt the heavy burdens lift.

At curfew, she escorted him outside. Coco and Miss Lucy, the security guard, watched his tight body lope down Crotona Avenue. They watched him disappear into the darkness, headed toward Tremont.

"He fine, Coco," said Miss Lucy.

"He just got out of prison," Coco said.

Coco felt guilty about the rendezvous with Wishman, but she also wanted to see him again. However, within three days of their meeting, he found himself another girl; Coco heard that she was a virgin. But he and Coco continued to speak occasionally on the phone. The conversations reminded her of those she'd shared with Cesar after his release from Harlem Valley—Wishman's voice brimming with direction, using big words she didn't know. He asked her what she planned to do.

"I'm gonna move, then the summer comes and I'll hang out," she said.

"What you planning for the *future?*" He wanted her to think ahead.

"I don't know," she said uncertainly.

"Girl, you gotta start planning now." He'd enrolled in Bronx Community College. She mentioned her tattoo. He scoffed. At first, she thought Wishman was disappointed that she had Cesar's name on her, but his reaction came from something more flattering than jealousy: he wanted her to better herself. Tattoos were for street girls. "You got a whole life ahead of you. You don't got to listen to me, but remember you is young," Wishman said. Coco wanted to keep the conversation going. She asked if he'd thought of getting a tattoo with his baby daughter's name.

"Why? I'm supposed to join you?" he said mockingly.

The Morris Heights Health Center was a gossip zone. Coco almost always ran into people she knew there. Luckily, that spring, when she took Mercedes and Nikki in for a checkup, there was no one she recognized to overhear her whispered request for a pregnancy test. The receptionist informed her that she had to schedule an appointment of her own. Coco was unlikely to ask twice for help on such a touchy matter. To return, she would need to find someone to watch the baby again, and she worried about being spotted by someone from her mother's block or Lourdes's. She'd once seen Giselle at the clinic. "I don't want to be seeing that girl around, because she'll start talking rumors," Coco said.

Cesar had a hunch that Coco had been intimate with Wishman. He recognized the pattern of avoidance and omission that emerged when she'd done something she felt terrible about. She had stopped sending him pictures, as though she hoped to disappear, and she wasn't writing much. What made him more than suspicious was Coco's behavior when she visited that spring. She and Rocco rode the Prison Gap for Cesar's twentieth birthday.

Coco tended to be subdued around Cesar's friends, but Rocco had relaxed her during the six-hour ride with his mugging and joking. He'd shaved his head, he said, because "there are so many problems in the world, who has time for hair?" His bottom teeth were gold. He flattered Coco about her mothering: "I don't know how you take the three of them, I give it to you, Coco." He and his wife had only a seven-month-old daughter and parenting still left him beat. Cesar had been feeling slighted by Rocco because he'd asked him to be Mercedes's godfather, and Rocco hadn't arranged the baptism. Rocco couldn't afford it; he'd unsuccessfully tried to explain to Cesar the essence of life as a working man with a brand-new baby—being broke. Cesar blamed Rocco's wife, Marlene.

Coco certainly understood. It may have been her empathy for Rocco that put her at ease. Whatever it was, Cesar noticed she wasn't self-conscious when she went to get his food from the vending machine. There was something vaguely confident about her short, squarish profile—maybe the way she held her head as she waited for the microwave to heat his barbecue chicken wings. He couldn't pin down the difference until later, in his cell. Her complexion was clearer. She seemed comfortable in her body. He became convinced she was pregnant when he received her next letter. Instead of signing "Love, your Wife Coco," she scribbled, "Coco the bitch."

Cesar's suspicions turned out right. This time, however, he didn't rage at Coco. He wrote a letter to Foxy instead:

> Dear Foxy: Hello! How are you and your loved ones doing? Fine I hope and pray. As for myself, I'm fucked up right now. . . . Foxy I already know that Coco is pregnant. Don't tell her I know. I ain't going to write her because I don't have anything to say . . . But I want to ask a favor of you. Please don't let Coco have that baby.
>
> If Coco has that baby it's going to effect all the girls up mentally . . . I really love Coco and I wanted a family. But I guess that's not what she wanted. I'll live through it, though. What hurts me the most is that I gave her another chance and she did it again. At least she could've used protection . . . I really want a lot of pictures of Mercy and Naughty, especially now that I won't be seeing them.

Cesar believed Coco was foolish to think Wishman cared for her. Cesar and Wishman were friends before Cesar met Coco, and Cesar had known Nikki's father, Kodak, too. Cesar surmised that Wishman might have gone after Coco to get at Cesar as payback for stealing Coco from him in the first place. Wishman wanted Coco to get an abortion so his girlfriend wouldn't discover that he'd cheated. Coco later said, "Ain't no one going to tell me what to do with my baby."

Coco knew that she no longer stood a chance with Cesar—the shameful pregnancy had put a stop to their exhausting back-and-forth. With Cesar gone, she could only hope that Wishman would come around. Coco had already reviewed the evidence of Wishman's potential as a father: he liked her daughters, and babies had a way of bringing out the best in people, of softening hardness, of gluing broken things. In his letters, Wishman had criticized Nikki's father for neglecting Nikki, and Wishman had mentioned how much he missed his other daughter, how he would have been there for that girl if the mother hadn't run away to Philadelphia. Coco wasn't going anywhere.

She invested a lot in small signs, such as the time he recently stepped aside to rub her stomach during a game of basketball. But she couldn't completely avoid the negative signs, either: when she and Wishman play-fought, he played a little too rough around a belly; when they made love, she sometimes felt as though he hated her. Sunny, Wishman's mother, assured Coco, "I know when you have the baby, he's going to be after you." Sunny couldn't know, of course, but she sounded willing to be a good grandmother. She told Coco, "At least this grandchild I'll see." Coco wished she could speak to Jessica.

CHAPTER TWENTY-ONE

As soon as it became clear to Jessica that Lourdes would never make it to Florida, she requested a transfer to a facility nearer home. In March of 1994, just as Milagros was packing her things to move upstate, the authorities shipped Jessica to a maximum-security prison in Danbury, Connecticut, an hour's trip from the Bronx. Jessica would serve the remainder of her term there. It looked like a high school with barbed wire, atop a rolling hill. Geese contentedly waddled about the large and manicured lawn. The floors shone from inmates' constant waxing, same as her old unit in Florida; the buildings had the same cinder-block walls— except here the paint was salmon, not beige. FCI Danbury had formerly been a male prison facility, and was still in transition. While the renovation was being completed, Jessica was temporarily assigned a cubicle in the gym. The inmate "cube" facing hers belonged to a young Brazilian woman named Player, who recalled watching Jessica unpack her property. "She was an extremely white-skinned person," Player said. "Lots of tattoos."

Jessica was assigned to a job at the compound's power plant, where she trained as a lagger, learning how to wrap pipes with fiberglass. She switched to the night shift. A Dominican correctional officer named Ernesto Torres supervised her. There wasn't much to do during the long nights in the boiler room. Torres did not believe in "bright work," the idle assignments that made up a fair share of prison jobs—mopping floors that were already clean, polishing gleaming copper tubing with steel wool, polishing shining brass railings, painting over paint. It bothered Torres that some of his fellow officers treated the women so harshly; the male inmates, he said, would never have put up with such insults and abuse.

The inmates Torres supervised reminded him of women from his old neighborhood. Torres had been raised in a poor community in Bridgeport, Connecticut. His first day on the job at Danbury, he'd run into a childhood friend—the friend was an inmate. He believed that the punishment was the prison term, and that officers should keep their opinions to themselves and do their job. So, when he could, Torres let the women be. He spent his shift in his office at the rear of the plant, and the women spent their shifts doing whatever—sitting and talking, writing letters, flirting, napping, listening to the radio. If Torres brewed fresh coffee, he shared it. He left his locker open so the women could use his cooking utensils and cassettes. To enliven the routine, he occasionally brought treasures of free-world food—Kentucky Fried Chicken, cranberry juice, doughnuts. "Mr. Doughnut" became his nickname. Every act of generosity was a violation of staff rules. Among the inmates, as in the ghetto, kindness was a risk. Even more baffling, Torres didn't seem to want anything in return.

Torres was accustomed to flirting; it was a chronic condition of an officer's life at a women's prison. Both the officers and the inmates were tremendously bored; the mood was a lot like the end of a long summer of the same people on the same street. Some of his colleagues regularly brought condoms to work. Torres probably got more attention than most guards because he was emotionally in touch with the women. He was also handsome, with fine features, impossibly long eyelashes, and brown-black eyes. He was short, but compact, and in the time warp of that environment, almost hip. He wore a tiny gold hoop earring and slicked his longish hair into a neat ponytail. Minus the ponytail, he shared an uncanny resemblance to Boy George.

Jessica responded to Torres's edgy appearance. She danced for him—in the supply room, in his office, on the catwalks around the boiler, provocatively unzipping her prison-issue coveralls. "There were other ones that did it," Torres recalled, "but she was very good at it." She serenaded him with ballads by Celine Dion and by Boyz II Men. He noticed her generous mouth when she laughed. She asked him for a birthday kiss, which he granted—not knowing that her birthday was still months away.

Soon, Jessica and Torres broke night talking. He told her about his two children and confided that he and his wife were having problems. Jessica told him about her daughters, especially Serena, who recently turned nine. Jessica recounted her own unhappy childhood, expressing sadness that Lourdes hadn't paid enough attention to her. She also told him that she had been molested for years. Torres clipped a magazine article about child abuse and gave it to her. She told him about Boy George and showed him the tattoos she planned to erase with laser as soon as she got out. Torres prepared linguine with clam sauce on his hot plate and surprised her with ice cream for dessert. He let her listen to his special house tapes. And he brought her a bottle of DNA, her favorite perfume.

Family Day was a big event for the women prisoners. Of those lucky enough to have guests, the festival was often the only chance they had to see their families. Family Day resembled a company picnic: there were performances and games, hamburgers, hot dogs, and Sno-Kones for the children. Jessica had looked forward to the celebration for five months. She hadn't seen Serena in more than a year; she hadn't seen the twins in the three years since her arrest. "It was all she talked about for several weeks," Torres recalled. Well beforehand, Jessica had sent Lourdes all the requisite forms and the free voucher for a bus that left directly from the Bronx. Then Family Day arrived, and no one showed.

Jessica was devastated. Back on her unit, she mouthed off to one of the officers, and he sent her into disciplinary segregation and wrote her up for insolence and disobeying an order. When she finally returned to work, Torres gave her a rose and a sympathy card. He offered to mail her daughters the gifts she'd made—another infraction of the rules for guards. He also improved on Jessica's homemade package by adding treats from the outside world: candy, a *Jurassic Park* videotape for the twins, and, for Serena, a bottle of perfume.

Until then, Jessica had considered Torres mainly a challenge, and winning him over a distraction to help pass the time. But his kindness toward her daughters touched her. She appealed to Amazon, an inmate who practiced Santeria, and one night, they performed a ritual to help the romance along. Jessica brought an apple to the boiler room. There, they removed the core. Jessica then wrote Torres's name on a piece of paper, rolled it up, and stuck it inside, like a message in original sin. Amazon topped off the apple with honey. Jessica hid it in Torres's locker. He discovered it and tossed it away. He thought "the voodoo" was a joke. Only many months later did he become convinced that Jessica was a temptress God had sent to test him, and that his failure to resist her had placed him under the devil's spell.

Torres told Jessica that she deserved better than to have quick sex with a married man in a locker room. He snuck in a self-help book—Marianne Williamson's *Women's Worth*—and presented it to Jessica. She interpreted this as a sign that he accepted the girl she had been in the past and that he wanted to help her become the woman she could be. She underlined passages that reflected the way she felt and recited them back to him.

In the meantime, Jessica's friend Player had developed a crush on an officer who supervised the recreation room. Eventually, Jessica and Player became roommates. Like schoolgirls, they daydreamed about their men. They hurried to the windows to glimpse them arriving for their shifts. They devised a secret code so they could discuss their would-be lovers freely—referring to the officers as inmate lovers, Jackie and Diane. Player's infatuation sped up the sluggish time of prison, but Jessica really fell for Torres. She began to daydream about their future, once he was divorced and she was released.

Jessica always took her time getting ready for anything, but preparing for her shift at the power plant became an all-consuming ritual. She showered. She rubbed herself with lotion. She never had much money in her commissary, but she supplemented what she could with whatever she could borrow from friends. She slipped into Player's lingerie, camouflaged by her olive green coveralls. She styled her hair and put on her makeup and dabbed perfume between her breasts. She always finished up with a beauty mark, dotted on the left side, above her lips, which made the cheap lipstick look lush when she smiled.

Jessica's shift at the power plant became the focus of her life: between shifts, she read and reread Torres's inspirational cards. She drove Player crazy, nagging her to read aloud Torres's letters, like bedtime stories to a child; Jessica mouthed whole passages that she'd memorized. Player, who was serving time for embezzlement, saw a pipeline of opportunity running beneath Jessica's starry love; she arranged for her mother to meet Torres in a nearby parking lot before his shift. Although Torres later denied it, Player claimed that her mother handed over black-market goodies—nail polish, colored contact lenses, Victoria's Secret lingerie. Jessica never asked anything for herself.

Jessica wrote Serena about her new boyfriend, telling her how they would all be together soon. She announced that she didn't want to return to the Bronx: instead, they'd all go somewhere happy, somewhere far away. The mention of another upheaval rattled Serena; she missed Jessica, but she didn't want to leave her siblings. Milagros chastised Jessica for filling the head of a nine-year-old with such plans.

CHAPTER TWENTY-TWO

Shortly after Cesar discovered Coco was pregnant by Wishman, Coco learned that Cesar had been courting Roxanne all along. Unknown to Coco still, Cesar had been writing Giselle and Lizette and several other girls. "He's a motherfucker and I'm a bitch. We're both the same and we'll never change," Coco said. Like Cesar, she worried constantly about money, and now, even more so, since her departure from Thorpe House was imminent.

For months, Coco had been scheduled for placement in a renovated apartment through the Special Initiative Program, SIP. The tenement was on 173rd and Vyse, not far from where Lourdes had once lived, but construction delays and paperwork kept postponing the move. In SIP buildings, a social worker would be available to help residents like Coco keep their disorganized lives on track, and ideally, with day care and other supports, Coco would find her way back to school or to a job. Coco's other options were Section 8—a federal rent-voucher program that paid the difference between 30 percent of a poor family's income and the fair-market rent—or the projects. It had taken Sister Christine some maneuvering to lure Coco away from the idea of the projects, where the housing authority covered the cost of gas and electricity. Coco didn't pay rent at Thorpe and already couldn't manage, even with her avid devotion to budgeting. Earlier that winter, Coco had agreed to take a look at the refurbished SIP building, and after seeing the bright, freshly painted place—near a park where her girls could play—she'd returned to Thorpe House thrilled.

But Coco's open excitement made her the subject of envy among her fellow residents, and she became a target for ridicule. Had she been able to move out quickly, she might have escaped the usual snittiness, but the delays gave the discouragement of others time to take effect. Some of the residents, and one member of the staff, told her how the nuns received a commission for every person they sent to SIP; that men weren't allowed even to visit; that the staff was nosier than the shelter's; and that the on-site social worker did double duty as an agent for BCW. The social service system deserved its criticism, and the women were justified in their caution, but Coco never had the chance to figure it out for herself. She desperately wanted to get discharged from Thorpe House, and also to avoid sharing the news of her pregnancy with the nuns. By June 1994, she was in what she called a fighting mood—looking for trouble to relieve the stress. She could always tell she was about to "mess up" when her hands started shaking.

The chance to fight was one ghetto opportunity that was both constant and encouraged, but Coco usually avoided it; she didn't want to fight in front of her kids. Now, however, Coco was ready, and she exchanged heated words with a girl at Thorpe who was pregnant as well. When the insults erupted into a physical fight, Mercedes pushed Nikki into the apartment but stayed in the hallway to watch over her mother; the security guard pulled the two women apart. Fortunately, the nuns agreed not to expel them since Coco was due to leave. Unfortunately, the pregnant girl's enormous boyfriend had just been released from prison. According to Coco's neighbors, he'd been pounding on her door, making it clear that when he did find Coco, he had every intention of avenging her disrespectful treatment of his unborn baby and wife.

Coco fled to Foxy's, but it was too crowded for a distraught pregnant woman with three small kids. She canceled her arrangements with SIP, requested her Section 8 voucher, and moved into the first place she saw—an apartment on Prospect, just a few blocks south of Thorpe House. The follow-up worker expressed serious concerns about her safety and the building's countless housing violations; Sister Christine worried about the risk of rape; Coco assured them she'd be fine. She didn't mention the man she'd met in the building's hallway who'd warned Coco about the rats; after all, her mother's apartment had mice.

The location was convenient. "It's big and near Tremont where the store's at, that's what I'm happy about. It's light," said Coco. The window near the fire escape didn't have locks, but if she craned her head, she could see the display of a bridal shop—three dusty mannequins adorned in white—next to a party-supply store, where she would go for her daughters' birthdays.

Drug activity was the life force of Coco's new building. There was no pretense of security: doors were always propped open, and the interior courtyard made for a nerve-racking trip from the sidewalk to the hall. Pigeon droppings formed a putrid sand castle in the building's crumbling fountain. The mailboxes were bashed in, their little doors dented and askew. People snatched lightbulbs from the hallways.

The disrepair was nothing new, but here Coco was a stranger, without her family to protect her. On Foxy's block, she was insulated by her connection to the local histories of blood and love. She also knew the personalities and could weigh the threats against knowledge and experience. In this courtyard, there were unfamiliar people, not her girlfriends or her neighbors' boyfriends or her brothers' friends. The dangers may or may not have been similar, but the unfamiliarity heightened the sense of risk: the potential for trouble felt random. Hector could no longer be whistled down to escort her and the girls upstairs. "My house scary," Nikki whispered, summing up the general sentiment.

Coco's approach wasn't much different from her approach to the pregnancy—she would do her best with what was in front of her and avoid the rest until she had to improvise again. She soothed her own anxiety by concentrating on Mercedes's and Nikki's and calmed their escalating panic by distraction: she plugged in the radio, cranked up the music, and tackled their bedroom first. With her $750 furniture voucher, Coco had bought them bunk beds, a set of couches for the *sala*, and a double bed for herself and Nautica. Beds, she proclaimed, were for sleeping, not bouncing, but she let the girls bounce anyway. She hung a framed picture of the Little Mermaid. Near it, she placed the clown she'd carved at Thorpe: *Cesar and Shorty and our unborn baby, Mercedes, Nikki. Done by Coco. Mom loves Dad, 1993.* She invited their opinions in her whirlwind decorating tour: should the shelf go in their room, for dolls, or in the living room, to display Abuela Lourdes's *figuras*? In the living room, Coco tacked up peach polyester curtains and spruced them up with a red Christmas bow. She unpacked her beloved pictures, which she arranged beside her girls' baby shoes.

The larger problems, however, Coco's touch couldn't mend: the clogged toilet; the leaking sink; the front door that refused to close without a karate kick; the drug dealer who managed the spot in the front of the building. "Hey, Shorty," he'd call out suggestively, and, "Shorty, what's your name?" Coco mumbled hello and hurried by. She also tried to ignore the gutter outside her kitchen window, trimmed with trash—a ball, a diaper (used), a child's sock, a gnawed Popsicle stick.

The rats made their debut her very first overnight; they were the size of skinny cats and shameless. Coco was shaken. One might bite Nautica. Coco dreaded going into the kitchen—the light didn't work—but Nautica needed a bottle, and the water from the bathroom sink wasn't hot enough. But as soon as Coco stepped into the hallway, a rat slithered along the wall and disappeared inside the kitchen door. Coco backed into the bedroom. Nautica howled until her voice became hoarse. She continued heaving long after she stopped making noise.

The next morning, Coco couldn't face the kitchen; food attracted rats; the girls were hungry. How could she cook? Wearily, she packed some clothes in plastic grocery bags, gathered up her girls, struggled to lock the apartment's disjointed door, and retreated to the comparative safety of Foxy's house. It was the summer of 1994; Coco had left home a year and a half earlier; now she was back, pregnant again.

The first day of July, Coco's brother Manuel's girl Yasmin gave birth to a baby boy. Their intense happiness took up space in Foxy's overcrowded apartment. By the end of the week, armed with a small entourage, Coco ventured back to Prospect; her crew included her three girls, Wishman's two younger sisters, Hector's gaunt friend Weedo, and Weedo's girlfriend, Lacey. (Weedo had earned the nickname because he was always smoking blunts.) Coco had been baby-sitting Wishman's sisters to give his mother a break, but they were wearing Coco out: she had to watch them every minute. They'd taught her girls curse words. Earlier, at Foxy's, Coco had walked into Foxy's bedroom and found the older one, who was rather plump, lying on top of Nikki. Coco went crazy; her hands started shaking, and she'd had to call Hector to intervene. But Weedo and Lacey were easy: they were fourteen and in love and hunting for privacy. Coco was also afraid to stay in the apartment alone.

When Mercedes heard that Weedo would stay overnight, she folded her arms across her chest and glared at her mother. "You said no boys in the house!"

"Mercedes, he can come in, but just once," Coco said.

"No!" Mercedes said. "You said no boys, only girls in the house!"

"This will only be one boy, for one night, because he's Lacey's friend," Coco said. "Don't you like Lacey?"

"You promised!" Mercedes said. Her upset wasn't the usual frustration she directed toward her mother before Coco caved in to her demands: this anger had a lower, despairing pitch.

At Prospect, the children played in one bedroom. Weedo and Lacey jumped into the shower. Their laughter trailed Coco as she roamed through the stifling apartment, trying to create fresh air. Their joyful noise made her happy. "Reminds me of me and Cesar when we was young," she clucked to herself. Most of the windows were misaligned and many had been painted shut. She fought one open—no breeze. She ripped the plastic covering off the couch. She wanted to preserve it, but she also wanted her guests to feel comfortable. She left Weedo and Lacey her only set of sheets.

Coco put the girls in their big room and retired to the tiny one, but soon they clustered by her door. They didn't want to sleep alone. She dragged her mattress onto the floor and they climbed on.

"Mommy suck my thumb?" Nikki asked. Coco had been trying to break Nikki of the habit, but Coco's directives, however well-intentioned, often got lost in the day's landslide of minor catastrophes. Coco shared with Nikki a story about Daisy, Jessica's cousin and old clubbing pal, who had a boyfriend who once complained that Daisy still sucked her thumb. The moral of the tale was eclipsed by Daisy's bravado, which was more inspiring. "Daisy do that and she's grown. She told her man, 'Take me like I am!' " Coco said. She peered over the mattress, down at Mercedes. "Your daddy sucks his thumb, too," she added kindly. Mercedes smiled. Wishman's sisters immediately placed their thumbs in their mouths.

Lacey peeked in, her pale body wrapped in a towel. "Why you all in the same room?" she asked.

"My girls aren't afraid to sleep on their own," Coco lied. She also didn't mention the flimsy kitchen knife beside her bed. The knife was a habit Coco had acquired from her mother, although it wasn't strangers but Coco's father whom Foxy had feared.

The children drifted off, but in the next room, Weedo and Lacey started arguing. Weedo had a violent temper. Coco fidgeted on the uncovered box spring beside Nautica, who pumped her pacifier, asleep. Coco could barely breathe. She worried about Nautica's asthma but didn't dare open the door because of the rats. She finally cracked open the window over the fire escape. Still, it was unbearably hot. Sweat dripped onto the plastic mattress cover. Lazy conversation from the sidewalk punched through the dead air. An alley cat cried without much conviction. Weedo, however, was hollering at Lacey with the whole of his raging heart. "I'm getting the fuck outta here," he yelled. She encouraged him to do that. "I'm going the fuck home," he shouted. She told him to do that, too. Coco was grateful that her girls slept through the next several rounds.

Coco hoped it didn't get physical; she'd have to get involved. In fact, Coco got involved whenever she saw other people—even strangers— fighting in front of little kids. She attributed this to the time that Nikki's father, Kodak, had gone after her in Foxy's courtyard. Mercedes was only two. The courtyard was packed with kids, teenagers, and adults. Kodak drove up in a fancy car with a new wife and demanded, "How come every time I come around you ain't with Nikki?"

"She's with your mother," Coco replied. "If you came around more often, you'd see me with her." Coco remembered that Kodak had gone berserk. Even with Mercedes screaming wildly for someone to help her mother, no one had intervened.

Recently, Coco had inserted herself into the middle of a fistfight a guy was having with a woman near Thorpe. She didn't know either of them, but she'd courageously told the man, "You a grown man. You want to do that? Take it in the house."

Finally, Coco dozed. Around three o'clock in the morning, she bolted up; she smelled smoke. Voices—men's voices—sounded awfully close, as though they were on the fire escape. She rolled over to look. What she saw made her leap—the tip of a sneakered foot on her windowsill, two hands tugging up the frame. She plopped Nautica on the mattress into the twist of sleeping girls, scrambled under the box spring she'd been sleeping on, hoisted it up on her back, flipped it against the window, then body-slammed herself against it to hold it up. The voices murmured. One man cackled. Eventually, they left. Had they wanted to, the men could easily have pushed their way in.

Coco jimmied the window shut with a screwdriver and returned the box spring to block it, pressed her back against it, and slid to the floor. She cradled the knife against her swelling belly. She tried to break night but nodded off. Once, she startled, but it was only Weedo or Lacey laughing in the next room.

By morning, the bedroom was hotter than a greenhouse, the children a tangled vine of arms and ponytails and legs. Mercedes moaned softly. Nautica gasped. Nikki, who had a sinus condition, snored raspily. Weedo and Lacey slammed the busted door behind them, and the noise woke Nikki up. She crawled over to the window and watched them go, her chin in her hands. Above the grubby street, Lacey's blondness dissolved into the summer haze. A garbage truck halted. The young lovers crossed over Prospect Avenue, looking disheveled, and headed south to catch the Tremont Avenue bus back toward University, the same bus that Coco used to ride from Cesar's to her mother's house.

Back at Foxy's, Coco and Foxy fought the way they had when Coco was a teenager. Coco complained bitterly about Hernan. "She don't want me with nobody," Foxy said. "She's got to let go." During one argument, Foxy threw a glass at Coco; after another, Foxy took extra prescription pills to knock herself out. Coco brought Mercedes and Nautica upstate to visit Milagros and let matters cool. Nikki was spending a few weeks with her father in Baltimore. When Coco returned to the Bronx, she announced that she was considering moving to Troy. The small city was boring, but it was pretty and quiet and the children had all kinds of space to play. Foxy kept her fingers crossed. "The girls need an environment. . . . Wishman's not gonna do shit for her. She's got to do what she's got to do on her own."

Coco and Wishman still got together, and Wishman continued to publicly deny that Coco's pregnancy was his doing. "I leave him alone," Coco said. But she hoped for a son.

At the end of August, Hector's Iris gave Hector his baby boy; they named him Lil Hector. A few nights later, Coco went dancing and met up with Wishman. Afterward, they went to a room he rented from a lady in a building around the corner from his mother's house. They made love three times; Coco later wondered if he was trying to hurt the baby. She had to go to the bathroom, and dressed for the walk down the hall. But when she stood up, a rush of blood came out. Wishman dialed his mother; Sunny dialed 911.

In the meantime, Wishman ushered Coco to the bathroom and helped remove the bloodied clothes. Then Sunny barreled in; Coco felt woozy; paramedics arrived; she continued losing blood. While two EMTs strapped Coco to a gurney, another was trying to get information from Wishman—Coco's name, birthday, and address. Wishman nervously kept repeating, "She's a Sagittarius." This amused Coco later on, when she was at the hospital.

The next few days were a jumble of emergency room visits. Coco continued bleeding heavily and was finally admitted to the hospital. For a week, the doctors tried to stop the bleeding; at one point, Coco was told, incorrectly, that the baby was dead. Finally, they wheeled her in for an emergency C-section at 3 A.M.

If Coco could have held the new baby, it would have fit into the palm of one hand. Its spindly legs were not much larger than a frog's, but they didn't kick; they just hung down. And it was another girl. Ruby Diamond Pearl was three months premature and weighed in at 636 grams, her veiny skin punctured with tubes the size of cocktail straws. Her chest heaved up and down; it was smaller than a chicken breast. Coco felt so undone that she wanted to believe they'd switched her child with another by mistake. "She actually looked like a crack baby would look," she said, mortified.

While the baby struggled in neonatal intensive care, Coco spent an anxious week on another floor of the hospital. Foxy snuck Mercedes in; Wishman didn't visit; Sunny did. The gossip had already started:

Wishman must be using something, Coco.

Someone doing something. That baby isn't right.

All of Coco's other children were healthy, so Coco called Sunny and asked if Wishman was using drugs. He only smoked weed. Wishman also assured Coco, and put his last name on the birth certificate. Coco was discharged and returned to Foxy's, and Pearl stayed on in the hospital.

In the midst of the crisis, Coco decided to make the move upstate. She felt that no good would come of staying in the Bronx. She rarely saw her sister, she couldn't pin down her own mother, and perhaps the distance would renew Foxy's interest in Coco and her kids. Coco also wanted to escape the neighborhood, which she felt was full of hypocrites—people pretending good while saying nasty things about her, and now, about her baby. Wishman had only visited the hospital once, and he'd brought along his new girl. Foxy condemned Wishman for abandoning a sickly infant, but Coco believed that he would eventually come around. "If it was hard for me and I gave birth, think how he must be feeling worse," she said. In the meantime, Coco reminded her mother that she'd raised her girls without two fathers, and she could do just as well without three.

Foxy agreed to oversee Pearl's care in the hospital while Coco went through the shelter in Troy and settled down. Richie agreed to keep an eye on the apartment at Prospect. Richie's brother had lent him enough money to get out of the shelter and rent an apartment, and Richie would use Coco's furniture until he could afford his own. In the meantime, Coco packed the important things she could carry with her—the girls' best clothes and her photographs. Richie promised to safeguard the toy chest Cesar had made for Mercedes until she came back for it. A friend offered to give her a lift to Troy.

Coco had three goals at the time of her brave upstate move. On her way to her new home, stuck in traffic on the Tappan Zee Bridge, she scribbled them down on a scrap of paper. The first, she circled: "my child out the hospital." The second: "Cesar in my life," beside which she drew a frowning face and added, "A dream now." The third: "My four girls to finish school and get married and do not come out like me!!!"

On another scrap, she drew a fat heart and placed her family inside: "This is my life Right here: Mercedes, 4 years old; Nikki 3 years old; Nautica, 11 months old (mother) Coco, 20 years old, Pearl 1 month old." She added comments in the remaining corners, as though hope, too, could be rearranged, like the figurines on the shelves of the apartment she'd fled:

Life is Bitch <u>BUT</u> I'm a strong woman!
I'll give these girls the world!
I'll never put anyone Before my Kids.

Then she graced the bottom with the sentence that would become the next tattoo of the seven she would eventually acquire—*Mercedes, Nikki, Nautica, Pearl. My four Pride & Joys.*

PART III

Upstate

CHAPTER TWENTY-THREE

To qualify for permanent housing in Troy, Coco had to prove that she was homeless. Shortly after arriving, she installed Nikki and Nautica at Milagros's and took Mercedes with her to a local shelter, Joseph's House, a renovated storefront downtown. The homeless guests had to clear out each morning; Coco and Mercedes would take the bus back to Milagros's apartment. The bus traveled along River Street, parallel to Troy's Hudson River industrial waterfront. The neighborhood had been a thriving working-class district. Traces of better days remained, but the area had grown shabby. Victorians that weren't boarded up had signs: *No Trespassing* and *Apartment for Rent.*

Out the bus window, Coco observed white girls pushing strollers with darker-skinned babies down the desolate blocks. She spotted a dealer in a rotting doorway. She passed a Burger King. Just before the entrance to Corliss Park, where Milagros lived, a strip mall offered a few stores. Gray patches of tar, like flattened mud pies, decorated the parking lot. Rent-A-Center stood beside the Town Village Laundromat and Dry Cleaners, where every thirteenth wash was free. Past the gas station, where the bus swung left, was a twelve-step gift shop called Living Recovery.

Corliss Park was nothing like the Bronx projects. Two-story garden apartments were plotted along a single looping street. Trees stood between units with front and back yards. Barbecue grills, protected from the elements by green garbage bags, loomed like giant mushrooms. Children left their bicycles, unlocked, outside.

Milagros had received her housing assignment quickly; she'd dealt with the paperwork before leaving the Bronx. Coco waited over three months; she'd arrived in Troy without any of the necessary documentation. Pearl's illness made her even more discombobulated than usual. She'd misplaced the girls' birth certificates, which she needed to register them at a clinic, which was required to update their immunizations so they could register at school—she'd forgotten their immunization forms along with other necessary documents. There were appointments and paperwork required for housing, and Coco didn't even have money for local bus fares because she had no benefits: the city was still paying rent on the apartment she'd abandoned in the Bronx and refused to transfer her welfare case upstate. Foxy would borrow $20 or $30 from Delilah, the loan shark, and wire it to Coco via Western Union, thus incurring an additional $15 cost. But whenever Coco had real money—$40 or $50 or $60—she interrupted her homelessness and took the three-hour bus ride back to the city to check on Pearl. Coco was so exhausted from the disruption and the traveling that she often fell asleep to the hum of the heart monitor as soon as she reached Pearl's bedside in the Bronx.

Foxy's maternal impulses were spent before her new granddaughter's birth, but the crisis brought out the capable woman Coco remembered and still yearned for. Foxy couldn't rouse herself to face Hector's probation appointments—for the time he'd brought a gun to junior high—but she visited the hospital every day. Hector's problems implicated Foxy, but no one blamed her for Pearl. The baby's condition remained extremely serious: she'd lost two ounces since the operation for a heart murmur, and infections still plagued her. She relied upon a respirator, which damaged her underdeveloped lungs. Foxy prayed in the hospital chapel before she headed home.

When Coco couldn't get to the city, she kept abreast of Pearl's condition through Foxy's neighbor Sheila, who had a phone. The child's condition improved as reports were passed along. The doctors' dire prognosis became Foxy's cautious prognosis, which Sheila spruced up. "This little baby's very sick" turned into "She's hanging in there" to "She's growing every day." One doctor had told Foxy that if Pearl survived, she wouldn't develop normally. Foxy hoped that by the time Coco finally settled in Troy, there'd be better news to share. In Foxy's experience, predictions rarely held.

Late in the fall of 1994, Foxy had a windfall. Richie's ancient lawsuit—concerning his fall from the fire escape—finally came through. Coco thought that it was no coincidence that her mother had reunited with Richie shortly before he received his check for $70,000, but Coco was still happy that they were seeing each other again. They burned through the money, some of which Richie kept hidden in the broiler of his stove: everyone ate takeout; Foxy cabbed everywhere; Richie gave his brother the $12,000 he owed him, paid for Foxy's sister Aida's funeral, bought himself a gun for protection, and got leather coats for everyone in the house. Coco told him, " 'You're all getting outrageous.' He's like, 'You never know if you die tomorrow.' " Every time Coco saw him in the Bronx, he would slip her some cash. Within a week, the family had also gotten good news about Pearl: she'd survived another operation and some of her tubes were taken out. Coco got to hold her for the first time. "It felt so good," she said, gratified.

Coco secretly liked the arrangement: in Troy, Milagros was watching Nikki and Nautica; in the Bronx, her mother was acting like a mother, and her stepfather was back in the picture. Coco felt like a teenager again. A girl could travel with just one, and Mercedes, who was four, accompanied Coco everywhere. The duo strolled down Troy's empty main streets, honoring the unspoken boundaries within which poor people could comfortably walk and congregate. They stopped by Barker Park, across from the abandoned Stanley's department store. They bought snacks at the Night Owl and hung around the Kentucky Fried Chicken. At night, back at the shelter, Coco and Mercedes stayed up talking with the other transplanted women. They had come to Troy from Brooklyn and New Jersey and the Bronx. Coco passed around a favorite photograph of Cesar—stepping out of the shower, grinning, his arms open wide. The women marveled at him.

Coco found her days at Milagros's boring. Milagros never played music or danced with the kids; she only wanted to watch TV. Coco wrote letters to everyone in the Bronx. The pace picked up when Jessica's children returned from school. Coco would do anything to make the children laugh. Sometimes they played school. Serena appointed herself teacher; if Coco wasn't an unruly student, she acted like a snotty parent who dismissed the teacher's criticisms of her problem child. Once, Serena, puzzled about what to do, ordered Coco to the principal. Coco drew out Serena's consternation but surrendered just in time; Coco was sensitive to the difference between teasing and mockery. Serena basked in the attention. Coco felt guilty about favoring one niece, but she believed that Milagros favored Brittany and Stephanie—she'd had them from birth—and Kevin, Milagros's oldest, was special just for being male.

Coco helped keep the girls in touch with Jessica. They dictated letters and drew pictures that she tucked into the envelopes. Coco wrote Jessica a long confessional: she couldn't explain what had happened with Wishman, but she knew she still loved Cesar. She enclosed a photograph of Pearl. The baby looked scrawny; Jessica wrote back that she was beautiful. Jessica assured Coco that no matter what, she would always be her sister-in-law. She told her to ignore what people said and to give her love to the girls and stay strong.

*   *   *

By January 1995, Richie's fortune was nearly gone. To make ends meet, Foxy rented a bedroom to Octavio, one of the Cuban brothers who oversaw several drug spots on her block. Octavio sometimes stored the day's drugs there. Grumpy and pockmarked, Octavio was probably young, but the street had ground him into middle age. He paid Foxy $40 a week and he occasionally sprung for cigarettes or milk. Pitchers and runners came and went, morning, noon, and night. They were supposed to load up and go, but they lingered unless Octavio badgered them to move along. They preferred to watch pro wrestling, survey the food prospects in the kitchen, or flirt with Hector's girlfriend's pretty friends. Foxy couldn't take the chaos and spent most nights at either Richie's or Hernan's.

The two men in her life lived near one another; she shuttled between them. Sometimes, to avoid detection, Foxy changed her outfits as a disguise. Once, Hernan suspected that she'd slipped over to Richie's, and he waited outside the building door for hours. Finally he gave up, but left behind a note:

> Foxy. Why do you lie so much?
> I waited here long and left my name to carry on.
>   Hernan.

That winter, when Coco came to the Bronx, her mother's apartment no longer felt like home. Foxy couldn't be badgered into staying the night there, even with her grandchildren, and the apartment she had forsaken had become a combination hotel, stash house, and teen fort. In the dim light, teenagers smoked blunts, watched bootleg videos of current movies, had sex, laughed and argued, playfought, and played cards. Babies crawled underfoot. On the living room wall was a swath of so many children's handprints that it looked like a stencil. The children were family—the block's sons and daughters, nephews and nieces, neighbors, friends' boyfriends' other kids.

Coco would once have loved all the action, but now it made her uncomfortable. Milagros usually kept Nautica upstate, but Coco worried about Mercedes's and Nikki's safety with what she called "all the in and out." She also worried about her uncle Benny's pitbull, Sugar, who—although she was kept in the bathroom—sometimes managed to escape. Coco corralled the girls in Foxy's room; they got restless and cranky; Coco lost her patience and hit them; then she would feel guilty and indulge them with candy or toys she couldn't afford from the dollar store. The company ate the cupboards clean. The fridge only held her uncle Benny's HIV medication. Once, while Nikki was posing in the bathroom mirror, she cut her hand on one of his razor blades. There had been no Band-Aids, clean towels, or toilet paper.

Whenever she could, Coco escaped to the hospital. Nikki and Mercedes weren't allowed inside the neonatal unit, and Hector's Iris offered to watch them at the house. But Coco worried—Iris smoked weed, and when she didn't she sometimes lost her patience with her one son. Coco preferred to switch buses at Tremont, request a transfer, and leave them at Lourdes's.

During one of Coco's trips to the Bronx, a pudgy brown-eyed boy, one of her brother's friends, kept coming around to the house. His name was Aaron, but everyone called him Frankie. Frankie recognized Coco from the neighborhood, but Coco didn't remember him. He was easy to overlook: his pale features were pleasing, but bland; he spoke little. He stuttered when he was nervous, except when he was stoned. Coco noticed that her mother perked up whenever Frankie came around. "He used to be bringing my mother weed, or my mother was always giving him weed, and he was just, like, constantly there," said Coco. Coco didn't generally favor guys with bellies, but Foxy's responsiveness to Frankie had caught Coco's attention. Then a bulletin from Cesar's gossipy sister, Elaine, accelerated things. Coco hadn't heard from Elaine for a while, but she tracked Coco down at Foxy's and informed her that Cesar had gotten married—legally. Cesar had made Elaine promise not to reveal the bride's name to anyone but family—*current* family. Coco was floored.

Around the same time, Pearl, who had spent six months in the hospital, was released to Foxy's care. Foxy agreed to keep the baby until Coco got her own place. Meanwhile, Foxy moved back to her own apartment, where Pearl's homecoming inspired a storm of cleaning. All guests were booted, including Octavio. Foxy had wanted to get rid of him earlier but had been afraid to kick him out; sometimes dealers refused to go. But even Octavio didn't doubt a sick baby's right to a good start.

Pearl's arrival stirred the somnolent building. The baby had so much gear that she required a small parade—her special crib, a brand-new asthma machine, tubing to hook her to the oxygen tank, reserve tanks, bottles of medication, ointments, and jars. Foxy bustled Pearl into the apartment, past the note she had taped to the door: "Absolutely no smoking!

The baby's home already. Foxy." Neighbors came by to look at her; the curiosity was not always kind. Pearl had Wishman's eyes, but watery instead of angry. Her thin face bulged at the cheeks as if she were eating gravel.

Hector, who, like Cesar, had long ago assumed the role of body-guard of his family, emerged as the primary protector of his infant niece. He moonlighted as a human smoke detector, ushering violators into the hall. He didn't keep his music down, though—Hector loved his hip-hop—and Pearl got little sleep. Nobody was sleeping much but Foxy, whose doctor had given her a prescription for her migraines called Toradol. The injections knocked her out completely. Pearl shivered constantly, as though she were being electrocuted, but the precise cause of this—music, slamming doors, shouting and laughter in the hall, or her illness—was hard to identify.

Still, the smokeless baby room was a haven. Wishman's fourteen-year-old brother, Shorty, visited his niece every day. Shorty had an ongoing beef with a gang, the Ñetas, and traveled in what he considered a disguise—he walked the few blocks from his mother's with a T-shirt pulled over his head. Perhaps he felt connected to the fragile baby, a soul whose life was as threatened as his.

Wishman, however, ignored his daughter. If he visited the apartment, he avoided Pearl's room. Once, he stepped in to check out a crew of girls there, but he didn't even glance in the direction of the crib. Foxy dismissed him as a bona fide hoodlum. Frankie, on the other hand, had warmed to the child immediately.

Frankie had grown up in the projects down the block from Foxy's build-ing. He lived there with his mother, younger brother, and stepfather; Frankie's own father, who was Italian, left home when Frankie was two. Frankie had a talent for sports. After high school, he moved to Florida, where he played minor league baseball and tried out with the Detroit Tigers but didn't make the cut. "It broke my heart, so I didn't try no more," he said. He returned to the Bronx.

Frankie had just split up with his son's mother when he met Coco. He was nice to Coco's daughters, and Coco liked that. One afternoon, Coco bought her daughters boxing gloves. It was too cold to go outside, and the girls needed something besides TV to keep them occupied. Hector's friends snatched the gloves—they were sick of TV also—but Frankie retrieved them for the girls and taught them how to spar. Mer-cedes and Nautica threw diligent punches. Nikki's were weak; her lack of toughness worried Coco. If other children grabbed Nikki's toys, or her cousins became too aggressive, Coco had to force Nikki to defend herself. Luckily, Mercedes, who was stocky, looked out for her.

Lots of boys lost their patience after a few minutes of play with children, but Frankie didn't. Coco observed him closely when her children were in his orbit, and his affection toward her daughters seemed real. They wrestled. Nautica dove on top of the thrashing heap and Frankie laughed easily: he didn't yell if someone's foot kicked his face. Coco offered Frankie eye-to-eye contact, registering her interest.

Frankie showed his respect and introduced his two children to Coco. He didn't get along with the mothers, but his own mother did, and he got to spend time with his kids when the mothers brought them to visit their grandmother. Mercedes and Nikki got along with Frankie's daughter, and Nautica played with his son. A few nights later, Coco put on thin pajamas that caught the outline of her legs. She plunked herself on the couch. Frankie sat on the floor before her. He asked her to please braid his hair and she said yes and he leaned back between her thighs. She did not move. "Can I put my head on your lap?" he asked politely. He hugged her belly and shifted upward, to her breasts. He soon formalized his intentions. He said, "You know, Coco, you know, I want to be with you."

On Valentine's Day, he handed her flowers and a heart-shaped box of chocolates. No one had ever done that for Coco. Valentine's Day was Foxy and Richie's anniversary. Coco found that auspicious. She spontaneously asked, "Yo, Frankie, you want to live with me?"

Coco reasoned that she had back evidence on Frankie: he was from the neighborhood, her big brother's friend. She'd shared with him her important secrets—her enduring love for Cesar, her hurt over Wishman's denial of Pearl. Mercedes seemed to be reserving judgment, but Nikki and Nautica already called him Papi. He said he felt so close to Pearl that she seemed his own. When Octavio gave him work, Frankie bought Pampers for Nautica. He contributed toward Foxy's rent. Coco believed if the proposal were a bad idea, Foxy would have stopped her. But Foxy wasn't paying close attention to Coco.

Coco planned to return to Troy and get settled. The housing authority had offered her a three-bedroom apartment in Corliss Park, near Milagros. Frankie would join her as soon as he'd earned enough for the move. He wanted to hook up cable because he liked the sports channels; he also promised to spring for wall-to-wall carpeting, an indulgence for Coco, whose size-four feet were used to linoleum. Said Coco, "Cesar's not the only one who deserves better, now that I found a man who loves me and my kids."

Coco and the girls moved on a windy day in March 1995. The first thing that Coco did—even before plugging in her radio—was to mail Cesar her phone number and new address.

Cesar did not love Giselle; he loved Coco. He liked Giselle, but the marriage was initially a mercenary move. He had to be legally married to qualify for conjugal visits, and he needed a girl who could be relied on to visit and to keep money coming into his commissary account. His friends occasionally contributed, but they were in and out of prison and in and out of solvency. Rocco remained his primary contact, but Rocco was changing. His wife had told him to straighten up or risk losing her and his baby girl; after he'd completed work release (scrubbing pots and pans at a restaurant), she'd steered him straight to AmeriCorps. Now Rocco was working as a youth counselor at a housing project. He still talked the hoodlum game, but Cesar sensed a shift.

Cesar badgered Coco and Roxanne to bring his daughters and they usually didn't. Elaine managed to send him the odd food box, but she struggled. Lourdes couldn't be counted on. Life on the inside wasn't anything like his previous bid as a juvenile in DFY. The lonely old-timers around him were depressing. Most never had visitors and didn't get mail. Cesar had proposed to Giselle as soon as he suspected Coco's latest pregnancy. Giselle suggested that they wait a year, but to his relief the engagement lasted just six months.

Giselle was wary of Cesar's hoodlum lifestyle; so many of her relatives were in prison that her mother had had to raise nine children who were not her own. She'd been cautious, even back when they were only passing neighborhood friends. Giselle remembered seeing Cesar zip by on his bicycle. He was always moving, playing, making faces, never staying still. Years later, she'd run into him on the corner of Tremont, his skinny neck drenched in gold. He'd reminded her of Mr. T. She worried about the risk of flashy jewelry. "Put them inside," she suggested.

"For what? That's what I got chains for, to put them outside," he said.

"You might get robbed," she warned.

"I ain't gonna get robbed." Cesar grinned. He lifted his shirt and showed a .45 caliber, snug in his waistband. The next time she ran into Cesar was at her sister's, when he was a fugitive.

Giselle hid the engagement from her mother, who remembered Cesar all too well from Tremont. The weekend Giselle snuck off to get married, she told her mother she was going away with a girlfriend from work.

Cesar had been transferred to Clinton, a maximum-security prison near the Canadian border; as Giselle's stomach churned with nervousness the entire seven-hour bus ride there, a few of the other women tried to calm her.

There was a network of support and loyalty among some prisoners' wives. The regulars informed other wives if a mistress had sat in their rightful visitor's seat. Guards, too, sometimes hinted to a woman about a guy's two- or three- or four-timing, or "accidentally" shone the ultraviolet light on another woman's signature that had been penned in invisible ink. Some of the guards seemed jealous of the inmates' ability to attract such pretty, young visitors. Some visitors ended up dating guards. Prisoners joked that the guards were so uptight that they must have had less sex with their at-home wives than the inmates had in trailer visits. Veteran wives counseled newcomers about regulations and circumventing regulations, important lessons they'd extracted from protracted dealings with the correctional bureaucracy.

The rural town of Dannemora, New York, was isolated and, to the minority women who visited inmates there, unwelcoming. The outer wall of the prison towered over one side of a stunted main street. Opposite, someone named Ting had a monopoly on local business: Ting's Store, Ting's Break-out Saloon, and Ting's Hotel. The visiting women pooled money and rented a room to shower off the long bus ride and freshen up before crossing the street and heading in.

Rooms at Ting's were dumpy but tidy. On the back of the door was a sign listing the prison's visiting hours, along with information about free coffee and where to find the ironing board. But Cesar had warned Giselle not to stay at Ting's; he'd heard that an inmate's girlfriend had been raped there, and he'd provided Giselle with the name of a local prisoner's wife. The woman had followed her husband to Dannemora and rented rooms to other visitors. The lady dispensed advice freely—she'd had her own prison wedding—and charged only $25 for three nights, including meals. Giselle checked in and found it difficult to sleep.

Giselle was organized. She brought every document she needed for the wedding—a $25 money order for the marriage license, proof of the premarital interview, a blood test, her ID, the rings. The next morning, she tugged on a black dress and slipped into a pair of black pumps. She said, "I looked like a widow instead of a bride." Cesar's maroon shirt matched his maroon Filas, which peeked out from under the cuffs of his prison greens.

Cesar was so nervous as they waited for the prison chaplain that he spilled a cup of Pepsi on his shirt. A friend of Cesar's and his girlfriend stood witness. The ceremony took three minutes, including the exchange of rings. Cesar had to remove his and pass it to the guard so it could be re-received. He later retrieved the ring from the package room, after it had been inspected for contraband and registered as his property.

The bride and groom couldn't take pictures on their wedding day. A marriage qualified as a "special visit," and the chits that inmates exchanged for Polaroids were only to be utilized during regular visiting hours. Giselle later thought it just as well she hadn't been photographed. She couldn't stop crying, and what kind of picture would she have made—a bride with bloodshot eyes.

CHAPTER TWENTY-FOUR

"Mercedes! Mercedes! Mercedes!" called out the priest during Mercedes's joint baptismal ceremony one late-April 1995 day. Dying lilies from Easter decorated the altar from which he exuberantly proclaimed his message to the perplexed parishioners; his accent was hard to make out. He was also having difficulty pronouncing the children's inventive names, but he spoke with great gusto about something having to do with their state of grace. Rocco and his wife, Marlene, had made arrangements for Mercedes's participation, and Coco and the girls had traveled down to the Bronx. Frankie was already in the city, dealing for Octavio outside of Foxy's building to make some extra income.

A lacy white dress with tiny pearl beads and a sparkly crown with its own veil had transformed the ordinarily jean-clad Mercedes into a child bride. They'd all shopped for the outfit on Fordham just hours earlier. Mercedes's beauty, and Rocco and Marlene's generosity, made Coco emotional. "It's like she's getting married, it's like I'm not ready for that," she said.

"Mercedes! Mercedes! Mercedes!" the priest sang out again. Rocco whispered to Mercedes, "It's probably the only name he knows how to pronounce." When it was her turn to approach the altar, Rocco held her hand and lifted her over the font. The priest gave unintelligible instructions.

Coco whispered, "Say 'I do,' Mercy."

"I do," Mercedes repeated. The priest spoke again.

"Say 'I do,' Mercy," Coco prompted.

"I do what?" Mercedes asked.

The water washed her forehead. Mercedes seemed crestfallen when Rocco placed her down. He brought back her smile with a funny face. The priest shouted, "Mercedes! Mercedes! Mercedes! Welcome into this new life!"

But it was the old one that exerted its pull. After the ceremony, they collected Rocco's daughter from Marlene's mother and decided to share a livery cab to Tremont. Coco wanted to show off Mercedes to Lourdes; Rocco and Marlene were going to visit Rocco's mom. Rocco amused the little girls on the ride over with his priestly gobbledygook: "Gadooms slaksfds larsedfiskish!" He explained to Coco that he felt bad that it had taken so long to get Mercedes baptized, but even though Marlene also worked and they lived with her parents, it had taken well over a year even to begin to get on his feet after his release.

On Tremont, near the steps of Lourdes's old building, Mercedes savored her last few minutes in Rocco's arms. Rocco shared a story: "Your daddy sat here with his head in his hands and cried and cried. 'You get in a fight?' I asked. He had a toothache!" Rocco laughed.

After saying good-bye, Mercedes led Coco and Nikki toward Lourdes's, causing a stir on the block. A drunken woman holding a miniature can of Budweiser crooned over her beauty until a man stomped to shoo the woman away.

"Everybody is staring at you, Mercy," said Coco.

"So?" said Mercedes self-consciously.

"You hear her? 'Everybody's looking at you, Mercy.' 'So!' I can't wait to be taking her to my mother's block, everybody be sweating her," Coco said. Mercedes turned left, headed for Mount Hope. Two men were standing outside the corner store.

"*Esa es la hija de Cesar,*" one said. That's Cesar's daughter.

"She's beautiful, God bless her," said the other.

"*Qué linda.*"

"She looks so grown!"

"She's making the whole block sweat! She's like a little Jessica!" Coco said.

Mercedes bolted for Domingo, who stood beside his hamburger cart. In warm weather, he sold burgers—and drugs on the sly—in front of Lourdes's building. Domingo knelt to the ground and lifted Mercedes up.

"Domingo, where's my present?" she asked. "Mommy, can I have a hamburger?"

"You know I don't have any money, Mercy," Coco said. Domingo plunked one on the grill and promised to bring it up.

Lourdes no longer lived in the studio with Domingo; she was staying in a small one-bedroom across the hall. The apartment belonged to a neighbor named Maria. Maria's young son had brought Lourdes home one evening, after he'd found her sleeping on the roof. According to Lourdes, Domingo had given Roxanne and Justine—Roxanne's daughter with Cesar—Lourdes's bed. Lourdes ended up staying on with Maria, who was dying of cancer. She nursed her and took care of her two unhappy kids. Maria's cousin, a tall, quiet Panamanian man named Emilio, also lived there. Lourdes and Domingo remained on fairly good terms, however; she seasoned the meat for his hamburgers and sometimes watched over the cart. They continued to sell drugs to friends and neighbors on the side, and he gave her tens and twenties in a pinch.

The day of Mercedes's baptism, Lourdes made the gestures of fussing over Mercedes, but she seemed irritable. Domingo delivered the burger in a napkin. Lourdes tucked a dishtowel around Mercedes's neck. "Be careful of your dress, Mercy," she said, lighting a cigarette.

"They went all out for her," said Coco. "The dress cost a hundred and twenty dollars. The shoes cost thirty dollars. The veil costs twenty dollars and they bought the tights." Lourdes murmured in response, but her eyes, which were glassy, stayed on the Spanish-language news. The silence seemed awkward. "Mercedes be crying for her sister," Coco tried. "Justine, Justine, always crying for her."

"Oh," said Lourdes.

"I'ma go now," Coco said.

Nothing.

Then Lourdes said, "All right then, Mami," and pushed herself up from the couch to see them off.

"Can I have a dollar?" Mercedes asked brightly. Lourdes ambled over to the dark bedroom, where Maria lay, and returned with one.

"Can I have a dollar?" Nikki echoed softly.

"You split it both ways," Lourdes said wearily. While the girls were putting on their coats, Mercedes held up the dollar, covered her mouth with it, playfully raised her eyebrows, then made the dollar snap.

"Don't do that, Mama," said Lourdes, and snatched back the bill. Mercedes jerked away, surprised. Lourdes added, "All the peoples touched this, it's dirty."

Coco headed toward the doorway. Lourdes ushered the girls after her and scolded Nikki, who'd crouched over to inspect a little shrine behind the front door. Mercedes absentmindedly placed the dollar near her lips again. Without warning, Lourdes backhanded her across the face. Mercedes howled—she seemed as surprised and betrayed as she was hurt.

"I told her not to put money in her mouth," Lourdes said flatly, grabbing Mercedes roughly by the head and pulling the child's face into her gut. "Mami, it's *dirty*, it's not good," Lourdes said, sounding soothing but stroking Mercedes roughly. The mixture seemed to work. Lourdes finalized the deal with a bruised banana, which Mercedes shared with Nikki in the hallway while they waited for the elevator, which never came. They took the stairs. Two boys leaned over the rail, spitting down to the entryway. "Lourdes, they spitting out here!" Coco yelled up. A door opened,

Lourdes said, "Stop!" without conviction, then the door slammed. "I feel she treats me different," said Coco of Lourdes. "I don't feel comfortable no more."

Coco liked upstate life at first, although nighttime scared her. She wasn't accustomed to being close to the ground, so near outdoors. The kitchen windows had no curtains. She said, "And the trees be flying. I feel like somebody's face be there." The stairs squeaked when she walked to fetch a bottle for Nautica, so Coco huddled up with her children on a bed of sheets on the living room floor. She didn't have any furniture yet.

She felt safer when Frankie visited. For Mother's Day, her sister mailed cookies and candy, which lifted her spirits. Foxy called. Cesar and Jessica called collect. Coco switched between Cesar and Jessica on call-waiting. "I was going back and forth and back and forth, 'Hold on, hold on,' giving them messages, then I said, 'Yo, Cesar, call me back later, your sister wants to talk to me.' But that was just to get him off the phone." She wanted Jessica to herself.

Jessica confided in Coco about Torres, albeit cryptically, mindful that the prison might be taping the call. "She sounded happy to me," Coco said.

Frankie, however, wasn't thrilled by Coco's nearly daylong calls, and it created tension between Frankie and Mercedes. One afternoon, after chatting with Cesar most of the afternoon, Coco hung up contentedly.

"Fuck that nigga," Frankie muttered.

"Don't say that about my father," Mercedes said. Or, if Frankie asked Mercedes to do something she didn't want to, she answered, "You're not my father. I ain't gotta listen to you."

Coco admired her daughter's nerve, but Mercedes and Frankie also drove Coco crazy with their bickering. Mercedes begged for cartoons; Frankie wanted sports.

Fun triumphed over rules at Coco's, where the door was always open: the neighborhood children congregated in and around her apartment. Frankie came and went; Serena whiled away her free time in the house or in the yard. Coco's grass couldn't withstand all the action. The surviving patches were soon worn down to mud, sprinkled with Cheez-it dust. The array of scattered broken toy parts resembled children's rooms in prisons. On the brick wall below the white siding near her front door, Serena chalked in screwball script "Coco's House."

Coco let Serena and her friends Rollerblade around the kitchen and the living room. The music was always on. Even after a church finally delivered donated furniture, the bedlam stayed pretty much the same. The house was hectic but usually happy—unless Coco was yelling, and even then, the children didn't pay her much mind. Her yelling was spontaneous and full-bodied, bursting with exasperation, whereas Milagros's could be scarier—colder—her anger so concentrated that the children automatically stilled.

If Jessica knew what to say to make you feel better, Coco knew what to do. Even on the worst days, Coco would drop whatever she was doing and dance. Dancing never needed an excuse. Mercedes swayed stiffly, self-consciously, but Nikki was agile and shameless—Foxy had taught her how to dance Spanish. Even Nautica, still in diapers, tried out the latest moves. She'd plant one hand on the linoleum, butt in the air, and squat in time to the music as she flapped her other arm like a butterfly. Everyone clapped. No matter how silly Coco was acting, she always noticed those children like Serena, hiding on the sidelines. She'd shimmy over and reach her short arms out. "Come on, Mami," she'd say. Serena was too bashful to join in, but she shone in the joyful lightness of her aunt. Sometimes Coco just pulled Serena in and got her moving. "You crazy, Títi," Serena would giggle.

Serena helped Coco with the kids. She changed diapers and doled out handfuls of dry cereal, filled bottles and cups with sugared juices, spooned rice into mouths. She comforted Nautica when she fell down the stairs. Nautica was always crashing into things. She had the same corkscrew curls and tightly wound physicality that Cesar had had as a kid, but she was slightly bowlegged and tripped when she ran. Coco's girls adored Serena. Coco often said, "I'd take Serena with the quickness." She welcomed Serena's companionship on her own as much as on her girls' behalf. If Frankie stayed over, however, Milagros did not let Serena stay the night.

Milagros's caution offended Coco. "Nothing is happening," Coco said to Milagros. In front of the children, she never so much as kissed Frankie. Like Milagros, Coco had trained her daughters to turn their heads away from the television whenever anything romantic or sexual came on. But Coco and Frankie's intimacies weren't what worried Milagros.

Milagros trusted no man. Night after night, she said, she'd seen her own mother beaten by her boyfriend, and the next men were no better. Too many friends had been molested by brothers or stepfathers or uncles or somebody's friend. One girl she knew had been raped by a police officer. Milagros had also had to deal with interrogations by the Bureau of

Child Welfare after she'd brought Serena to the doctor for a complication from her earlier abuse. Her rules about men were nonnegotiable— exempting blood family. Sometimes Serena snuck over anyway, and if Milagros paid a surprise visit, Serena hurried upstairs and hid. But mostly, Frankie was out and Coco cooked and Serena sat on the counter, swinging her legs, keeping her aunt company. Then Coco leased a washing machine from Rent-A-Center for $39 every other week and Serena sat on that.

Browsing through Rent-A-Center—a few minutes' walk from Corliss Park—was like wandering through a catalog. Coco strolled through the model rooms, each a tiny stage set, but completely coordinated, hooked up. The living rooms had stereos and lamps flanking couches behind coffee tables on rugs. The TVs had their own home cabinets. Firm mattresses lay beneath fluffy puffs and bright quilts. Stuffed animals adorned bunk beds. Kitchen appliances lined up for duty. Sets of glass dishes waited patiently, stacked in see-through cabinets.

The furniture beckoned to you: a mirror said, *Rent me!* None of the cheap wood bore scrapes or stains from spilled juice or children's fingerprints. A sign listed the price variations, depending upon whether you wanted to buy or rent: *brand-new cost, cash price; previously rented; total rent to own.* There were rings you could have for $16.99 a week. *Free jewelry cleaning while you wait! Free setup for your stereos!* Everything was cheaper at Wal-Mart, but Wal-Mart required a car. Rent-A-Center didn't make you wait while you paid layaway. They delivered free.

The Rent-A-Center people treated Coco respectfully. "Miss Rodriguez, we just want to know a time when you gonna come in for the payment" was the kind of thing they said. She was supposed to pay on Saturdays, but they gave her until Mondays, and whenever she was late—which was usually—it was a $5 fee. Five dollars was a lot, but it was better than borrowing from Delilah, the loan shark in the Bronx.

Although Cesar was married, he continued to call Coco—first twice a day, then four and five times, always collect. Coco ignored her growing telephone bill. They reminisced about their youth like sentimental senior citizens. The precision of his memory flattered her. She said, "He remembers everything—the last time we made love, all of the positions. I told him, 'That's cuz you have all that time in there, to think.'"

Cesar congratulated Coco on her independence. He alone acknowledged the significance of her move away from her mother and the Bronx: "You did it. You live there, are you proud of yourself? You should have done it when I was on the run." She shared her next ambition—to learn how to drive. They imagined his release date and fantasized about taking Mercedes and Nautica somewhere far away—maybe the Poconos—where they could be a family just once, before Cesar returned to Giselle. He said, "I wish all the kids I had by other girls I had by you."

Coco pretended more generosity toward Giselle than she felt: "Who knows? You could fall in love with your wife. It happens over time." Cesar asked for photographs—sexy ones of Coco, happy ones of their daughters. Serena took photographs of her aunt for her uncle. Coco posed seductively in underwear. She turned coyly over her shoulder with her hands up against the wall, as though being searched. She sucked on one of Nautica's pacifiers. She added suggestive captions on the back. But Coco worried that Serena, at ten, could understand the nature of the posing. "Even though she's a girl, that ain't right," said Coco. Eventually, the picture-taking became Mercedes's job, because she was only five.

During her phone calls with Cesar, Coco promised to send photographs, but also told Cesar she was better off for not having married him. "I woulda been working my ass off trying to impress you, and you would be having these bitches on the side," she said. They avoided the subject of Frankie, except for Cesar's admonishments that Coco make sure his daughters didn't call Frankie Daddy. Mercedes didn't, but Nautica did.

Toward the end of one conversation, Cesar said, "You don't know how much I want to break down and cry. I got no family out there, just my kids." Coco used to brawl with girls who so much as looked at him when he was on the street; now she no longer even declared her love for him. He added, "You don't tell me no more, I gotta keep asking you."

Coco still loved him absolutely, but felt foolish telling him—not so much because he'd married, but because she'd let him down again. "I feel so fucked up what I did," she blurted out. He began to cry. She held in her tears until the connection cut off, as it did, automatically, after half an hour.

Soon enough, the telephone company shut off Coco's service for the unpaid bills, and she and Cesar were back to writing again.

CHAPTER TWENTY-FIVE

Two months into her affair with Torres, Jessica discovered she was pregnant. Panic-stricken, she claimed that she'd been raped in the bathroom, thrown to the floor by someone—perhaps a repairman—whom she was unable to identify. Unfortunately, she didn't give close thought to the details of the fabrication; in a report chronicling her allegation, she described the crime scene as the bathroom in her old unit, a part of the prison she no longer had access to. The investigation, however, was already pointing toward Torres.

Even before the pregnancy, guards and prisoners alike had volunteered their suspicions about his relationship with Jessica. The reports seemed to be less concerned with the sex than with the benefits their relationship brought: official memos noted the "big" pizza and "big box" of doughnuts; a prisoner mused about the frequency with which Torres washed his hands ("must be getting himself a handful"); another sniped, "When Torres walks by he smells like Martinez's perfume." One guard used Torres's declining popularity to file a four-page typewritten complaint about his politics, all in caps:

> LAST I WOULD LIKE TO SAY IN PAST CONVERSATIONS WITH TORRES ABOUT TOPICS SUCH AS GUNS, DRUGS, AND WELFARE, THAT TORRES HAS SAID TO ME THAT HE FELT ALL DRUGS SHOULD BE LEGALIZED AND THAT ANYONE IN PRISON FOR SELLING DRUGS SHOULD NOT BE, FOR THEY WERE ONLY TRYING TO SUPPORT THEIR FAMILIES AND MAKE A LIVING.

The prison authorities had given Jessica a pregnancy test that August, which was negative; but by October, the blood test came back positive. Jessica asked for an abortion but said the prison refused to give her one unless she paid for it. She didn't have the money. She called her former pro-bono attorney, but by the time he had intervened and the abortion was scheduled, Jessica had spoken with Torres and changed her mind.

Jessica's devotion to Torres complicated an already complex situation and put her at further risk. First, by signing an affidavit claiming rape, Jessica had committed perjury; if convicted, she could face additional jail time. Because the alleged attack had taken place on federal property, the FBI opened its own investigation.

In early November, Jessica retracted the story about the rape, admitted she'd had sex with Torres, and refused to say anything more. Torres was eventually suspended. Jessica's loyalty to Torres had unwittingly earned her the reputation of a snitch. Ostensibly for her own protection, she was transferred to what was known as the camp, a minimum-security facility up the hill. Shortly after the move, Jessica's old cellmate Player was transferred to the camp as well. Their room, which they shared with four other women, had three bunk beds, lockers, one window, and enough space for a small table with chairs. Jessica took the bottom bunk and covered the underside of the upper bed with pictures of her girls.

Minimum security meant fewer restrictions. They still had count three times a day, but the women could roam the unit, make ceramics, or sit at picnic tables beneath the trees. Like mothers and grandmothers shut in their Bronx apartments, the inmates watched soap operas and played spades. On Saturday nights, the camp screened outdated movies in the visiting room. Someone always saved Jessica a seat. On Sundays, the women enjoyed listening to *Radio Suave*, a salsa music program broadcast from New York. To amplify the small sounds emitted from prison-regulation Walkmans, the women crafted speakers out of empty toilet-paper tubes. They danced and held hands if a friendly guard was on duty; otherwise, they danced with regulation distance between them.

Jessica took little pleasure in her new freedoms. She rarely left the darkened space of her lower bunk. "She was in her own little world," said Ida, one of her roommates. Jessica corresponded with Torres, using Player's mother as a mail drop. Jessica memorized his words and flushed the letters. She fantasized about the family she and Torres would have with their baby, his two other children, and her three girls. She said that one night, aided by a sympathetic colleague, Torres came onto the prison grounds and met her on the camp's back lawn. Beneath an enormous elm tree, they kissed.

Meanwhile, the investigation droned on, parallel to the pregnancy. Jessica reported to a job in the camp's kitchen. In the morning, she dragged herself to work. She complained a lot. She'd always surrounded herself with women who indulged her, but the investigation created extra burdens on her friends. Bending rules was necessary to make prison life bearable, but Jessica's notoriety meant that she—and anyone she hung out with—was held to the book. Guards would tear apart the room in search of evidence.

Still, the women gave Jessica extra leeway because she was pregnant—and then even more leeway when it turned out she was having
another set of twins. Babies were about hoping and growing, not just surviving. They pulled you into the future, even if you were literally impris-
oned by your past. Any belly—inside or outside of prison—required at
least the perfunctory gestures of optimism. One night, a guard with
whom Jessica was friendly placed his hand on Jessica's belly to feel the
babies stirring and blessed it with a kiss.

Ida was the cook of the bunch, and she made it her business to keep
Jessica full of food. Ida had been pregnant when she was arrested and
still regretted her abortion; Jessica's pregnancy offered her a second
chance to do right. Jessica loved Ida's special treats—banana pudding,
plantain-chip cake, and chilikidas—a special jailhouse dish made by
mashing together everything sweet (or savory) you could lay your hands
on and spreading it over crushed Oreos (or plantain chips). The women
also made hooch by mixing fruit with bread from the cafeteria and
stowing it above a ceiling panel to ferment.

The FBI wanted to run a DNA test on the fetuses, but Jessica refused.
At one point, the FBI agents checked her phone list and visited her sister in the Bronx. Elaine worried that Jessica was about to get her heart
broken again. But Jessica maintained her faith in Torres, even when he
dropped out of touch.

That spring, in 1995, Elaine and Coco brought her daughters and Jessica's girls to Danbury. Jessica was nearing the end of her pregnancy. The
visiting room at the minimum-security camp was light and airy. Vending
machines lined one end. At the other end a play area posted an intricate
list of rules. Another sign said *Welcome Back!* Because some children
believed they were visiting their mothers at work or in the hospital, visitors weren't supposed to say *prison* or *jail*.

Jessica carried a clear plastic bag of crocheting. She wore a teal cotton
sweat suit. Her white T-shirt, which was perfectly ironed, hung loosely
from her belly, which was firm and big. The red jailhouse dye in her hair
had grown out, revealing her brown-black roots. She wore no makeup,
except for lipstick. Her face looked full and vulnerable.

Serena and the twins ran to her and hugged her. Brittany and
Stephanie drifted toward a dollhouse they'd spotted, but Serena hovered by her mother. Jessica tried to defuse the awkwardness between
them by showing what she'd made: two sweaters for the unborn twins, a
cloth-covered photo album for Elaine for Mother's Day, and, for Ser-

ena, a peach-and-yellow coverlet that matched a skirt set she'd sent her long ago.

"That's one good thing about being locked up," Coco mumbled encouragingly. "You get all creative."

With an eye on the guard, Jessica slid out a sheet of plastic from one of the photo albums. It was a copy of her most recent sonogram. She introduced Serena to her brothers. "See, Baby A, that's his head, his eyes, the ears." Jessica carefully traced the body with her fingernail. "There's Baby B. His eyes there, his ears? You can't really see him on that one, but there's his head. They real big, right? That's what the doctor said, they got big heads."

Jessica untied Serena's straggly ponytail and combed out the knots with her fingers. She scooped up the strands and twisted a perfect topknot on the crown of Serena's head. Her hands moved unconsciously, expertly. Serena loved to be touched. She leaned into Jessica's side and bit her lip. Jessica rested a hand on her large belly. Serena lifted it and placed her own hand beneath.

"Mommy," Serena whispered. She reminded Jessica of what had become their special ritual since their visit in Florida—sharing a bagel from the vending machine. Jessica helped Serena count change and, holding hands, they walked over to the bank of food. Serena slipped the coins in the slot and pressed the button; inmates were not allowed to touch money.

The click-click—the inmate photographer—suggested they take a picture outdoors. Ordinarily, Jessica loved having her picture taken. When George was in the MCC, he would say, "Baby, take a roll of thirty-six." He sent her magazine pictures of poses for her to copy. In prison, on picture days in her unit, she and her roommates planned and traded outfits. They styled their hair and experimented with makeup and choreographed each pose as if they were on a fashion shoot. Jessica never went into debt for food in prison, but she often borrowed money for toiletries. That day, however, outside the camp's plain entrance, Jessica seemed uncertain. Instead of turning to the side to show off her profile, as most pregnant girls did, she faced the camera with an expression of apprehensive resignation. She removed the clunky prison-issue eyeglasses she detested and stood beside a prickly bush.

Serena never liked being photographed. At birthday parties, she had to be dragged to join her sisters and her cousins and cajoled to look pretty, to be sexy, to unpeel herself from the wall. Now she looked as though she wanted to hide behind the bush's scratchy branches. "Come on," Jessica said quietly, hugging her in. She clasped her daughter's hand. Serena placed her other hand on her hip and tried to smile.

Children born to women in federal custody must be taken by family within forty-eight hours of their birth, or they become wards of the state in which the mother lives. Jessica gave birth to two baby boys in a local hospital near the prison. Some inmates were required to give birth handcuffed, but Jessica's doctor wouldn't tolerate it. He had no say over the armed guard, though, who stood watch during the labor. Right up to the delivery, Jessica had held on to the hope that Torres would come to see their children being born, but she didn't hear anything from him. The birth had been his cutoff date. "Whatever I felt for him, it all turned dead when he didn't turn up in the hospital," she said coolly the following afternoon. She claimed she'd named the boys Michael and Matthew out of affection, but the impulse seemed closer to longing and spite. Michael was Jessica's father's name. Matthew was the son of a prison friend whom Jessica had met earlier in the MCC; the friend had been released, but Jessica then coincidentally befriended Matthew's sister, who was serving time at Danbury. Jessica and Matthew talked a lot on the telephone. He and Jessica were becoming closer as Jessica became more disenchanted with Torres. "I'll never regret my sons," she said stonily.

She hardly saw them in the hospital, however; the guards on duty weren't always willing to walk her to the nursery. When they finally agreed to let her peek at them, she inched slowly down the hall, the guards flanking her as she pushed her rolling IV. She tried to engage in small talk, perhaps to defuse the embarrassment of the stares of the other patients. She complimented one guard on her diamond engagement ring.

In her room, the guards jotted down notes of Jessica's conversations with visitors. Handcuffs lay on the table at the foot of her bed, beside a rose that Matthew had brought. He also surprised her with some Crabtree & Evelyn lotion from the hospital gift shop. He later returned with Lourdes and Elaine to collect the babies, and Jessica was discharged from the maternity ward. She managed to sneak the Crabtree & Evelyn lotion back into prison, but the female officer assigned to escort her confiscated Matthew's and Michael's baby footprints; they were considered contraband.

Lourdes promised to help raise the babies, but the burden fell to Elaine. She and her husband, Angel, had agreed to look after them while Jessica completed her prison term. Angel had recently graduated from a drug treatment program and was maintaining himself on methadone. He worked long days at a factory in Queens. Elaine had completed her GED and volunteered at her sons' school as a teacher's aide. She wanted to work, but her husband discouraged it, and she felt obligated to stay home and try to bring together her scattered family.

Elaine had gone into therapy to learn how to control her temper with her children, especially her youngest son, who had Cesar's quick energy. She felt ambivalence about the strong instinct for self-protection that might have saved her from her siblings' fates. She'd discussed her guilt about not helping Cesar more when he was a child and also while he was on the run after shooting Mighty: she'd worried about exposing her sons to his lifestyle, and with her husband's history of drug use, she had feared unexpected visits from police. Even though Angel now seemed to be shaping up, she was losing confidence in the marriage. She was ashamed to have a man who lined up for his Dixie cup of methadone. Elaine had no clue how she'd manage with two infants—the apartment she and her husband shared with their two growing boys was no bigger than a studio—but she also couldn't live with the thought of her nephews in foster care.

Shortly after the boys were born, Lourdes finally appeared at Danbury. Jessica was not initially welcoming. Although Jessica had been in prison for four years, Lourdes had visited only twice. Jessica was tired of her mother's excuses: she had no way to get there, she had no money, she was supposedly pregnant, she had husband trouble, she felt sick. Lourdes later said she couldn't emotionally handle the lengthy visits. Jessica thought she didn't want to be away from her block for too long, which was a roundabout criticism of Lourdes's dependency on men and drugs; Lourdes insisted there was no dependency.

Mockery was Jessica's way of reestablishing her connection with her mother; their wounded repartee kept a safe distance and neutralized the tension that always sat between them. Jessica spoke harshly to Lourdes, but she craved her attention and love. Now she cruelly assessed the older woman's body.

"She finally getting tits," Jessica said, and rolled her eyes. "Ma, you fat. You aren't just chubby, you are fat. So tell me, what are you, pregnant, or is it a tumor, or what?"

"I don't know, Mami," she said beseechingly, pouting into her double chin. Lourdes told Jessica she had to leave the visit early: "I have to go to the doctors. That's why I can't stay, Mami, I have to see a social worker."

"You don't need to see no social worker. You can talk to me," Jessica said, giving in.

"Mami, do my hair?" Lourdes asked. When Lourdes lifted her long hair from the nape of her neck, Jessica noticed that her mother was wearing the two boxing gloves that Boy George had given her on a slim gold chain. She touched them tenderly. "He'd be surprised that I still have that," Jessica said. "Probably thinks I sold it," she added sarcastically. Then she launched into the questions she always asked of Lourdes, reciting a litany of lost objects, as if Jessica could never accept her mother's failure to safeguard what she'd held for her. The purple shearling coat? The leathers? The chains? The rings?

Lourdes repeated her lines: "I don't know, Mami" and "I told you." She let the implication of the pauses do the work. Jessica bent forward. "Give me your earrings," she whispered. She sat back and said casually, "Let me try your earrings on."

"Be careful, Mami," Lourdes warned, glancing at the guard on duty.

"One hand washes the other," Jessica said, explaining that the guard was a "friend."

Lourdes pursed her lips as though she'd eaten something rank. "Sometimes the right hand doesn't know what the left hand is doing."

After the visit, Lourdes stood at the top of the hill overlooking the maximum-security facility below. As she waited for her daughter to be searched so she could appear in a window for a final wave, Lourdes retrieved a charm bracelet from her pocket and slipped it back over her bloated wrist. The letters spelled out *LOVE*. One of Domingo's drug customers had offered it in lieu of cash, and Domingo had passed it along to Lourdes. "Good thing she didn't take this," Lourdes said. "I'd have to get another one new! See how she took my earrings like that?"

Finally, Jessica's figure appeared in the window. From a distance, without the power of her expressive face, the sultry voice, the intelligence in her hazel eyes, Jessica looked beaten down. Lourdes waved. Jessica waved back. Both seemed diminished, small. Lourdes waved with each step down the hill toward the parking lot until she could not see her daughter anymore.

By summer, Jessica was feeling completely abandoned. First, she had lost Torres; then she had lost her boys; then she learned that her friend Matthew was spending a suspicious amount of time with Elaine. The prison authorities placed Jessica on suicide watch. Her vicious moods alienated her from her roommates, who had enjoyed the brief reprieve of her hospital stay. They weren't thrilled to have this particular Jessica back; the blunt impact of Jessica's depression was hard to escape in the small room. She was clearly suffering, but suicide watch meant that a guard checked in on them every hour.

For a while, Jessica dove back into the prison mix. The mix was to prison what the street was to the ghetto. Although the camp mix was watered down compared to the yard in maximum security, Jessica courted the damage she could: she gossiped and dated widely, ignoring the established wives and girlfriends, and she welcomed threats. "She started getting crazy," said Player. Jessica hooked up with a loudmouthed girl who offended Jessica's roommates with her belligerence, yet Jessica continued to invite the girl into their room. Jessica's roommates were "getting short"—their release dates were approaching—and they wanted to finish their time quietly; eventually, they asked Jessica to leave. She moved into a corner cube.

Jessica tried to turn to her family. Her older brother Robert had attempted suicide again. Lourdes and Coco had blocks on their telephones. Elaine had little tolerance for Jessica's sadness and complaining and requests for commissary money. The additional financial burden of Matthew and Michael was making it hard for her to cover her monthly bills, and her hard-won patience with her own sons was dissolving in the constant wash of the twins' needs. Matthew's ceaseless crying kept Elaine's sons up, so that they were cranky when it was time to get ready for school. Elaine became afraid that she would hurt Matthew and temporarily gave him to her downstairs neighbor. She was making arrangements to send them to Milagros.

Jessica wanted to return to the maximum-security unit, where there was less pressure to behave. She pursued the easiest way back—administrative segregation, the prison's version of solitary. Some inmates ironically referred to SHU, the secure housing unit, as "a vacation," because it removed them from the mix, and they could take pills and avoid work. Refusing a direct order was the ticket. So one evening, at count, Jessica remained in the TV room. She sat truculently on the couch in the summer version of her uniform: khaki shorts and a prison-issue shirt. She wore a baseball cap turned to the back.

"Count—you gotta go to your room," the officer said to Jessica.

"Yeah and what?" Jessica said. "Count me here. I don't want to go to my room." Of course, the defiance worked.

A guard escorted her to SHU. There, she vacillated between her choices: opting out or acting out. She wanted to escape, and she wanted to be noticed. Sadness was like falling; sleep was temporary; rage let her feel alive. She slept, then demanded to be screened for bipolar disorder, the diagnosis a doctor had given Robert following one of his suicide attempts. She sought oblivion through medication, which prison medics liberally provided—Naprosyn, Flerexil, Dolobid—and then fought against it. "They think I need to be kept in the fucking dark," she said resentfully. Imagining her reunion with Serena got her through the worst stretches, with a little help from the voices of the other isolated women on SHU harmonizing to old R&B. The songs lulled her to sleep.

CHAPTER TWENTY-SIX

Pearl joined her family in Corliss Park on Mother's Day, 1995. Milagros collected her from the Bronx and brought her up by Greyhound bus. She was nine months old, with a roaming eye and an oversize head. She was still attached to an oxygen tank; the tubing stuck into her teeny nostrils, which were usually encrusted with snot. She had bulbous eyes, like her grandmother Foxy, who suffered from a thyroid condition. Instead of conveying a distant sadness, though, Pearl's eyes were disconcertingly wise. Coco felt as though Pearl were trying to teach her a lesson, but Coco couldn't decipher it yet.

Pearl required at least three daily half-hour treatments on a nebulizer for her severe asthma. Crisis focused Coco's attention, so the more trouble Pearl had breathing, the better Coco responded. The distended hernia was Coco's signal to give Pearl a treatment; it was often the size of an apricot. Otherwise, Coco, overwhelmed already, ended up treating the asthma as she did so much else—haphazardly. Pearl's congested breathing came to seem normal, much like her constant vomiting. Coco was more consistent in her affection; she loved babies, and she played with Pearl for hours. She kissed the stitch marks traversing Pearl's stomach like the tracks of an angry bird.

But Pearl's fragility frightened Coco and she had to rely on Milagros more than she wanted to; Milagros, who had worked as a home aide, had nursing expertise. And although Milagros didn't ask for anything—except once in a while, when her food ran out, for food stamps—Coco's dependency incurred debts of other kinds. Coco resented the freedom with which Milagros now spoke her mind. It was no one else's business how Coco raised her kids. Even if Coco didn't have to take Milagros's advice, however, she had to hear her out.

Milagros's biggest complaint was Coco's softness toward Mercedes. If Mercedes didn't get her way, she sometimes muttered, "Shoo," or kicked Milagros, or told Milagros to shut up. Once, Milagros grabbed Mercedes by her collar, and Mercedes ran to her mother, indignant, clamoring that Milagros had hit her—no one but a mother had that right. But Milagros was resolute; no child was going to curse her, not in front of her other kids. After the spats, Coco kept Mercedes at home until Mercedes drove

Coco crazy. Milagros cautioned Coco about what she saw as an even larger problem: If Coco couldn't make a five-year-old respect and listen, what was going to happen when Mercedes was no longer a child?

From an early age, even before she was a toddler, Mercedes garnered attention for having attitude. A fog of despair so pervaded the ghetto that the smallest gesture of rebellion could seem like a bold, piercing light. *Bad*, said with fond exasperation, was almost always a compliment.

Babies who grunted with frustration at an uncle who intentionally scared them or who kicked when a cousin shadowboxed too close were bad. Bad meant the opposite of cowed or frightened—like Lil Hector, Coco's three-year-old nephew, when he tossed brand-new sneakers out of Foxy's window to summon his parents away from their weed-smoking friends. Bad was also behavior that amused teenagers and adults: little girls dancing sexy and talking about "getting mines"; little boys grabbing their own crotches or rubbing women's thighs; smart-mouthed toddlers using smart-ass words like *yo* and *ho* and *bitch* and *punk*. One of Nautica's first words was *puta*, and for a time, if she didn't get her way, she narrowed her eyes and spit.

Bad was encouraged in small children, but its meaning changed as they got older and their cuteness waned. Adults' impatience might have had something to do with the extra labor of caring for spirited children, and the looming realization that as the children grew in size, they could physically back their badness up. Whatever caused the sudden shift, it took children years to sort out the subtleties, as they learned by excruciating trial and error. Errors took place publicly, and humiliations were routine. For the early years of Mercedes's life, though, bad remained an affirmation.

Mercedes had long known the value of attitude, but she was coming to appreciate the power of telling Coco what she wanted to hear. Women tended to discourage older boys from gossip but routinely asked girls and younger children, "Who Daddy with?" Children were good sources of information because they were always hungry for attention. Mercedes had the important themes down—love and allegiance and betrayal—long before she developed a sense of proportion or the knack for connecting sequences. She eagerly tailored her stories to her mother's interest— intrigues concerning Cesar, revelations of neighbors' hypocrisy, dirt on Foxy's boyfriend Hernan, whom Coco still despised. Violence always worked as the dramatic lead: "Hernan smacked me." If Coco threatened to confront him, Mercedes retreated into nonsense songs. By the time she was five, Mercedes's tall stories had eroded her credibility in nearly all but Coco's eyes. Other people secretly called her nosy and bossy; among children her own age, she had difficulty making and keeping friends.

Neither did she get along with Frankie. Too many nights, Mercedes stomped to bed, screaming, "I want my father," raging until, exhausted, she fell asleep.

Coco longed for Cesar, too. One night, she lay next to Frankie on the blankets she had spread out on the floor of the living room. Pearl slept beside them, breathing congestedly. Frankie said quietly, "You don't love me."

"But there's so many different kinds of love," Coco replied. "You show me how you feel, we go playing, you treat my kids okay, I guess that's why I love you."

"Do you love me like the girls' father?" he asked.

"I can't. Like—I don't," she said. She later wondered if she should have lied. She hugged him. Her love for Cesar was something altogether different; for Frankie, she felt something more akin to gratitude.

"That's why I love you, Coco, you so open," Frankie said.

Coco said soberly, "That's cuz I been through fucking hell for twenty-one years old."

Upstate life temporarily freed Frankie from his reputation as a punk. In the city, he was an ordinary, small-time, part-time drug dealer, an employee, a bit of a schemer, a wanna-be. In Corliss Park, among the local white teenagers obsessed with inner-city culture, Frankie was a live representative. He took advantage of their adulation, boasting about his Bronx exploits and presenting himself as tougher than he really was. Coco warned him, "You better stop acting like Mr. Hercules. I'll be laughing when somebody beat your ass." But, for a time, Frankie's reputation covered what he lacked in actual power. He ran drugs up from the Bronx. He was what Coco called "the quiet type," not brassy and aggressive, less likely to draw attention from police.

The busier Frankie became, the less time he had for Coco and her girls. He joined Coco in bed late at night, long after she had fallen asleep. In the morning, he showered and ate and announced, "Ma, I'm leaving." He lost interest in playfighting. Soon enough, he stopped bringing dinner dishes to the sink. "Whenever he comes in the house, all he does is play that Sega," Coco said. Drugs changed boys, and Frankie was becoming less like the boy she'd settled for and more like other boys she knew. Coco needed help with the girls, but she didn't feel that she could demand it because they weren't his. She taunted him about leaving, though.

"Coco, one thing you aren't going to do is control my life. I'm not gonna be in lockdown," Frankie said. But people flocked to Frankie if he stayed indoors. The phone rang constantly. Cars idled in front of Coco's living room window, which overlooked the strip of the parking lot. Boys stuck their heads inside her door:

Frankie in?

He home?

Where he at?

Coco knew it wasn't good to have boys hanging out in her apartment, but she grew bored stuck home with the children alone. She tried imposing house rules. She shooed her company outdoors to smoke their cigarettes and weed because of Pearl's asthma, but the neighbors complained about the noise. She let the boys smoke upstairs, in Mercedes's bedroom, as long as they opened the window and shut the door. But when Mercedes returned home from school she would complain about the smell and the mess they left, making a ruckus until Coco shooed them outside again. Rick Mason, the head of security for Troy's public housing, also brooded over what was going on at Coco's: he regularly drove through Corliss Park and slowed down as he passed the cluster of dejected boys who often stood on Coco's three-by-three-foot porch. Four months after moving into her apartment, Coco received an eviction notice citing violation of the long-term-guest clause of her lease.

On the walls of a converted room of the Victorian house occupied by the Troy Housing Authority, photographs hung of derelict houses renovated, broken homes now fixed. Coco's eviction hearing convened in an old living room that still had a fireplace. Beneath the eighteen-foot ceilings, Coco looked especially short. The ears of her recent bunny tattoo peeked above the neckline of her short-sleeved striped shirt. She'd dressed the girls neatly and styled their hair in tiny nested buns. Coco hunched over at the end of the long conference table, clutching Pearl on her lap like a shield.

Rick Mason sat by a suited housing administrator at the other end. Coco recognized Mason from his frequent laps of Corliss Park. She gulped out her explanation before the hearing opened, falling back on the same story used by hundreds of women in public housing before her— no man lived in the house, it was just her and her children. She was so anxious about getting evicted that the urgency of her explanation sounded worse than the truth. She said Frankie visited every day from the city—three hours, each way—but never spent the night.

"Is he employed?" the administrator asked.

"Um, no."

"That must be pretty expensive," he remarked. "Coming up from the city every day."

Coco had to be careful not to say anything that would threaten Frankie's monthly Social Security check; she wasn't really sure why he was eligible for it, but she knew that it was how he got by. And if he lost his SSI, his mother risked losing her subsidized apartment in the Bronx, where he was still registered as a dependent.

Luckily, the Troy Housing administrator prattled on with the questions Coco expected. Frankie's address. Whether he had friends in Troy. Had he fathered any of her kids? Coco emphasized Frankie's restriction to her porch. The administrator seemed unconcerned; the hearing was the first step of a longer process, and he was bored. "You are going to be sure to tell him that if he comes to Corliss Park, he will be arrested," said the administrator perfunctorily. All that was left was the paperwork.

Throughout the hearing, Rick Mason waited, his muscular arms folded across his well-pumped chest, leaning back in his chair like a smart-aleck boy in a boring class. "Is it my turn?" he finally asked.

Mason knew about drugs firsthand; he'd had a serious cocaine problem when he was younger. He had also grown up in Troy public housing; he and his mother and seven siblings had moved into Troy's high-rise Taylor Homes after his father died. Mason credited public assistance with saving his broken family. He believed that girls like Coco and their children deserved chances they weren't going to get otherwise. Over the last few years, he'd watched, with some amusement and plenty of pride, the excitement with which the new arrivals from New York and Puerto Rico greeted the ordinary public housing apartments he patrolled. But Troy was bankrupt; industry had fled, and local politicians had used a HUD grant intended for public housing to bring the city a hockey team. Now drugs were wrecking what was left of his embattled hometown. His son and a brother were Troy police officers, and they'd told him about the drugs coming up from Brooklyn and the Bronx. He didn't blame boys like Frankie for Troy's problems, but Mason was a pragmatist, and the drug dealers were identifiable targets.

He looked directly at Coco and spoke; he was neither rude nor friendly. "There are people constantly in and out. I've gone over there and knocked on the door. You were not there and your children were not there. There is your boyfriend, and all his little friends, in and out of the house. Tell me, what's going on? I go to the door and an old man in an undershirt opens the door. There are little kids all over the place. Tell me what's going on."

"He doesn't stay in the house," Coco lied. "He stayed outside, on the porch."

"Don't tell me what I did see and didn't see. I was there, and you weren't."

"I don't know what you mean, an old man in his underwear. Frankie don't even be in his underwear," she said nervously. The fight for the lease was momentarily forgotten. Mason had waged the most hurtful allegation anyone could—that she wasn't protecting her children.

Mason's voice rose. "There were all kinds of people in and out, in and out, and your boyfriend, sitting on that lawn chair like he was the big king of the castle. We may not be from the Bronx, but we ain't stupid," he said. "Your kids shouldn't be exposed to that, and neither should other people's kids."

The administrator interrupted, eager to conclude: "Do you understand now, is it agreed, that should he come on the premises, he will be arrested? Will you sign a statement agreeing to that effect?"

Mason continued, "Because if I see him around there, he's going to be arrested."

Coco agreed to sign an interim contract, which would be effective for eight months. She promised that she had no other tenants besides her and the girls. If all went well, she would return to a regular lease.

The administrator arranged his papers and packed up, saying, "Now, we don't want to have any more trouble. Life is hard enough without getting evicted." His eyes darted over Mercedes and Nikki and Nautica, their backs pressed against big kelly-green chairs lining the wall, their legs sticking straight out; they looked scared. He added, "And you have your hands full."

"Mommy?" Nikki croaked.

Mason rose and offered Coco his hand. "There are enough good men in Troy to keep you outta trouble. He's gotta stay out."

The first thing Coco did when she got back to Corliss Park was drag the lawn chair to the sidewalk and dump it in the garbage. Then she marched straight to Family Dollar. Mercedes wheeled Pearl's oxygen. Coco bought several packages of decorative white picket-fence pieces, trooped back to Corliss Park, in no mood for nonsense, and shoved them in her lawn. She clamped a bouquet of plastic red and yellow flowers to one of the ankle-high picket-fence posts and waited for Frankie to come home, so she could tell him that he had to go.

Frankie didn't last in the Bronx. He later confided to Coco that he had felt displaced at his mother's house. His younger brother had claimed his old bedroom. His mother, who worked part-time for a bookie, did not approve of sons whose nights extended through to afternoons on her couch. Outdoors, he risked encountering people he owed money to: Octavio, the drug spot manager; Delilah, the loan shark; the mothers of his two kids. He returned to Troy. After several furtive nights at Coco's, he started spending most of his time with some friends who stayed in a rickety second-floor tenement on Second Avenue, near River Street.

The apartment served as a hangout and a stash house for crack arriving from the Bronx. They dealt out of the Phoenix Hotel, using a room that had been rented by a crackhead. Business was great. The gram that brought $30 in the city brought in $100 in Troy, and they could unload fake product because upstate customers were easier to intimidate and dupe. "There are a lot of dummies up here," said Frankie. "In the city, they ain't playing that."

But the pace of dealing crack was too much for Frankie—"Too *fast*," he said, "too fast, it like gets you scared." He was constantly coming up short, and he was also lousy at collecting debts; overdue addict accounts, even in Troy, required threats and the occasional beat-down. His languid personality was better suited to dealing weed.

So he started dealing weed out of the Second Avenue apartment, where he split the bills with another recent Bronx transplant and two white boys, who opened the flimsy door to a shifting collection of bored friends, acquaintances, and customers. Frankie had been smoking weed so long that he could estimate the weight of a bag by sight. He wasn't ambitious; he mainly wanted to earn enough to keep himself in smoke. He went weeks without going to the city, then might go every day for a week. He sometimes took the bus, but the police occasionally patrolled the buses and the stations; he preferred his local teenage customers to drive. The teenagers relished the opportunity to go to the inner city on a mission evocative of—albeit more unsettling and less exciting than— those adventures depicted in rap videos on TV. The white boys provided Frankie with a cover—their cars were less likely to be stopped on the Thruway. The ride was also more comfortable than the bus, and they didn't ask for contributions for tolls or gas.

What Frankie loved most about his new arrangement, however, was the freedom. He'd lived under women's rules most of his life. Now, at twenty-four, he blasted music at any hour—not Coco's slow jams, but rap, much of it hard-core, which Coco forbade. On Second Avenue, there were lots of abandoned houses, and the people who lived there rarely called the cops for small disturbances. He could watch his pornography whenever he felt like it. Baseball games weren't interrupted by Mercedes's whining for cartoons. There were fewer reminders of all the people he was letting down. The best things about his relationship with Coco continued much as before. Only their intimate life quieted.

He still showered at her apartment, because his roommates left the bathroom a mess. He ate at Coco's when his ulcer flared up from all the greasy pizza and microwave cheeseburgers. But Coco was usually asleep whenever he surprised her at night, and stealing privacy during daylight with four children was impossible. In the morning, if he managed to pull her into the shower, Mercedes would be pounding on the bathroom door before they'd even kissed. Even without interruptions, the situation was fraught; when Frankie told Coco that she was beautiful, she'd start crying. She had been picking her face and arms and the reachable parts of her back.

Pearl's illness flattened Coco. Frankie no longer accompanied her on the merry-go-round of doctor appointments, and she couldn't manage the long waits alone with a baby, a toddler, and two kids. Just taking the bus was risky because Nautica was prone to tantrums and Coco's hands were full with Pearl and her portable oxygen tank. Sometimes Mercedes would fall asleep so deeply that she couldn't be politely roused.

Frankie had to be badgered to stay home with more than two. Nor could Coco burden Milagros too frequently because Milagros now had Jessica's baby boys, and Matthew and Michael were fearful and clingy. When Milagros did watch the girls, Mercedes and Brittany and Stephanie got into fights, so Mercedes always ended up accompanying Coco.

Coco never had enough money for a taxi. Money was tight. Frankie generally kept his earnings to himself. Coco had to make $10 last the three weeks from the day she did her grocery shopping until the end of the month; Pearl had been approved for Social Security income for her disabilities, but the checks hadn't yet been transferred. The girls still needed coats and beds. Coco would say, "I know these ain't your kids, Frankie, but you ain't helping out in any way." For a spell, Frankie would pass along food stamps given to him by one of his customers. But Coco always needed—comfort, Pampers, milk.

Mercedes started combing through Frankie's pockets for spare change when he was in the shower or sleeping. One night, a glassine of crack fell out, and she brought it to her mother; Frankie claimed he'd picked it up when another dealer had tossed it, midchase, while running from cops. Coco secretly wondered if Frankie was using. Something was also up with Mercedes; she complained constantly that her teeth were hurting her, and by the end of November 1995, she was taking up to five baths a day.

Coco shared her frustrations about Frankie with anyone who would listen. She urged Serena to recognize what was going on beneath appearances. "He look like he haven't changed, he be all nice and sweet, but he has changed," Coco said. But Frankie did look changed. In fact, he looked terrific. His posture had improved. His shirts no longer sagged. Somehow his eyelids had quit drooping. His face shone from fresh shaving; his sneakers were brand-new. Coco noted wryly, "You more fly."

"For real?" Frankie responded, mistaking the hard nut of assessment for a compliment.

In December, just as Coco was reaching her breaking point, Frankie brought his son up from the city for an extended visit and left the child with Coco. She began to suspect that Frankie wanted her stuck in the house, saddled with the kids. Coco had never considered him a player, but neither had she known him to be popular, and now he was. She dispatched Mercedes, with Frankie's son, to investigate. They spent a day at the stash house. Aside from some gossip, Mercedes had little to report. Coco visited the apartment unannounced, bearing food. "I don't want you starving. Whatever goes on between us, you have to eat," she said disarmingly.

Half-dressed white girls, the wives and friends of Frankie's friends, lounged on the old couch, knobby legs holding up their chins. They struck Coco as shameless—parading around in nothing but oversize T-shirts not only in front of Mercedes, but in front of their husbands' friends. White boys did not seem to mind their girls' obvious disrespect. Coco heard they gave up sex easily. Boys didn't have to buy Troy girls Pampers or milk or let the girls keep the change for cigarettes. Coco didn't barter, either, but she allied herself with the demeanor of the Bronx.

Even though Coco had been the one to tell Frankie to leave, she felt that he'd abandoned her. She blamed Rick Mason and castigated the Troy Housing Authority. She fantasized about returning to the Bronx. In the meantime, Frankie prospered and hung framed prints of his favorite pro wrestlers in the stash-house living room. He assured her that the arrangement was only temporary, but when he signed up for cable, Coco believed he'd never come home.

In the meantime, Mercedes had continued to complain about her toothaches, and she was still taking lots of baths; Coco brought her to the clinic. The dentist said that five of her teeth were rotten and needed to be removed; the doctor diagnosed Mercedes with genital warts. He explained that he had to notify BCW. Coco was devastated. Mercedes had always had warts, ever since she was a little girl, but the pediatrician in the Bronx had never treated it as a problem. Suddenly, this doctor was saying that her daughter might have been molested. Although there were other possible explanations, now that the suspicion had been voiced, Coco assumed the worst.

The sexual threat men posed to little girls was so pervasive that even the warnings meant to avert it were saturated with fatalism. For the mothers of girls, this threat hung over the whole of life, like a low cover of dread; it was one of the more commonly given reasons why expectant parents wanted boys. Good mothers didn't go from man to man not only because promiscuity was frowned upon, but also because protecting children meant limiting the number of men that passed through a house. The rules sounded clear if you listened to what people said: never leave your girls alone with a man who wasn't blood. In practice, however, that expectation was unrealistic, and women frequently failed to meet it: a neighbor would mind a baby while the mother made an emergency visit to the hospital; a sister would need to run to the store and her brother's friend would watch her niece; a friend would offer to keep an eye on the kids to give an exhausted woman a break; children often stayed awake long after their mothers fell asleep. And all of this was further complicated if adults were drinking and using drugs.

Coco believed she was vigilant. From their infancy, she'd admonished her girls to keep their legs closed and to stay off men's laps. She never let them go away with strangers but, given her profound insecurities and the fluid kinship relationships on which she depended, it was impossible—and sometimes rude—to draw a hard line between who was like family and who was not. A lifetime assault of contradictory messages—to be sexy, to respect, that all men were dogs but that without them women were nothing—reinforced her sense of powerlessness and futility. In a sense, Coco had been both fighting this eventuality and waiting for it all her life, so that now her guilt and failure trumped the very real question of whether the abuse had actually happened or not. Mercedes's own confusion showed during her examination with the doctor: her mother had always told her not to let a man touch her. The doctor had to bribe her with a lollipop.

Cesar had been transferred to Sing Sing. Coco felt that she had to tell him immediately, and in person. Foxy agreed to watch Nikki and Pearl. Coco, Mercedes, and Nautica took the train to Ossining.

Coco was frightened. She hadn't been able to sleep the night before. In the visiting room, she approached a guard who stood at a podium. She explained to him about Mercedes's warts and said, "I don't know how my husband will take it." He moved her to a table nearer him. Coco pulled Nautica onto her lap. "Don't tell Daddy, Mercy," Coco said.

"Why?" Mercedes asked.

"If Daddy gets mad, they will keep him in jail longer," Coco said. Mercedes moved into the empty chair facing the officer. "Move here, Mercy, that chair's for the inmate," she added.

"What's an inmate?" Mercedes asked.

"The person that's in jail. Naughty, take the gum out your mouth." Nautica refused. "Naughty, take the gum out and Daddy will take you to play in the playroom," Coco tried. She spotted Cesar. "Mercy, Naughty—Daddy," she whispered. Nautica clambered off her and ran after her sister. One on each arm, Cesar carried his daughters back to the table. Mercedes settled on his lap. Nautica tugged him toward the playroom. "You want to sit on Daddy's lap?" Cesar asked Nautica. Nautica smiled bashfully. "Naughty, you wanna sit on Daddy's lap?" he asked again. She declined. "Aw, all right then," he said, hurt. He faked a punch to her belly.

"Mercedes," Coco said, and sucked in her breath. She didn't pause after that: "You know the warts on her that she had from the time I wrote you in Harlem Valley when Mercy was a baby? Well, down here, they never paid them no mind. But up there? They real strict, right, Mercy? They look hard into everything. I went to the doctor and they said somebody was messing with her, and on Monday she's going to have a physical because she has to have one before they get removed, but they got BCW and everyone involved, and I have to find out from the hospital down here to get the records from how old she was. The only two people she was left with was my mother and your mother, and your mother says it might be Richie, but if he was going to do something, he would have done it to me and my sister. . . ."

Cesar stared at Coco; Mercedes looked at her mother, then turned up to her father, then turned back to her mother again. Coco finished and smiled dumbly.

"You find something funny?" Cesar said icily.

"No."

"What so funny then?"

"Nothing." Coco didn't know why she smiled.

"You finished?" he said impatiently. She nodded. "We'll talk about this later," he said, then reached for his daughters' hands. They spent the rest of the visit in the children's room. They built houses with bright blocks and ate the plastic food Nautica served them on dishes she washed in a plastic sink. They played dominoes. He gave them pony rides so fast that between the bumps and the laughter they couldn't catch their breath.

Back in the Bronx, Coco stopped by Lourdes's to report what had happened, but Lourdes was "all into her business." Coco next tried Elaine, who was down the block, visiting her mother-in-law. Coco hollered up to the window and Elaine and her family met her in the lobby. Mercedes was hungry, so Elaine's husband, Angel, went off to get french fries. Since the last time Coco had seen her, Elaine had put on a lot of weight. She'd returned to school. She and Angel were having problems. The children started a game of tag. Elaine asked Coco how she was. Whole minutes passed before Coco could stop crying enough to be able to speak. "Don't you think if Richie woulda done it, that he would have done it to me and my sister?" she asked.

"It never happened in your family," Elaine said quietly. "It never happened in your family," she repeated, her voice getting firm. "It happened in my family. I said to my mother, 'Mom, if it happened in our family, and the only place the baby was, was with our family and her family, don't you think that it means it probably happened in our family?' She said she never left the baby with her boyfriend except for when she went to the store. And you know my mother, Coco. She wasn't at the store for no five, ten minutes. Forty-five minutes every time. 'And who gave the girls a bath while you were cooking? And who went to liit the girls to go to bed? And who stayed with the girls when you went to the store?' My mother just cried."

Coco cried during the ride back to Foxy's. Mercedes and Nautica watched her silently. Coco's thoughts returned to something Elaine had said about Jessica—how Jessica didn't do anything when the doctor discovered Serena's abuse. Elaine had emphasized the point. "She chose to not hear. She *chose* it. But you are doing something about it, Coco. You are trying to find out," Elaine had said. It also touched Coco that in the eight years she'd known Elaine, it was the first time Elaine had ever given her a hug.

Back at Sing Sing, after Coco's visit, Cesar trashed his cell. "It was mad dark. It was deep," a friend said. "I ain't never seen Cesar like that." Cesar tore up his letters and ripped apart his books. He shredded his clothes and his bedsheets. He destroyed everything he owned but the photographs. The guards let him be.

Coco told everybody she spoke to in the Bronx that day about what she believed had happened to Mercedes—neighbors, cousins, Rocco's wife—as though the craziness she felt could find relief by raising the general level of alarm. She also told them so she could anticipate their judgment, receive their comfort, and assuage her guilt. Mercedes pulled Coco aside: "Why you telling everybody for?" Mercedes seemed humiliated, but her mood improved as soon as she got back to Corliss Park. The following day, she told Stephanie and Brittany that she had been abused and bragged that she'd gotten to miss a day of school and spent the whole day playing with her dad—an unexpected treat.

That evening, the girls trooped upstairs to the bathroom; since her trip to the dentist, Mercedes had anointed herself the family dental czar. She lorded over the bathroom sink, above her smaller sisters, dispensing toothpaste generously. Nikki closed the lid of the toilet, climbed up, and placed one foot on the rim of the sink. Like an accomplished general, she turned the water on—blasting—with her toes.

"*I* brush my teeth at night," Mercedes boasted. More softly, she whispered, "Naughty don't." Nautica, who had several rotten teeth herself, preferred to play with the dolls beside the bathtub. Mercedes, still full of her day with Cesar, dedicated a song in his honor.

"'This is the song I sing at night, when I cry for my dad," she said solemnly, launching into R. Kelly's "I Believe."

"Me, too! I cry for my dad at night," Nikki added.

But Mercedes was the chosen one. She saw her father more often, and he always sent letters and pictures and birthday cards. All Nikki had from Kodak were some outfits he'd surprised her with for her last birthday. Lately, whenever Mercedes received yet another letter from Cesar, Nikki asked, "Mommy, why my daddy don't write?"

As Mercedes belted out the blues, Nikki tried to join in, but when Mercedes hushed her, Nikki retreated to her room. She took the crimson velvet skirt her father had sent her out of the closet gently and smoothed an imperceptible wrinkle. With her free hand, she reached for a dog-eared photograph curled on top of her broken TV. It was a picture of her with her mother. Every day, Nikki carried the picture with her to school. In it, Nikki was a baby, sleeping blissfully in Coco's arms. Coco, whose eyes were also closed, rested her chin on Nikki's head.

Nikki pressed the picture to her chest. She pulled out Mercedes's pink satin first-birthday dress and twirled around the room, watched by her bedraggled dolls. "I'm always a prin-cess, I'm always a prin-cess," Nikki sang softly to herself.

Unlike other people's children, whose sicknesses seemed low-grade and intermittent, Coco's girls' conditions now seemed to alternate between serious and extremely serious. Mercedes was uncomfortable and disconcertingly quiet; Pearl vomited constantly—sometimes ten times in a day. Coco tried letting Pearl scoot around in just a T-shirt and diaper, but Pearl kept catching cold; the apartment was drafty, and Mercedes and Nikki and Brittany and Stephanie were always running in and out of the house. Pearl still needed three asthma treatments a day, and there were plenty of times that Coco didn't have a chance to change her clothes until the other children were going to bed. Even when Pearl wasn't attached to her oxygen, she required more supervision than Coco was accustomed to in a toddler—more than Nautica, who, at two, was still tripping and banging into things.

One morning in mid-January, while Coco was taking a quick shower, Mercedes broke into the bathroom, screaming, "Something's wrong with the baby!" Pearl had turned blue. Coco ran Pearl over to Milagros. As Milagros administered CPR, Coco froze. Milagros coaxed Coco, who was shaking uncontrollably, to phone the ambulance. Milagros watched Coco's other children until Coco and Pearl returned home from the hospital. Then, in February, Mercedes suffered from a recurrence of the warts; Coco would wake up in the middle of the night to pee, or to take Nautica to the bathroom, and she'd discover her daughter asleep in the now-cold tub.

Even after Mercedes had the warts removed, Coco couldn't stop crying. She cried over the segment of *Sally Jessy Raphael* in which a teenage girl acted snotty to her mother. She wept when another guest left her baby with the child's father and claimed her back after six hard years. She cried over the happy stories, the sad ones, for the girls who were angry, or stupid with love. She wondered if she was having a nervous breakdown. She said, "Everything, God, I'm sure I cry." She picked the skin on her face until it bled. Nikki started to mimic her. Coco begged her not to and looked in the mirror and interrogated herself: "Why I pick my face? Why do I have this bad habit? I wonder, did my father have this bad habit? How come I'm the one that got it?"

One afternoon, when Frankie passed through, Coco read to him from a brochure from a sleepover camp. Camp Ramapo was a country camp for at-risk children, and Coco was considering sending Mercedes and Nikki. She thought they were too young to be away for three weeks, but she also wanted to get them out of the house, away from all the arguing. She had fond memories of her own experiences as a camper with the Fresh Air Fund.

Coco felt self-conscious reading aloud to Frankie. When he chuckled at her halting pronunciation, she broke down in tears.

"Damn, Coco," he asked, "you crying again?"

Coco's despondency unsettled even Milagros. Milagros gave little thought to her kids' appearance—she just aimed to keep them clothed and fed—but Coco had always been vain about the girls' looks, and now she seemed not to notice their mismatched outfits and sloppy hair. Mercedes and Nikki were also missing school; in the mornings, Milagros would send Serena over to Coco's to make sure they were awake. One morning, Pearl's health aide could not rouse Coco despite hearty pounding on the door. She scolded her later for sleeping through Pearl's treatment and threatened to call BCW.

Foxy made an emergency visit. Ordinarily, Coco cleaned her house top to bottom for company, but now she trailed her mother through the mess. Coco said, "You don't know what it's like, I cry for you every day up here, Mommy. I miss you so much." When Foxy left, she took Nautica back to the Bronx for a week, to relieve some of the pressure.

Coco's sister, Iris, suggested Coco see a therapist. "With all Pearl's appointments, you think I got time for another appointment?" Coco asked derisively. Increasingly, Coco's hopes for relief hinged on Frankie. His absence had enhanced his appeal; without his companionship, his willingness to baby-sit, and the little extras his cash made possible, life was lonely and grim. "Every cab pulls up flashes in my window and I get excited, and then it's not him, and I get so upset," she said. Coco's playfulness had disappeared, and her children hovered close. Nikki repeatedly assured her she was pretty. Mercedes kept a sober vigil by her side.

Then Coco received the $1,734 back payment for Pearl's disability income and decorated the apartment. She bought furniture and a large-screen TV from the white lady next door, who was leaving Corliss Park. The burnt-orange-and-brown velveteen couch was just like the one

Lourdes used to have back when Coco had met Cesar, but the rest of Coco's inherited decor was green and pink, with a cow theme. She was glad to have a coordinated style to her apartment, even if it wasn't her own: the cow mobile, cow cookie jar, and cow utensil holder matched the cow wallpaper trim. The trim bubbled slightly because the lady had ripped it from her wall, but Coco hammered it in to make it stick.

She tacked up green polyester curtains, a green straw fan beside her print of the Last Supper, and another beside a print of an elegant black panther in midleap. She placed a picture in a frame Iris had made from Popsicle sticks and papered the wall of the dining room with photographs. There were several of Jessica and her friends.

Frankie came back to the newly hooked-up apartment shortly afterward. Coco wanted to think his homecoming came from one of her many ultimatums—that he stop dealing—but he was having trouble covering his rent. His mother had also had a dream that he was going to get locked up or hurt. It seemed like a good time to take a break.

Frankie's hiatus from selling drugs wasn't unusual. The low-level jobs of the drug trade resembled other low-level jobs: employees got laid off with fluctuations in the shipments or the business; or they got bored and restless; or hopeless, just as they did in Troy's few remaining factories. Technically, Frankie was still forbidden from living with Coco but, luckily, trouble elsewhere granted Coco a reprieve. Rick Mason had turned his attention from Corliss Park to Fallon Apartments, the housing project where Iris and her family now lived.

Without work or much weed to distract him, Frankie grew possessive. He noticed Coco checking out Large, a neighbor, another dealer, who parked his car in a space outside her front door.

"What you putting lipstick on for?" Frankie asked.

"Cuz I don't want to be pale," she said smugly.

"Pull the shade," he snapped. The interrogations multiplied. Why did she wear tight clothes to appointments and baggy clothes around the house with him? Why did she have kids with other guys and not him? Coco agreed that the situation wasn't ideal: "I finally got a relationship and I don't wanna have a baby. And then when I was dealing with them, I wasn't in a relationship and I had them. So it's weird." But she also understood that she could not manage another child, not just yet, even though she still wanted a boy.

Fortunately, Pearl bolstered Frankie's sense of belonging. He was always lifting her up and cuddling her. He would administer her asthma treatments and let Coco rest. Some nights, Pearl slept on his chest so he would wake up if she couldn't breathe. But he was reluctant to baby-sit all the girls, even when he had nothing else to do. At least now that the weather was warmer, Coco could bundle Pearl in a towel and escape to Milagros's. Serena wheeled the oxygen tank. Milagros placed Pearl near Matthew and Michael, whom she'd set up on a sheet laid out on the floor. Coco and Milagros would watch TV and play cards and gossip. At some point, Frankie would poke his sullen face inside Milagros's door. "Coco, come home," he'd say.

"I'm here," she'd say.

"Coco, cook, I'm hungry already."

"You had your fun, now I'm having mine," she answered, but her resolve would already be weakening.

After Frankie left, Milagros would say, "I got to give you credit. For a young mother, you do good. You don't just leave."

Coco sighed. "Where I'm supposed to go?"

One afternoon, Frankie surprised Coco and invited her to play a game of football. She barreled upstairs to change. She had not been outdoors for four days. But by the time she came back downstairs, he'd already gone. She pushed open the door to the porch: he was halfway down the block, headed toward the basketball courts, surrounded by his friends.

Mercedes ran up to her mother. "Can I go with Frankie? Ma?" Mercedes asked breathlessly. Her hair looked fantastically wild; strings of curls had sprung free from her ponytail. Her face was flushed with excitement. Coco turned from her and stared after Frankie in the distance.

"Ma?" Mercedes repeated. "*Ma!*"

"I don't know what you want to go for, he ain't going to let your ass play," Coco said. Mercedes sprinted toward the boys, wove her way to Frankie, and reached for his hand.

"Don't think I need you! With Pearl's check at the beginning of the month, I got enough to pay my bills by myself!" Coco shouted, watching her man and her daughter walking into the first hole of spring.

CHAPTER TWENTY-SEVEN

As Coco's situation continued to unravel, Jessica was attempting to piece her life together. "My little girl's getting breasts, I gotta get out soon," Jessica said. That January 1996, she had transferred to the residential unit of the prison's Drug Abuse Program, DAP. Graduates earned a full year off their prison term. Access to social service programs, inside or outside of prison, wasn't always based on need, nor was the access logical: the inconsistencies and red tape tried everyone's stamina, clients and staff alike. The arbitrary nature of bureaucratic processing led many poor people to approach government assistance as another state-sponsored lottery.

Jessica had never had a drug addiction, but she qualified as an "inmate in need of recovery," which turned out to be a stroke of luck. Before she was sentenced, she'd been interviewed by a probation officer for her biographical profile for her pre-sentence report. During the interview, Jessica had admitted that she'd used weed and cocaine socially. She had also used coke to lose weight when George thought she was getting fat. The mere mention of the drug use, which the probation officer had jotted down, gave Jessica a chance to acquire practical skills that would substantially improve her prospects.

Compared to her lolling prison routine, DAP resembled boot camp. Guards strictly enforced dress codes. They barred the geometric designs that women ironed onto their khakis to individualize their uniforms. Morning meditation launched weekdays. Meetings and themes and acronyms—NA, AA, SMART—organized the week. Each resident acquired a designated buddy, with whom she had to write a report on their required conversation about the week's chosen recovery theme. DAP convened community meetings, group meetings, and individual counseling sessions.

DAP required five hundred hours of therapy and education in five areas—Thinking Skills, Communication Skills, Criminal Thinking, Relapse Prevention, and Wellness. Just as she had in Florida, Jessica responded enthusiastically. She said her favorite class, Feelings, helped the most. She seemed interested in examining the connections between the present and her memories of the past. She became animated about subjects other than love, and even somewhat curious. She said, "So much

258

chunks of my childhood has been erased, I guess cuz of the trauma and everything." It was hard to tell if her new confidence stemmed from having absorbed anything useful or simply from having become part of a new culture of recovery, with its terminology and sense of legitimacy; either way, she seemed better than she'd been in years. "The way I see it," she said, "in co-dependency you re-create your parents' problems."

Jessica came to believe that her exposure to Lourdes's abusive boyfriends had caused her to confuse love with violence. She remained loyal to George, with whom she was still in touch, but she grew publicly less protective of him. And she blamed herself less. She began to discuss scary memories, such as the times George played Russian roulette with a gun to Jessica's forehead. After she realized that the gun was loaded, she figured that "the bullet wouldn't hurt me because I was so numb from fear."

Yet she resisted categorizing herself as a victim of domestic violence; she felt that the dynamic between them was much more complicated than the analysis allowed. She preferred to remember what George had given her, rather than what he'd taken; and she'd also been rotten to him. To deny George's goodness or to downplay his generosity and guidance—to the authorities, no less—ran counter to her personal code. "Take it like a woman," Lourdes had told her after she was arrested. "You can walk clearly in the streets."

Jessica was also reevaluating her behavior as a parent. She wrote Serena that there was nothing Serena could say that Jessica hadn't felt herself: anger that Jessica was incarcerated, anger that she had put herself in a position to get arrested in the first place, longing for her own mother, crying in bed at night. She assured Serena that it was okay to hate her and not write back.

But while Jessica attempted to address the problems of the past, new problems intruded. Coco wrote Jessica about what was going on with Mercedes, and Jessica was flooded by memories of her own and Serena's abuse. Suddenly, her newfound faith in the value of self-examination felt far more tenuous, and old habits began to reassert themselves. Six weeks into the program, on Valentine's Day, she allowed an amorous couple to use her top bunk for a moment of privacy. Inmate couples violated DAP's guidelines, and someone in the unit snitched.

Characteristically, Jessica protected the guilty couple, but the director interrogated the women individually, and one of the lovers caved in; Jessica could tell by the shamed look on the girl's face as she left the director's office following the interview. Jessica glared at her.

The confessor said, "You know, Jessica, I don't like to fight."

Instead of backing off, Jessica blew up. "I'm not asking you if you like to fight," she said heatedly. "You just better be ready to protect yourself from the blows when they come." Jessica had already received a strike for her role in the rendezvous, and another for keeping the secret to herself. "STRIKE," the memo read. "Ms. Martinez received a strike today for enabling a physical relationship on the unit. It was her responsibility to come forward and she did not." Now she had earned a third: threatening to assault. She was thrown out of the program. She had also forfeited the year off her prison term.

Jessica changed from the standard khakis into a bright orange jumpsuit. Her loyalty had earned her a three-week stint in SHU. The segregated housing unit denied inmates all privileges, including personal property. An officer locked Jessica in a bare cell. Jessica had snuck in two favorite photographs, glued back to back, which she kept in the plastic frame that held her prison ID. On one side were the twins in pink satin dresses. On the other was Serena, grinning broadly in Jessica's lap. The photograph had been taken during the prison visit in Florida. Serena wore a red, white, and blue outfit, with her hair in a French braid. It was one of the few pictures of Serena in which her happiness outshone the worry. Between the two pictures, Jessica had tucked a four-leaf clover. The clover had been given to her by Tamika, her old girlfriend from Florida, who had plucked it from the prison yard at the beginning of her bid; Tamika had then passed it along to Jessica the night before she got out.

Jessica lay on the thin mattress. She flipped the photograph over and over, her daughters' faces tumbling, like a puzzle she couldn't crack. She comforted herself by telling herself stories about the life she longed for, rather than the one she had.

Jessica emerged from segregation with a reassignment to the general population and a stack of mail: she'd placed a personal ad in a newspaper and now had lots of pen pals from all over the country. One of her most interesting correspondents claimed to be an attorney, who lived in the same town as Cesar's latest prison—Elmira, New York. There was also an eight-page letter from Cesar's buddy, her ex-love, Tito; Tito had been transferred to Sing Sing, where he was serving twenty-five to life on the murder charge. She received a note from Big Daddy, her favorite stepfather, who reported that Lourdes had rejected his recent invitation to the Poconos. Jessica also received a letter from the locked-up son of a fellow inmate, who'd been inspired to write because he'd been looking through his pictures and was reminded of how fine she looked. Her older brother, Robert, mailed a homemade computer-generated greeting, tucked in with another Jehovah's Witness brochure. There were belated Valentine's Day notes from her daughters, including one from Serena, with hand-drawn hearts and a computerized unicorn. Serena had gotten two F's in school: "I couldn't bleive it, But I am doing better now."

Amazon, Jessica's inmate friend who practiced Santeria, offered Jessica a free consultation in honor of her upcoming birthday. They met in Jessica's unit after evening count. Amazon had visions of Serena: "She's going to run away. You're never gonna see her again." She still saw Serena running even with Jessica free.

Jessica's twenty-eighth birthday fell on a cold day in March. Her friends started her special day with a corsage made of Tootsie Pops. One pinned it onto her uniform, while another handed her a bouquet snatched from the desk of a guard. During her shift in the kitchen, Jessica spotted her friends sneaking out contraband—tomatoes in pockets, peppers behind books, onions tucked into waistbands. They prepared her favorite chilikida—crushed Doritos, cheese, peppers, onions, tomatoes, and chilies together, mixed with water, zapped in the microwave. They baked a cake.

But Jessica could not shake Amazon's prophecy, and she tracked the older woman down for a follow-up. Jessica believed in Amazon's visionary powers. Before she'd fallen in love with Torres, Amazon had predicted that Jessica would give birth to two children fathered by a man in a uniform. This time, Amazon saw another man. This new one would be tall and strong. "He would complete me," Jessica said in the same dreamy voice she used whenever she described the early days with Boy George. Amazon told Jessica that this new man would make her feel love as she had never known it, and Amazon envisioned Jessica's belly growing again.

Jessica was back in therapy. Throughout the spring, the doctor noted her progress:

> . . . Ms. Martinez presents as angry and seems to deal with frustration by acting out those feelings. She reports cursing people out as well as having frequently beaten people up while on the outside. She says it provides her with a sense of pleasure and satisfaction to see the person suffer as she feels they have made her suffer. Inmate reports a history of suicide attempts

(9 times) and says the only reason that she is alive today is because of her children particularly her ten-year-old daughter. Appears to have borderline features with a narcissistic bent.

Inmate . . . discussed the sexual abuse she received from her stepfather which occurred over a period of many years. She had a great deal of anger toward him and her mother who she felt did not protect her or provide her with the nurturance that she needed. She again repeated that the only time she feels alive is when she is feeling pain. . . . We agreed to meet again and begin work in the workbook *The Courage to Heal.*

Presenting problem: Explosive rage reactions, long-term depression, unresolved issues of sexual abuse.

The doctor also noted a pattern: Jessica's emotions were extreme at the beginning of the sessions, but visibly improved after even the briefest of talks.

Again and again, Jessica returned to her "lack of trust in others and a deep-seated fear of being hurt." She spoke frequently of her daughters. In May, the doctor noted:

She . . . brought in pictures of her children that she received yesterday. Ms. Martinez proudly shared pictures stating that it was the children that were helping her to stay focused and not lose control. . . . Especially her ten-year-old daughter.

What Jessica imagined of Serena she extracted mostly from memories of herself at Serena's age. Besides Serena's letters, and the odd update from Coco, Jessica had little information about what was really going on in her daughter's life. Jessica mined her own adolescence for clues. She'd cut herself to relieve anguish, scratching the thin flesh of her underarms and comb marks on her inner thighs. As a woman, Jessica preferred somebody else's blood. "I'm getting so fucking fed up, I don't care who has to pay, and whoever has anything to do with this is gonna pay, every tear I shed," she said. "I try to tell myself, 'Forgive, forgive, forgive,' but my heart's filling up with revenge. But revenge—that's the only satisfaction I'm gonna get." She wondered if her fierce attachment to men like Torres and George was due more to hatred than to love.

That August 1996, Torres showed up late for his sentencing at the federal courthouse in New Haven. He wore a navy uniform from the boiler company where he now worked. He looked like Boy George as he rose to stand before the judge—except for the short ponytail and his obvious nervousness.

Torres had agreed to plead guilty to a misdemeanor charge when confronted with the positive results from the twin boys' DNA saliva swabs—which an FBI agent had traveled to Troy to obtain. Jessica wasn't allowed to attend the sentencing, but she asked her attorney to request three things on her behalf: first, that Torres acknowledge paternity of the twins; second, that the children bear his last name; third, she wanted him to help support the boys financially, or, at the very least, provide bus fare so that Milagros could bring them to Danbury.

The judge dismissed all three requests—they were civil court matters—although he told Torres that losing his wife and job was punishment enough for the criminal charge. He gave Torres probation for violating Title 18, U.S.C., Section 2243 (b) of the Federal Criminal Code—Sexual Abuse of a Ward.

CHAPTER TWENTY-EIGHT

Ramapo Anchorage Camp, in Rhinebeck, New York, sponsored a special program called Mild Month. Mild Month was a supplemental program for children having social and educational difficulties, which ran in May, during the school year. Mild Month aimed to provide children with consistent structure, close attention, safety, and fun within routine. The young counselors were college students studying education, social work, and psychology. The counselor-to-camper ratio was one-to-one; if attention was the problem, the staffing fulfilled the need. Ramapo's philosophy was that if the campers felt secure, they could master the life skills necessary for school. Children were rewarded not for accomplishment but for effort and attitude.

Coco had signed up Mercedes and Nikki for camp during the winter, and when May finally rolled around, she bravely stuck to her decision. It was a bold, unprecedented move—to willingly place her children in the hands of strangers—which incurred the disapproval and scorn of her family and friends. In her community, good mothering was premised on keeping one's children away from authorities. Coco had been trying to deflect the criticism and begrudging comments and ill will for weeks. "You gotta take risks in this world," she said.

On the day of departure, Milagros sternly received Mercedes's and Nikki's good-bye kisses, standing on her slab of porch. She wore a large T-shirt and Lycra leggings. One of Jessica's twin boys lay on his stomach on the dry dirt before her bare feet. He seemed content, intermittently fanning his legs. Milagros certainly doubted Coco's wisdom. What kind of camp had male counselors for little girls?

All week, Coco had quizzed her daughters about good-touch and bad-touch, which the children had learned from an abuse-prevention coloring book. Milagros dictated from her step as the girls kissed their cousins: "No mens going to touch you. There ain't no reason for no mens to touch you, you remember that?" Coco reminded them to wear shirts beneath their tank tops.

"I love you, Mommy, I love you, Frankie, love ya'aw," Nikki blandly repeated to everyone.

"She been saying it for days," Coco said, scrutinizing Nikki. Frankie wasn't even outside. Coco told the girls to go inside and say good-bye to him. He brooded on the couch, listening to his Walkman while watching sports. He accepted their kisses, but didn't say anything. Frankie didn't like good-byes. Coco didn't either, but she still had a few more hours with her daughters.

When they arrived at Ramapo, Nikki led Coco and Mercedes down a wooded path covered in pine needles. The camp sat on its own freshwater lake on 240 acres of wooded hills, fields, and streams. They heard singing in the distance. Coco carried Nautica; Mercedes gripped Coco's free hand. The singing got louder nearer the drop-off point. Counselors poured over the sloping hillsides, skipping and clapping. They greeted their charges and helped carry their bags. Most of the campers, who lived in New York City, had come by bus. Mercedes clutched her mother's leg. Coco was swept up in the excitement.

"Hei-di hei-di hei-di ho!" some of the counselors shouted.

"Rickety-rackety rickety-rackety row!" others called back.

Coco joined right in. "I like that. That they ain't worried about making a fool of themself. That they want the kids to laugh," Coco said. She wondered how people got jobs like this.

Nikki's bunk counselor, a dark-haired college freshman named Sarah, reached down and shook Nikki's hand. Nikki held her white teddy bear beneath her other arm like a briefcase, turned to Coco, and said, "Bye, Mommy."

"Ain't you gonna give me a hug and a kiss?" Coco asked.

Nikki quickly kissed and hugged her mother and sister. Then Nikki retrieved Sarah's hand and walked away. Nautica called after, "Can I go with you?"

Sarah walked back over to Nautica, knelt down, and looked her in the eye. "I'll make a deal," Sarah said. "How about this? See that dirt at the end of the grass? You can walk us up to there." To Coco's surprise, Nautica let Nikki go at the boundary and watched her sister disappear into the rowdy crowd. Mercedes, however, refused to move.

Mercedes's counselor, Beth, suggested that Coco escort her to the bunk. Beth was a Ramapo veteran. She led the way through a wooded path to a brown cabin. Name tags decorated the beds. Welcome notes lined the wooden walls. Beth invited Mercedes to find her nametag. Mercedes turned her head shyly into Coco's belly. "It's in green," Beth suggested. Mercedes bit her finger.

"Think, Mercedes, concentrate! You getting nervous. You looking at the names too fast!" Coco said.

"You have a good bed. It's right by the table where there are books," Beth hinted. She confided to Mercedes that each night after they brushed their teeth, the bunk mates selected a story and she read it aloud.

Coco scanned the cabin. "Oh, I didn't know they could bring a radio!"

"It's the counselors'," Beth said.

"I don't wanna go," Mercedes said.

"What's wrong, Mercedes?" Coco asked.

"Mercedes, we can go to the—" Beth started.

"I said I don't wanna go," Mercedes said.

"Ai, Mercedes—" Coco said.

"I *ain't* going. I am going with my mother," Mercedes declared. She gulped down a cry. Coco mouthed to Beth over Mercedes's head, "Can she be with her sister? She'll be okay if she can stay with Nikki."

"Mercedes, your sister won't be far away. It's time for your mother to go," Beth said. Mercedes shook her head. Other staff members, sensing impending trouble, joined them as they walked toward the sing-along. Out of earshot of the counselors, Coco whispered, "How about a bribe? Mercedes, when you get home, I'll try to get you anything you want."

Mercedes stopped. She stared at her mother, tears still wet around her eyes. "I don't believe you," she said, considering.

"You don't believe me?"

"Get ready to go now. The longer this goes on, the harder it is," Beth warned.

The counselors trailed Coco, who followed Mercedes, who headed for Nautica, who had planted herself in a sandbox. She'd wet herself. Coco lifted Nautica and headed for the car. Mercedes rushed toward Coco, and the counselors picked up speed. They trotted beside Mercedes, listing all the things that camp meant you could do: pick strawberries (and eat as many as you wanted), go to the play center and build with blocks, take boat rides on the lake, eat dinners of burgers and fries.

"I ain't staying," Mercedes called back over her shoulder. "I am going with my mother."

"Your mother is going to go now," Beth said, panting.

"I ain't staying."

"Bye, Mercedes," Coco said. Mercedes dove for Coco's leg like a shortstop grasping for a ball. The counselors pinned Mercedes to the ground. Coco broke free and ran. Nautica bounced and looked back and forth at her wailing mother, her screeching sister. Clumps of sand fell from Nautica's wet butt.

Coco glanced over her shoulder and saw Mercedes kicking and bucking in a human web. "I guess that's what they do, they hold them in a hug," Coco said, pausing to catch her breath. Her voice cracked. Wrenching herself away from this vision, she broke into a run again, flying past the trees. When she reached the parking lot, she cramped up and plopped Nautica down on the hood of a car. Coco placed both palms flat on the hot metal, her chest heaving, tears pouring down her cheeks. She could hear Mercedes wailing through the woods. Leaving Mercedes was the hardest thing she'd ever done. With the exception of those nights she'd left her with Lourdes as a baby, it was the first time Coco and her daughter had ever been apart.

On the way home, Coco stopped at Price Chopper and bought Serena a cake to celebrate her graduation from middle school. Milagros hadn't planned a party; she felt that parties were for birthdays. Coco thought the special day should be acknowledged. She decorated Serena's cake with a tube of blue frosting. Serena ran over as soon as she spotted Coco. Coco held out the cake; Serena had anticipated a gift. She silently read the homespun message and scrunched her face in disappointment. Coco dropped the cake in Serena's hands. "That's life!" Coco said, wounded. She turned her back on Serena and ran into her house.

Coco filled the first uneasy day of the girls' absence with music and the smell of King Pine. Cleaning gave her a sense of control. Frankie swept. He wiped up a sticky puddle of soda that had been inside the refrigerator door for months. Coco scrubbed the dishes, then the sink. She tossed away piles of papers and stray toy parts and sorted through clothes. She emptied drawers. She did load after load of laundry.

Pearl liked to lie on her back on the floor beneath the glass table from the Rent-A-Center, watching her mother move about the kitchen. Every few laps, Coco would bend over the tabletop and Pearl would look up, as though she were gazing at a star. Coco would try to get Pearl to speak. She'd raise her arms and say, "Say, 'I'm a miracle. God bless me, I'm alive.'" Pearl, smitten, would throw her hands up in the air.

Ordinarily, Coco hung her laundry indoors, even on gorgeous days; sometimes she just felt too rotten about the marks on her skin to be seen. Plenty of folks shunned the indictment of daylight and stepped out for fresh air only in the forgiving dark of night. In warm weather, Coco avoided tank tops and short sleeves. But that day, she felt good enough to wear her T-shirt and to hang the wet clothes outdoors. Nautica trailed her. Pearl clutched the railing near the steps. Coco playfully clamped clothespins over Nautica's jumper, making her into a contented porcupine. One by one, with determination, Nautica passed the pins back. "Mommy's little helper," Coco said. Nautica grinned into her neck with feigned nonchalance.

Coco dragged the baby pool to the sidewalk. Pearl grabbed on to the edge and watched it fill. She loved water. Whenever Pearl's sisters were in the tub, she crawled in and joined them—a few times, fully clothed. Now Coco plunked her in the pool, and she splashed with pleasure. Frankie chased Coco with a hose. Pearl was so excited to see her parents playing that she threw herself backward gleefully, and sank. Coco rounded the corner just as Pearl slipped under. Coco scooped her up.

After lunch, the girls napped. Frankie went off with his friends. Coco wrote Mercedes and Nikki letters (she'd already written each girl twice the night before). The laundry dried beneath the sun. A lawn mower buzzed in the distance. A dog barked. Coco listened to her talk shows and organized her prized photographs of her children in an empty box of baby wipes.

Frankie came home early with a movie appropriate for children, a gesture Coco appreciated. Coco cooked and everybody ate and watched the movie together on the living room floor, which had been mopped and spread with fresh sheets. Coco always rested better with Frankie beside her, especially since Pearl had joined them. Once, he'd saved Pearl's life. She was having a violent seizure, and he'd woken up to her head slapping against his leg. That night, they all drifted off to sleep together, Pearl's oxygen machine hiccuping predictably.

A few days later, Coco ripped open Mercedes's first letter. It had been dictated to a counselor onto a donated pharmaceutical memo pad:

Dear Mom,
    I miss you and I miss home, even though I like it here. I love boat riding! I like learning center. We had a party, and we ate ice cream, and we played a game called, "What Time Is It, Mr. Wolf?" with all my friends. We are going boating again tonight. I love you, and want to see Frankie. This letter is for him Frankie. I miss Pearl. I will love you forever (even when you are mad at me). We played Frisbee, too. My favorite song is "Boom Chicka Rocka Chicka Boom." I will sing it for you. I want you to call me. I have friends here.
                               Love, Mercedes

Toward the end of the week, Frankie declared that he was going camping himself. Coco was suspicious. He was uncomfortable changing clothes in unfamiliar places. She couldn't imagine him undressing in the woods.

Frankie lugged his boom box upstairs. He pulled dried clothes from the radiators and doorknobs. Coco tracked him through a garden of her daughters' underwear—California Raisins, Winnie-the-Pooh, Three Little Kittens, Beauty and the Beast. On the waistband of his boxers, she'd written *Coco and Frankie*, a firm tug at his thickening waist.

"And there ain't no girls. *Right*," she quipped. She followed him downstairs. He headed back up. She flung herself onto the couch and clicked to the Weather Channel. The forecaster predicted a severe thunderstorm for the afternoon.

"You so stupid, camping, my ass, in weather like this?" Coco said. "What he need three pair of boxers for?" she asked Nautica and Pearl. "Girls!" Coco said, answering herself. Frankie ignored her on his way out and kissed the girls good-bye. The screen door slapped. A friend stepped out of the passenger seat and let Frankie in the waiting car. Coco bolted to the door. "Frankie, you—" she called out.

"Whatever, Coco, whatever," he said.

"Why don't you take the rest of your things, you fucking asshole!" she shouted.

"Because I don't want to," he replied coolly, his face expressionless.

"I hope that lightning *strikes* your ass!" she screamed. Her hair was still wrapped in a towel, her hairline irritated from picking. Frankie's friend glanced at her and smirked. She slammed the door and yanked the curtain shut and slid down into the couch. She did not want Frankie's friends to see her, but she wanted them to hear: "They going to the Bronx, I know it!" she hollered almost maniacally. "*Camping my ass!*" Somebody in the car turned up the volume of the music. "Why you talking like that, you yelling at my daddy. Don't do that," Nautica said.

Pearl made a snorkeling sound. Coco ripped the wrapper off Pearl's medication, dragged the machine to the socket, and jammed the prong into the plug. She lifted Pearl and roughly arranged her on her lap and gave her two treatments, back to back, to make up for the ones she'd missed. Pearl was being weaned off oxygen, but she still needed her asthma treatments. She shuddered. Coco stewed. Eventually, the two of them relaxed.

Night fell. Pearl fidgeted. Coco couldn't sleep. Crickets chirped.

Coco spoke quietly. "If I leave Frankie, will another man want me and my girls?"

First thing next morning, Coco called her sister, Iris. She wanted to know how Foxy had found the courage to leave their father, Manuel, who was unemployed at the time and addicted to heroin. "You remember with Mommy, how people said that Daddy died because she kicked him out?" Coco asked anxiously. Iris believed that their stepfather, Richie, had given Foxy the courage necessary for the final split. But the trouble had gone on for years beforehand, and the beatings for as long as Iris could remember—Iris still recalled the horror of the time their father tied Foxy to the bed and raped her, and how his parents, with whom they were living, pretended not to hear her mother's desperate screams for help. Manuel's violent outbursts terrified the entire family, but everyone attributed them to the drugs; no one knew yet that he was schizophrenic. Police came to the house so often that they would say, "Manny, come on, you know the routine." Once, he'd even robbed the house clean, after Foxy had kicked him out. Eventually, she took him back, but he beat her again and ended up in jail.

It was during Manny's incarceration that Foxy met Richie at a children's birthday party, although Richie recognized Foxy from the neighborhood. She had passed by him on her way to a cosmetology class she was taking at Wilfred Academy. Richie immediately noticed her long, blond braid; next, he noticed the black man she was walking with. "A good-looking Puerto Rican white girl going with a black guy, that makes me sick to my stomach," Richie said. At the birthday party, Foxy assured him the black guy was just a friend.

Foxy would invite Richie over, and he'd tell her he was broke, and she'd offer to pay the fare for the cab. His living situation at the time was precarious. "I wanted a roof over my head, she took care of me—cooked, cleaned, clothes," Richie said. He fell in love with the children first.

Coco drew the resemblance between Foxy's exasperation with Richie's heroin habit and her own nagging after Frankie. "I feel like I do so much like my mother," Coco said. "I do what a man and a lady do. I feel we the same but for the drugs. Well, the drugs—but not as much, a little bit." Weed was better than heroin.

The morning of the girls' last day of camp, Coco hopped out of bed before the alarm went off and dressed in an outfit she'd laid out the night

- before. Her hair was already styled. She delivered Pearl and Pearl's machinery to Milagros's. Coco dressed Nautica in a canary-yellow shorts set matching her own. She'd bought similar outfits for Mercedes and Nikki and had them neatly folded in a bag. She'd also packed their gold jewelry, which they hadn't been allowed to bring.

Bernie Kosberg, the director of Camp Ramapo, welcomed the parents in the dining hall. The city people looked meek against the blond wood and the bolts of natural light. Kosberg, a garrulous man in his fifties, wore an earring and a Hawaiian shirt. He listed skills the children had learned—how to sit down during meals, how to listen to one another, how to use utensils—and encouraged the parents to follow through. He emphasized the importance of predictability. Each night, he said, the counselors had explained to the children what the next day would bring. He warned the parents to keep an eye out for the symptoms of Lyme disease. Coco didn't hear a thing. She desperately wanted to hug her girls. She sat through the rest of the greeting impatiently. Finally, Kosberg invited everyone to explore the grounds. The parents shuffled out, some blinking, looking somewhat lost. He encouraged the adults to let the children lead.

Mercedes spotted her mother immediately. She ran to Coco and flung her arms around her. Coco cried. Her daughter's fresh face was ebullient. The circles were gone from beneath her eyes. She smiled broadly. Nikki approached Coco tentatively. Sniffling, Coco hugged them both with one arm. With the other, she burrowed in her bags for their jewelry. Mercedes spoke excitedly about her new friends, but Coco was untangling earrings and necklaces and chains and slipping rings on their small fingers. She presented Mercedes with an ankle bracelet with two special charms—a horseshoe for good luck, and a pacifier. Coco pinned Nikki's earlobes with earrings and clipped her necklace. She put her own rings on, too. "Mercedes was probably the most popular girl in the camp," said Beth, the head counselor from Mercedes's bunk.

"Thank you," Coco replied. "Who did your hair?" she whispered to Nikki.

Nikki mumbled, "My counselor."

"For the camp people, it don't look so bad," Coco said reassuringly. Coco busied herself changing Nikki's clothes. She lifted off Nikki's *Camp Ramapo* shirt and held open new yellow shorts for her to step into. Nikki's lack of enthusiasm for the outfit deflated Coco. Mercedes put on the clothes somberly. The sisters stared at one another in consternation. What was going on? Coco straightened Nikki's waistband and centered her gold chain, then leaned back and appraised her re-dressed daughters. Then she seemed to sense the general shift in mood. She turned to Nikki's counselor and said, "But she looks so pretty in jewelry." No one had said a word.

Mercedes led her sisters and her mother to the Learning Center, a space with high ceilings, child-sized tables, and shelves of books. Campers' art covered the walls. Mercedes located her package—a large green garbage bag brimming with three weeks' worth of art. She removed a spider that she'd created out of straw.

"What's that, Mercedes? Your father?" Coco laughed.

"No, a spider," Mercedes said, seeming confused.

The Learning Center teacher introduced herself. She said, "One of Mercedes's favorite books is *Girls Can Do Anything.*"

"I wanna be a doctor!" Mercedes announced. Coco looked surprised. A flash of worry passed over Mercedes's open face. Coco smiled dumbly at the floor. Mercedes added, "I want to be a mom." Coco went off in search of Nikki.

The teacher tended another needy parent and, quietly, Mercedes gathered her things. Like a lawyer assembling her papers after another weary court battle, she organized her drawings and sketches. She folded the large envelope of artwork beneath her arms. Her mother was standing outside, squinting in the sunshine, trying not to cry. Coco said weakly, "I have a headache, I think cuz I'm smiling so much."

Nikki, who ordinarily relished performing, made a lackluster appearance in her bunk's talent show. Halfway through the Fugees rendition of "Killing Me Softly," she burst into tears and burrowed into Coco's gut. The family proceeded to the picnic lunch. As Mercedes escorted Nautica through the buffet, she outlined Nautica's choices and carried her paper plate. Mercedes made sure that everyone had enough of what they wanted. Only when everyone was eating comfortably did she fill her own plate. Nautica had a hearty appetite, like Mercedes. Nikki picked at her food. Nautica polished off her portion of chicken nuggets, then ate most of Nikki's and eyed Mercedes's. Mercedes handed them over—no whining, no fight.

"Oh, but I'm not used to her like that. Oh, she changed so much in three weeks!" Coco said uncertainly.

Mercedes assured her mother, whispering, "Every morning I woke up and said, 'I wanna go home.'"

"Give me a kiss," Coco said.

Coco's discomfort lessened each time Mercedes returned to their shared, familiar ground. Mercedes clasped Coco's hand and led her to a huge tree, beneath which sat a tall man in a silk shirt and dress slacks. A tiny boy sat on a chair beside him—his son. The boy's shorts hung over his knees. Mercedes stood directly in front of him, as though he were an exhibit she had seen many times and was no longer particularly interested in.

"Mommy, that's him," she said plaintively.

"That's who?"

"That's the boy. That's the boy I have a crush on." He shrugged and turned his chin into his shoulder. Mercedes turned to get a drink. He dropped onto the grass and padded after her. Coco and the boy's father watched them. At the table, Mercedes filled a cup for the boy, then served herself.

The campers and parents and counselors convened at an open-air stage for the closing ceremony, the all-camp sing-along. Mercedes and Nikki and Coco belted out the camp songs. They all held hands.

The parting point was a chorus of lamentation. Counselors consoled the campers. Counselors consoled one another. The campers boarded the buses, bound for New York City, pressed their noses to the windows, and waved good-bye. Nikki's counselor, Sarah, clung to Nikki and sobbed.

"I can't believe how attached they are to my daughters," Coco said. Then Coco started crying. Sarah placed Nikki down and hugged Coco. Then Nikki started to cry. Nautica became alarmed and began weeping. Mercedes moved through the monsoon like a veteran relief worker. She lifted Nikki in one arm and held Nautica's hand with the other. She waited patiently for Coco. Slowly, Coco collected the girls' garbage bags of artwork and clothing and followed Mercedes, who led the way to the parking lot through the woods.

On the ride home, Coco wondered aloud if Mercedes's counselor had lied to her about Mercedes's popularity. It was hard for Coco to imagine the Mercedes she knew as beloved among her peers. Mercedes was a problem child. A fighter. Nikki had always been the likable one.

Mercedes's obvious success at camp pointed to Coco's failure to care well for Mercedes herself. Mercedes seemed to intuit this and began to revise her camp experience, proclaiming as boring activities that hours earlier she'd loved. She downplayed the importance of her new friends. She denounced her accomplishments, just as her mother had at Thorpe, when she was on the brink of striking out on her own. Mercedes swore she was never going back to the awful camp. Then, like a tittering schoolgirl, she called her counselor, Beth, with whom she'd been affectionate, "fatso" in Spanish. Coco laughed greedily. "I know I shouldn't," she said, but she did, covering her mouth.

Back at Corliss Park, Mercedes could see that her ordinarily tidy room had been occupied. Her teddy bear still hung from the wall, beside her Christmas stocking and the poster of Roberto Clemente Frankie had lent her, but the Pocahontas tent that Coco had bought Nikki for her birthday had collapsed, and the furniture that Cesar had made was covered with laundry. Someone had used the window's tracking as an ashtray and left a small burn mark in the metal. A lucky money candle leaned against the rim.

That night, Mercedes invited Nikki to join her in the revived Pocahontas tent while, downstairs, Coco chucked her daughters' artwork in the garbage. She called it "extra mess." She spared the letters and photographs. She stared at a prison Polaroid Cesar had mailed Mercedes. He'd been working out; his biceps bulked beneath his shirt as he crouched before a mural with his arm around Gabriel, his wife Giselle's son. The next morning, Coco asked Mercedes, "Does it bother you that Daddy sends you pictures of that boy?"

"No," Mercedes said, and opened the refrigerator door. Coco watched Mercedes closely. Mercedes added, "Oh, that boy's *hand*some."

"Check you out," Coco said, relieved.

After its hopeful beginning, Coco's summer went from bad to worse. One night, after a serious fight with Frankie, Milagros and the kids came to keep Coco company. At 4 A.M., all the children asleep around them, Milagros said, "I'm just going to stay here, it's too late." Kevin's long legs draped over the couch. Later, Coco said she woke to find Milagros snuggling into her. Appalled, but still pretending she was sleeping, Coco shoved her away; Milagros collected the twin boys and left. Afterward, the two women stopped watching movies together; Mercedes or Serena would deliver videotapes back and forth; they also would relay notes if Coco or Milagros needed rice or Pampers or milk. When Coco and Milagros did get together, the relationship felt strained. Coco said, "We even play spades with attitude." Milagros laughed at Coco's suspicions; she insisted Coco had misinterpreted her. They never spoke about the incident, but it had got Coco thinking about Milagros's relationship with Jessica, and Coco plucked the photographs of Jessica and her prison friends off the wall.

Back in the Bronx, Coco's cousin Jesus had finally been released from Rikers. Foxy had taken him in because his mother, Aida, had died while he was in prison and Jesus had nowhere else to go, but her generosity had consequences that spread all the way to Troy. Jesus had a temper before he was locked up, but when he came out, it was worse. He could get scary when he drank, and he seemed determined to catch up on all the fun he'd missed. But too much fun always led to trouble, and Jesus was on parole. He participated in an armed robbery during which another boy got shot. Jesus fled. Coco's brother, Hector, however, got the brunt of the law's suspicion. Hector was staying indoors, trying to keep out of trouble, but it meant that he was always home when the detectives or Jesus's parole officer came to call. Meanwhile, Jesus was moving from place to place. He crashed with Coco's older brother, Manuel, and Yasmin, Manuel's seventeen-year-old wife, who in addition to their young son was raising Manuel's other two kids. Their mother was in and out of hospitals, and the aunt who usually cared for the children needed a break. Yasmin took them in to keep them away from foster care. Yasmin's sister was also staying in the apartment with her two children, and she and Jesus hooked up. Soon both men were partying elsewhere and chasing girls, and Yasmin's sister was pregnant with Jesus's kid. Manuel started getting mouthy with Yasmin, and Hector started following his brother's lead. At the end of her rope, Yasmin shipped Manuel's older two up to Iris, but Iris quickly discovered that she couldn't handle them and passed them along to Coco. The boy was always trying to follow Coco into the bathroom; both children had rotten teeth and cried constantly from toothaches. Coco would try to distract them with hours of kick-the-can. They played outside even in the rain; she was afraid she would hurt them, otherwise. Foxy soon retrieved the children and brought them back to Yasmin. Coco was relieved, but worried and full of guilt.

At the same time, Frankie was hanging out with a white man who beat his girlfriend, and he'd started getting more belligerent with Coco. One morning, he demanded Coco make him breakfast, and the situation disintegrated into a fight loud enough to bring out the neighbors. When Coco started tossing Frankie's clothes out the second-floor window, he shoved her. Nikki, usually unflappable, bolted outside to get Mercedes, and Mercedes came running: "Mommy, you okay?"

"Look at what's happening in front of my kids! My motherfuckin' kids! They are not going to see this, you motherfucker!" Coco screamed, and told him to get out. Solemnly, Mercedes watched him pack. He gave her his Roberto Clemente poster and a watch. He told her that he never intended to hit her mother. "I was just embarrassed," Frankie said. "I didn't know how to handle it."

*　　*　　*

Soon afterward, Coco's great-grandmother died. Coco felt badly that she didn't have the money to travel to the Bronx. On the day of the funeral, Frankie came over for a visit and asked Coco if she wanted to get high. Coco surprised him and said yes. Coco hadn't smoked weed since the one time she tried it when she was thirteen years old. Later, she admitted that she simply wanted to feel close to Frankie. The first time they smoked, she felt paranoid, but the second time was better. The third time, she fell asleep in the afternoon and slept through a good part of the night; Milagros took the babies, and when Coco finally woke up, the older children were still out in the street. Milagros told her that the stillness in Coco's apartment had reminded her of the homes of girls she'd known who were hooked on drugs. Afterward, Coco could recall little of the episode other than at one point looking in the bathroom mirror and seeing her mother's face. She swore she would never get high again.

By late August, the obvious influences of camp life had dissolved. If Coco cursed, Mercedes no longer said, "Mommy, please don't swear." After failed attempts at employing her fledgling skills as a diplomat in her dealings with her sisters, Mercedes resorted to petulance, then bullying. Her battles with Brittany and Stephanie resumed. Mercedes still sang the camp songs, though. She taught "Boom Chicka Rocka Chicka Boom" to Pearl, who made song sounds as she splashed in the tub. Mercedes taught Nautica, who sang sternly to her dolls. Mercedes even shared the songs with Brittany and Stephanie, who set the lyrics to cheers. Matthew and Michael were too young to say the words but they liked to watch their sisters do flips and cartwheels. Mercedes even sang as she cycled, which was how Coco could tell when she pedaled by the front window and was about to turn at the tree. The way she held the handlebars reminded Coco of Cesar.

Mercedes loved riding her bike through Corliss Park. She would coast down the sidewalk hill and take the shortcut by Milagros's to avoid the boys hanging out at the basketball court. She would wave to the white ladies who sat at a picnic table smoking cigarettes and drinking coffee all afternoon. She knew the sidewalks, exactly where the bumps made the front wheel hop. She knew where to slow down for the turns on the dangerous sand. The ladies at the picnic table could sense it—the pleasure she took in her sturdy legs, the confidence suggested in the determined chin, the delight of the freedom and the fresh air. They seemed to share her exuberance, even as it passed them by. The smoke from their cigarettes rose in the sun, like haze, and made its way above the poplar trees.

PART IV

House to House

By December, Coco and Frankie were back together, but rarely having sex. She told her mother, "I feel like a damn nun." Foxy replied that she couldn't imagine Coco with anyone but Frankie. "Show me a perfect person," Foxy would say, "and I'll kiss their ass." Frankie sometimes kept his drugs at Corliss Park, but he himself was usually out: he had gotten a car. Coco wanted him home, but when he was home, she didn't like his treatment of her girls. One morning, she caught Frankie snapping scissors in Nautica's face. He said that he was fed up with her demands for food she never ate, but to Coco that was no excuse: "It's okay if you trying to show them something, trying to teach them, but not to make them feel fear." She told him that he would never treat his own kids that way.

The violent bickering between them was contagious: Coco yelled at Nautica, who then pulled her mother's hair and kicked her in the back. Mercedes pounded Nikki, who scratched to draw blood. Pearl clawed at herself, as Coco used to as a child. One morning, Nikki woke up in tears. "I feel like it's seeing my mother all over again with Richie," Coco said. The next thing she knew, just before Christmas, Frankie got arrested.

He called Coco crying; she called his mother, who said to Coco, "He made it all this time without getting in trouble, why's he going to start acting stupid now?" Frankie had been stopped for not wearing a seat belt. He gave the officer his license, but his name had an arrest warrant attached to it. As luck would have it, the warrant was for a murder. Frankie panicked: both he and Coco knew people who'd been arrested and convicted for crimes they did not commit, just as they knew others who'd committed crimes and were still at large, committing new ones; crimes and punishments rarely added up. Even Iris's husband, Armando, a solid working man, had been stopped by police. Luckily, fingerprints cleared Frankie, and his mother wired Coco money and Coco bailed him out. The episode made Coco seriously consider moving back to the city, where she and her troubles would feel less conspicuous and Frankie could live with her without being subjected to this level of scrutiny from the police. In fact, whenever Coco felt trapped, she fantasized about moving.

But Cesar, whom Coco had written to about her restlessness, told Coco to stay put. He was in solitary confinement again, and he'd been thinking a lot about his daughters. If Coco returned to the Bronx, she was resigning herself to a lifestyle they'd both tried to escape:

> *I understand what you mean about Albany being too much for you and Mercedes, but I really don't want my daughters growing up in the Bronx. Try to move and stay in Albany think of the kids and stop thinking of yourself all of the time. . . . You had those kids for all the wrong reasons, and now you're paying the price. I know I'm in jail for something I did, but with your selfish ass self and your selfish way of living you've made things psychologically worse for my daughters and yours. I am not saying you are a bad mother. You take very good care of my kids and I will never take them away from you, but you ruining their minds. But you don't see this because you're too busy fucking and having babies after babies by dudes who don't give a fuck about you or your or (THEIR) kids. . . .*
>
> *Coco I've made my mistakes but I didn't want you or Roxanne to have these babies because I knew I wouldn't stay with either of you, but you both gave birth to those girls for the wrong reasons and now my daughters are paying the price along with me. Mercy was the only baby I agreed on having. Don't get me wrong, I love all my daughters equally and with all my heart. But it hurts me to know they're suffering because of OUR inconsiderate actions. . . .*
>
> *You may think that being a good mother is enough but it's not. I know the effects of growing up in a household with brothers and sisters from different fathers and seeing different men with my Mom and all the other shit you're doing. It's not good. . . . I am trying to open your eyes to see the pain you're going to cause those kids. I know I been through it. The pain is paramount. Start thinking with your mind and stop thinking with your pussy. A child can be physically healthy and seem to be alright, but psychologically trauma is a very serious disease that can effect the healthiest of children and cause serious problems in their life. Look, learn from your mistakes and stop making them over and over again. Why do you think I haven't had a baby with my wife? . . . You know I'm dying to have a son, but I can't allow my child to go through the psychological torment that me, Mercedes, Whitney, and Justine and Naughty are going through. . . .*
>
> *. . . I'm not saying to stop having sex. I'm saying to stop having babies like if it's okay. Your having them for all the wrong reasons and all your going to do is cause them pain in the long run. And they are*

going to see you and say, Oh, my Mommy's a hoe. And if she has had
kids from a bunch of different men, then it's okay if I do it. I don't want
my daughters to come out like you or me. . . . Anyway this letter wasn't
meant as a bad one, it was meant to open your eyes. I'm really tired
of staying shut and watching you destroy the lives of you and your
kids. I hope you take my advice because it's for the good not bad.
Anyway, I want for you to send me a lot of flicks of my kids. . . . Lis-
ten, I also expect to see my kids with YOU. Those are our kids, and
OUR responsibility. . . . I want to see Mercedes and Naughty with
their Mom. I'm bringing this to a close bye bye.

Coco read the letter, then reread it and said, "It makes me feel dirty. It's
bad enough I have them, he don't have to remind me what I did." That
very afternoon, she left the kids with Milagros and took the bus downtown
to the offices of Planned Parenthood.

Coco's attempts at birth control had been much like her attempts at
many other things—well-intentioned and wholehearted, dwarfed by
other problems, and eventually forgotten. After Pearl was born, she'd
asked the doctor if she could have her tubes tied, and he told her to ask
her regular doctor, but Coco didn't have a regular doctor. She had also
asked a hospital nurse, who wasn't sure whether the procedure would be
covered by Medicaid. Coco had meant to pursue it, but within a month
she and her girls were homeless, upstate. Since then, she had considered
other options, but she also knew her limitations. If she couldn't always
remember to give her own children their medications, how could she possibly remember to take the Pill? Her sister, Iris, had Norplant, which she
swore made her queasy, and Coco thought it was creepy to have small
cylinders lined up on the inside of your arm. She'd also heard from friends
the rumors that the government needed guinea pigs to test Norplant and
was encouraging its use mainly among Puerto Ricans and blacks. Coco
had debated getting "the shot," Depo-Provera, but she'd been turned off
by the rumors of its side effects. Elaine claimed that it had ended her sex
drive; Iris heard that it made girls lose their hair and lose weight, and
Coco, at four feet eleven inches and 133 pounds, was still trying to get fat.
But Cesar's letter was the push she needed; she made an appointment for
the following morning.

That night, as Coco labored over her response to Cesar, reconsidering
and editing each sentence, Mercedes asked her mother if she would
write down a letter for her. Mercedes dictated as Coco scribbled:

Dear Daddy,

How you doing? Fine I hope. As for myself I'm confused about something. Mommy's boyfriend got locked up and she bailed him out. I want to know why she didn't bail you out. Daddy I'm sorry about telling you about Mom's boyfriend. I don't understand. Mom tried to explain to me. I want to hear what you have to say now. Daddy I'm telling Naughty every day that you love her, and when we went to the city she was crying for you. Daddy write back once you get my letter. I love you. 👁 ❤ *U Daddy*

> *Love,*
> *Mercedes and Naughty*

Coco carefully copied it onto a fresh page of paper ripped from Mercedes's notebook from school before returning to her own letter. She picked her face as she mulled over the final version. "My face is destroyed," she said miserably.

"And you still picking," Mercedes said tartly. She listened as her mother read her rebuttal aloud:

Dear Cesar,

What's up? I wish you were not in there. I know shit is hard for you. What you need to know is that just cuz you're the one in there, that it's not hard just for you. It's hard for me also. If you wasn't in there, it would've made our daughters and my life easier for real. I'm tired of you demanding for me to bring your girls. I'll bring them if I could. You always made me feel like I had and still have to do as you say, and it's not like that. . . . I'm tired of acting scared of you or feeling like I have to stay shut from you. I want you to hear me out. You made me cry by the letter you wrote me. You always want to bring the past up too. Whatever I did in the past I want it to stay in the past. I love my future now.

. . . You told me once there's no one going to love a girl with four kids. Well I'm proud to say you was wrong. My man loves me and my girls. He's the only one I been with and fucked for two years. I'm not a ho. I changed a lot. I'm not proud of the shit I done, but I learned from my mistakes and I don't regret my four girls. Probably I did have them for all the wrong reasons, but hey, I'm doing all that I can for them. . . . I'm not a ho no matter what anyone says. I take care of what's mine. I've been, and I fucked one guy in two years.

Probably if you was out here long enough I wouldn't have cheated on you. You wanted me to suffer for mistakes you made, the times you got locked up. When you were out here I did you right, even when we wasn't together. Also knowing that you out fucking bitches without a condom. Yes I know that's my fault. I loved you that much that I took so much shit from you. You told me one time if I fucked someone that you don't want to have anything to do with me anymore. That's when you were out here. That's why I didn't cheat, because I didn't want to lose you completely. Anyway. The reason for saying what I just said is cuz I don't want you to hate me cuz I got shit off my chest. And cuz of all the stuff I learned from you I learned how to be a bitch from you, I learned how to fuck good and also cheat the way you did. I learned from the teacher. . . .

As for his daughters, Coco wrote:

I will bring them when I can. It's hard. There's no babysitting. I don't leave them just with anybody. . . . You act like shit you tell me don't hurt me. But it does. I wasn't a great girlfriend, but I feel that I was there for you. . . . Anyway take care. Your girls love you. Write to them <u>soon</u>.

Coco kept her appointment at Planned Parenthood and decided on the Depo-Provera shot, but she didn't react well to it. She bled heavily for a solid week; when she reported to Planned Parenthood again, she was instructed to continue taking Motrin. Coco asked if she could get her tubes tied and was told she had to make several appointments, including one for an hour of counseling. Between her chronic problems with Frankie and with Pearl, she never made it back.

CHAPTER THIRTY

Things were far worse for Cesar than he'd admitted to Coco. From the box, he wrote Jessica that he no longer valued his own life. He feared that his hate and anger ruled him. In the same way that Serena had been Jessica's inspiration to get out of prison, Mercedes became Cesar's lifeline to survive:

> Jessica, the only time I feel at ease is when I'm with Mercy. Naughty and Justine are lost to me. They don't treat me like their father. . . . Mercy is all I have left. And she's slowly slipping away. . . . Once she's gone I'm going to lose it. I can't lose her Jessica because then I will lose myself. She's everything to me.

Cesar had been extorting people to finance his increasing drug use. "There's a lotta people in here you can talk into anything," he said. "You can extort them and they don't even know you've extorted them." But threats always created other threats. Unlike Tito, who'd joined up with the Latin Kings gang for protection, Cesar took care of business on his own. "If I want to rob somebody, I gotta ask?" he said. "I can't see asking no man about what I can do." But in order to operate without backup, he had to prove that he was capable of doing anything. When five inmates jumped him, Cesar fought back. Afterward, they all got searched, and Cesar was found carrying a shank—a homemade weapon—and he was thrown in the hole. Then he dug his trouble deeper: outside the hearing room, he attacked one of the five guys, who he believed was about to snitch.

The authorities put Cesar in the box. He faced nine months for the internal weapons violation, for which the state was considering pursuing an additional criminal charge. If he was convicted of possessing contraband in prison, years could be added on to the nine to eighteen Cesar already had to serve. Serving time for killing his best friend was justice, but serving time for needing money for drugs he'd sworn he'd never use filled Cesar with self-loathing. Even though he shared his unhappiness with Jessica, he kept his drug use secret.

Dear Sis,

. . . As for why I had the knife. Jessica, nobody in N.Y. sends me money. The family done forgot about a nigga, my wife hasn't been on her job for a while now, so I've got to live off the land or starve. Now when I chose to live off of the land I made a lot of enemies in the four years I've been down. So I don't have to explain the rest. If you're not ready or I'm not ready, I could end up with a cold piece of steel in my chest. I've lived the life of a warrior in here & to change will mean signing my death certificate. What keeps my enemies at a distance is my rep. . . . If I change now, I'll starve & they will hit me up in a matter of days. I have enemies throughout the state and I'm always getting transferred from jail to jail so I can't change. It's not a matter of pride it's a matter of surviving. Plus Jessica I got a solid chain link, $300.00 nugget wedding band & $125.00 Guess watch. I will get robbed day one if I ain't ready. Jessica this isn't the feds. This is the jungle. This is where all of the murderers, rapists, stick-up kids & societies worst are all put under one roof. If you walk away from a confrontation you'll get treated like a bitch & the next thing you know somebody's going to be trying to make you their bitch I ain't with that. I'm going to live the thug life until the day I'm released!

Plus Jessica nobody sends me no money at all from N.Y. Elaine brought me $30.00 in like June of 1996. Mom sent me $25.00 last month. That was my income from NY in the past 8 months. So you know I have to do my thing. If Mom & Elaine sent me at least $40.00 a month I could chill out. But I ain't going to starve.

. . . I don't need a psychiatrist. I saw one of those for almost two years when I did my last bid. All he kept saying was that "I was too young to be full of so much anger & rage." But he never helped me. They get paid to listen, they don't want to. I'm okay without one. You'll be my psychiatrist. You love me & care & that's what I need. But Jessica it's going to take forever to finally get everything out.

You see Jessica, while I was growing up I put up a shield. I couldn't let the neglection get to me so I closed up. But that was how it affected me. It caused me to become frustrated. That's why when I was a bit older I took to the streets. I was acknowledged out there. I was taken in and they showed me love (or so I thought). But now I realize that all they loved was that hatred inside of me. They fed it. And I kept that shield up for all that was good & vibed off of the evil.

Jessica, I went & took my problems out on innocent people. Because my family was bad I made other people suffer. But never to ladies, old *people, or kids. . . . I regret what I've done because it wasn't fair. I hate what I've become Jessica. . . . I'm so fucked up inside. But I'm going to straighten it out. My kids need me! . . . Yo, about me, & Mom talking & letting out our secrets. She's too old & sick for that Jessica. I don't want to cause her anymore pain. . . . I don't want to speed her death up. I want her to live in peace. What I got inside will hurt her too much because she'll know it's true. Mom knows how her & the family neglected me. But I forgive Mom, she's been through so much as it is. I get angry at her a lot but she's still Mom. . . . Boy do we come from a dysfunctional family! Smile! I guess some people go through hell to end up in heaven. Only God knows why we go through the things that we do. But I do hope for better days.*

Jessica, "God willing," when I make it out of here I never want to return. I never want to see a jail cell again. I'm tired of this bullshit. . . . Yo! Jessica please tell your lawyer to call the DAs office up here & speak to the DA assigned to my case. Tell him to make some noise & say all the fancy stuff about the law & talk that Private lawyer stuff & they might not pursue the case. Please Jessica it's important. . . .

Love always,
Cesar

Pretty Lone Cesar
Thug Life: Survival of the fittest
The Law of the Land

Jessica understood that relationships were tools of survival. She immediately hooked up Cesar with Lovely, one of her better-off prison friends. In the meantime, to hold him over, Jessica mailed Cesar $20 from her commissary. (After Lovely and Cesar started corresponding, Lovely's mother made occasional contributions to Cesar's account.)

Next, she scanned her phone book and attempted to tackle Cesar's legal mess. Over the years, Jessica had maintained her many outside contacts, even those that were fleeting. (Once she'd called a guy she'd met on Fordham Road. He didn't remember her name, but she refreshed his memory by describing how she'd been dressed.) She called Boy George's attorney, who placed a call on Cesar's behalf. She tried the activist lawyer who ran the prison clinic at Yale. The lawyer, also the mother of twins, held a special place in her heart for Jessica. Yale couldn't help Cesar—they didn't take New York State criminal cases—but, as it turned out, they could help Jessica.

*   *   *

Following the twin boys' birth, Jessica's health had continued to deteri-
orate. She suffered from migraines and abdominal cramps, and she
believed the prison medical staff didn't take her ailments seriously. If Jessica joined the long line for sick call, some staff members mocked her:
"What's wrong, Martinez, pregnant again?" The harassment upset Jessica.
During her phone calls with the Yale lawyer, she mentioned her frustrations. She also referred several other inmates to Yale who believed they
were being mistreated by the medical authorities at Danbury.

While Jessica worked the phone, Cesar wrote voraciously; he mailed
letter after letter to Mercedes, who was balking every morning when Coco
woke her, physically exhausted from staying up late. Coco, however, mistakenly attributed Mercedes's reluctance to attitude. Cesar tried to make
a connection: "Daddy used to hate school, too. . . . The better you do the
quicker it will be over. You don't want to be ignorant and on welfare when
you get older. Stop giving Mom problems in the morning and get your
lazy butt up and go to school alright!" He responded to the photographs
of her: "All of your little girl teeth are falling off and your big girl teeth are
coming in." He also advised her about Frankie: "Don't ever disrespect
Mom's boyfriend, but don't never let him take my place okay."

Cesar was also counseling Jessica. Sometimes they exchanged two or
three letters in a single week. Jessica worried about her brother's reaction to her lesbian relationships: "Who am I to say you're wrong
because you enjoy women?" he wrote. "Shit! I Love women so much I
understand." He offered her his expertise: "So you say she's a player
right. . . . So if you stay with her you're going to suffer for the whole time
you're with her. . . . And just because she said 'I Love You' doesn't mean
it's true." Jessica told him that she'd reconnected with George. "Anyway, tell B.G. I said What's up. Why do you still keep in touch with him
if you said he caused and causes you so much heartache? You are very
confused." He encouraged Jessica to write to Giselle—"Coco, Roxanne, Lizette & all those other bitches I've had combined couldn't
stand in her shoes"—and Jessica did.

Although Cesar marveled at the advantages of federal time—"You'se
get to throw birthday parties and all that shit over there. Boy that's
proper. We can't throw shit"—he worried about Jessica taking prescription pills. "Listen up Booga," he wrote Jessica, "& listen good—DO NOT
GET ON ANY MEDICATION/I know you may feel you need it but you
don't. . . . Medication is nothing but temporary relief."

The prison authorities might have been begrudging about providing

inmates with certain types of medical treatment, but prescription medications were provided liberally. This discrepancy concerned the law students at Yale, who were—in part, through their conversations with
Jessica—educating themselves about the female prison experience.

That spring, Jessica attempted to get a time cut for what she'd been
through with Torres, but her request was dismissed. That summer, Cesar
pled guilty to possessing the shank and received an additional one to three
years. By fall 1997, Jessica and a team of Yale law students decided to file
suit.

Jessica's case, like so many prison cases, was a difficult one. In a letter to
Jessica, the clinic students admitted, "We feel the chances of winning
either of these actions on the merits are not good." Nevertheless, the law
school decided to take it on. Many of the candidates who contacted them
for help shared similar backgrounds to Jessica's and had traveled the same
worn-down paths—sexual abuse and teenage motherhood, family violence and violent men, overcrowded housing, inferior schools, dangerous
neighborhoods, few decent jobs, high stress, lousy health. Yet Jessica was
the one they'd chosen, among the thousands of locked-up women desperately in need of free legal aid.

Jessica's looks probably helped, but the students also liked her. She was
broken, but unlike so many other women in prison, her damage was
harder to see. Her anger didn't show through—at least, not at first. The
students were both conservative and liberal, and the fact that Jessica
refused to view herself as a victim contributed to her appeal.

Jessica's concern about the legal aspects of her case came and went,
but she was always interested in any new information about Torres and
his whereabouts. To some of the students, she seemed ambivalent about
pursuing the case. Some believed that she was still in love with Torres.
During the legal consultations, Jessica's appearance and moods changed
drastically. At one consultation she looked so lifeless that, at first, a student didn't recognize her.

That fall, the Jerome N. Frank Legal Services Organization of Yale
Law School filed a complaint on behalf of Jessica Martinez of the Danbury Federal Correctional Institution in Connecticut district court. The
federal civil suit sought compensatory and punitive damages. It waged
two charges against the authorities: that the prison had failed to protect
Jessica from becoming pregnant while she was in their custody, and that
once she was, the administration remained indifferent to her substantial
medical needs. The prison denied Jessica's claims.

Jessica's aims, however, were slightly different from those of her lawyers. She cared most about the paternity claim. She didn't care about child support—Milagros, she said, would manage—but she wanted Torres to publicly admit that the children belonged to him. His refusal to do so was like Puma's denial of Serena, and her father's neglect of her. Yet Jessica lost her resolve for battle. She received word through an old colleague of Torres's that Torres was angry about the lawsuit and immediately asked Yale to drop the paternity action.

The students also argued that prisons should require guards to receive comprehensive sexual-harassment training appropriate to the populations they oversaw. (A Yale student who researched the consent issue for Jessica's case determined that guards' sexual-harassment training consisted mainly of the distribution, during orientation, of a booklet called "Games Inmates Play.") Prisons were required, by law, to conduct background screenings of their inmates. Danbury had in their possession reports that documented Jessica's history of self-destructive behavior and depression related to her abusive involvements with men. Jessica's sentencing judge, who had requested that she receive counseling, noted her tendency to be led astray. Women like Jessica should never be assigned to work the night shift in remote locations with inadequately trained male officers, the lawyers argued. Only one month after Torres became her supervisor, Jessica had been required to submit to the first pregnancy test. The results were negative, and she returned to work, despite the ongoing suspicions raised by other inmates and staff. Yale asserted that the pregnancy testing proved that the administration had taken the rumors seriously. Given what the prison knew of Jessica's psychological history, the administration had acted with negligence by not rescheduling Jessica's shift away from Torres's or reassigning her to another job.

Medical negligence against the prison was even harder to prove. On New Year's Eve of 1995, when she was four months pregnant, Jessica had rushed to the phone to call the girls: there was always a mob, and even more of one on the holidays. In her hurry, she had tumbled down a flight of stairs and landed on her stomach. The Yale students were arguing that the prison had refused to perform a sonogram, and had only done so after Jessica's pro bono attorney got involved. Besides that, the strongest challenge in Jessica's favor was that it had taken more than fourteen months for Jessica to get a laparoscopy that her doctor had ordered after the twins were born. The procedure had discovered a substantial cyst on her ovary.

The students were becoming disturbed by what they were learning about prison life through discovery. "Telling her to have an abortion, her falling down the stairs and them giving her no medical treatment, and her not knowing whether or not one of the babies she's carrying is dead," one student said. "The power of the prison can sort of seem transparent for a while and then appear very starkly." Jessica had grown numb to much of prison life, but the students' reactions gave her fresh eyes through which to view what she had assumed to be her lot. Their sincerity inspired her and she became politicized. She volunteered to testify about prison conditions when a United Nations *rapporteur* visited Danbury to investigate violence against women for a report that was eventually presented to the Commission on Human Rights. Out more than a thousand inmates, Jessica was one of only three who dared to step forward.

To hold the prison legally accountable for Jessica's predicament, the students had to prove that the injuries she had suffered were intentional. The legal challenge was a lot like the challenge of demonstrating the impact of racism or poverty or substandard housing: How could you untangle the structural injustices from the self-inflicted damage? How could you separate neglect from malice, the intended from the unintended harms?

By the spring of 1997, Coco and Frankie were driving down to the Bronx almost every weekend, and as a result of all the moving around, Coco's life in Troy was falling apart. In the Bronx, the car would regularly die, and Coco and the girls would be stranded at Foxy's; Frankie stayed at his mother's. Parking tickets stacked up against the windshield, Coco missed the collection day for her food vouchers, Pearl missed her doctors' appointments, and Mercedes and Nikki missed day after day of school. By March, Mercedes had accrued so many absences that Coco received a visit from a social worker from Child Protective Services. Then in May, Coco missed a recertification appointment and her welfare case was closed. Nikki bravely returned to Camp Ramapo, but Mercedes, who was seven, didn't want to leave Coco alone. One afternoon, she was leaning out of her second-floor bedroom window, looking haggard, and one of Frankie's friends mistook her for a grown woman.

Mercedes no longer shared her mother's love for the city; she wanted to stay in Troy. By summer, she declared dramatically, "I have suffered enough." Her Tío Rocco had given her a new bicycle, and she just wanted to stay home and ride it; the little cement square of her grandma Foxy's courtyard couldn't contain her. Mercedes also worried about the gangs. She'd overheard stories from the boys who'd stayed in her house. "I wanna wear red, I don't wanna go to the Bronx," she complained.

"You a fucking spoiled brat, Mercedes," said Coco.

"It's not fair," Mercedes replied. "We always have to do what you wanna do. I don't wanna go back to the Bronx."

"You have trouble wherever you are, Mercedes, you a problem child!" shouted Coco. But on one July run, Mercedes convinced Coco to let her stay with Iris.

In the Bronx, everyone was out on the street, everyone was talking, and the news of other people's problems muffled Coco's own: Foxy's neighbor's daughter was held hostage, at gunpoint, by her man; Wishman, Pearl's father, was back out on the street, dealing; Wishman's girl was pregnant again. Coco was pleased—despite her feelings for Wishman—because the couple had lost their infant son the year before. A friend had been carrying him across University and they had been hit by a car. For months, Wishman's girl couldn't believe her son was dead; at one point she had spooked Wishman's mother, Sunny, by buying the lost child a pile of new clothes. Maybe the baby would help heal her.

During that visit home, Coco brought Nikki, Nautica, and Pearl downstairs to play outside. Wishman seemed to make a point of passing by Coco's mother's way.

"Pearl's gotten beautiful," Wishman said. He complimented Coco on her mothering. He peeled two twenties from a roll of bills, locked those green-blue eyes on Coco, and added an extra ten.

Except for one time two years earlier—when Coco had cajoled Foxy to ask Kodak's mother to ask Kodak to buy Nikki's winter coat—Coco had never asked her daughters' fathers for help. She was proud of her independence. Some girls denied a baby's father access to his child unless he handed over cash. Other mothers claimed they needed money for the baby, then spent the money on clothes for themselves or clubbing or beer or cigarettes. Sometimes money was the main reason girls had sex with boys. But Coco wanted her intimate relationships to be better than that.

After Wishman gave her money, she bought Pearl sneakers and handed him the receipt as proof. Coco hoped that Wishman's attention meant that he was finally interested in becoming Pearl's father. "I guess he's ready when he's ready," Coco said. Foxy believed that Wishman's sudden discovery of his two-year-old daughter was simply the most direct route to getting Coco into bed, and that Coco ought to get money from Wishman while she could. Foxy was right.

Foxy was in a distinctly mercenary frame of mind; she'd taken a job as a scout for a marriage broker. The broker paid her a couple of hundred dollars for every man or woman she convinced to marry an illegal immigrant for cash; the American bride or groom received up to $1,000—and sometimes a wedding outfit and celebration dinner—as soon as he or she stepped out of city hall. She'd married off whole families—parents, children, their husbands and wives, their common-law in-laws. Some of the husbands were unexpectedly generous: one of Foxy's in-law's husbands bought her a used car after she passed the final immigration interview. Now Foxy was working on Coco, who desperately needed the money without her welfare benefits. But Coco worried that a marriage would jeopardize her welfare eligibility for the future. "One thousand dollars would go through my hands like water," Coco said, wounded that her mother didn't seem chastened by the serious risk.

Foxy had witnessed weddings in each of the five boroughs and she had learned a lot. She'd become a whiz at the paperwork and had devised her own ranking, by nationality: Indians were the most generous; Panamanians were fair enough; she couldn't speak truthfully about Ecuadorians because she hadn't handled too many of them. But she resolutely refused to deal with Mexicans, and Dominicans were, as ever, the worst. You couldn't get a wedding outfit or a reception dinner from a Dominican.

Sometimes the real girlfriends of the men acted as the witnesses. Sometimes, after Foxy hooked up the men, she found husbands for their girlfriends, too. She'd heard of an arranged couple who fell in real love. If the arranged marriages worked, the immigrants inched closer to citizenship, and the American wives and husbands were paid in installments for every naturalization hurdle they cleared. But most of her clients took the first payment and disappeared.

Foxy became friends with her clients and their real wives. They periodically got together to take lots of pictures; immigration needed ongoing documentation of ordinary life—domestic proof. "Howse my gold-digging hussy of a mother?" Iris asked sardonically, as Foxy pulled out her best wedding photographs. She liked the one of the bride looking regal in a traditional red-and-gold-embroidered sari; the Indian groom had paid for her hair, at a beauty salon, and the wedding party celebrated at Jimmy's Bronx Café. Sports figures and celebrities and drug dealers partied at Jimmy's; Foxy had lived most of her life only blocks away, but she'd never been before.

One afternoon, Coco and her children were in front of Foxy's building when Wishman appeared in a livery cab and invited Coco to play pool. Nautica threw tantrums whenever Coco tried to leave her behind, just as

Mercedes had as a child. But Nikki jumped at the chance to assist her mom. She shooed her little sister into the building, so that Coco could make a run for the car, cheering her mother on: "Naughty's inside, Mommy! Go! Go! Go!"

It had been years since Coco had been alone with a man without having to worry about her children in the house. "I haven't been spoiled for a long time," she said later. "We went to a hotel. The room looked like the Poconos." She floated on the soft cloud of Wishman's whispered voice—*Let's get busy*—as he lifted off his shirt. His stomach still had cuts from workouts during his prison bid. *Damn, Coco, you used to kiss good. What happened?* She pulled him toward her and corrected that. She loved how he said with certainty, *This shoulda been mine. This is what I always wanted, Coco, one whole day with you.* Until then, even with a baby between them, they'd never had such privacy.

After they'd made love, Coco confessed that it hurt her feelings that he'd ignored Pearl. She would have liked to ask him other questions, but she didn't want to push and spoil what they'd just had. Wishman gave Coco another $50 for Pearl.

The next night, Coco brought Nikki and Nautica down to Foxy's courtyard. Pearl was up the block, at her grandmother Sunny's. Mercedes was still upstate with her aunt. Coco wanted to be outside in case Wishman passed by, but it was a perfect summer night that needed no excuse. The children had spent the whole day indoors, waiting and restless, and they were eager to run around.

Coco still felt high from Wishman's attentions, but she tried to temper her excitement. She felt pretty sure Wishman had other girls on the side. Cesar always had. Nikki's father, Kodak, too. "All my girls' fathers is like that. They all be with a lotta girls, and the girls they like is young," she said.

As she got older, though, it seemed to Coco that the girls her old boyfriends liked were getting younger. During the recent spate of visits to New York, Wishman and his friends had commented more than once to Coco about how fly Mercedes looked. Ordinarily, Coco relished compliments about her daughters. But these felt different. Mercedes was seven. "*Too* fly," Coco said. "The way they say it—'Coco, yo, that girl is *fly*, your daughter is *fly*.' These are boys I grew up with, I have a history with. It ain't right." Even Kodak, during a trip from Baltimore, singled out Mercedes. Coco wanted to say, "Pay attention to your own daughter," but she didn't say a word.

That night in front of Foxy's building, Coco let the children play outside for hours; before going back upstairs, they even took a walk around the block by Wishman's building, but they never caught sight of him. A few days later, the car broke down yet again and Coco and her kids took the bus home. They were stuck in Troy for the rest of the summer, where Coco became increasingly irritable.

Coco knew that her fling with Wishman would have been almost impossible if Mercedes had been with her. If new boys came around to visit Frankie, Mercedes's body tensed. She seemed to understand that something in the combination of attentive boys and Coco's sexual interest posed a threat to Coco and Mercedes both. When Coco wanted to be what she called strong, her watchdog daughter made it easier to "do right," but if Coco wanted to be what she called bad, she resented her daughter's checks. Coco was honest with her daughters about her relationship with Frankie, but her resolutions changed with her mood; for Mercedes, who took her mother very seriously, Coco's vacillations were bewildering. Coco would yell at Frankie, "I ain't having nobody in my house who don't do for me!" Then she'd yell at Mercedes if Mercedes supported the idea of kicking Frankie out: "I won't let you tell me who I can have in my house!" Even though Mercedes had told Frankie straight-up that she hated him, Coco believed that Mercedes would still have alerted him to her mother's indiscretion, if she'd known about it. Mercedes regarded Frankie as family, compared to Wishman.

Lately, everything Mercedes did seemed to bother Coco: Coco relied on her as a helpmate and confidante, then yelled at Mercedes for acting grown. She chided Mercedes for forgetting to change Pearl's Pampers or for scolding Nikki, but neither was Mercedes free to be a child. When she tried to be affectionate with her mother, even her hugs seemed to weigh too heavily around Coco's neck. "You ain't a baby, Mercedes!" she would threaten, or, "Mercedes, you too big!" Mercedes had always been tall for her age, but her obvious neediness made her seem more cumbersome; her unhappiness demanded attention, which was in short supply. As a child, Mercedes had only pouted at Coco's inconsistencies, but now she got angry. When she couldn't get Coco's attention, she would hit one of her sisters or pick a fight with a neighbor's child. By late summer, Mercedes was getting into fights almost every day.

One August afternoon, Coco answered her door to find a police officer staring down at her. She assumed he wanted Frankie. Instead, he asked, "Do you have a daughter by the name of Mercedes?"

Mercedes was at church. A local church occasionally lured Corliss

Park's children to a youth group with promises of pizza and a ride in a van. Coco wasn't particularly religious, but she was glad the children had something constructive to do. The pizza also relieved Coco of the worry of one more meal.

The police officer said Mercedes was potentially guilty of harassment—she'd allegedly called a neighborhood woman fat and threatened to send her cousin after her.

"Do you know how old my daughter is?" asked Coco. The officer expressed surprise that Mercedes was seven. He suggested Coco have a talk with her, before she ended up in juvenile hall. He said he heard Mercedes's name a lot.

Mercedes admitted to harassing the woman. Coco approached the woman, who was new to Corliss Park and white. The woman told Coco she didn't want problems from a little girl. "Exactly," Coco agreed, "*a little girl*. But why you calling the cops? You want my daughter to get arrested? I know you ain't the type to cause trouble. If you have a problem with my kids, knock on my fucking door."

On the street, Coco usually defended Mercedes, so as not to shame her. But at home, she reprimanded her daughter for instigating fights. Sometimes she grounded Mercedes—"Go to your room. You're not seeing no street," she'd say—but Coco found it difficult to stick to the punishment. Although she didn't approve of Mercedes's combativeness, she understood; she, too, took her frustrations out on her kids.

One hot sticky evening, Coco's rage exploded over everyone: Coco chased Mercedes, yelled at Nikki, and warned Nautica, "You're next!" Smacks punctuated every syllable—"You [smack] been [smack] ask [smack] ing [smack] for [smack] it [smack] all day!" Mercedes screamed, "*I want my daddy!*" Her sisters watched her blankly. Nikki looked dazed.

Coco checked her answering machine, cranking the volume to drown the girls' crying. The first message was from her caseworker, who was trying to process her Section 8 application, so Coco could leave Corliss Park: Coco wanted to move to a place where Frankie wouldn't have to hide like a fugitive. Frankie's voice followed: "Yo, Ma, yo, I been calling you all day, yo, but you ain't there, I'll see you." She rewound the tape to hear his voice again, then dragged herself into the kitchen, where the girls had gone in search of food.

Mercedes scanned the refrigerator. Besides a dozen eggs, it was nearly empty. She held a bottle of sour milk at arm's length. It had spoiled while they were in the Bronx. Mercedes clipped her nose. "Mommy! It stinks!"

"Toss it, Mercedes," Coco said wearily.

"Mami!" Mercedes said helplessly. Coco snatched it and flung the full container into a corner generally designated for trash. She sent Mercedes to the store for milk. Nikki wanted cereal; Pearl wanted instant potatoes; Mercedes wanted Spam and scrambled eggs; Nautica needed to know the whereabouts of Baby Matthew, her pet rock. Nikki requested the plastic bowl with the straw attached. Coco opened and shut a cabinet, and a Barbie leg caught Nautica's eye. Mercedes rescued Barbie. Nautica had by then spotted Nikki's miniature box of Froot Loops. Coco offered cornflakes. Nautica slumped inconsolably to the floor. Nikki tiptoed by, carefully balancing the cereal bowl she'd topped to the rim with milk. Coco propped Pearl against a wall and placed a bowl of instant potatoes between her feet.

"*I* want potatoes," Nautica said. Coco cooked a second batch. She cracked open the last of Mercedes's eggs. Mercedes changed her order to tuna fish.

"Eggs and Spam ham, Mercedes!"

Mercedes flung herself onto the couch.

"I want Spam ham!" Nautica started.

"Naughty," Coco sighed. She wiped the knife on her leg and sliced her a hunk, and gave Pearl another dollop of potatoes, since most of the previous serving now frosted the floor.

Nikki pointed to the smear. "Mommy, look!"

"You don't think I see?" Coco replied.

"I need a spoon!" Nikki added.

"Go find one, then!" Coco said.

Nikki found a dirty spoon. She found Baby Matthew, too. "Nautica, look!" Nikki declared.

"Gimme that!" Coco said, grabbing the spoon from her daughter to rinse.

"I don't need a spoon, Mommy," Nikki said reassuringly, slurping the milk from her bowl to demonstrate. Nautica dropped the hunk of Spam to pick up Baby Matthew and happily sauntered off.

Coco scooped up the potatoes and Spam and dumped them in the garbage. She stepped onto the reeking bag to stuff in the overflow and dragged it outside. The girls dropped the dirty dishes in the sink. Coco arranged the comforters on the floor and told the girls to lie down.

"I can sleep here?" Mercedes asked, full of hope.

"What I say, Mercedes?" Coco said. Pearl scooted to the edge of the blanket and rested her cheek on the floor. The linoleum was pleasingly cool. Nautica escorted her rock through the forest of sisters, balancing Baby Matthew precariously above Pearl's head.

"Naughty," Coco warned as she rewound the answering machine. She listened again to Frankie with a grim face, her hand on her hip, and rewound it once more. She searched for the cartoon channel. Nikki snored—her sinus trouble.

Mercedes propped herself against the couch. As the night wore on, she struggled to stay awake. She would doze and slip to the side, then jerk back up. Coco, gazing glassy-eyed at the familiar cartoon stories, eventually fell asleep. Only then did Mercedes allow herself to drift off.

By the end of the summer, Coco began to accept that there was nothing for her in the Bronx. She couldn't stop her mother from running around; Wishman was committed to his girl; her own girls had to return to school. Coco resolved to tackle her small-city life. She appreciated Frankie more than she had in a while. "Frankie isn't the best man in the world. He gives me headaches, but he's been there for me. He helps me with the girls," she said. He promised to pay for their school supplies.

In the meantime, national changes in welfare policy had finally caught up with her, and Coco either had to return to school or go to work. Pearl's medical disabilities had bought her a little time, but now she had to report to a "transition agency." Coco supported the welfare-to-work policy, but she was afraid to place Pearl in day care until she was old enough to speak; how could Coco know if anything went wrong? Coco had come to blame her failure to protect Mercedes from the alleged sexual abuse on the two weeks she'd worked at Youngland, the clothing store in the Bronx; during that time, she'd left Mercedes at Lourdes's, and Mercedes couldn't yet talk. But Coco had no choice with Pearl: Milagros was enrolled in a GED course and going back to work herself, and Coco didn't entirely trust Frankie to pay close attention to Pearl's medical needs.

Luckily, Pearl thrived in day care; then, better still, she got accepted for Head Start. Coco called Pearl "Little Teacher" because she wore tiny pink glasses. Her enthusiasm for school reminded Coco of her own, when she was younger. Coco remembered Foxy taking them to the dollar store for school supplies, and how she had sharpened her pencil so many times in anticipation that she had ended up with nubs. Pearl went nearly crazy with excitement as she waited by the picture window each morning for the Head Start bus.

Coco decided to return to school and pursue her high school equivalency diploma. She believed a GED would help her find a better-paying job and set the best example for her girls. With the exception of the brief stint at Youngland, and baby-sitting, Coco, at twenty-three, had never held a job. On her academic assessment test, she scored at a fifth-grade level in reading, and sixth-grade in math.

After the first week of classes, Coco proclaimed herself transformed. "Welfare, just the word makes me sick. Before it used to be, 'Oh, I'm just getting my check, whatever.'" Now she was headed to a career. She would work in medical records until she could learn photography. Serena quizzed her from a list of vocabulary words: *Compassion. Humble. Jeer. Brutality.* Coco scored a perfect grade on the second test. Cesar's letters would no longer intimidate her with big words she could not pronounce. She denounced his requirement that the photographs she send exclude Pearl and Nikki. His children were his children, but they had sisters, and she was proud of all of her daughters. "I'm tired of having to hide what's me," she wrote.

To Coco's surprise, Cesar didn't lecture her about mentioning her other children. His time in the box was prompting him to reconsider things. "You go girl," he wrote. "Get that education together. You could do anything you put your mind to. Don't let anyone tell you different." In her next letter, she signed off, "From the love of your life Coco."

Frankie, however, got anxious about the implications of the new Coco in his midst: he predicted that she would abandon him. Coco agreed. "He can't afford me," she said pertly. But Frankie surprised her, too, and found an off-the-books job laying cement slabs for a sidewalk construction crew. It was the first almost-legal job he'd ever held.

Coco cranked up the volume on the radio when she heard Frankie's news, then grabbed him and danced. Frankie rarely danced; he felt self-conscious, and Coco sometimes made fun of him. But now he held Coco's hands and the girls piled in: Mercedes hulked over Nikki, who shimmied her skinny hips and coyly flicked her wrists; Pearl bounced slightly off-beat to the music; and Nautica, with perfect timing, did her crowd-pleasing butterfly. The moment later reminded Coco of happy times when she was growing up, when her stepfather, Richie, would dance Spanish with her mother in the middle of the afternoon. Said Coco, "It was music everywhere. Music all around."

CHAPTER THIRTY-ONE

Prisoners while away hours imagining what they would do if they were released. Cesar wanted to take a plane ride and travel. Boy George wanted to take the subway to Harlem, get off at 125th Street, and walk home to the South Bronx over the Willis Avenue Bridge. Jessica wanted to open Club Fed, her own nightspot, where she would dress up and hostess. She envisioned palm trees, a waterfall, decorated drinks. Federal IDs would let ex-felons in for free.

With less than two years remaining on her sentence, however, Jessica began to think more seriously about the prospect of her release. Her optimism about the future derived in part from the restorative powers of a new love. Jessica had met Nilda, a shy, old-world Puerto Rican girl, in the recreation room. Nilda resembled Milagros—short and stocky, with a pug nose and cagey eyes.

"Take your hat off," Jessica had said suggestively. "You got long hair under your hat." She smiled her fantastic smile. Nilda removed her hat. "You got real pretty hair," complimented Jessica. She then invited Nilda to give her a birthday kiss—although it wasn't her birthday. Before the week was out, they had fallen in love.

But Nilda was scheduled to start DAP, the drug-treatment program Jessica had earlier been kicked out of, and Nilda didn't want to have a long-distance relationship with a girl on another unit. "If you want to be with me, you have to go," Nilda said.

Jessica didn't want to reapply to DAP. She claimed that she hated the staff, but seemed more worried about the shame of failing a second time. Jessica's hesitation brought out Nilda's conviction in her, a dynamic that would come to characterize their relationship.

Nilda was raised in a family of fourteen. She'd married briefly, in a failed attempt to convince her mother that she wasn't a lesbian. "I related to Jessica," she said. "I was raped when I was young, the hitting and the beating. It was like I decided I was going to change Jessica, and I felt if Jessica could change, I could change." She reminded Jessica that her five children needed a mother, and that DAP meant a time cut: it was Jessica's responsibility to try. Jessica reapplied, and Nilda relocated to the DAP unit. Jessica joined her there ten days later. Miranda, her old rival who'd managed Boy George's table, had been transferred to Danbury, and was starting DAP as well. She and Jessica became friends.

Jessica's other girlfriends had been possessive, but Nilda didn't discourage Jessica's socializing; if Jessica wanted to go to the rec room and Nilda didn't, Nilda said, "You go." When Jessica was blue, Nilda would put Spanish music on the radio. "Come on, baby, dance," she would say. Nilda herself wasn't much of a dancer, but she would do anything to amuse Jessica; once, she started breakdancing in the dinner line. But when Jessica got belligerent, Nilda knew to let her be; a few times, Jessica provoked Nilda and dared Nilda to hit her; Nilda refused. Once, however, Nilda did shove Jessica—when she caught her making out with Lovely, Cesar's pen pal. "You set that girl up with your brother!" Nilda charged. Jessica was amused at Nilda's prudishness. She assured her, "My brother is like, 'The three of us will go at it, there's no problem right there.'"

Always, Jessica missed her children. She traded stamps and manicures for birthday cards made by the more artistic inmates. She sent candy to Kevin and Brittany and Stephanie. She blamed Milagros for their coolness. Once, after Jessica had kissed the twin girls at a visit, they wiped her lipstick off their cheeks. They called Milagros Mommy, which continued to humiliate and enrage Jessica. Nilda said, "Your job is just to love them no matter what they call you."

As Jessica progressed through DAP, her abandonment of Serena increasingly haunted her. She worried less about the twin girls—they belonged to Milagros—and she admitted that she felt little connection to the baby boys. But the bond with her eldest daughter stayed strong. She mailed gifts to Serena—crocheted hangers, crocheted slippers, an address book. She consigned a friend to make Serena a T-shirt featuring the Tasmanian Devil with the inscription *Mommy's Little Angel, Serena.* At one point, Jessica even forwarded Serena her diary, but Milagros intercepted it, saying that it was too sad for a child to bear. Nilda urged Jessica to keep writing the girls letters whether or not they responded. Years from now, her daughters could look back upon her efforts and understand that, even though she wasn't with them, they were always in her thoughts.

As Nilda tutored Jessica about motherhood in prison, Coco and Milagros argued about the best way to raise Jessica's daughter back in Troy. Serena was twelve, and showing signs of Jessica's sleepy beauty. Both Coco and Milagros divided her world into two options—a belly, or school and a future—but they disagreed about how to steer her in the right direction. Milagros's approach was to repress all signs of Serena's womanhood, whereas Coco thought it wiser to impart life's truths as she knew them. When Kevin, now fifteen, confided to Coco that he and his girlfriend were having sex, Coco gave him condoms and urged Frankie to speak with him. (Frankie claimed he tried, but Coco thought that Frankie and Kevin just ended up smoking weed.)

Serena continued to do poorly academically, but she had learned how to circumnavigate the school dress code. When necessary, she'd zip up her jacket in the hallway to hide her midriff-exposing top. She earned attention from the boys who hung around Corliss Park, Kevin's friends, older boys. They commented when she and her best friend made a point of passing by the basketball court.

Jessica spoke to the children on the phone after she'd resettled into DAP. "Why haven't you written me?" she asked Serena. "You chillin'? You love me?"

"Yeah," said Serena.

"How much you love me?"

Serena answered without much heart, "Two fingers put together so nobody can come between us." Jessica reminded her that, if she earned a time cut, she could be home by the end of the year. Stephanie grabbed the phone. Jessica said, "You still see your daddy, then? Tell him to send me money."

"He still with his wife," Stephanie said.

"Your father's full of ca-ca," Jessica said, before remembering her newer approach to parenting. "Even though youse are big, I'm gonna take you to school."

Brittany reported an 85 average and recited the days of the week in Spanish. "Love you smushies," she chirped.

"Bunches and bunches," said Jessica. Serena came back on the line. Jessica asked Serena to sing a song, remembering how, as a child, she'd loved to croon into a hairbrush. "Make believe the phone is a microphone," Jessica urged.

Serena said, "I don't want to."

"Why?"

"Cuz my voice is all cracky."

"It's a feeling, you'll get over it," Jessica said, hurt. Serena passed the phone to Kevin. Jessica marveled at his deep voice. "You are sounding like a whole man. Before you was a little cutie, now—you are using the condoms, right?" She reminded him to protect his sisters and to take care of himself. He'd been getting into trouble—placed on probation for stealing a bicycle with a group of his friends and suspended from school for fights. Jessica added, "This ain't no life for nobody. It's boring. Yo, you be good." If he mailed her some pictures, she promised to hook him up with some pretty prison girls.

Milagros finally had her turn. Jessica teased her, too. "You gotta keep him away from me. You know how I am with the young boys."

"I'll beat you up if you show him things," Milagros replied cheerfully.

"How the boys?"

"They bad."

"Serena?"

"Bad. She got a body and a half." Usually, Jessica deflected her dependence on Milagros with sarcasm, or by criticizing Milagros's mothering, soaking her own wounds in blame. This time, she tried something different. "Thank you for everything, girl," she said, venturing to speak aloud what Milagros understood. Then Jessica quickly changed the subject, as if embarrassed not only by the help Milagros had given her, but also by the expanse of the need that remained.

Serena seemed to understand that despite her longing for a mother, her most vital connection to Jessica was as a friend. Boys, for example—her mother's favorite subject—appeared in Serena's letters far more often than they did in her day-to-day conversations:

> Oh Mommy guess what you know the boys I told you about they was at this dance I went to. When it was over we all went outside and I walked around by myself and one of them walked by me and was like "Beau-ty-ful" then he went on walking and then he was like "Serena don't denie it you know you was the prettys girl up in that dance" and then all the boys was like Yap. I said, "thank you very much." Well that is all I have to say. Peace and love Serena . . . P.S. The boys names are Anderson, Ernesto, Mike, Cris and Thorey. Ernesto was the one who called me Beautyful.

In another letter, Serena described a trip to the store:

> . . . they'es boys was outside and kept on looking at me. So I didn't want Mommy Milagros to leave me by myself in the store but the baby's had to use the bathroom so she went around the corner to take them + ask me to pay for the stuff so I did, but when I came out

the boys started kicking it to me you know trying to talk to me. One boy was like what's up cutie and was like hi, he was like, don't you live on 14th street, I was like no, he was like yeah you don't remember me I was riding my bike I was like no, then he ask me for the 7 digits (my #) I told him no because I am already taken. This boy was so cute. I only said that I was taken because I am not allowed to have no boyfriends. . . . this other boy try to kick it to me in front of my mother and just ignored him cause he was butt ugly. Well mommy, I gotta go I love you so very mush and of course miss you more then Nething.

By New Year's 1998, Milagros had completed her GED and returned to work full-time; she'd found a job as a home health-care aide. She needed Serena to help watch the twin boys after Kevin picked them up from day care and brought them home. The Troy buses ran infrequently and Milagros's workdays sometimes ended at nine or ten o'clock. Serena chafed at the responsibility. Kevin was supposed to help baby-sit, but he spent his time with friends or his girlfriend, and Milagros had a higher tolerance for his irresponsibility because he was a boy. He was also impatient with the children and sometimes hit them.

Coco felt that Serena ended up with too much of the burden, but understood the situation from both sides—from the perspective of her niece, with whom she shared a sense of lockdown, and from the perspective of Milagros, with whom she shared the feeling of being overwhelmed. Milagros also regretted relying on Serena; it reminded her of her own childhood, having to watch little children indoors when she wanted to go outside with her friends. Sometimes she managed to get home early and relieve Serena, but instead of playing outside, Serena would make a beeline for Coco's, which irritated Milagros: What was the difference between one house full of children and the next?

That same January, Coco dyed her hair black and immediately decided it was a mistake. "I feel I look tough, mean. I don't want to look like that," she said. "I want to get over my past. I want to learn how to get over it. I just want to move on." There was too much come-and-go at Corliss Park, and when she received another eviction notice, it seemed like a blessing rather than a curse: "I feel once I'm out of this stupid building I'll be much, much better, and my life will be great," she said. By February, she'd found an apartment in a drafty house on a hill near the girls' school.

"There's drugs there," said Frankie; he preferred to keep street and home life separate.

"There's drugs everywhere," Coco replied.

But if Coco was readying to make her break from the Bronx, the Bronx wasn't done with her. Her new place immediately filled up with the latest wave of refugees. Some of her visitors had recently been living at Foxy's, but Foxy got hauled in during a drug raid—"I was in the wrong place at the wrong time," she said—and her apartment was temporarily off-limits. Like her mother, Coco had trouble saying no to anyone in need.

Trouble broke open like a burst of billiard balls. Hector, his pregnant wife, Iris, and his son had gone homeless in Troy; Hector had been dealing drugs in the Bronx, and he wanted a fresh start before the new baby arrived. Hector's Iris's childhood friend Platinum had followed Iris up with her son and gotten kicked out of the shelter for mouthing off. Sheila, Foxy's old neighbor, was hiding from her favorite son, who'd been released from prison and gone back to crack; Sheila dreaded having to involve the police. She had found an apartment in Troy, but she couldn't afford to buy any furniture; when she stayed in her place overnight, she slept on a thin blanket on the linoleum floor. Hector's family had also gotten a housing placement, only to learn from the pizza delivery boy that the previous tenant had been stabbed to death by her husband, which explained the stains on the stairs. They all preferred Coco's house.

In a sense, all folks going house to house were fugitives: sometimes it was a debt or a stepfather or a boyfriend who scattered a family; other times, a marshal's padlock drove you from your door. That's what had happened to Hector's Iris before she'd moved into Foxy's: following her mother's arrest for dealing, the apartment was seized, and Iris had to crawl in through the window to retrieve some clothes.

Day in, day out, life in the overcrowded house was hard for Coco to bear. Sheila and Platinum smoked cigarettes and Pearl's asthma worsened; Coco tried doing her homework while administering extra treatments, but often fell asleep herself. Now Mercedes was arguing with Tío Hector, instead of with Frankie, but the arguments covered the same tired themes. Hector would reprimand Mercedes for not listening to Coco, and Mercedes would blink her eyes insultingly and suck her teeth. Or she'd shout, "I ain't gotta listen to you. You ain't my father!" Hector, who was only eighteen himself, would yell, "What, you threatening me?" He would order Mercedes and his son to stand in the corner, which Coco found humiliating. On the other hand, Mercedes was exasperating, and Coco would smack her; blank-faced, Mercedes took her licks. Her fortitude impressed Hector's wife. She said, "Coco whips Mercedes's ass and she pays no mind." Mercedes's apparent toughness reminded Coco of the stories she'd heard about Cesar as a boy. Mercedes listened carefully to the comparisons made between her and her dad.

Soon, Head Start effectively expelled Pearl: she still had seizures and vomited whatever she ate, and they were understaffed. The situation devastated both mother and daughter. Every morning, as Pearl's sisters put on their coats and grabbed their knapsacks, she said, "Mommy, give me my bookbag. I want to go to school."

"Mami, but you sick," Coco would say, and Pearl would start to cry. Coco tried to distract her with a Barney video. Pearl adored Barney; she often walked around the apartment humming the theme song to the show and clutching her beloved Barney book. Coco left Pearl at home and went to class, but she knew that her daughter could be fine one minute and in jeopardy the next. Coco worried that her friends might overlook the signs that preceded her attacks—how the color of her fingernails changed, or her nostrils flared, or the constant swallowing.

Pearl's removal from Head Start also jeopardized her benefits; SSI needed proof that Coco wasn't responsible for keeping her out of school. Luckily, Pearl's teacher wrote a letter describing Pearl's condition, and Coco brought a copy of the letter to Pearl's doctor, who finally seemed to hear what Coco had been saying to various medical professionals for more than two years. He diagnosed Pearl with reflux—a condition greatly eased by a simple operation. Frankie nursed Pearl through her recovery because Coco couldn't bear to see her baby with a feeding tube.

In the midst of everything, upsetting rumors about Cesar's wife, Giselle, had been reaching Coco upstate. Giselle owned a car; Giselle was studying law; Giselle was in Elaine's wedding (Elaine and her husband, Angel, remarried in church, and Elaine's father threw them a reception, from which Lourdes was barred). Giselle took her son, who looked distressingly like Cesar, to Disney World. Most hurtful to Coco was the news that Jessica was corresponding with Giselle, her new sister-in-law.

CHAPTER THIRTY-TWO

In fact, Giselle had never responded to Jessica's letter, and the rumors made Giselle's situation sound better than it was. The car she used was borrowed from her godmother—in exchange for repairs and gas. Giselle's son, Gabriel, had been the ring bearer at Elaine's wedding, and it was true that Giselle had taken him to Disney World, but it was their first vacation in six years, and she was still paying for it on an installment plan. She was enrolled in Bronx Community College, but she'd had to borrow $400 from a loan shark for tuition because of the vacation debt. Since the Disney World trip, however, she was considering switching her major from business to criminal justice because she'd heard that Florida had a shortage of prison guards. In the meantime, as she had for the last three years, Giselle plugged away in the office of a factory that produced menus. She earned $8.75 an hour, without benefits. But she still felt lucky; her mother worked the factory floor, and compared to that, office work was a luxury.

On her desk, Giselle kept a photograph of Cesar, taken during one of their trailers. You couldn't tell from the picture that he was in prison—he stood near what passed for a small cabin, on grass. Giselle kept Cesar's incarceration a secret from her colleagues. "People are ignorant, they start treating you stupid," she said. Love wasn't something anyone could understand. When they asked why her mysterious husband didn't pick her up after work or take her dancing, Giselle said, "He works." Four nights a week, she went to school—she had no time for playing. From school, if it wasn't too late, she collected her son from her mother, and they went back to the orderly apartment where they rented a tiny room.

The apartment was only blocks from East Tremont, where Giselle had been raised and her mother still lived; she yearned to leave the neighborhood but couldn't afford to. In the meantime, the trailer visits with Cesar provided her with some escape. Once she cleared the prison gates and had her bags searched and got processed, there was Cesar, waiting for her. They would painstakingly put away the groceries or arrange the videos she'd brought to watch. She had finally weaned Cesar of the gangster movies he'd loved when he was on the lam; now she subjected him to her own favorites—romances. He had cried at the end of *Romeo and Juliet*. She was eager to show him *Titanic*, but she had to wait for the certified release, because the Department of Corrections banned bootleg tapes. The initial awkwardness between them on the trailers enchanted Cesar; it bemused him how nervous he could be with his legal wife. But once they kissed, things relaxed.

Giselle had her own kitchen and her husband to cook for, and her son was free to jump about the way a growing boy was supposed to, without someone yelling at him, "Be quiet, Gabriel!" or, when he watched cartoons, "Turn down the TV!" Here Gabriel's exuberance wasn't inevitably met with an adult's irritation, and his requests to play Go Fish and Spit got Cesar's grateful *Yes*, instead of *No*. In the afternoon, he and Cesar played basketball.

For the first few trailers, Cesar didn't sleep at all—he didn't want to miss a moment—so when Giselle fell asleep, he woke up Gabriel and they played chess, a game Cesar had taught him in the regular visiting room. The only reminders of prison, besides the consciousness of time passing, and the barbed wire, and the occasional crackling announcement from the loudspeaker, were the three times a day Cesar had to step outside for count.

Although Giselle yearned to understand Cesar's prison life, she didn't like to pry. She watched the TV show *Oz* for insight, and weighed it against the small tidbits that he shared. She kept her worries about his safety to herself, although she shared her fears that he would go back to being a heartbreaker as soon as he returned to the free world. "I'm not saying I will be faithful, but I will never leave her," he said. But the real threat to their marriage was much closer to home. Cesar had yet to tell Giselle that he had received an additional one to three years for possessing the shank; nor did she know he was using heroin.

In the spring of 1998, Cesar asked Giselle to make arrangements to bring Mercedes and Nautica along on the next trailer, and Giselle agreed. She knew that Mercedes had been writing Cesar about her unhappiness at home, and that he was worried about her. When he got out, he wrote Mercedes, she could live with him and his wife.

The trailer visit would coincide with Mercedes's eighth birthday. For weeks, it was all Mercedes spoke about. Some of the staff at her school pitched in for the bus fare. Coco had bought the girls new outfits, sneakers, toothbrushes, socks, and underwear. No one would have any reason to discount her daughters, and she instructed them to speak up if anything made them uncomfortable, or if they wanted to sleep with their father or sit on his lap. Mercedes and Nautica were packed to go days before they were due to leave.

Then, the night before the girls were going to meet Giselle in the city, Giselle called Coco: the trailer visit had been canceled—there had been a fight at the prison and Cesar had been slashed. He'd been thrown into protective custody, with thirty-two stitches across his back.

Weeks earlier, Cesar's friend had been attacked. According to Cesar, the men involved decided to jump Cesar rather than wait, because they feared Cesar would retaliate. Cesar had been standing in the chow line when they assaulted him.

Cesar didn't want the children to visit until the beef was resolved. The visiting room on a weekend would provide a prime opportunity for a revenge attack on his family. He didn't want to put the children at risk, or put himself in a position where he would have to defend them, thereby further compromising his already shaky status with the authorities.

When Giselle arrived that Thursday, Cesar nervously scanned the room before he would let her hug him. He hadn't shaved, and he had dark circles beneath his bloodshot eyes. Ordinarily, he ate three packages of barbecue chicken wings and three packages of microwave french fries, but Giselle had to get after him to finish even one. He told her he could finish his own sentence because it was punishment for killing Mighty, and for all the bad things he'd done for which he hadn't been caught. But he couldn't live with being the cause of harm done to his family. Giselle found that she was unable to comfort Cesar this time: "All the serenity he had was gone."

Before Giselle could make it back to see Cesar, he got shipped to Southport again.

When Lourdes and the girls visited Jessica, that same spring, they found her in a reflective mood. In therapy, she had been analyzing her relationship with her family and reconsidering her relationships with men. After greeting her with hugs, the three girls headed into the prison's playroom, a glassed-in space with bright decorations and comfortable furniture and toys. Jessica eyed Lourdes narrowly. "I had to write a family history and I put that you was codependent on men." Lourdes fidgeted in her seat. "I don't even know the reason my father died."

"I told you, Mami," Lourdes said.

"Why he died, then?" Jessica asked accusingly.

"Mami! I *told* you."

"Did you love him?"

"I loved him, but he hurt me a lot," Lourdes said as though her throat were bruised.

The children drifted back. Jessica started her usual primping and grooming. She styled the twins' hair, using her fingers as a comb. She picked lint from their clothes. She noticed a plastic price-tag thread on Serena's shoe and bit it off. She braided Serena's hair. She described the kind of nightlife they would share when she got out. If she continued to do well in DAP, she would be home by Christmas. "They gonna think we sisters. We gonna dye our hair blond. We don't have to ask anybody. I be like, 'C'mon, Serena, get dressed! We going to a club!' "

"Ai," Lourdes cautioned.

"You just jealous," Jessica said. When Jessica had been a teenager and taken her mother dancing, she'd made Lourdes pretend they were sisters. Now, though, the ruse could never work. Lourdes had aged. She lumbered instead of scurried. She looked matronly. The anger that had animated her eyes had been replaced by resignation. She wore smocks and turtlenecks instead of tank tops and leggings; Hush Puppies instead of strappy sandals with heels.

Serena flapped her knees distractedly.

"Mami, your legs! Keep your legs closed!" Lourdes said sharply. Serena rolled her eyes. "He beat me up," Lourdes murmured.

"Why you stay with him then?" Jessica asked, her tone wet with disgust.

Lourdes's indignation barely stirred. She mumbled, "You have to be sure you want to leave when you leave. You can't come back. You be towed around like a dog."

Jessica then came at her mother again. "I want to get a job, any job. I will do anything. I want to support myself." Lourdes didn't retaliate, and Jessica backed down, adding, "Mommy, I gave your address to the parole. They'll be calling you. They need to come to the apartment to look to make sure everything's okay." The Troy Housing Authority had already rejected Jessica's application to live with Milagros; they did not accept felons. Jessica hadn't heard back from Elaine, and she'd never taken Coco's offer seriously. Lourdes's cramped one-bedroom was her only choice.

"You going to live with me? My baby's coming home!" Lourdes exclaimed. She sidled onto Jessica's lap. "I am so happy, Mami! I knew you were coming to me!" She kicked her feet a little, but the enthusiasm felt fraudulent.

"Your man," Jessica said gravely. Lourdes slipped back into her seat and cast her eyes down. Jessica bent forward and placed her elbows on her knees. "Your boyfriend," she repeated, staring up at her mother, making sure Lourdes heard all that could not be said. The silence lasted only seconds, but it contained decades of their history. Jessica then relieved her: "If you start messing up, I'm gonna be behind you on that." The threat hung between them hollowly, before it gave way to levity.

Jessica leaned back. She breathed in the uplifting sight of a young boy, who stood beside another boy peering at the selection in the vending machines. They were visiting their mothers. One was the son of one of Jessica's friends. "Serena, come on, look how cute that boy is!" she said.

"You so bad," Serena said.

"Come on! Come on, Mami! You so pretty! Look how cute he is!" She pulled Serena's hand and clasped her shoulders and positioned her in line. Serena waited and bought candy like a soldier, all the while with her eyes down. When she was through, she pressed into Jessica's belly, happy and relieved.

"You so bad, you so bad," Serena repeated.

Jessica smiled.

CHAPTER THIRTY-THREE

Coco survived another winter, but she was run down by the demands of school and the days and nights of Baby Motrin, steaming showers for Pearl's asthma, and the endless sippy cups of apple juice. She struggled to finish her schoolwork, but during class she found it nearly impossible to concentrate: she would start wondering if the girls had made it home safely from school, if Frankie's friends were in the apartment, and if they'd devoured her daughters' snacks. One morning, she snuck back to check up on Frankie and caught him bagging crack in the kitchen. She dropped out of school to keep watch over him. He balked at her policing, and one fight got physical. Mercedes ran to a nearby hospital, where there was a telephone. She called her uncle Hector and begged him to hurry over and help.

Coco's affection for Nikki's father, Kodak, had ended that day he hit her years before. Cesar had never laid a violent hand on her. Coco threw Frankie out. To make ends meet without his assistance, she took in baby-sitting, adding three children to her bedraggled four. At the end of the week, for five days of child care from 6 A.M. until 3:40 P.M., she was paid a total of $40. Added runs to the church pantries didn't make the food last. By the weekend, Coco felt as though she was going crazy. It was spring, and the girls needed air, but the backyard was a slide of mud.

Coco sometimes walked down the hill to Fallon, the garden apartments where Iris lived. Iris was making progress toward the realization of a lifelong dream—she wanted to own a funeral home. "At least dead people are quiet," she said. The local community college had a mortuary-science program Iris hoped to take; she had nearly completed her GED. Her husband, Armando, toiled at Garden Way, a nearby factory. Iris worked part-time at a hobby shop; she got discounts on the supplies for ceramic lamps and statues, which she liked to sand down and paint in her spare time. She also taught ceramics at the community center at Fallon, where she'd received an award from the tenants' association for her good works. Mercedes had enjoyed attending her classes for a while.

Hector and his wife and son also visited Iris's. One afternoon, Hector got into a shouting match with the drug dealer who lived next door; the drug dealer made an allusion to Coco's affair with Wishman, Hector told him to shut up, and things deteriorated from there. Next thing you know, the dealer's brother pulled a gun. In the past, Iris had asked this neighbor to lower the loud music, but she was careful to control her temper; Hector didn't know how. Later Iris's husband, Armando, said, "We been here three years without trouble, and look, here it is, when your family comes."

Without Frankie to baby-sit, Coco's situation stagnated. "I'm dying," she said. "I can't go nowhere. I can't go shopping. I'm just pinned." Summer provided some relief, although, unfortunately, the sloping backyard that the girls had longed to play in for months was spiked with dangerous junk and infested with fleas. But Coco adamantly stuck to the positive things. She might have had to drop out of school, but Iris had graduated and made a beautiful speech. She had spoken from her heart in front of everyone: she had told the audience how she was nervous, and that she'd moved to Troy to get a better life; that she'd left school at fifteen because she was pregnant, and that the years had passed, and she didn't feel like going back. But when her kids asked what she was going to be when she grew up, and she didn't know what to tell them, she realized it was time.

Foxy had traveled up for the graduation; it always pleased Coco when her children got to spend time with their grandmother, and she was also relieved to see that Foxy didn't seem to be partying so much—she was fat. The public swimming pool that was within walking distance of the apartment buoyed Coco's girls through the dog days of summer heat. Pearl loved the water; Nikki loved her shimmery bikini; Nautica mastered the cannonball.

But Mercedes tested her mother's patience with comments like "I'm gonna get a tattoo and get me a man" and "I want a boyfriend."

"Wait till you father hears you want a boyfriend, Mercy," Coco warned.

"How old do I have to be to have a boyfriend?" Mercedes persisted.

Coco shouted, *"You don't even know what a boyfriend is!"*

To Coco's relief, Mercedes spent two blessed weeks with her grandmother when Foxy went back down to the Bronx.

Since Coco had kicked him out of the apartment, Frankie had been living with one of Coco's cousins, Leo, who'd moved to Troy from the Bronx. One August afternoon, Frankie rode his bicycle down River Street, past mangy dogs and pit bulls trotting along the busted sidewalks, half-breeds and rottweilers and skulking mutts. He was headed to a block party at Fallon sponsored by the tenants' association, in which Iris was involved.

Frankie dodged potholes. His tires crunched the shattered forties glass. His tank top billowed in the breeze. He emerged from the shade of the overpass and cycled onto the sidewalk that trailed the Hudson. He coasted off the sidewalk back onto the street. He passed the furniture warehouse that was too expensive and did not deliver, the Napoli bakery, where the lady behind the counter still snubbed you, no matter how many loaves of Italian bread you bought. By the dreary Happy Lunch luncheonette, the old tavern, the rows of empty tenements. A thin white guy with long, feathered hair kicked a box toward a U-Haul. Moving vans were a familiar sight along River Street. The bored women watched Frankie pass.

Fat women, scrawny women, women on broken steps drinking diet no-name soda out of promotional cups from Burger King. Two middle-aged ladies sat on the sidewalk in bucket seats salvaged from a car. Frankie turned left at the intersection of River and 101st. He looped around the back road that led to Fallon and glided to a stop.

Frankie was trim from no home cooking and tan from afternoons at the community swimming pool. He wore sunglasses, which Foxy had given to Mercedes and Mercedes had given to him. The lenses were a cool light blue. The hard sun glinted on his newly shaven head. Coco spotted him instantly.

She had been hearing rumors since their latest split: at the pool, Frankie had tossed a girl in the water, then jumped in after her. Serena knew the girl, who was a friend of Kevin's girlfriend's. The girl had met Frankie while visiting her aunt, who lived in the apartment above Frankie's basement room. The aunt had a crush on Coco's cousin and sent the girl downstairs with plates of food. Coco reasoned, "What man isn't going to want a hot little ass walking into your door delivering a plate of homemade food?" The aunt also had real dishes and pretty cups and silverware that didn't bend.

During one of Frankie's sojourns to the Bronx, Coco searched his room in the cellar apartment and unearthed a photograph. She said she also found a poem that began, *Roses are red, violets are blue.* "Come on," Coco snorted, "my girls could do better than that." And if she, Coco, were going to send a man a picture, she'd send a sexy one: this stupid girl had sent Frankie a regular picture of herself looking regular, on a couch. Coco conceded that the girl had pretty, fat lips. "But when she talk to you, she look all ugly cuz she have a mouth full of yellow teeth," she added. When

Coco confronted the girl, her lack of sophistication was evident even in her denial that she'd messed around with Frankie at all: "She said, 'You know I have a man, cuz I have hickeys all the time'"

But the girl's age disturbed Coco most. Frankie was twenty-seven; the girl, fourteen. "Fourteen. That's a child. Come on, that's a child," Coco repeated softly, as though she were still trying to absorb it. Coco confronted Frankie about the girl at the party. He denied that they were involved; when Coco persisted with her accusations, he said, "But, Coco, you ain't got no proof." Coco reasoned that if he was attracted to such a young girl then her own daughters were vulnerable. He said, "Coco, if you don't know me now, talk to my mother. You know I ain't like that." Still, the possibility unnerved her. Said Coco, "I want him to go, then when he leaves I cry." As a precaution, she instructed her daughters to wear shorts under their nightgowns whenever Frankie visited.

That same summer, Kevin's girlfriend came out pregnant. The girl-friend's cousin approached Milagros with the sobering news on the Number 80 bus. Milagros was furious. Kevin's girlfriend had just turned fourteen. "How you gonna support a child when you can't pay for a haircut?" Milagros asked.

"Welfare," Kevin said. How, Milagros wondered, could he choose a life whose hardship lay right before his eyes? In fact, Kevin had walked through Corliss Park carrying the positive tab from the home pregnancy test like a miniature banner. But the pregnancy was only one car in the pileup: the girlfriend's mother was in and out of prison; the girlfriend shuttled between her grandmother and an aunt; the aunt's fast lifestyle was hectic. On weekends, Milagros took Kevin's girlfriend in.

The girl's name was Donna. She was a white girl—skinny, with brown hair, a tendency toward quietness, and a habit of keeping her fingers in her mouth. She and Kevin broke up by her third month, but Serena and Donna became quick best friends. Milagros hoped at least Serena would learn from Donna's mistake since she could see, firsthand, the day-by-day discomfort of a belly. But Coco suspected the opposite could happen; Donna looked prettier the bigger her belly grew. Maybe it was the baby, maybe it was all the attention, or the confidence of sex. Coco knew that love and babies didn't operate on logic. And Serena was thirteen.

"You better keep an eye on Serena now," Coco warned. Guys certainly had their eyes on her. Mercedes had recounted to her mother what boys said to Serena out of the earshot of adults. The harassment reminded Coco of the way she'd been taunted when she was a virgin, but these boys sounded nastier than the boys of her memory. Comments like *When I'm gonna get that?* and *When can I slap on that?* were common. Serena acted oblivious to the comments; Coco remembered hollering back at the boys who used to harass her on Andrews Avenue when she was Serena's age, walking home from school; a few times, Coco had broken down and cried. Foxy had told her to stop walking home by Andrews, but Wishman had defended her on the street. "Stop disrespecting the girl," he'd say.

Serena denied ever having kissed a boy, but Coco knew otherwise. Kevin had caught Serena in the woods kissing one of his friends. It was less than a year before Jessica's release date. "Serena had a I-don't-give-a-fuck attitude. She knows her mother's coming out," Coco said.

Soon the threats posed by and to the various teenaged girls in Coco's life were muted by a larger, more immediate crisis. For months, Coco's landlord had ignored her pleas to fumigate the apartment, which was flea-infested. By fall 1998, the girls scratched so much that the skin around their ankles looked like thick pink socks. The school sent them home with lice. Milagros suggested that Coco call the Department of Health, and Coco did. Requesting help from agencies was always risky, but Coco was desperate. She didn't want her girls to be ashamed of something that wasn't their fault. Instead of sending an exterminator, however, the Department of Health dispatched a housing inspector, who condemned the place. Con Ed shut off the electricity, then sent her a $900 bill. Coco drew an extension cord to the refrigerator from the apartment next door and rushed the girls through their baths at night. The lady told Coco to feel free to use the shower during the day while she was at work, but Coco didn't feel safe with the lady's boyfriend in the house. She also hated to be a burden. She then received a notice that if she didn't move off the premises within seventy-two hours, the Department of Health would report her to the Bureau of Child Welfare for neglect. She was homeless again, for the second time in a year.

Frankie was also about to get kicked out of Coco's cousin Leo's for not paying his share of the rent. But Frankie looked to Coco to resolve the situation; he was making no effort to find them all a new place to live. When Jessica heard about Coco's troubles, instead of the sympathy Coco expected, Jessica lobbed back a hard note of advice: "Stop giving, start getting. How can you say they love you and not help you? Say he love you if he ain't doing? If he ain't doing, get rid of him."

Coco criticized herself: "I been through so much in my life, if I can't pass through this, something is wrong with me." She drew strength from remembering Lourdes: the distance between them had grown, but she still felt a connection. "All the times Lourdes been in trouble, owed rent. How the hell she get out of her mess?" Coco asked herself. Lourdes had a block on her telephone line, so Coco couldn't call collect, and Coco didn't have enough money for a telephone card. But if she had, she would have dialed Lourdes up and asked her, as she had when she was a teenage girl, "What you did?"

CHAPTER THIRTY-FOUR

At forty-eight, Lourdes continued to cobble together an existence, as she always had. She'd joined up with Emilio, the six-foot-three army veteran who'd lived with Maria, the neighbor with cancer who had taken Lourdes in. After Maria's death, Lourdes had briefly inherited custody of Maria's children and the apartment, until the authorities decided otherwise. The eight-year-old reported Lourdes to BCW, claiming that Lourdes wouldn't feed her and her brother, and that she locked them out in the hall. Lourdes claimed she fed them, but refused to let them eat her pantry clean—how, she asked the caseworker, could they be hungry and so overweight? Social Services placed the children in foster care; shortly afterward, Lourdes and Emilio came home to find a padlock on the door and all of their belongings piled in the hall.

Emilio's veteran's status qualified him for rent subsidies, and they found an apartment on a leafy residential street at the end of one of the Bronx subway lines. Lourdes believed that she'd left Mount Hope for good. She called her new neighborhood "civilized." She regularly complained of chest pains and shortness of breath, and the proximity to doctors and a decent hospital reassured her.

She earned extra money baby-sitting Justine, Roxanne and Cesar's daughter, and Justine's half sister. Roxanne, who was pregnant again, dropped them off on her way to the Laundromat, where she worked long hours folding clothes. Lourdes also rented the couch to Angel, her soon-to-be-ex-son-in-law. Elaine had left him and the Bronx for Yonkers, where she lived with her two sons in a working-class neighborhood. Lourdes did Angel's laundry and cooked him dinner. He worked at a law firm in Manhattan as a mail-room clerk.

Still, Lourdes had to hustle to get by. She reapplied for SSI and was rejected. She applied for emergency food stamps and got lucky—$50 worth came through. Her ex-boyfriend Domingo occasionally gave her an extra $20 or $40 when he brought a crate or two of vegetables up to her apartment, his truck double-parked. One time, when Serena visited, they bused to Tremont to hit up Felix, the old family friend who'd offered his Mount Hope apartment to Lourdes, years before. Felix gave Serena money, just as he had her mother, when she was Serena's age. In the long run, though, Lourdes, like Cesar, was banking on Jessica.

Lourdes no longer partied much; she no longer broke night. Darkness no longer haunted her; her prescription medication, Ambien, knocked her out completely, preventing the anxiety attacks that had for years kept her awake. She saw a psychiatrist, who had diagnosed her with depression, a condition that intrigued her. No one had ever attached professional words to her anguish: they had said she was "having problems" or was "all into her business" or "doing wrong" or "messing up."

The relative serenity of Lourdes's new life made the ravages of her old one more apparent: her face had taken on a ruined and vacant air. "She looks that way because she is not avoiding her pain," Cesar said. Like the onset of diabetes that followed years of obesity, or the rotten teeth that came from candy and poor diet, Lourdes was showing the disappointments and disasters she'd weathered to reach middle age. But Lourdes's ailments would recede some in her cozy kitchen, when she stood among Domingo's donated produce. Sacks of onions and garlic slumped against crates of avocados and lemons and tomatoes, and starched ruffled curtains blew in the alleyway breeze.

Domingo attended school at night in pursuit of a trucking license. Sometimes he would stop by after work and practice vocabulary words with Lourdes while she cooked. Emilio spent most of the time quietly watching television in the bedroom. He only became animated when Justine made screwball faces up close to his unhappy one. Her giggles were infectious, and if he tickled her, she tickled him back.

One morning six weeks before Jessica's release, Lourdes changed into a T-shirt and leggings; she already had a tea towel over her shoulder, the way she used to wear her braid. She scrubbed the kitchen sink, filled it with hot water, chopped the tips off the green bananas, slit them, dropped them in the sink, and added in a handful of salt. She peeled the white *yuca*. She skinned the pumpkin and scooped out the seeds. All the while she tended to the codfish she was boiling for the *bacalao* for lunch. She railed against her latest favorite culprit—Elaine—who was snootier than ever since getting promoted at her job. How miraculous it was, mused Lourdes, that her daughter's back wasn't broken for all the sex she was having. If Elaine's working ass was so superior, why didn't she help out her mother? Why wouldn't she take Lourdes to see Cesar in her new used van? Elaine would only drive Cesar's wife. But the ranting no longer revived Lourdes; the complaints seemed a habit, drained of expectation.

By dusk, Lourdes's *pasteles* covered the counters and table. She counted them aloud like a child newly confident with numbers—sixty-seven altogether—and said contentedly, "I'm gonna smoke me a cigarette." Her fingers were stained from the *achiote*. One of her favorite songs, "Suave," came on the radio. She took two *pasteles* and held them elegantly in her swollen hands, as though she were releasing little birds. "When I danced, there was always a circle around me," she recalled wistfully. Now she lacked the optimism for dancing: "Why did God take away from me the one thing that I loved the most?"

A male voice beckoned to her from outside. Lourdes popped her head between the curtains. A workingman stood beneath her window, wearing coveralls. "*Esa comida que huele tan rica, es para vender?*" he asked politely. Was the good food he was smelling for sale? She answered, "The food is for my childrens." His wife had no talent for *pasteles*, he explained—she was Panamanian—would Lourdes teach his wife some afternoon? After he left, Lourdes smiled pityingly. Her food was unique, her creation, like a baby—specifically hers to give. "That's what I'm proud of," Lourdes said. "Whoever tasted my food always come back for more. What *you* have made, not what anybody *else* have made."

Another Christmas was approaching. Cesar had been transferred to a facility only ninety miles away. She sensed the potential of the move, even if Cesar hadn't yet; he was closer to home, one step nearer family. "God does the right thing, in his own time," Lourdes said. Giselle had promised to bring him some of Lourdes's *pasteles* on their next trailer. And Jessica would be home in time for the holidays.

It would be hard to keep the *pasteles* safe once the word got out. Lourdes neatly stacked them in the freezer. Her delicacies filled it up.

Following her evacuation from the flea-infested house on the hill, Coco reapplied for Section 8 certification and also for public housing. (Part of the application asked her to write an essay, "Why I Want to Live in Public Housing." "Because I'm homeless," Coco wrote.) She and the girls shuttled between Hector's and Iris's to give each host a break.

Coco felt bad about imposing: the timing seemed especially bad. Hector had just started working. He was also housing Iris's mother, who had been moving house to house in the years since her release from prison; Iris's sister and toddler; Platinum and her son; and Hector had the new baby on the way. His two-bedroom apartment didn't have much furniture yet—only two beds, which people used in shifts. Coco was sensitive to the strained language of worn-out welcomes—exasperation with the naturally unruly ways of children, observations about the shrinking food ("I just *bought* soda"), the way Hector spoke of his new van as if it were a human being ("It needs a rest"). Luckily, Hector Jr., who was four, qualified for SSI. He was hyperactive, which worried his parents, but the first SSI check—which included retroactive payments for all the months it had taken for processing—had paid for the secondhand van. The van made it possible for Hector to take a job packing fruit at night. Troy's limited bus service often made evening jobs prohibitive. Soon, Hector got Frankie hired, and the two rode together to work.

Coco's sister's apartment was uncomfortable in a different way. Iris had just started college and was struggling to keep up with her course work along with her household obligations; Armando had agreed to let her enroll only as long as their home life remained unaffected. She was dog-tired, Armando could be impatient and humorless, and Coco's presence meant five more mouths to feed. Iris and Armando's six-year-old daughter, Brandi, loved Nikki, which made Mercedes jealous. Nautica regularly balked when it was time for the tub, but the battle seemed louder in Iris's house. There was never music on. The TV was, and Armando wanted the children to hush so he could hear it, and he regularly ordered them upstairs to play. Iris's children had two sets of identical toys—one for display, one to play with—and Iris noticed if the display set had been touched. Pearl fussed at night and gasped and puked during the daytime; Coco had run out of her medicine. Armando made Coco take every diaper to the trash outdoors because he hated the smell. Coco said nothing, but she felt unwelcome.

Galvanized, Coco applied for several jobs and got hired by the deli at Price Chopper, slicing meat. At times of crisis, there was no denying that her family could not carry her, much as they tried to help. She'd moved to Thorpe House after Cesar's arrest, while pregnant; she'd relocated to Troy in the middle of the upheaval with Pearl; now, homeless again, she rallied herself to work. Dire need cut through the chaos, much as the anticipation of a lover heightened an otherwise boring afternoon on the street. The greater challenge was surviving the daily grind.

Price Chopper paid $5.14 an hour. Coco spent the evening before her very first shift cradling Pearl in the emergency room. The night cracked open into day. In the mornings, Troy's streets could seem almost unbearably bleak. It may have been the abandoned tenements, or the forties bottles emptied of beer and filled with pee, or the boarded-up doors, or the cars whirring by. Coco hadn't slept, and the world filtered in around the edges of her exhaustion. She quietly dressed her girls in the morning dark of Iris's house. She walked them around the corner, to River Street, and stood at the bus stop in front of a Laundromat. She was shorter than some of the kids.

Coco had witnessed gunfire on the same block a year earlier. She and Mercedes and Frankie had been waiting for the bus home after Sunday dinner at Iris's. Two white boys robbed a Spanish man at the River Street Store and were firing as they ran out; Frankie had been in the store when the shooting started, but somehow he was suddenly next to Coco and Mercedes, covering them and flagging down a car and ushering them into the backseat. The driver recognized Frankie from the neighborhood and delivered them to the relative safety of Corliss Park. This morning, though, the block was tranquil, and amid the sounds of the mundane world, the future presented itself through a cloud of bus exhaust. Coco spotted a sign in a broken window of a first-floor tenement across the street—*Apartment for Rent.*

The intersection of River and 101st Streets was at the heart of Troy's growing ghetto, the place where the migrants from the big city and the stalwart residents of the now-poor part of the small city mixed. Hip-hop clashed with the heavy metal that wafted from the windows of the cars idling at the traffic light. Row houses that had once belonged to white working-class families had been hacked up into rentals, drywalled, and painted in ugly colors for the working and unemployed poor, who were white, Puerto Rican, and black.

Milagros urged Coco to keep looking in other neighborhoods. River Street was no place for growing girls. It was a known drug spot. "It's not as if I have a choice," Coco huffed. What were her options, exactly? Other people's floors? Homelessness made her private business public; everyone had opinions about how she raised her kids, whether or not they spoke them. And what kind of mother would she be if her girls were homeless for the holidays? Having no apartment made any apartment look good. Coco said, "The store is right across the street. The bus stop is there. The rent is three-fifty, so all I think about is that."

The glass in the bay window, shattered from another shooting that had driven out the previous tenants, could be replaced—perfect to show off her Christmas tree. Coco already envisioned a backyard with her daughters playing and ignored the actual crumbling square of tar with its mangled shopping cart and trail of gnawed chicken meat. The two empty units above her, one of which had burned and still smelled faintly of smoke, meant no nosy neighbors—no one judging what they couldn't know, eyeing Frankie's friends, calling the police. The girls didn't have to transfer schools. The store had a pay phone she could use when the telephone company cut off her service, and Iris lived around the block. While Coco waited for the Section 8 inspector to approve the apartment, she and Hector snuck back into the condemned house on the hill to retrieve some pots, pans, and clothes.

Coco kept a close eye on Mercedes and looked for any change in Mercedes's feelings about Frankie, whose return from Hector's was imminent. Coco didn't want her daughters to put up with what she had from men, but the best example she offered was her willingness to point out her own weaknesses and hypocrisies. Girls were surrounded by women who ignored the contradictions between what they said and what they did. Women routinely made grand pronouncements about all they wouldn't tolerate, but the particulars were another thing entirely. Women didn't ask questions of men in public directly, unless they were angry, and then the questions weren't really questions but indictments that called attention to their own wounds. Iris asked Armando's permission to lend Coco money or give her a lift, and every night—whether or not she actually did—Frankie expected Coco to cook. And Coco had her moments of defiance: at family gatherings, instead of serving the men, the children were the first to get their plates of food.

Mercedes believed in Coco's best self, and when she recited Coco's ideals back to her mother, the old refrains would strike Coco anew. But the idealism required vigilance. Mercedes cautioned her mother about spending too much money on birthday presents for other people's children and reminded her, when the house swelled, that they didn't have enough food to feed everyone. Mercedes publicly rebuffed the guests whom her mother privately scorned ("How come you always show up right when we about to eat?" Mercedes asked Platinum once). If Coco talked about putting $50 toward new outfits for her daughters on layaway, Mercedes would discourage her, advising instead, "Fifty to the house, not to us." Yet it was Coco's awareness of Mercedes's dissatisfaction with Frankie that had become the focal point of their relationship. "I'm not going to give you what you want, but I am going to listen to what you want," her mother would say.

While Coco settled into her new apartment, Cesar settled into his latest prison. He'd emerged from the grueling five-month stint in the box weakened, enraged, and somewhat dazed. He and Giselle had undergone a period of estrangement, but she wanted to salvage the marriage. She believed in the relationship with a faith he could not imagine for himself. Cesar loved her and knew he needed her, but he still felt at a crossroads between need and his pride. It had been over a year since he'd seen any of his children. Coco's letters filled his head with only more problems—usually, complaints about Mercedes, who was getting into trouble at school and upsetting Coco whenever she talked about boys.

Cesar's avalanche of trouble did, however, create a pocket of opportunity. The latest addition to his institutional file labeled him as depressive—"violent-suicidal type"—and the categorization merited something called a double-bunk override. A double-bunk override was a coveted stigma in the crowded prison system, rather like SSI. Cesar was assigned his own cell.

For the first few months at Shawangunk, the authorities placed him on keep-lock—twenty-three-hour lockdown in his own cell. Keep-lock had restrictions, but it was much better than solitary, because Cesar had access to his property. He could open his locker, or peruse the sneaker box he stored beneath his bed, where he kept his letters, filed by writer and by date. He could look at his hundreds of photographs. He no longer pinned up his pictures, like some of the other inmates. The first few years he was locked up, he'd posted the pictures—wanting the world to see his beautiful daughters and his sexy girlfriends. But now the photographs were too painful. "I was getting really stressed seeing my children grow and not being able to be there."

Back on River Street, Mercedes placed Cesar's picture prominently in her new bedroom, on top of the toy chest he had made. Next to it, she put another picture of her father and her godfather, Rocco, taken in the Harlem Valley visiting room. The bedroom, a narrow, dark space off the kitchen, overlooked an alleyway. Mercedes mopped the floor and covered the drafty window with a sheet. There was no closet, but she folded her clothes neatly and stacked them on the floor. She arranged her toys beside them. She made up her bed, which was only a box spring, and posted a notice on her door:

RULES
Take your shoes off when you come in.
Don't sit on the bed.
Knock when you come in.
Don't come in if I'm not here.

Mercedes had her own bedroom because she was the oldest, and also because Coco didn't entirely trust her with her sisters alone. "She shakes Pearl as if she really wants to hurt her," Coco said. Sometimes Mercedes became so angry that she hit Nikki or Naughty, not the way you would hit a sister, but as though she were fighting a stranger on the street. Once, when Coco was reluctant to take her along on an errand because of the chorus of wailing sisters, Mercedes said, "You gotta take me, I'm a problem child. I'll get into a fight."

As usual, Coco had her Christmas tree and all her decorations up long before Thanksgiving. She spent most of her first two Price Chopper paychecks on gifts. She reimbursed Mercedes $35 she owed her. Mercedes said, "I'm going to save it. So when Mommy run outta money, or don't got no gas, or if we hungry, I can give it to her."

As before, Mercedes and Frankie argued if they were left alone too long. One day, Iris and Coco returned from shopping and found them wrangling on the *sala* floor. Coco and Frankie yelled a lot themselves. They had a big fight in November. To cheer up the house, Coco let the girls open all their Christmas presents, then she immediately began to worry about how she would replace them. Frankie, contrite, tried to help, but then he got arrested for boosting videocassettes from Ames. He'd stolen a gangster movie for himself and a Barney tape for Pearl. Then, the next thing you know, miraculously, gifts from Cesar arrived in the mail. Cesar had gotten the money from Rocco, who'd had a windfall.

Rocco kept Cesar abreast of the news on the street, and Cesar kept Rocco up-to-date with the goings-on inside. Plenty of times, the news overlapped. Those friends and acquaintances who were involved in what Rocco and Cesar called the thug life—full-time or part-time—were constantly shuffling among the prisons, getting arrested or rearrested for parole violations or for new crimes, and occasionally getting released.

Rocco hadn't returned to prison since his 1993 bid at Rikers. He had succumbed to what he derisively called "a Rick's life"—legally married, renting an apartment in the north Bronx on a quiet street, holding down two jobs, still not meeting all the bills. The apartment had been robbed while he and his wife and daughter were vacationing in Disney World; Marlene was so upset that she ripped up her birthday gift—theater tickets Rocco had bought for *Miss Saigon*. Now Rocco was back with his in-laws, "back to a rougher place where they have more respect for me and know who I am." Days, he drove trucks in Jersey; nights, he worked as a support technician for a software company.

Rocco hated the predictability of the straight world. He said he felt dead. He pined for the old glory days of spontaneous brawls and shoot-outs; he missed the excitement and the camaraderie. Much to Marlene's annoyance, he played Wu Tang Clan constantly. He flirted with a Chinese girl he'd noticed at the desk of a car dealership he passed on the way to his trucking job. But chess was the only thing—besides crime—that engaged Rocco entirely. He competed on-line in the morning and played on the computer at his second job. The first thing he did whenever he visited Cesar was to challenge him to a game.

Around the time Cesar got moved to Shawangunk, Rocco's situation had begun to unravel. His wife had won a graduate scholarship to New York University; she wanted to become a high school guidance counselor, but even with three jobs between them, they couldn't cover their expenses. With school, Marlene was too tired to restrict Rocco to living life the harder way. She later said, "He was a pit bull, and I let go of the leash." Rocco assembled a crew of younger boys and started robbing drug dealers again. "When the struggle's put on me, this is the only way I knew how to deal with it," he said. Just before Christmas in 1998, Rocco and two other boys made a successful hit. They came away from a stash house with $150,000—$50,000 each. Rocco bought himself a motorcycle, surprised his disgruntled wife with a Honda CRV, indulged his daughter in presents, and deposited $400 in Cesar's commissary account.

Cesar spent down the money on sneakers for his three daughters, which he ordered from a catalog; he sent Giselle's son a $30 money order for his birthday; and he used the rest for Giselle's third-year anniversary gift. He mailed a rose enclosed in a bell jar to Giselle's office, with a card that read, "With all my love from your husband, Cesar."

PART V

Breaking Out

Inmates at Danbury called the restless discomfort common to women near release S&SS—short and shitty syndrome. Jessica had a case of it. She slept fitfully, had diarrhea and migraine headaches, and hadn't been able to hold down food for weeks. She anxiously awaited her box: she was allowed a box of clothing in preparation for her return to the outside world. Jessica's box arrived with eighteen days remaining on her sentence. "Now I really know I'm leaving, now that my clothes are here," Jessica said. The friend who'd sent the box had herself just gotten out of prison; she'd planned on dressing Jessica sexy, but sent a sporty style instead—beige sweater, beige underwear and bra, with matching overalls. Jessica tried on the outfit and suffered an anxiety attack. "She couldn't breathe," said her roommate, who was happy for Jessica but not looking forward to being left behind.

Release dates were onerous. Inmates with longer terms had been known to try to "steal a date," which meant intentionally provoking a fight with a woman who was due to leave. Despairing lovers jumped girlfriends to keep them close. Nilda kept a distance, not because she would hurt Jessica, but because she didn't want to dampen Jessica's spirits by letting Jessica see her cry, and she'd been crying a lot.

Other risks awaited Jessica on the outside—mainly, the utter precariousness of her life. Boy George, from his antiseptic cell in a supermax prison in Beaumont, Texas, wrote, ". . . I've got a couple of brothers outside who if you find yourself in need they could be helpful. I have no malicious thoughts towards you Jessica, trust in me. . . ." The cement fortress where George lived was connected to a vast compound shining with state-of-the-art high-security technology, laid out in a wasteland of dried-up oil rigs. Some of the small-town guards affected the slang and mannerisms of their inner-city prisoners. George said the only difference between the street and prison, besides the absence of cars and real women, was that it was more dangerous inside. He wore a four-ounce eighteen-karat-gold chain around his neck.

Boy George still knew how to make the most of the little he had to work with. He read more than he had in the free world—Machiavelli, Thomas Harris, the *New York Times,* and *Maxim,* his latest favorite magazine. His cellie passed along books about Puerto Rican heritage and George read them, mainly as a courtesy. "I don't care if I got white in me, black in me, European, it don't make a difference. I'm me." He was more interested in the Internet.

He'd never inscribed Jessica's name onto the blank space of his heart tattoo, but on his shoulders, he'd inked the skyline of Manhattan, including the Statue of Liberty and the Brooklyn Bridge. Below the city, *BOY* arched above two shooting pistols, near 27, a reference to a gang that controlled a piece of the prison black market. On his stomach, he'd added an apple, with a New York Yankees insignia, pierced by two swords. It amused him that in all the years he'd lived in the Bronx, he'd never thought to go to a Yankees game.

Prison had further refined Boy George's philosophical leanings; he'd become a bit of an avuncular sage. He believed he still knew the best route for Jessica: to find an educated man who was also streetwise, "a person who could teach her and stand to be taught by an individual who has had a life like her," he said. Jessica's susceptibility to the influence of others worried him, just as it worried everyone who knew her—her blood family, her prison family, the friend who'd mailed her the clothing box. "She's easy to convince," said George. "She thought that sex was the right thing, to give it up to everybody. She's got to say, 'Am I gonna be a free-for-all? Or am I gonna be a person who has limits here?' Is it all about sex, Calvin Klein, is she gonna parlay with that? Or is she gonna say, 'I got five children. Now that's a lot of children'?" He paused. "If she doesn't find the right man, she did all that time for nothing. She did all that time for shit."

George was thirty-two years old. He'd served nearly a decade and still had a life sentence left. He claimed that he was optimistic about winning his latest appeal, but his confidence sounded strained; there wasn't much money left for the legal battles. His mother still worked as a hospital aide. But when George spoke of Jessica, he exuded certainty.

Nilda warned Jessica to stay away from anyone who had anything to do with George. Other close friends advised Jessica to keep some distance from her siblings; they didn't like the childhood stories they'd heard about Jessica's older brother, Robert, and they didn't trust Elaine. Where had she been all these years? Nilda understood that Jessica had to reckon with her mother. "Open up your heart," she told Jessica. "Tell her how she hurt you. Accept it, but what happened, happened. If she denies it, hey, go on."

With only days to go, Jessica took the last lap of the outposts that comprised her daily prison routine, what inmates called the merry-go-round:

She signed herself out of security and gathered her files from education. She checked out of religion and released herself from medical. A few of the guards wished her well. Nilda prepared a chilikida for Jessica's last supper, which she served with a can of Coke. Jessica's closest friends gathered in her cubicle. They sang her favorite song (the Red Hot Chili Peppers' "Under the Bridge"). She distributed her property; it was bad luck to carry anything from prison to the free world. She gave Nilda her most cherished objects: two sample-size bars of Dove soap, which she'd snuck home from the hospital, on which she'd carved *Matthew* and *Michael*; her red plastic Hamster cup (Hamster was Nilda's pet name for Jessica); and a crocheted vest. Jessica also left Nilda a pile of pictures of herself. She broke night her final night in custody and finished a sweater she was crocheting for Nilda's mother; she would mail it from a post office, so that the gift wouldn't have a prison stamp.

At 8:30 A.M. on December 17, 1998, Nilda walked Jessica to R&D — Release and Delivery. At 8:50 A.M., seven years from the day she was sentenced, Jessica walked out of Danbury Correctional Facility. She had one streak of gray hair below the crown of her head, a skunk's tail, and she carried twenty extra pounds. She was thirty years old. Prison, she wrote to a friend, had transformed her from "a naive young girl that thought without a brain," to a woman with a longer view.

While Jessica rode the bus from Danbury to New York, Nilda opened the notes Jessica had hidden in their secret places for her to find. Jessica sat beside a fellow ex-inmate whom she recognized, but didn't know well. They were both so nervous that they barely spoke, but they held hands. Jessica looked out the window at the farm stands, the highway. She gazed over the Bronx as the bus headed toward Manhattan, then watched the people on the city streets.

Finally, the bus pulled into the cavernous garage of the Port Authority. At the gate, Jessica and the woman disembarked; they didn't have luggage. The woman stepped into the glare of the terminal to no one, clutching her crocheted knapsack, her hand clamped on a scrap of paper with her halfway house address, petrified. But Jessica was surprised by a small crowd of well-wishers who surrounded her with a happy burst of instructions and laughter and nervous anxiety: Inez, a Danbury friend, who was pregnant, had brought her a bag of clothes; Cathy, another Danbury friend, had brought along her new girlfriend and gave Jessica a Metro-Card (tokens had been the standard the last time Jessica was in New York). The group protectively led her to the express train, which rushed them all to the Bronx: Jessica had just under an hour to report to the halfway house to which she'd been assigned. On the ride, they caught up on the gossip—which guards had divorced or retired, which physician's assistant was dating which ex-inmate, who'd gone back to being straight and who stayed gay. Arm in arm, the women escorted Jessica to the block where they had already been, pointed out the building, kissed her, hugged her again, and let her go. It was a violation of everyone's probation to fraternize.

Meanwhile, Lourdes, with the fragile hope of surprising Jessica, waited underground in a nearby subway. She stood on a platform with Emilio, who hunched over her, nervous and tentative. He'd been hearing about Jessica, it seemed, forever. Framed photographs of her dominated Lourdes's *sala* walls. For the special day, Lourdes had worn her new eyeglasses with gold trim, and a brand-new pink-and-green sweat suit. She'd even gotten a neighbor to French-braid her hair. But Lourdes had mistakenly gone to the wrong station. After an hour, she gave up. Emilio tenderly held her elbow as he helped her slowly climb the stairs.

Whatever expectations had accompanied Jessica's homecoming quickly dissolved into the strange twilight haze of postprison existence. Jessica had physically returned to her old world to begin a supposedly brand-new life that hadn't quite started yet. The dreary halfway house hunkered down on a gritty block just north of Fordham Road. Institutional renovations and a glossy blue coat of paint had added a fluorescent sheen to the dingy tenement, not unlike the probationary life Jessica faced: the governing rules imposed a superficial order on the old vulnerabilities, but there was a deeper sense that nothing much had changed. She attended her required Narcotics Anonymous meetings, walking past familiar drug spots that operated in a nearby park. She could have walked to the hooky house where she'd met Puma. Her children were elsewhere, her little brother was locked up, her mother was broke.

Almost immediately, Jessica got romantically involved with a fellow resident. At night, she skulked beneath the security cameras and snuck into his room. She posed for photographs—straddling his bed, squatting on the floor, her hands up against the cinder-block wall, wearing his gift of black lace lingerie. Boy George soon received news of her adventures; a member of his prison gang was stationed at the halfway house.

In her loneliness, Jessica also resorted to the pay phone, as she had so many times before. Her first call out went to Edwin, Wishman's little brother. He was studying to become an X-ray technician and working at a Bronx hospital. He couldn't see her—he was married and his wife was pregnant—but his mother, Sunny, met Jessica on Fordham to celebrate Jessica's first two-hour pass. ("I'm still the same?" Jessica asked hopefully, to which Sunny replied warmly, "You still got that fat ass!") Ghosts of Jessica's former life, both kind and unkind, seemed to haunt her everywhere. She ran into one of the boys from the hooky house. Lourdes surprised Jessica by showing up at the halfway house with Big Daddy, who'd lived with them on Tremont. Jessica made a snide comment in front of him about Lourdes's continued use of drugs. "That's right, baby—the kind that a doctor prescribes," Lourdes said archly. "Mami, want me to pee for you in a cup?" Jessica even passed by George's mother's apartment. Rita still had the reversible mink and leather coat George had had specially made for Jessica ten years earlier. "To get it back I have to kiss ass. It's not worth it," Jessica said. George's little brother had become a man. He'd acquired more confidence, a wife and children, and reminded Jessica of George.

But it was her children who were truly transformed: Serena was a young woman; Brittany and Stephanie had stretched into slender adolescent girls; her infant sons were now little boys. Milagros brought them all down for Christmas, which they celebrated at Lourdes's. Lourdes set out a feast—her *pasteles*, *arroz gandules*, potato salad, a special ham. Jessica's grandmother came in from Florida; Jessica's favorite aunt—Lourdes's younger sister Millie—came with her girlfriend, Linda; Elaine and Robert brought their children; Jessica's cousin Daisy showed up with her little boy. Jessica surprised the children with winter coats from Old Navy. She said, "I was happy cuz I was with my kids. That was the best gift." They took lots of pictures. In them, Jessica smiled broadly, back in the bosom of her family.

Although the job market for ex-felons was severely limited, Jessica's release from the halfway house depended upon her finding employment. Elaine got Jessica hired at the warehouse where she worked. Elaine managed the office; Jessica took orders and called clients, reminding them in her sultry voice of overdue bills. At an office party, she met a married schoolteacher, whom she briefly dated. She gave her daughters her toll-free number: Jessica couldn't travel upstate to see them because of probation, and Milagros couldn't usually afford the time or money to bring them down. Serena called frequently.

In January 1999, Jessica was approved to move in with Elaine. (Her application to live with Lourdes was denied because Lourdes's boyfriend had been convicted of a felony.) Jessica still had to pay $50 a week to the halfway house, which was part of a court fine imposed a decade before. The day she was leaving the halfway house, Jessica ran into Talent, an old colleague of Boy George's from the early days. Talent was being admitted, having finished an eight-year term for drug dealing. He and Jessica exchanged numbers and promised to keep in touch.

Although Jessica and Elaine were getting reacquainted, Jessica privately doubted the arrangement could last; historically, the sisters' periods of peace had been short. Elaine now had the large life: she had a good job, a wardrobe, credit cards, a car. She was in the midst of an intoxicating romance. Jessica suffered anxiety attacks. She wasn't accustomed to the lack of rules. She missed the daily support of her prison friends, and sometimes she felt so overwhelmed that she half-wished she could go back—at least there she knew what she was supposed to do. Her weight made her painfully self-conscious. She was in a perpetual panic about money, and she needed eyeglasses. Jessica could barely manage her court fine and her share of Elaine's household bills.

Elaine kept a tidy house, but Jessica cleaned obsessively. She lost her patience with her nephews, who slammed the door as they ran in and out of the house and plunked their dirty dishes in the sink. Each night before she crawled into Elaine's bed, she swept and mopped the floors, as she used to in her prison cell. The bed frame was the same one Jessica had given Elaine years earlier, from one of the apartments Jessica had shared with George. On Sundays, Jessica's boyfriend from the halfway house visited on his free pass, but the couple had no privacy unless Elaine went out. The only bureau Jessica had was the edge of Elaine's computer desk. She crowded it with photographs and toiletries.

Elaine relished her mentor's role. She explained to her older sister how to budget. Jessica needed and resented her. Elaine was undergoing a sexual awakening, and it was as though she and Jessica had traded places. Elaine went clubbing, and to strip joints with her girlfriends, and away for weekends with her lover, to the Poconos; Jessica baby-sat. Serena would come to visit, and it sometimes seemed to Jessica that Serena loved Elaine more; they'd grown closer over the years of Jessica's incarceration, and Elaine could buy things for Serena. Elaine had even kept in touch with Torres, the twin boys' father, who was clamoring to meet his sons. Milagros reluctantly agreed to bring them down. "He just wants to get in Jessica's pants," she said, her voice clipped.

The initial meeting went badly. Jessica had an anxiety attack and hid in the bathroom; Milagros blankly observed Torres, who sat with his hands clasped on Elaine's couch, while the boys ran in and out of the living room. Elaine kept pace with them, buzzing back and forth between Torres and Jessica like a harried diplomat. But Torres and Jessica reconnected on the phone. They began having long, flirtatious conversations. He called her from the boiler plant, where he now worked nights. Jessica switched between Torres and her boyfriend on call-waiting, and some nights fielded a torrent of other calls.

She and Torres scheduled a meeting in New Haven the day of the settlement conference for the Yale lawsuit, which had yet to be resolved. By then, her lawyers had learned she was back in touch with Torres and urged her to settle, which she did—for $5,000. After the conference, she lunched with the law students and spoke to the prison clinic class. (Years later, one student summarized the lesson Jessica had taught him as "the importance of and the impossibility of nailing down the facts.") Torres picked her up at the train station and drove her back to Elaine's. By the end of the ride, it was clear to both of them that rekindling the relationship wasn't likely—Torres had become a born-again Christian and wouldn't even let Jessica listen to pop music in his car. But Jessica needed the attention and seemed glad to have men back in her life.

It wasn't long before she fell in true love again: with a twenty-three-year-old ex-marine who walked right up the stairs onto Elaine's porch and knocked on her door. He'd been looking forward to meeting Jessica; the colleague who was training him as a home confinement officer had described her as "Wow." He later said he knew he was in trouble when he first laid eyes on Jessica: she was stepping out of the shower, wearing only a towel. He introduced himself; Jessica believed it was destiny that his name was George. She joked about already having his tattoos. Jessica asked him in her prettiest voice to please wait while she dressed. George didn't tell Jessica that he had a girlfriend, whom he considered a wife.

CHAPTER THIRTY-SIX

Every opportunity Coco seized on improved her life, but sustaining the improvements proved impossible against the backslide of poverty. The financial advantage of a minimum-wage job for a family of five was imperceptible, but the disadvantages were quickly becoming clear: Coco was the spirit and the anchor of her household, and her unpredictable absence—given the irregularity of Price Chopper's hours—made it difficult for the family to settle into any routine. What was good for Coco—getting out of the house—wasn't always great for her children, and Frankie made a lackluster substitute.

He'd had to quit his job at the fruit-packing plant not long after Hector moved on to a slightly better-paying job as a security guard at a nursing home. At first, another coworker gave Frankie lifts to work, but the man then started on the day shift, and the buses didn't run late in the evenings, so Frankie was back on the street. Coco had pretty much resigned herself to Frankie's "doing what he do out there," but Frankie seemed increasingly demoralized. Coco worried that he might hurt himself—one of his brothers had committed suicide—but other problems vied for her attention, such as Mercedes's ongoing trouble at school. The school where Mercedes attended third grade was having its own problems. Its test scores were abysmal and it had a reputation for not being able to control its kids. The principal had suspended Mercedes several times and had told Coco that unless she got Mercedes to counseling, Mercedes would be expelled. Coco wrote Cesar and asked for guidance; when she explained to Mercedes that the situation was serious, Mercedes seemed to understand because she cried. Mercedes didn't often show the softer side of her emotions; her tears usually came from frustration and rage. Coco thought her difficulties at school started at home: "I think it's Frankie, but I can't blame her because we always having problems in front of them, and I guess she feels, I don't want my mother to deal with that."

Mercedes watched her sisters while her mother worked. Sometimes she sounded exactly like Coco, such as the time when Nautica pointed out the "raper" in Corliss Park—a man rumored to be a sex offender who walked around the neighborhood pushing an empty shopping cart.

"Shut your mouth, Naughty," Mercedes said. "Don't you say that, and besides, you don't even know what that means."

Coco quit Price Chopper after several weeks because of the erratic hours, but yearned for another job. "I want it so that when the kids ask for something at the store, I can say yes," she said. Just before Christmas, she joined Hector at the nursing home where she served meals to the residents. The hours were steady—she worked the 6 A.M. to 3 P.M. shift—and her house benefited from the predictable schedule. To Coco's surprise and relief, the fighting between Mercedes and Frankie calmed down.

Coco made it as easy for Frankie as possible: she got up at 4 A.M., woke the girls and dressed them, cooked breakfast, then jumped into the shower after she'd settled them in front of the TV with their food. They ate and went back to sleep. Coco reset the alarm for Frankie; all he had to do was wake them up again, help them into their coats, and give them their bookbags, all of which she'd left on the couch beside the door. Frankie didn't even have to step outside; he could watch from the front window as Mercedes safely ushered her sisters across the busy street and onto the bus. Frankie stayed with Pearl, and Coco was back by the time the other children got home, after which he was free to go out.

Coco loved working. Her coworkers resented the old folks' picky behavior, but Coco found their quirkiness interesting. By her second day, she'd memorized the names of each resident. At home, she cooked dinner, the girls did their homework, bathed, ate their evening snacks, then fell asleep, each in her own bed. Coco went to bed herself by ten.

A few weeks later, Pearl underwent another vomiting siege, and shortly after that, Coco, who had begun to suspect she might be pregnant, started vomiting as well. Without a car, Coco couldn't manage the doctor's appointments, which she couldn't always schedule during the two free hours she had after work. So she quit the nursing home and tended to the most pressing problems first: she bused Pearl to her doctor in Albany, which required a minimum of three hours of travel—no local specialists were willing to accept Medicaid. Frankie stayed home with the other children, who couldn't tolerate more waiting rooms. Coco understood: "I get impatient, and I'm a grown woman. Imagine how it be for a child." Pearl, who was four, sometimes got so frustrated that she'd grab fistfuls of her uneven hair, yank herself backward, and smack her head on the floor.

At home, Mercedes baby-sat whenever Frankie stepped outside to conduct his business. Without Coco around, however, Frankie allowed the customers into the house. Mercedes would leap to the door at every ring of the bell—which, sometimes, seemed like every few minutes. Quickly, the household returned to chaos. People were always hanging out. As usual, Coco didn't have the heart to tell her lonely friends to go.

"It's just like my mother's," said Iris. Most of the guests were the same as well: Bambi, Coco's cousin, had just left Foxy's in the Bronx and moved in next door to Coco's with Weedo, Coco's old neighbor. Munchie, another boy from Foxy's building, now rented the apartment upstairs. At night, Platinum and her son slept on Coco's couch cushions, which they arranged on the floor.

Iris accompanied Coco to the clinic for a pregnancy test toward the end of January 1999. But there were lots of young women waiting, and the clinic only tested eight girls a day. Coco's stamina continued to weaken. In winter, she usually prepared her daughters warm breakfasts — microwave waffles, or eggs and toast — but now she overslept. Mercedes did her best to get her to school, but she overslept as well. When she did get to school, she couldn't seem to get along with her teachers or her classmates; at home, the battles were more familiar, but she lost them just the same.

On Super Bowl Sunday, after smoking a fat blunt with his homeboys in the bedroom, Frankie floated through the house in a happy cloud. He reclaimed his chair directly in front of the large-screen TV. His neighbors flanked him — Munchie to the left, Weedo to the right. The bowls of chips and nachos moved back and forth. The boys either didn't notice the children's hungry eyes or they ignored them.

Mercedes tried to negotiate. She asked Frankie to share. He wouldn't. She went to the kitchen, where the women were preparing dinner. "Mami, Frankie won't share," she reported.

"Mercy, oh, please," Coco sighed. She didn't feel like having an argument with Frankie, so she surrendered her last $2 of food stamps, and Mercedes gallantly went to secure more snacks from across the street.

With all the houseguests, Coco had been going to three food pantries and still wasn't managing. A fair amount of the food went to a pear-shaped seventeen-year-old with stringy hair named Marisol, who lived upstairs with Munchie; besides a bed, they didn't have any furniture, let alone pots or pans. Marisol had just moved upstate but she already wanted to go back to the Bronx. "I'm too young to be here. I'm a girl. I don't have no kids. I shouldn't be living with a man," she said. On her arm was a bite mark, the size of a lemon; Munchie had caught Marisol looking through his pants for his pay stub.

"I wouldn't put up with that shit," Platinum said.

"So, Marisol," Bambi asked pointedly, "what are you going to do?" Bambi wasn't one for small talk. She had served seven years for armed robbery and and had lost five kids to foster care. She had little patience for girls who thought they had all sorts of time to fix their problems. Just then, Nikki skidded into the kitchen. "Ma! Ma!" she shouted. Mercedes banged into her from behind. Nikki held up an empty bowl. "Frankie wants chips MA!"

Mercedes interrupted breathlessly. "Ma! Ma! Frankie-wouldn't-let-us-have-any-of-the-nachos-and-the-cheese-dip-but-now-he-wants-ours!"

"Then give him some," Coco said.

"Why we have to share, Ma?" Mercedes asked.

"Give them to him, Mercy."

"It's not fair!"

"I don't care if it's fair, dammit!" Coco said. "Give him them, Mercy!"

"*Ma!*" Mercedes wailed. "MAAA!!"

"Mercy, if you don't shut up, you going into your room." Coco ripped the bag from Mercedes's hand, gruffly dumped the chips into the bowl, and shoved the bowl back at Nikki, who strutted away holding it too-cutely above her head. Mercedes spooked her with a fake punch.

"Ma!" Nikki cried, just as fake. Coco grabbed Mercedes under the arm, dragged her into her bedroom, and slammed the flimsy door.

"She like that. She always gets into it," Bambi said softly. Marisol bit her lip. Platinum, who was usually never at a loss for words, stared silently ahead. The three decided to step outside to share a cigarette. Coco returned to the scrubbing, her lips tight. She clanked the pot.

The pork chops were ready. Coco put them on the plates and plopped the rice on top. The children ate on the floor. They anxiously awaited halftime, when their goddess, Mariah Carey, was going to perform. They knew all her songs and dance steps and had been practicing for her Super Bowl appearance. Just as she was to rule the screen, Frankie flicked the channel to pro wrestling.

"Aw, Ma!" Nautica moaned.

"What I'm supposed to do?" Coco yelled.

Nikki slapped herself.

"*Ma!*" Nautica cried again.

"Frankie," Coco said.

"Ma," he whined, and ignored them. He loved pro wrestling. Meanwhile, Pearl circulated among the company, holding out a new Barney book. "Read my book?" she asked. No one took the bait.

No, *Mami, later.*
After the game, Pearl.
No, *Ma, go play.*
But Marisol suddenly lifted Pearl onto her lap and read the book. "Again!" Pearl said. By the third reading, Pearl had the story down.

Coco slept her way through February. The girls missed school. Nautica cried bitterly; she loved school. Under the latest round of welfare changes, $60 was deducted from Coco's check for each child who had more than two unexcused absences. Coco lost most of her cash allotment. Mercedes unsuccessfully orchestrated breakfast for her sisters, who wanted to prepare breakfast themselves. "Do you want to burn yourself? Do you want to burn yourself?" she yelled. "I'ma gonna punch you. MA!" Even Frankie was openly worried. Then Coco found out for sure that she was pregnant again.

The response to Coco's fifth pregnancy was mixed. Frankie was pleased; he rarely saw his children. A new baby would give him a chance to do things right. He also wanted Coco to be the mother of his child. Unlike other girls he knew, Coco always put her children first. He confided to her, "I hope I'm the one to bless you with a son." Iris was so upset that she refused to speak to Coco. The grandmothers worried about Coco's health, given Pearl's difficult birth. Milagros surprised Coco and didn't even give her a lecture. All she said was "It's going to be a lot of work and nobody dies from hard work." Hector told her, "I support you no matter what. You my sister. Frankie's my man, I love that nigga, yo. But not for nothing, Coco, he's a loser. He ain't going anywhere. You going to be raising that baby on your own. But you do what you gotta do." Coco accurately imagined Cesar's response—*Why you having another baby when you can't take care of the ones you've got?* Coco called Sunny, Wishman's mother, during a visit to the Bronx, and Sunny relayed the news to Wishman, who came over to see Coco at Foxy's. He tried to talk to Pearl, but she ignored him. Wishman asked Coco, "How did it happen?"

"It just happened."

"But why this?" he asked, poking her belly with his finger. She shrugged. Nikki's father, Kodak, wished her luck.

The guests drifted away, but still there was never enough food in the house. Distraught, Coco returned to the Department of Social Services and applied for emergency food stamps. She mentioned the pregnancy to her caseworker.

"I don't know whether to congratulate you or say I'm sorry," the case-worker said. Coco smiled weakly; she didn't know herself.

Coco wanted a son but was terrified of having a nervous breakdown as a result. How could she manage another child? "I feel like I'm gonna go crazy if I have this baby, for real. I'm gonna end up like my mother, in the hospital and taking all kinds of medication," she said. Fresh red spots lined her hairline. Some bled, like sickly freckles. Coco considered getting an abortion, but then she thought about what people would think of her for murdering an unborn child. One night, she polled her girls on the way to the dollar store. "Mommy might take out the baby. I went through the same thing with the four of ya'aw, but I thought I could do it, and there's so much I want to do for you—you know how Mommy wants to go to Great Escapes? And I swear, I'll get you there this summer if I have to rent the damn van myself. But I can't do this."

"Mommy, that ain't right," Mercedes said.

"I know, Mercy, but Mommy can't do it. You see the problems I got with Frankie now?"

"But, Mommy, it ain't right," Mercedes said again.

"We'll help you, Mommy," Nikki said. "We can make the bottle."

"Mommy had ya'aw when she was young, but now ain't a good time."

Nikki seemed convinced. "It be better when we older, like eighteen, cuz we can do for you then. We can buy the baby's bottle, buy the Pampers."

"I be stuck with Frankie the rest of my life," Coco said. "No matter what he do to me, if Mommy has the baby, I be stuck with him; no matter what, I have to stay with him. I ain't joking. You girls could grow up and Mommy still have to be with him." Coco began to cry, heaving, desperate cries. When she calmed down, she looked upward and asked God, straight-up, about her odds: "What if this is my son?" she said in a voice close to panic. The girls watched silently.

At the dollar store, Coco treated her daughters to three things each. Nikki tried, in kind, to lift up her mother's spirits: "Mommy, thank you for all you do for us. You a nice mommy. You take us to nice places. I love you."

"Why you love me?" Coco asked.

"Cuz you do for us. You buy us things."

"You love me only cuz I buy you things?" Coco asked.

Nautica said, "Yeah!"

"Listen to her!" said Coco.

Nikki tried again: "I love you cuz you do for us."

The night felt silent and huge. "I'm waiting for the right answer," said Coco. "I'm waiting."

Mercedes knew it: "Because you're my mother." Coco was pleased. That was the right answer in her book.

Sometimes Coco slept through dinner. She dragged herself out of bed and vomited blood. "I make them suffer, I feed them out of cans," she said sadly. She ignored the telephone, which always seemed to be the school, calling about Mercedes:

Mercedes refused to listen to her teacher.

Could someone collect Mercedes from detention?

Mercedes fought with a classmate.

Mrs. Rodriguez, we've suspended Mercedes again.

Again the school demanded that Coco get Mercedes into counseling.

Coco did not believe in counseling. Her family had been required to go into therapy after their father died, when Coco was eight years old. The therapist had continued to see Hector individually, and he'd placed Hector on Dilantin, but Hector remained the most volatile one in her family. Foxy's condition hadn't improved in the six years of weekly therapy since her three-week stay in what she called "psychiatric." As far as Coco was concerned, the doctors had only made Foxy's drug use more dangerous; in addition to the cocaine, now she took prescription pills. Coco didn't think her mother was equipped to be her own pharmacist. Besides, pills turned into their own problems. If Iris didn't take her antidepressants, she became frighteningly ill. Said Coco, "I see how it brought my brother down, I see how it brought my mother down, and how my sister can't be without it."

When Coco finally did take Mercedes to a therapist, Mercedes spent the first session hiding beneath her coat. That counselor told Coco that giving in to Mercedes's demands was unproductive—an observation that Coco found obvious. "I give in with all my girls," Coco later said. "I guess they always going to end up blaming me, anyway. It's a waste of my time. Mercedes won't say nothing. Counseling ain't for me."

For Mercedes, counseling presented different obstacles. To speak forthrightly with a therapist meant navigating a minefield of secrets, which meant betraying her mother and placing her sisters in jeopardy. Welfare couldn't know about Frankie, because Coco could be disqualified for her housing subsidy and cash benefits. And what about the drugs that Frankie sometimes hid from Coco in the house?

CHAPTER THIRTY-SEVEN

For the first few years of prison, sitting in his cell, Cesar had imagined a limited future: He'd get out and go back to what he called his "crimey ways." He'd reappear on Tremont, stronger than ever, and exact revenge upon those enemies and former friends foolish enough to have written him off. He'd enjoy lots of girls. He could already hear the comments women would make about his chiseled body. "Damn, he been in nine years and he come out looking *young*. He look brand-new!" If he blessed Coco and Roxanne with a nighttime visit, they would remember why they should have waited for him.

But the length of the enforced separation from Tremont and the distance from the day-to-day struggles of his family had granted Cesar an unanticipated reprieve. He hadn't been able to see the shape of his life until he'd been removed from it. Giselle's lack of interest in Cesar's toughness had also cleared a way for him to explore less familiar parts of himself. While Cesar was growing up, if Lourdes or Jessica or Elaine ran into trouble, they would say, "Cesar will take care of it." His friends expected him to resolve their beefs; Cesar remembered the time Rocco got into a fight in the pool hall on Mount Hope and Cesar pulled out his gun, after which Rocco disappeared. Mighty had been the only one who equally shared the burden of being the tough guy. Cesar had gone into these situations willingly, but now his naïveté disturbed him; he'd begun to wonder whether his friends' and family's dependence actually qualified as love. In the box Cesar couldn't intimidate, protect, or save anyone; his physical powerlessness was complete. The box had also forced Cesar to contend with what he later called his greatest demon—the terror of being alone. He thought about the comfort he'd received from all the girls who he'd been with. Sleeping with a girl beside him, he said, "was the only time I felt safe, at peace." The enforced solitude had also made him reevaluate what it meant to be a son, a father, and a man. "The box gives you time to think why your kids act the way you do," Cesar said. Protecting family was too large a responsibility for any child. Mercedes was weighing heavily upon Cesar's mind.

The proximity of his new prison to the city also made it much easier for family and friends to reach him, and his clarity about his old life and his resolve about the future improved as he had more contact with the outside world. Elaine visited with her sons and her new boyfriend. Giselle took the shuttle, which was less expensive than the longer bus rides, and the frequency of their visits made them less charged. Since their reconciliation, she'd been talking about having a baby, although Cesar wanted her to wait until he was released. He wanted to help the children he already had. Rocco would ride up on his motorcycle and play a game of chess before he reported in for the night shift at his software company.

Rocco, who continued to vacillate between the criminal and the straight worlds, was feeling guilty about his good luck. He'd been thinking about his old crew. Mighty was dead. Tito was still serving time in Sing Sing, and he wasn't doing too well. Rocco had visited Tito a few times and found him paranoid. Tito believed the authorities beamed voices to taunt him from his transistor radio and obsessed over a far-fetched theory for another appeal he couldn't afford to wage. Cesar was locked up, too, but at least he was surviving. "In a way, I started them all," Rocco said. "Why am I still here? Why am I with my family? Why did I manage to get married? Why are things so cool for me, when I am the main dude?" He wanted to make it up to Cesar. "I'll show him Windows 95, Windows 98, I'll show him DOS—so that he won't get lost again," Rocco said. "I'm on this new route." Giselle's vision of the future also included Cesar as a family man. That's who he was during their visits. "I don't care if he works at McDonald's as long as we have enough to pay the bills and have a roof over our heads," she said.

Cesar didn't let on, but he sometimes believed Giselle's love for him was close to miraculous. During visits, he'd watch her cross the room and wonder why such a beautiful woman stuck by him. She did not need Cesar in the ways to which he'd been accustomed to being needed. His ability to physically protect her was limited. Trailers were the only time Cesar could satisfy her sexually. She earned her own money. Said Giselle, "I can do for myself. I don't need to be with someone because of what they can do for me." She performed her wifely duties but did not become intimately involved with his family. She called to wish Lourdes her happy birthdays and Mother's Days; she passed through at Christmas and Thanksgiving; she called Coco on his behalf and checked up on the girls; but she left Lourdes to handle Cesar's tenuous relationship with Roxanne. Giselle visited Cesar, but when she didn't, she did not apologize.

Shortly after Cesar got off keep-lock, he stopped the drugs cold turkey and used the remainder of Rocco's money to pay off fines he'd incurred from the recent charge. He stepped out of the mix and kept to himself. Cesar said, "I was either gonna end up killed or murdering someone, and I thought about how that would make my daughter feel, to come to my funeral for that." He confessed to Giselle that he'd been using and devoted himself to her in earnest. He stopped writing other girls. He signed up for a parenting class.

Meanwhile, Jessica was slowly establishing herself on the outside, struggling to balance the needs of her current life with the habits of the old one. She showed photographs of her Boy George days to her current George. He couldn't relate to the bejeweled girl in leathers and fur coats. "I see her as simple. The pictures didn't seem right. She's just Jessica," he said. They didn't go to expensive hotels; they snuck over to his mother's empty apartment. Jessica no longer lounged in Benzes and BMWs, smug on the ostrich-skin passenger seats; now she amicably ducked beneath the dashboard to avoid being recognized by fellow probationers when she accompanied him on his rounds.

The couple had more privacy when Jessica moved into her own place in May 1999 and George quit his job. The owner of the company where Elaine and Jessica worked had helped Jessica find the newly renovated studio apartment, which occupied the basement of a privately owned home on a pretty block in Pelham Parkway in a middle-class neighborhood. Elaine had shared her worries after Jessica showed her the apartment she'd originally planned to take. "No sister of mine is living in a dump like this," Elaine said of the moldy cave in a dismal building in a dangerous neighborhood. "You served your time," she told Jessica. "You don't have to live like this anymore."

Still, Jessica spent some harrowing nights alone in her new digs. The couple who lived upstairs had brutal fights, which she could hear through the ceiling. She'd curl up in bed and try to drown out the sound of the children's screaming, covering her head with a pillow that Serena had embroidered with *Welcome Home*. Other nights, Jessica distracted herself from the stillness by calling whomever she could think to call—Serena, although she had to watch the long-distance; George; her prison pals Ida or Miranda; or Talent, Boy George's old friend, whom she'd bumped into at the halfway house.

Since Jessica's release, Boy George had been trying in vain to reach her. He'd written letters in care of Lourdes, but the last address he had was Mount Hope, and Lourdes had moved five times since then. He had also written Jessica in care of his mother, but they hadn't kept up after Jessica's initial visit. Jessica wasn't interested in her old lifestyle, but she did miss the anchor Boy George had provided. She was doing what she was supposed to—working, trying to reconnect with her children, trying to make a lasting relationship with a man—but a lot of the time she felt unmoored. She was still dating George, who had become a security guard. His wife was pregnant, but Jessica still hoped for more than he was giving. She worried constantly about money. She'd promised to help Cesar and to send her ex-girlfriend, Nilda, her box—Nilda was about to be released—but Jessica was barely getting by. The children always needed something; Jessica wanted lots of things herself.

A few times, George drove Jessica upstate to see the children; Jessica had lent George $3,000 of her $5,000 settlement to repair his car. On one trip, they ran into Coco and Frankie and Coco's girls in the park. From a distance, Coco mistook George for Serena's boyfriend because they were holding hands. Coco and Jessica exchanged hugs, but neither had much to say. The encounter disappointed Coco, who attributed its awkwardness to Jessica's allegiance to Giselle. Coco later said, "Jessica falls in love too fast."

The warehouse where Jessica worked shut down for a month in the summer. She invited her daughters to come to the city and share the vacation with her. The twins weren't as eager to spend time with her as they had been when they were younger, but Serena seemed excited, and Jessica wanted to act like a mother, even though she wasn't entirely sure how. In anticipation of the visit, she hung three new toothbrushes on her bathroom wall.

That July, the girls bused down to Jessica's. Brittany and Stephanie quickly grew homesick and returned to Troy, but Serena stayed on. Jessica dyed Serena's dark brown hair blond. They spent afternoons at the swimming pool at Roosevelt Park. They went to the clinic, where Jessica had a pregnancy test (it came out negative). She and George doubledated with Serena and Frederico, George's younger friend. They went to Coney Island, Serena said, "about a million times."

Serena sometimes placed calls to George on Jessica's behalf—as a lure, or as a front to bypass George's wife. Jessica's openness in the company of her daughter surprised George: "Jessica treats her like she's thirty. Certain things you shouldn't say—in a way it's-good, but in another way it's taking away childhood." At the same time, George counseled Serena about the dogging ways of men. "Mostly I would tell her what I would think if I saw a girl," he said. He invited her along with his friends and their dates: after they'd dropped off the girls, George would let Serena overhear the deprecating comments the boys made about the girls they'd just been sweet to in the car. Serena celebrated her fourteenth birthday in the city; George treated her and her cousin Tabitha to the movie *American Pie*. Afterward, they all went to a diner, and Serena received a cupcake with a candle. The waitresses sang.

The tentative changes that Cesar began in the box accelerated with the crises that hit him back to back in the spring of 1999, within weeks of turning twenty-five years old. First, Rocco had a devastating accident: he was riding his motorcycle on the Grand Concourse when a woman made a U-turn in front of him, and he smashed into the side of her car. The crash left him permanently paralyzed. One week later, Lourdes suffered the first of two major heart attacks. She was admitted to the same hospital as Rocco. Cesar had long feared that Lourdes would die while he was locked up, and he didn't want his mother to leave the world disappointed in him. He became even more determined to figure out a way to help the people in his life, even from prison. "My mother's health had a lot to do with it," Cesar said. "My wife. My children. I had to make a list of my priorities." Cesar couldn't reach Rocco on the phone during the months of his hospitalization, so Cesar befriended an inmate who was wheelchair-bound and started educating himself.

Giselle took Mercedes and Nautica along with her son, Gabriel, to visit Cesar that summer, but Mercedes returned home morose. She'd overheard Gabriel call Cesar Daddy.

"Why you calling him Daddy? He ain't your father," she'd said, and Cesar had reprimanded her. She'd been taught that she wasn't supposed to call Frankie Daddy; she was supposed to teach Nautica that Cesar was their father, and she had always taken the responsibility seriously.

Cesar didn't even know where to start; if Mercedes was confused, what about his other children? Mercedes had visited him since birth, and they'd had those precious seven months together between Harlem Valley and his current bid. What about Nautica, whom he'd rarely seen? Or Justine, whom he was just beginning to know? Or Whitney, the daughter he'd yet to meet? How would he explain yet another sibling to his daughter? For, unknown to Mercedes, Giselle and Cesar were trying for a child. Cesar held serious doubts about the wisdom of Giselle's timing, but he felt he was in no position to refuse. He wanted to reassure Mercedes, but he was also disturbed by her attitude. Giselle advised Cesar to be gentle with Mercedes. She told him, "Mercedes only does what she sees." His job, as her father, would be to counteract it, to show her another way.

As Cesar groped for new ways to help his troubled daughter, Rocco was in a state of shock. He only began to sense the gravity of what had occurred through the reactions of his friends. "Stone-cold murderers, killers, crying, 'Yo, man, I can't see you like that,'" Rocco remembered. He still couldn't take it in: "'Is it bad? Get out of here! Is it that bad?'" In a panic, he checked himself out of the rehabilitation hospital months ahead of schedule.

Rocco's wife, Marlene, was immediately overwhelmed: she was working full-time, going to college, raising their daughter, and now nursing Rocco, who was home and at a loss as to how to manage the most basic tasks. Within months, their credit cards were maxed out by all the charges for the medical supplies. Marlene started drinking and chain-smoking cigarettes, and despairing that her life would never be hers again. She said, "He is his own person. He will survive this and I'll lose my mind." Rocco had finally given himself over to his family, but his surrender had come too late: "He straightened out. Because he's got no choice. He can't go anywhere. He can't do anything illegal. He's in a fuckin' wheelchair," Marlene said.

That fall, she put Rocco's name on a waiting list for a wheelchair-accessible apartment, signed him up for SSI, found him a good doctor and a bearable home health-care aide, installed him back in his old bedroom in his parents' apartment on Tremont, and left. Cesar criticized Marlene's disloyalty: "Your boys are still there, but Marlene left." Rocco defended her: "But my boys haven't been through what Marlene's been through."

Rocco didn't listen to music because it made him want to go outside, and he couldn't go outside unless his brother carried him down three flights of stairs. He couldn't roughhouse with his daughter. For a time, he couldn't even manage the bathroom alone. Rocco began wondering if this was his punishment for all the bad things he'd done. He wanted to die. During their phone conversations, Cesar didn't offer consolations; he respected the immensity of Rocco's loss. But his letters and phone calls helped bring his friend back from the edge.

Mercedes was also having a hard time, but she didn't have Cesar's counsel; Coco couldn't afford collect calls to her phone. As it turned out, Coco *was* having a boy, and her baby shower was to be the summer's big event. Coco's cousin Leo, whom she'd asked to be the baby's godfather, had gone all out and reserved a picnic area in a park: there were games and a sound system and a pile of gifts and balloons and tin trays toppling with food and a huge cake and a barbecue. An enormous pacifier dangled down over Coco's wicker chair, which was decorated in baby blue. Then Frankie got arrested and ruined everything. During the festivities, he slipped away to buy weed for some white kids, anticipating a small cut for himself. On the ride back from the pickup, a police officer pulled them over and Frankie got so nervous that the officer became suspicious and conducted a search of the car. Instead of opening the gifts alongside her baby's father, as Coco longed to, she sat miserably beside Iris, who gleefully ripped open the packages before passing them on to Coco, undone.

Coco encouraged Mercedes to return to Ramapo Camp, which she did, for two weeks that July. She learned to swim underwater and jump off a diving board. But as soon as she met up with her mother in the Bronx afterward, Mercedes's family responsibilities returned. When Octavio, the drug dealer who managed Foxy's block, made a nasty comment about Coco, Mercedes bravely told him, "Shut up." Octavio then swatted her—only half-jokingly—and she hit him back with all of her might. Then she spent the rest of that night baby-sitting her sisters in the waiting room at Bronx Lebanon because Pearl had fallen in the bathroom and seriously cut herself.

Mercedes was baby-sitting even more than usual because Coco was supposed to be on bed rest. Coco's doctor had expressed concern about this delivery, and he'd scheduled a cesarean for the early fall. "How you be on bed rest with four children?" Coco asked. Frankie, who had been released after the drug charges were dropped, was nowhere to be found. Or he'd appear when it was too late to do Coco much practical good. "Ma, you want something to eat?" he asked sheepishly at two o'clock one morning, trying to pat down Coco's anger as she lay beached on the floor at Foxy's among her daughters and the rumpled sheets.

"What do you think? The girls had oatmeal for dinner, with a package of hot dogs! I have a belly to feed!" Coco yelled. He stood dumbly, still waiting for the order. She screamed, *"Chicken and cheese!"* Mercedes was relieved when they returned to Troy.

At home, Mercedes escaped to the street and rode her bicycle to visit her Títi Iris. Like Mercedes, Iris loved upstate life. She could walk to the store and not worry, "Is someone gonna take my money?" Kids didn't ride bikes around the kitchen, but on sidewalks and lawns. But even Iris's didn't remain the refuge Mercedes needed. In August, the Troy Housing

Authority police raided Iris's apartment, which they'd mistakenly targeted instead of the drug dealer's across the way. During the bust, the police grabbed Mercedes's uncle, Armando, who was watching TV in the bedroom, shoved him to the floor, and handcuffed him. They told Iris, who was screaming, to shut up as they rifled through closets and upended bureau drawers. Their oldest son ran all the way to Coco's: Coco knew it was an emergency because Iris's kids were never allowed on the streets alone. Only when one of the police officers saw the award from the tenants' association on the wall did he recognize Iris from the community center and call the raid to a halt.

After the raid, Armando became more rattled than ever; Iris's kids started having difficulty sleeping, afraid that the police would break in and take away their father. Iris quit college and fell into a depression; her determination didn't return, even after the family moved. Her doctor put her on an antipsychotic medication called Risperdal. Mercedes's formerly ambitious aunt now stayed locked up in her apartment and started putting on weight. Iris couldn't tell how much of her anxiety came from the trauma of what had happened, or from the fear she felt about her new neighborhood, which was around the corner from Mercedes's school; every fourth or fifth house was condemned or abandoned. Drugs always managed to wreck her life no matter where she went.

CHAPTER THIRTY-EIGHT

Serena returned to Troy in time to start high school. After the summer with Jessica, Serena and Milagros argued more than usual. To Milagros's consternation, Serena now called Jessica's boyfriend "Daddy George," and she had a photograph of herself and George in a frame inscribed *Daddy's Little Girl*. Milagros said, "Don't you tell me that every man your mother gets involved with, you're going to be calling them Daddy." Serena got angry; she told Milagros Jessica and George were getting married, that he called Serena his daughter, that he called her on the phone. Milagros told her the relationship wouldn't last. She warned Serena, "Believe me, your mom is gonna be with a lotta guys before she even settles down."

That same September, Serena met her first boyfriend. Cristobal sported a profile from a Roman coin. He professed true love for Serena. Milagros proclaimed that a nineteen-year-old with earrings and a tattoo wanted a fourteen-year-old for just one thing. She ordered Serena to end the relationship. "All she was doing was caring, but caring for me in the wrong way," Serena said. She and Cristobal snuck around. Milagros found out and confronted Cristobal's parents, reminding Cristobal's father that Serena was underage; she threatened to call the police. "I wasn't going to give Serena up for anything," Cristobal said doggedly.

"I grew to love him, I had to see him," said Serena. "I'd call him when she was in the bathroom, tell him, 'Meet me at Video World.'" She would run through Corliss Park, taking the dirt path that led behind Family Dollar, and jump into his idling Sunbird. He whisked her to McDonald's and treated her to her favorite Value Meal. "He always made sure I had, regardless," Serena said.

Coco scrunched her small nose disdainfully at Serena's choice. "He too ugly for Serena—she's beautiful, God bless her," Coco said. But Jessica supported the relationship. Love mattered more than looks. The threesome spent hours on the telephone; Jessica switched between Cristobal on one line and Serena on another, consoling him and chastising her.

Jessica got scolded for making calls at work and Milagros grounded Serena for failing all her classes. Serena spent much of the lockdown scribbling in her journal. She called the black-and-white Mead composition notebook her portfolio. Cartoons and magazine cutouts and pictures of her friends and family decorated the Magic Marker prose. She copied poems and passages from her favorite authors—Maya Angelou, John Steinbeck, Gandhi—and her favorite teacher, Mrs. Morace.

She composed a letter to her dead father, Puma. She interviewed classmates and cousins. She practiced spelling and played solitary games of tic-tac-toe. She penned poems. She listed what she liked ("sleeping, nice people, amusement parks, bright colors, food, money, jewelry, boys") and what she hated ("meatloaf, homework, racism, preps, stuck-ups, snobs, dumb people, scrubs, and nappy hair"). She honored her favorite people—Kevin's baby son, Coco, and Milagros—naming the sketches "The New Baby," "My Older Friend," and "My Second Mother," respectively. She wrote this, in part, about Coco:

> *She has four girls and a unborn baby boy. Her son's name is gonna be La-Monté. She is a very nice person. She is always there when I need her no matter how much it is. When I'm confused she helps me out a lot and I thank her for that. I used to live with my aunt when she lived with my grandmother, and that was like the funniest days of my child hood. When we moved up here I almost died cuz my aunt was not near us. Until she moved up here and moved in with us and then that was even funnier then before. . . . My aunt is like my second mother cuz when nobody was able to listen to me my aunt did no matter what time it was. If I was ever to decide to move out of my house or run away I will go to her house with the quickness. Well my aunt is the bestest of them all and that is why I love her so much.*

Of Milagros, she wrote:

> *She took me in when my grandmother and my uncle couldn't take care of me. She is so nice because she raised 6 kids that she didn't even give birth to all by herself. My real mom was sent to jail when I was five years old. . . . Then my mother had twin boys and even though she had five kids (because she is also raising her friend Nellie's son) she still took my twin brothers in. . . . She trys her hardest to keep a roof over our heads, clothes on our backs and food on the table. She is very strong because she managed to do all this by herself with nobody's help. . . . She treats us all the same. If somebody gets something every-*

*body gets something not better not worst. She is the strongest lady in
the whole world.*

Serena was less generous with Milagros in person. Milagros scolded
Serena and Serena sassed back. Sometimes, after school, Serena took the
bus to visit her aunt. Serena said, "If I had a problem, if I lost my virgin-
ity, I would go to my Títi Coco. When I had my period, I told Títi Coco.
When I got hair under my arms, I went to Títi Coco. When I'm bored,
I go to Títi Coco's."

Coco would tell her, "Growing up ain't the move." She wanted
Serena's life to not "go down, but up." And yet Coco no longer emphatically sided with her niece. Her understanding of Milagros's strictness had
deepened. She regretted the covert alliance she'd forged with Serena
against Milagros's rules. "I wish I never talked about Milagros that
way. . . . Now that I got a nine-year-old asking when she can have a
boyfriend? It's just scary," said Coco.

Milagros said wearily of Serena, "She's all into Jessica."

One day shortly before Coco's due date, Jessica surprised her with a visit;
Shirley, Robert's ex-wife, and Jessica had driven up to Troy to see her kids.
"I don't know what the fuck is up with your brother, girl," Coco said. She
showed Jessica Cesar's latest letter, in which he promised to rescue
Mercedes from the chaos and berated Coco for having another child.

Jessica said, "Don't let him stress you. You pregnant. You're doing a
good job, Coco. You make them take time out to write to their fathers;
how many mothers are going to do that?"

They spoke easily that day as though the years had not passed. Jessica
treated Nikki and Pearl as warmly as her blood nieces. Her presence
reminded Coco of just how much she'd missed her. But Shirley wanted
to go, so the visit was short. Jessica always seemed to be on her way to
someplace else. Coco walked her to the door. "Damn bitch, you don't
live in the city no more," Jessica said.

Coco said, "I know." She was a country girl now. Jessica hugged
Coco and rubbed her belly for luck.

Coco had, in fact, begun to sever her deepest ties with the city: she
had decided that the Bronx did not deserve to be the birthplace of her
first son. But, as luck would have it, the day before her scheduled
cesarean, she and the girls got stranded at Foxy's. Coco had driven down
on a mission to fetch Frankie, determined to start her son's life with his

father standing by, "away from the nosy people who look at a baby and say, 'Oh, he's beautiful,' then go away and say, 'Oh, but he ugly.' " Coco was so anxious to get back to Troy that she abandoned the useless car and called a livery cab to take them all to the Port Authority—but they missed the last bus. Fortunately, the cabdriver agreed to bring them upstate for the equivalent fare—$200. The cabdriver and Frankie listened to the radio; Pearl and Nautica and Nikki fell asleep; Pearl and Nikki snored; Coco watched Mercedes watch the road.

The next day, right on time, La-Monté Carmine Antonio John joined his family. He had his father's lovely round head and melancholy mouth, and his mother's happy disposition, and button nose, and brown eyes.

Coco was supposed to convalesce in the hospital for a few days, but she convinced the doctor to discharge her early because Frankie wasn't able to manage the girls back at home and Mercedes was overburdened. The baby's arrival was hardest for Pearl. Her demotion in the household shocked her: in the weeks that followed, she wandered about the apartment like a tiny bumper car. She pawed at Frankie's legs while La-Monté sat on his lap or tried unsuccessfully to wrap her arms around her mother's neck while Coco cradled her precious son. If Coco put La-Monté on the floor on a towel, Pearl pushed against him, pretending she just happened to be going that way. Coco and Frankie's relationship was in the best place it had been since they'd met, four years before— Frankie was helping and Coco wanted him to be involved—but they were both losing patience with Pearl's cloying and clutching. Frankie would shoo her and Coco would say, "Ruby *Pearl!* Go *away!*" Nautica observed her baby brother without too much interest; Nikki, however, blossomed into the little helper Mercedes no longer wanted to be.

Mercedes bragged about her baby brother to her teacher and her classmates, but for the first time in years, her primary focus was school. The principal with whom she had frequently clashed had been transfered, and Mercedes liked her replacement. Miss Scutari was funny. She had a black belt in karate and an earring-studded earlobe. She invited Coco in for a conference, and Coco brought the baby and Frankie. Coco immediately liked Miss Scutari as well. She could tell the lady cared about kids.

But the most important thing was that Mercedes loved her fourth-grade teacher, Mrs. Cormier. Academic performance had never been Mercedes's problem; she passed with little effort; the trouble always had to do with discipline. When confronted, Mercedes became defensive, but her fear was hard to see because she acted so tough. She was opinionated.

She also had a slang street style, which some adults found off-putting or intimidating; it was actually her way of testing people's interest and reaching out.

But Mrs. Cormier enjoyed her spiritedness and had deciphered from her meetings with Coco that Mercedes's chores at home included parenting; she understood that having such a young mother made Mercedes older than her age. "Mercedes wants to achieve, but she also wants to be in charge," Mrs. Cormier said. So she expanded Mercedes's responsibilities whenever possible and overlooked the small things—the shoulder rolls, the feet on the desk—and she completely ignored the outbursts, Mercedes's "bids for negative attention." Almost always, Mercedes came around. Mrs. Cormier also spoke Spanish and translated for those Hispanic parents who had recently moved to Troy and spoke little English. Mercedes still didn't speak much Spanish, but the connection helped. Mercedes was showing interest in her Puerto Rican heritage. She continued to cause a ruckus in art and stack up warnings for refusing to change her clothes in gym—an acute physical self-consciousness Coco had noticed ever since the discovery of Mercedes's warts—but she behaved, and sometimes thrived, under Mrs. Cormier's ironic tutelage.

With her mother at home, Mercedes seemed more childlike. She sprawled across the couch and moaned, "Ma, all the attention's on the baby." Coco, however, wasn't as fully absorbed as her eldest daughter imagined. La-Monté delighted her, but—to her own surprise—she missed work. One of the provisions in the revamped welfare legislation required that Coco start looking for paid work when La-Monté turned three months old, but she found herself fantasizing about a job just weeks into his life. She missed the freedoms and pleasures of a paycheck—taking the girls to the movies and treating them to meals. The car—still stranded in the Bronx—needed fixing. Her son's first Christmas was just one month away. But her tubal ligation surgery was scheduled in a few weeks' time, and in the interest of her family's future, Coco was doing her best to stay put.

She had asked for the procedure during her cesarean for La-Monté, and the doctor had been willing, until a nurse warned him that Coco could sue and that she required counseling. Coco made the initial appointment shortly after she was discharged from the hospital. In the meantime, she'd opted for another three-month Depo-Provera shot. But Coco heard through her brother-in-law that Garden Way was hiring, and Garden Way was one of the only jobs available to Coco that paid more than minimum wage. They hired at $9 an hour. The downside of Garden Way was the layoffs.

Garden Way, which produced garden tools and lawn mowers, was one of the few factories left in Troy. The steel plants—Allegheny Ludlum, Adirondack, Republican, Cluett—had gone. Arrow Shirts, which had given Troy its Collar City moniker, no longer existed. Coco had briefly worked at Garden Way after she'd left the nursing home, but she'd been laid off. This time, however, Coco was hired to start the following week. Coco asked her boss if she could delay her start date; her doctor had told her she'd need to rest after the operation, and she didn't want to start a good job, then call in sick. Her boss said, "I hope attendance is not going to be a problem." Coco canceled the appointment for the operation and reported to work.

Coco splurged her first paycheck on Christmas. She even gave her daughters money so she, too, could be surprised with gifts: Mercedes bought her a calculator, to help her budget; Nikki bought a bathtub pillow to rest her head; Nautica bought candy; and Pearl gave her a coloring book. Frankie gave her a dish set and silverware.

Coco was grateful that Garden Way was within walking distance of River Street; even after the car had been fixed, she knew she couldn't rely on it. To open the driver's door, she had to bring down a glass of hot water to unstick the lock. She sat on two pillows so she could see over the dashboard. When the car wouldn't budge, she hurried along the icy sidewalks, her arms wrapped around herself. She'd given Mercedes her winter coat.

Since Coco left early and Frankie slept late, Mercedes woke and fed and dressed her sisters. During the day, Frankie watched La-Monté; he didn't trust strangers with his son. If the car was working, Coco sped home during her half-hour break; while she believed that La-Monté was physically safer with Frankie than he would have been in day care, Frankie watched a lot of television, and Coco worried that he'd neglect to play with the baby. Coco made it home before the girls returned from a latchkey program they attended after school—all but Mercedes, who had been kicked out for mouthing off. Some afternoons, Coco returned to find Mercedes alone with La-Monté; Frankie would have ducked out early, even though he and Coco had agreed that he was supposed to wait.

Coco tried to lighten the extra burden on her oldest daughter by driving her to Secrets, the teen nightclub where Jessica's twins daughters liked to dance. Serena snubbed Secrets, but it was thrilling to Mercedes still. It gratified Coco to see Mercedes relax and act like a young girl. Every few weekends, Coco and Mercedes traded places—one baby-sat, the other went dancing—so long as Coco had money for the cover charge and gas. But before long, she got laid off again.

Serena spent Christmas with Jessica, who arranged a rendezvous between Serena and Cristobal in the Bronx. The second night of the getaway, Milagros, who still had legal custody of Serena, found out and called the police. Cristobal was sent back home, and Jessica, furious, had to make arrangements for Serena to spend the night at her grandmother's house. Lourdes held little faith that Jessica would ever be ready for her children. Her oldest daughter had never had the patience, and since her release from prison, Jessica seemed more easily overwhelmed.

One Friday in February, Jessica departed for Troy. It would be her first overnight on her own with her children in the fourteen months since she'd been released. Milagros had welcomed Jessica's offer to baby-sit and made plans for a weekend in the Bronx without any kids. Unknown to Milagros, Jessica had made plans to go out dancing as well, with Coco. Jessica had also brought along extra company—Elaine's two sons and Robert and Shirley's daughter, Tabitha, who was fourteen. Jessica made a deal with Serena: Serena would watch her siblings that night, and Jessica would stay home the next. As planned, Milagros headed for the Bronx straight from work. Jessica arrived four hours late.

Milagros's temporarily unsupervised house was overrun with teenagers when Jessica finally pulled into Corliss Park: Music pulsed from the apartment. Girls danced on the lawn, and other girls watched them. Someone's baby lay facedown on the dirt; Milagros's broken screen door flapped open and shut like the wing of a hurt bird. Matthew? Michael?—Jessica couldn't tell her sons apart—zipped by on bicycles. If one veered into the street, someone yelled "Michael!" or "Matthew!" and they obligingly swerved back onto the sidewalk. Big Kevin had left his son, Baby Kevin, strapped in a stroller while he courted a girl new to the neighborhood. Baby Kevin screeched hysterically as his father chased the girl's baby daughter, who giddily drank in his attention. Brittany and Stephanie breezed by with weak hugs. Serena kissed Jessica and looped her arm through her cousin Tabitha's. Mercedes stepped to the side to allow Serena and Tabitha to pass, and watched the older girls as they disappeared upstairs.

Jessica kissed Mercedes. "Mami, aren't you hot?" Jessica asked.

"No," Mercedes said. The apartment was extremely warm, yet Mercedes wore Coco's oversize down coat. Jessica walked upstairs with her bag of dry cleaning. Mercedes followed, leaned against the doorway of Brittany's room, and watched her legendary aunt get ready to go out.

Brittany had done what she could to spruce up her space: she'd hung Barbie curtains from some shoelaces, which she'd knotted together; she'd arranged her three Magic Markers neatly on the bureau; she'd lined up the bottles of lotion and stacked her toys in one corner. Jessica ripped open the plastic of her dry-cleaning bag. She peered at her outfit closely and plucked at invisible lint. The knee-length black jacket had see-through polyester sleeves. Jessica held the hanger at arm's length, scrutinized it as though she were still at the store. Then she foraged through her bag. She pulled out a clutch of candy and offered Mercedes some. Mercedes declined. She didn't much like candy. Her favorite treat was fruit—oranges and melon. The level of noise in the house went up.

"My father's taking me to wrestling," Mercedes said.

"Oh yeah?" said Jessica distractedly. Mercedes called Frankie her father in front of people she wanted to impress. She and Frankie were going to the World Wrestling Federation Gala at the Pepsi Arena in Albany. Mercedes couldn't wait; she told Jessica that the event was going to be broadcast on TV. Frankie had waited overnight in line just to get the tickets, which he'd given to Coco to celebrate their fourth anniversary, but Coco wasn't keen on wrestling.

Mercedes watched Jessica lift off her T-shirt and unpeel her jeans.

"Close the door, Mami," Jessica said.

Mercedes's eyes fixed on Jessica's tattoos. "Everything on your body says 'George, George, George.'"

"Cuz that's my man," said Jessica.

"Your *ex*-man," Mercedes corrected.

"My *man*," Jessica said emphatically, meaning the current George, although their relationship was effectively over. George disapproved of Jessica's ongoing flirtations with other men; Jessica resented waiting for George to sneak away from his wife. The situation had became so bad that Jessica had resorted to blocking the door when George tried to leave her apartment; a few times, she'd hidden his keys. George wasn't returning Jessica's pages and, lately, not even Serena's.

Jessica tugged on a pair of black leggings, pulled on the jacket, and adjusted the zipper low on her chest.

"What you call that? Funky Brewster style?" Mercedes asked.

"Freaky style," Jessica said. Meanwhile, Serena squealed with delight and ran past, Big Kevin chasing after her, trying to retrieve his CD.

"You better calm down!" Jessica shouted to anyone. Baby Kevin cried from somewhere. The baby daughter of the new girl from Brooklyn roamed around untended, sobbing rhythmically; Brittany eventually led the child into the kitchen and fed her. Jessica hollered for someone to get the boys. Outside, Matthew and Michael were pouncing on a discarded mattress that was teetering like a seesaw on a pile of trash. The kids ignored her. "How can I leave if they don't behave now? When I'm here? Why they gonna behave when I'm gone?" she complained. "If you keep it up, I'm not going out!" Jessica threatened to no one in particular. "How am I supposed to trust you alone if this is the way you're acting HERE?"

"Don't worry, Títi, I'll calm them down," Mercedes said reassuringly.

Jessica's cleavage earned an appreciative glance from the off-duty cop at the entrance to Casablanca, a small club in Albany. The bouncer took her $10 and requested her hand for a stamp. "Who is George?" he asked, smiling. Jessica grinned and drifted after Coco, who headed to the dance floor in a small back room with a low ceiling.

Two muscular men in their thirties or forties in dress slacks leaned against the opposite wall. A woman in a leopard Lycra top with black-feather trim sat at a tall cocktail table, the heels of her stilettos hooked around the bar of the stool. Three obese white girls in thick sweaters huddled beneath an air vent clogged with dust. Coco wanted to dance— she had prayed for Spanish, but it was hip-hop night. Still, music was music to Coco. She was out on the dance floor before she'd even finished her drink.

The DJ, thrilled to have a customer, crooned to the beat, "New York's finest! New York's finest!" Coco beckoned to Jessica. Jessica demurred, nursing her White Russian. She was captivated by her reflection in the mirror that ran along one wall. "See that bouncer? He's looking at me," she said, but Coco had danced off, out of earshot. Jessica watched herself possibly being watched in the mirror.

Attention worked differently with Coco—it opened the door for the undiluted Coco to break out. On the dance floor, a boy orbited her like a happy vampire. She returned his challenge and shimmied right up to him. He backed off. Coco reached for Jessica's hands. Jessica swayed a little bit but said she needed a Spanish song.

More people arrived. Younger boys danced in groups. They kept on their name-brand coats despite the rising heat. Albany styles—Pelle Pelle leather, puff coats—had already risen, peaked, and died in the Bronx. Someone busted a beer bottle over someone else's head. "Everyone here to have fun, everyone here to party! Manhood," the DJ intoned, "could be proven on the street!" The crowd got sticky. Coco danced until it became so crowded that she couldn't move. Finally, Jessica and Coco decided to leave.

Coco stood on her toes to ask the bartender for a cup of water and hurried ahead to de-ice the lock on her car. Jessica lingered around the exit, and the bouncer stared at her breasts again. Jessica slowly followed his gaze, as though she were looking at someone else's body. Their eyes locked on the way back up. Jessica laughed richly.

"Who's George?" the bouncer tried once more.

"My son that passed," Jessica said, raising her eyebrows mournfully, her lips in a sexy pout.

On the ride back to Milagros's, Jessica looked out at Troy's empty streets. It was nearly 4 A.M. She regretted dressing up; Albany's style was casual compared to clubs in the city. Jessica gazed at the empty factories, a furniture warehouse, The Alpha Lanes, where Serena and Cristobal would go bowling the following night. Past the Sno-King, boarded up until summer, and the strip mall where Price Chopper had been replaced by Family Dollar.

"I miss my kids," she said.

CHAPTER THIRTY-NINE

Jessica still wanted to be a mother. When she filed for full custody of Serena, Milagros didn't contest the application. She believed that Serena would be safe with Jessica, and she was exhausted by the months of battling—with Serena in person, and with Jessica by telephone. Milagros still had Brittany, Stephanie, Matthew, and Michael to raise, and now—on alternate weekends—Baby Kevin. She also said she was losing patience with kids.

Shortly before Serena's custody hearing, Jessica went to celebrate a friend's birthday at Jimmy's Bronx Café. There she met a weight lifter named Máximo. Máximo's body was outrageous: his chest was cut, fatless; his back was V-shaped; the muscles on his butt were visible through his slacks. Máximo asked Jessica to dance. He glanced at her cleavage and suggested she pull her jacket closed. Jessica appreciated the gesture of concern. His demeanor was reserved, polite. "He sounds Italian," Jessica said.

They became a couple. Máximo worked as a recreation specialist at a state park, and to supplement his income, he sometimes performed as a stripper. He lifted weights six times a week. Inspired by Máximo's healthy example, Jessica no longer fried her steak; she baked it. Instead of cake for snacks, she nibbled fruit. Máximo dreamed of a career in law enforcement. There were always going to be criminals, he said, and there would always be a need for people to catch them. He had five children, about whom, Jessica said, it upset him too much to speak.

Jessica hoped Máximo was "the one." He called her back when she paged him, and she paged him frequently. He kept her informed as to his whereabouts. He wrote Jessica love notes on his computer, left her tender messages on her answering machine, offered little gifts—a Beanie Baby, vanilla flower gel. She expressed interest in losing the weight she'd gained in prison, and he promised to help her, although he told her that he liked her body just the way it was. Within days of their meeting, she eagerly brought Lourdes to meet him. Lourdes promptly warned him to treat Jessica properly because "my daughter's been abused enough." Lourdes then crowned him her son-in-law and ordered Jessica not to play head games with him. On the ride home, Jessica told her that Máximo attended John

Jay College of Criminal Justice, although, in fact, he hadn't actually started classes yet. Lourdes worked up a yelp. "Not everybody gets to go to that college," she shouted, as though a victory had been won.

In March of 2000, Jessica quit her job; she said that her boss was disrespectful to her. Moreover, the hours had not been ideal. Jessica wanted a job that was strictly nine-to-five, so that it wouldn't intrude upon her responsibilities. "When five o'clock comes," she said, "and I have to go home and cook and take care of my daughter, that's exactly what I'm going to do." Lourdes and Emilio, who had recently been evicted again, moved in with Jessica and agreed to help with the rent. Emilio's height and the apartment's low ceilings gave the place the feel of a bunker; the couple did their best to dodge Jessica's foul moods.

But Jessica's was better than the friend's place where they'd been camping out since their eviction—a one-bedroom with two young children and six other adults. The friend didn't always come home, and Lourdes got saddled with her grandchildren. On weekends, her housemates snorted coke and broke night, amused by the macho antics of the three-year-old who eagerly passed the blunts around among the guests. Lourdes couldn't go to bed because the party was in the living room, and the living room was where she slept. She was getting too old for such nonsense, and swore she was going to have another heart attack.

At Jessica's, Lourdes and Emilio slept on a futon in the narrow hallway, which also served as Jessica's kitchen. Jessica was compulsive about keeping a clean apartment: she wanted the floor swept and mopped each night; the bathroom sink and shower wiped after each use; no dirty dishes or crumbs—ever—in the kitchenette. Jessica also threatened to evict her mother if she caught Lourdes smoking cigarettes. Like an adolescent, Lourdes snuck them at a nearby park, where she killed time while Emilio aimlessly circled the block. Lourdes bought detergent at the dollar store, wheeled the dirty clothes to the Laundromat, did the grocery shopping, and prepared dinner every night.

Máximo soon joined the household. Lourdes resented Jessica's blind generosity toward him—at least compared to Jessica's stinginess toward Lourdes herself. Máximo held a state job; the man flashed a credit card; Lourdes labored; Emilio shared his veteran's benefits. So why did Jessica glare at Lourdes when the mail brought in the bills? So the man bought her daughter a pair of sneakers. What about the house that needed the food he happily ate, not to mention rent? Lourdes mocked her daughter's ability to sustain such open faith in love.

Yet Lourdes still prided herself on the very same thing. When she had become pregnant at seventeen, by her first love, Jessica's father, her mother had ridiculed her for her stupidity and kicked her out. "My mother used to tell me, 'Take the mens for what they got,' " Lourdes recalled. "If I woulda used my figure and my beauty, I wouldn't be in the Bronx, honey. I would be in a mansion, living." Her logic was convoluted, but it got at a deeper truth: both mother and daughter had often used their looks to get by, but that only made the times when they hadn't more meaningful to them.

Jessica's ambitions weren't gigantic, although they might have seemed so when set against her circumstances: she dreamed about getting a house big enough for her five children, and Máximo's five, and not having to work. She was no longer employed, but she was working hard at the relationship—feeding Máximo, listening to him, giving him money, tweezing his facial hair.

That same March, Jessica and Lourdes traveled to Troy for the custody proceedings. They stayed at Milagros's. The following morning, Milagros went to work and planned to meet them at family court. Serena fed and dressed her twin brothers and put them on the preschool bus; then she, her mother, and her grandmother watched the movie *Gremlins*.

Serena and Jessica cuddled on the love seat. "You didn't notice my new tattoo," Jessica prompted Serena coyly. She lifted her chin to the light and showed the mole. "You like it?"

"I told you already," Serena said, brushing her away good-naturedly.

Jessica told Serena that the friend who'd given her the mole had promised to make over the six Boy George tattoos for free. She outlined her revamped body with her fingernail—the poem on her shoulder she'd cover with a butterfly. She then turned, gracing her shoulder with her chin; she'd blacken the *George* in the heart high on her right thigh. She wanted a new tattoo on her ankle: the two masks of drama, the inscription inverted—*Cry now, Laugh later*—in recognition of her new approach to life.

"What are you gonna be," Lourdes asked, "a newspaper?"

"That's art," Jessica said.

"That's fucking disgusting," Lourdes said. "When a man kisses you—"

"If a man can't handle it, that's his problem," Jessica interrupted.

"—*Property of George* across your ass?" Lourdes finished. She kept her eyes on the TV.

Serena went upstairs and dressed. Serena's bedroom walls were cov-

ered with magazine cutouts of Puff Daddy, Whitney Houston, Gin-
uwine, and Lauryn Hill. Beside them she'd hung photographs of Coco
with her cousins, and of Jessica, alongside drawings Jessica had mailed
from prison. In one, a melancholy angel dropped a handful of hearts from
a sorry cloud. On the old entertainment center that she used for a
bureau was a favor from her cousin's *quinceañera*: a virgin bride afloat in
a champagne glass, purple and white ribbons spilling from the rim.
Serena and Jessica had already started to plan Serena's sweet sixteen—two
years would give them time to save. Jessica wanted to rent a hall and a
limo. Serena daydreamed about passing out pamphlets the way promoters
did for nightclubs; about the banner, announcing her party, ribboning
behind the Goodyear blimp. She wished Cesar could be her ceremonial
father, but he wouldn't be out in time. Jessica popped in a house tape
she'd brought, which Máximo had lent her.

"Jessica! Serena! Turn down the music!" Lourdes yelled. Then she
joined them upstairs.

Serena outfitted her grandmother in a pair of sweats and guided
Lourdes's aching feet into sneakers, a gift from Cristobal. Lourdes shimmied to the music. Serena giggled. "I don't know how I got to fit in my
granddaughter's shoes," Lourdes said dramatically.

Cristobal had also given Serena a necklace that read *I Love My Baby*,
but she couldn't wear it because the clasp had broken. Serena chose
Mickey Mouse earrings and the nameplate necklace Jessica had given
her; Jessica had bought all her girls gold nameplates with the money from
the lawsuit that hadn't gone into George's car. Serena liked jewelry, but
she forbade her mother to wear the necklace with the boxing-glove
charm that Jessica had retrieved from Lourdes; Serena had heard about
how Boy George used to mistreat Jessica, and she didn't like what it represented.

Everyone at family court but Serena agreed that Serena should finish the
school year in Troy. Serena would also stay with Milagros for the summer and complete her internship at The Ark. The Ark, a nonprofit art,
technology, and job preparation center, operated out of a first-floor
apartment in a high-rise project. The mood of the space was airy, even
though there weren't many windows, and not much natural light. Serena
loved going there. After school, she would drop her bookbag and plunk
down in front of a state-of-the-art computer. As she waited for the modem
to connect, she spun around on the office chair. Self-portraits of public-
housing kids surrounded her, alongside message posters—*Keep It*

Afloat—and African proverbs and quotes from Olive Schreiner intended to boost the teenagers' self-esteem.

One project involved developing her own Web site, on which she posted her autobiography, divided into sections—past, present, and future, as though the categories were conceivable and clear. It read, in part:

> *My name is Serena. I am 14 years old. I am Puerto Rican, 100%. . . . My favorite subjects are English and Math. Lunch is my favorite time of the school day because I get to talk with my friends. . . .*
>
> *I lived in the Bronx for 8 years. I miss it. Whenever I have vacation, I go down to my grandmother's house. . . . I always go to the corner store to buy candy. The candy is much cheaper down there than up here. . . . My birth mother was put in prison when I was five years old. . . . I decided to move in with my twin sisters' godmother because they were living with her. She took me in with no problem. None of us are her real kids, but she still took all of us six kids in and raised us as her own. My birth mother is now out of jail, and I am moving with her to catch up on our relationship. . . .*
>
> *In the future, I would like to be a teacher. I would first like to finish high school and go on to college. When I'm done with school, I would like to work on getting a nice house and getting a good job. Then I would like to get married and have two kids, a boy and a girl. Then I just want to raise my kids. When they are all grown up, I want to travel the world.*
>
> *I want to teach kindergarten class because they are easier than older kids. I would like to go to Fordham University. It is in Bronx, NY, where I used to live.*

Serena never finished her Ark internship, though; her grades in school were so awful that Milagros made her quit. As soon as the year finished, Serena moved to the Bronx.

CHAPTER FORTY

Frankie's heady weeks as a doting father had for the most part ended by the time Coco took a job at Ames. Frankie still bought things for La-Monté, but during Coco's shifts at work, Mercedes was in charge. She was exhausted, like her mother, and cranky. She lost her temper with her sisters, and sometimes she hit them—hard.

Meanwhile, a measure of peace characterized Cesar's days. He was receiving a lot of visitors. Elaine loved to drive. She took her sons and Jessica's girls to visit their uncle; when she could, Elaine took Justine and Giselle and Gabriel as well. Much to Lourdes's disgruntlement, Elaine didn't always invite her along on these expeditions. After Jessica got clearance from probation and a proper ID, however, Elaine arranged a family reunion. It was the first time Lourdes and her four children had been together in almost ten years.

Upstate, the twins would brag about the visits and show Mercedes the latest Polaroid photograph of Cesar. Her cousins seemed to know more about her father than she did. Giselle was pregnant, and her belly was bringing her closer to Cesar's sisters, especially Jessica. Coco fumed, "So much they talk about family. Why they pushing my daughters to the side?" In July, the fighting between Frankie and Mercedes reached a crisis point. Desperate, Coco sent Mercedes down to spend a few weeks with Foxy.

Foxy was living with Hernan, the Vietnam vet, of whom Coco still disapproved. Hernan had moved from his barren room in a boardinghouse to a small studio off the Grand Concourse, which Foxy had transformed into a cozy nest. She had been approved for SSI because of her psychiatric condition, and her matchmaking days were done. By all appearances, Foxy was enjoying retirement: she had her new homegirls and her Newports and her bottle of Yoo-Hoo. Hernan, a few yards over, had his beer and his buddies and his dominoes. It was summer; the women from his block didn't know her personal history; they hadn't witnessed her hard times, and Foxy kept the conversations light.

Mercedes found staying with Foxy peaceful but dull. She accompanied her grandmother to the stations that comprised an older woman's life—medical appointments and visits to the hospital to visit Foxy's own mother, who had been for months moving in and out of consciousness. A few times the old woman called out for Mercedes; another time, she became agitated and begged Foxy to take care of an overdue debt at the corner store. At night, Mercedes and Foxy watched pro wrestling and cheered for their favorite contender, Stone Cold. But nights with old people ended early: Hernan sometimes drank, and Foxy's medication knocked her out. Coco worried about the combination of Hernan, her mother's heavy sleeping, and her young daughter; Coco didn't have a phone then, so she bought calling cards and checked in with Mercedes by pay phone. Ordinarily, Hector would have kept an eye on her, but he was locked up on a drug charge. Coco assured herself that her daughter was the type to speak out if anything was wrong.

Mercedes worked the phone: she called her Abuela Lourdes, who complained about her ailments; she called her Títi Yasmin, but she and Tío Manuel had broken up, and Yasmin had her hands full with their new baby (Tío Manuel's oldest two had been placed in foster care). Mercedes called her godparents, Rocco and Marlene; she wondered if they could come and get her for an overnight, but no one called back. Coco explained, "They aren't together no more."

Mercedes replied, "That ain't got nothing to do with me." Mercedes also called Serena, but Serena and Jessica were busy with Cesar's new family.

Cesar had wanted to be sure that his marriage would survive before having another baby, but he also felt he had to prove his commitment to Giselle. He said, "I feel that the only way she'll ever believe in this marriage is if I believe in her, that I'm not going to search anymore. She's set on having that baby. I figured, 'Well, you know, because you the one out there. Well, I'm behind you one hundred percent.'" Giselle believed the pregnancy reinforced Cesar's commitment to a positive future for himself. "I think it helped a lot when I got pregnant," she later said. "That was a reality hit right there."

Cesar was doing so well that the authorities reduced his security status from maximum to medium. Among the privileges of good behavior were festivals, which were like high school field days for prisoners. By coincidence, one festival took place while Mercedes was in the Bronx. Cesar already had tickets for Jessica, Serena, Giselle, and Gabriel; Mercedes desperately wanted to go along, but it was too late to include her; the reservations had to be made months in advance.

Soon afterward, Mercedes announced that she wanted to come home early. Because of work, Coco couldn't travel down to get her. Foxy suggested a guy who offered to take Mercedes for $40—he drove upstate every day to deliver fruit. Although Mercedes seemed anxious to return to Troy, Coco refused to take the risk of sending her anywhere with a stranger. On payday, Coco wired a money order to Manuel, who agreed to escort Mercedes back by bus. The fare ate up almost all of Coco's check.

Back in Troy, Mercedes exploded. She swore she'd hang herself if her mother didn't kick Frankie out. "I'm stuck between my man and my daughter," Coco said. Frankie tried to dodge Mercedes's fury: he stayed outside a lot and kept to his room. Two weeks later, Serena called, bubbling with the latest news: Mercedes had a new baby sister—Giselle Alana. Cesar sent Mercedes a prison Polaroid of himself with the baby. Mercedes responded by mailing her father a photograph of La-Monté, around which she'd wrapped a note: "Please accept this picture as I accept yours."

Matters did not improve when Mercedes returned to school. Unlike Mrs. Cormier, Mrs. Hutchins, Mercedes's new fifth-grade teacher, employed a traditional classroom approach. Mercedes bucked against Mrs. Hutchins's authority. Mrs. Hutchins's attempts to manage Mercedes resembled Coco's: she tried reason and bribery and punishment and raising her voice, but, eventually, she gave in. It was easier to let Mercedes sleep than to battle, as it had been easier, that winter, to let Mercedes wear her puff coat in the hall. Sometimes Mrs. Hutchins shipped Mercedes off to the nurse's office, where Mercedes napped some more. Three months into the academic year, her school instituted what they called "Mercedes's Behavioral Plan," which formalized the consequences for Mercedes's infractions—not opening her book, not saluting the flag, banging computer keys. Unheeded verbal warnings resulted in the appearance of a hall monitor, who escorted Mercedes to the guidance counselor's office, where she also slept. Detention made up for whatever class time got lost between the warning and its resolution. Despite the fact that the plan ignored Mercedes's physical exhaustion, it worked briefly, just as every other official response had. Except for Ramapo Anchorage Camp, Mercedes had never had access to exceptional programs, but even the mediocre ones had always done some good. For a while, Mercedes responded well to a time-out arrangement that involved reading to younger kids. To make a lasting difference, though, the help itself had to last.

Mrs. Hutchins did notice Mercedes's wariness about taking chances. The child demanded to know answers before she tried to find them. She refused to do anything in front of the class. If she had a good day and Mrs.

Hutchins invited her to move her desk from the back of the room into a regular row, Mercedes declined. She felt safer on the sidelines, in the ghetto of her isolated desk. Mrs. Hutchins said, "It was as though she didn't trust herself."

Serena moved in with Jessica in the fall of 2000 and she started ninth grade all over again. Lourdes and Emilio pushed on to Robert's, in Brooklyn; Domingo, Lourdes's ex, moved them with his truck. Almost immediately, Serena and Jessica began having arguments. Serena felt Jessica spent too much time with Máximo; Jessica felt Serena spent too much time with her friends. Jessica hounded Serena about cleaning; Serena called Jessica a "clean freak." Serena spent weekends with Elaine in Yonkers, which alternately relieved and wounded Jessica; sometimes Serena went to Lourdes's. If Máximo or Jessica gave Serena money, she took the bus to Troy.

Milagros worked full-time and studied nursing four nights a week. During one trip up, Serena passed by her aunt's. Coco had moved again. She was living in a dilapidated, picture-cluttered apartment in a tenement a few blocks from her old place, but the blocks were long on River Street.

Serena held La-Monté while Coco brushed Mercedes's hair. Lately, Mercedes had become more interested in her looks, and Coco had been waking up early each morning to style her hair for school. Serena chattered on about a boyfriend. He worked at a store near Jessica's and had welcomed Serena into his group of friends. The inclusion eased her first nervous days of a new school. "He bought me sneakers," Serena said. He'd even given her money to pass along to her sisters, although they'd never met.

"Mami, it's not all about buying," Coco said. "Take all he gives. But it's not all about buying, cuz they usually do that till you give in. Once you give in—not all men, I can't say all men—but once you end up giving in, then you'll see the change." As Coco braided, she spoke frankly with her niece about sex and Frankie and the value of independence. "Make sure that he respect," Coco said to Serena, but as much for her daughter's ears.

Then, just as Serena was readying to leave, Mercedes called out to her mother from the kitchen. She sounded frightened.

"What, Mercy?" Coco said. Mercedes's face was wet with tears. "What happened?" Coco asked.

It took a while for Mercedes to calm down enough to speak. She told her mother that during the summer visit to Grandma Foxy's, Foxy's boyfriend, Hernan, had done something nasty to her.

* * *

It was impossible for Coco to find out exactly what had happened: Mercedes said that Hernan had made comments as she came out of the shower—that he'd suggested she remove her towel and that, in turn, he would expose himself to her. Hernan said that he'd discovered Mercedes smoking cigarettes in the bathroom, and that in the ensuing argument about who was old enough to do what, Mercedes had said that she was already having sex. Coco believed her daughter. She took her to the doctor, who said she was fine, and gave the doctor Hernan's address and phone number, so that he could be questioned by the authorities.

When Coco first called Foxy and told her what Mercedes had said, both mother and daughter cried and cried. Foxy told Coco that she had been repeatedly sexually abused as a child, and then Coco confessed that she had been molested several times by a cousin, when she was nine. Foxy was shocked that Coco had never told her. Foxy also promised to confront her boyfriend the following day, when he was sober.

An official inquiry was begun in the ensuing weeks: Mercedes and her sisters were individually questioned at school, and an investigator went to Hernan's and interviewed him, but did not pursue the matter.

Coco had never held her mother responsible for what had happened to her when she was a little girl. But that fall, when she realized that Foxy wasn't going to leave Hernan—even though Coco had made it clear Foxy was welcome in Troy—something in Coco's feelings for her mother changed. Coco's years of anger and frustration with Foxy had been based on the belief that Foxy could fix her life if she really wanted to—if not for herself, at least for her grandkids. Now Coco understood that her mother didn't have the strength. Finally, Coco saw that her home was no longer in the Bronx. Within weeks, she was called back to Garden Way, and this time, she would remain there for almost a year.

The following spring, Coco finally got her tubes tied. Then her grandmother passed away after almost a year in the hospital. For the first time, Coco debated whether she should make the journey home for an important family occasion. The practical dilemma—whether the car she had bought with her tax refund would get them to the wake—got tangled with the eternal one: choosing what was best for her and the children, or trying to help her family. She didn't have enough money to get there and contribute to the collection for her grandmother's funeral costs, but then Frankie surprised her. Unasked, he filled the tank with gas and handed her $200. Coco suspected he wanted her away for some reason, but she didn't interrogate him.

The girls had already gone to the corner store to buy snacks for the drive when Coco surprised herself. The trip to the Bronx was simply not worth what it would cost her: the girls would miss school, and she'd miss work. "My grandmother's dead, God forgive me, but after this I go on. My life goes on living," Coco said. She decided to take her family to dinner at King Buffet instead, and she invited the two white girls who lived in the apartment downstairs to come along.

The two sisters, eight and ten, lived with their religious father. Coco pitied the girls, who were wispy and pale; their mother lived hours away. "I know they all into the church, and not cursing, but you have to live a little," Coco said. The group packed into the clunky car and it got them there, and they had a beautiful time.

It pleased Coco to see her children comfortable in restaurants. She still remembered the awkwardness she'd felt the time when she'd eaten out with Jessica and a drug dealer Jessica had been dating while Boy George was in jail; Coco had felt so self-conscious that she hadn't been able to fully enjoy the meal. But at King Buffet, Mercedes and Nautica confidently ate plate after plate of vegetables and salad. Nikki bided her time until Coco freed her to join the lengthy line of children at the soft-ice-cream machine. Pearl smothered mashed potatoes with melted cheese sauce. La-Monté ate pretty much everything. He was an easy baby, generous and sweet.

He offered food to an elderly lady seated behind him; she received the mushy gift. Serenity fell upon the table. Nautica didn't cause a ruckus. The two sad white sisters got happier. Pearl didn't vomit up her meal. Even Mercedes seemed contented. Life was a feast. A man approached Coco. He said, "What, you got these children on tranquilizers?"

"Thank you," Coco said, aglow with pride. She whispered in Nautica's ear, "Naughty, see? When you do right, and somebody compliments you, how good that feel?"

The old lady La-Monté had befriended finished her dinner and gave him a kiss good-bye. A busboy cleared the table, and a new couple soon sat down. La-Monté welcomed them wholeheartedly. The new lady didn't speak English. La-Monté gurgled a few words of Spanish and held out a gob of chicken. The lady remained uncharmed. Coco covered her mouth but didn't suppress her laughter. She pressed her face close to La-Monté's food-smeared one and planted a loud kiss on his fat cheek. "Go, La-Monté, that's my son," she said, swiping his mouth with a napkin quickly before he balked. Some people were nice and others simply weren't. La-Monté was a friendly baby, hopeful. There was no shame in that.

CHAPTER FORTY-ONE

Mercedes had been doing better in school since her trailer visit with Cesar and Giselle in December, but in April, her teacher said, "she went back to being the old Mercedes again." Shortly afterward, she launched a bold plan for attention, which landed like a dud. According to Iris, who worked at Mercedes's school as an aide, one Friday, during school, Mercedes told the parent liaison, Ms. Sanford, that she'd had sex with a boy. Ms. Sanford conferred with Mrs. Cormier, Mercedes's favorite teacher from fourth grade; Mrs. Cormier suggested that the parent liaison ask Mercedes's permission to share the news with the principal, and school authorities say Mercedes agreed. In fact, she seemed eager for Miss Scutari to hear: she trailed Ms. Sanford to the principal's office and hovered outside the door.

Glass windows lined the school office, and Miss Scutari saw Mercedes watching her; intentionally, she showed no reaction to the news and returned to her paperwork. Mercedes lingered for well over an hour, until Miss Scutari finally stepped into the hall.

Mercedes blurted, "Did Ms. Sanford tell you something?"

"No," Miss Scutari said. She later said she didn't want to give Mercedes the reaction she seemed to want. In the meantime, the news was spreading up and down the hallway. Iris sensed something amiss that afternoon when she reported to work. She asked Ms. Sanford, who briefed her, then Iris called Coco, and Coco, furious, immediately called the principal. How could the school phone her if Mercedes refused to open a book but not call her about something this serious? Coco confronted Mercedes, who denied saying anything; the principal apologized. The question of whether or not Mercedes had, in fact, had sex, or why she had spoken to three adults about it, somehow got lost.

A few days later, Mercedes made her second spectacular bid for attention: she walked out of detention and then out of the school altogether. She strode down the steep hill toward River Street, past the bleak block where Iris and her family now lived. She cut across the pounded turf of a small park where boys sometimes sold crack from a wobbly swing set, past the field where she played softball and the picnic area where her Girl Scout troop sometimes met. The block was one of the bases of Troy's growing gang activity: lots of the boys on the block wore bandannas; a few were Frankie's customers. Mercedes passed La Placita Market, Troy's first Spanish store, and ten minutes later, she was home. The school suspended Mercedes for five days.

That next Friday, Coco received a certified letter stating that her attendance was required at a superintendent's hearing the following Monday morning. She had a right to be represented by an attorney, to cross-examine witnesses opposing Mercedes, and to present witnesses and other evidence on Mercedes's behalf. Mercedes would be punished further if she was deemed guilty of insubordination. Thirty-one pages of disciplinary records were enclosed. Coco didn't know what *insubordination* meant, but she knew the situation was serious. In her panic, Coco mistakenly assumed that the superintendent's hearing concerned the sex allegation of the previous week, and that the school was going to take Mercedes from her.

Coco did what she usually did when frightened—she compulsively talked to friends and family in the hope that someone would know how to help. No one had much experience with constructive outcomes, but everyone had a story about losing a problem child: Milagros knew a mother who'd lost her daughter through PINS; Frankie's friend White Bobby's son had been shipped to a group home; three of Coco's cousin Bambi's kids were fugitives from foster care. Foxy predicted that her granddaughter was going to run away, just as she had, just as her older sister— Bambi's mother—also had. Foxy was thirteen years old when she took off with Manny, Coco's father, who was twenty-three. "He swept me off my feets," said Foxy, although her father's brutality had contributed to her urge for adventure. They stayed with Manny's uncle in Philadelphia, until Foxy became pregnant and Manny messed around with the uncle's girlfriend and the uncle told the young couple to get out. Manny started beating Foxy upon their return to the Bronx, where they lived in his parents' house.

But Foxy claimed that she had never regretted running away, as harrowing as the experience had been. She was a girl when she left, and a woman when she returned. She said, "I was real good until I ranned away. That's when I became a bitch." Bitchiness was an important survival tool.

Foxy believed Coco shouldn't fight the authorities if they wanted to send Mercedes to a group home. Coco, however, remembered how Foxy had fought when the authorities had tried to take Hector. Coco agreed with Mrs. Cormier, who took an affirmative approach: she thought Mercedes needed someone to take her places and give her things to do.

Otherwise, Mrs. Cormier could imagine the alternative—a boy's car stopping to give Mercedes a ride, or the lure of gangs that were migrating to Mercedes's neighborhood. Hector, still smarting from his year in prison, believed that fear was the best teacher; how else would respect get instilled in his hardheaded niece?

But Mercedes had already had more than enough hardship and fear and humiliation for several lifetimes—nights in unsafe buildings; cold waits on the hard benches of homeless shelters, police stations, courtrooms, and welfare offices; she'd been uprooted eight times in eight years. Her mother struggled every single day of her life. Her father was in prison. Terrifying seizures plagued her little sister. Drugs rendered the adults she loved incoherent; her godfather was permanently paralyzed. Sadness threatened to engulf every corner if her anger couldn't keep it at bay. She'd witnessed countless acts of violence involving parents, grandparents, aunts and uncles, cousins, friends, strangers, police. Raised in poverty, Mercedes had weathered innumerable sudden crises, but perhaps even more insidious was the fact that—despite them—little changed. Fear organized whole seasons of Mercedes's experience, and she was probably still frightened: she just didn't show it anymore.

Coco reread the official-looking letter. She couldn't bear the thought of losing Mercedes. It was this kind of moment, during Coco's own adolescence, that had made the drugs so hard for Foxy to resist. Coco said, "So much is in my head, I feel I'm gonna crack." Then the phone rang; it was Milagros. Did Coco want to go dancing to celebrate Mother's Day?

Milagros seemed to have lost interest in nursing school and had lately been going clubbing every weekend. Coco disapproved of Milagros's partying, and her women friends, but Coco needed music, and she was in no position to turn her nose up at the company. She wanted to shake off the stress. She put La-Monté to sleep, threw on some clothes, and left Mercedes in charge of the children. She met Milagros at Broadway, a new club in Albany.

Usually, Coco strode straight to the dance floor. That night, she sat at one of the tiny cocktail tables and watched other people dance—Milagros laughing with her girlfriends, older couples dancing Spanish. She slumped down, like Mercedes at her classroom desk. But instead of sleeping, like her daughter, Coco placed her heavy head in her small hands and wept.

Foxy's call woke her the next morning; she wished Coco a happy Mother's Day, a ritual Foxy never forgot. After they finished talking, Coco shuffled into the kitchen to warm La-Monté's bottle and discovered Frankie, tears streaming down his face, his barrel chest heaving, his hands gripping the edge of the dish-filled sink. He'd recently discovered that his mother had cancer, and the prognosis wasn't good. Coco had been trying to get him to talk about it, but they'd get interrupted by one of the children, or he wasn't in the mood, or Coco was too tired from work. Frankie left.

Jessica called next. She and Coco had not been in touch often, but they kept up with each other's news through Milagros and still felt close. "It could be years, she never forgets me," said Coco. Throughout Jessica's incarceration, Coco had always sent Jessica Mother's Day cards. The recognition meant a lot to Jessica, who still acutely felt her own failure as a mother.

Jessica had had a difficult year with Serena. Serena was failing ninth grade yet again, and Jessica had recently come home from work to discover her daughter in the apartment with a boy. When Serena took the phone, she sounded as unhappy as her mother. "Happy Mother's Day, Títi," said Serena.

"Thank you, Mami," Coco said.

At the hearing, the associate superintendent suspended Mercedes indefinitely and ordered the principal to file for a PINS petition on behalf of the school. Before Mercedes would be considered for reentry, she was required to attend at least two sessions of counseling. In the meantime, a tutor would visit her at home and she would report to a probation officer. Coco was relieved; she had expected worse.

Outside, Coco hurried after Mercedes, who broke into a run. "You all right, Mercedes?" Coco called after her.

"It don't matter. It don't matter," Mercedes said, her voice cracking. By the time her mother caught up with her, she'd succeeded in beating back the urge to cry.

At home, Mercedes retreated into her dark bedroom, which sat off the kitchen at the back of the apartment, climbed beneath her comforter, and turned on her TV. On the paneling hung a drawing Cesar had commissioned from a prison artist shortly after Nautica was born—three inscribed hearts chained together—*Daddy, Mercy, Naughty.* Coco hovered in her doorway. "I feel sick. I can't talk," Mercedes said, and Coco let her be.

There was no need for words. "I know exactly what's wrong with my child," Coco said. "I know, that's why I don't need counseling. I am tired of saying the same thing. They ask me, 'Do you know what's running

through Mercedes's mind?' I know exactly what's wrong with my child."
She paused. "I know what the answer is—Cesar. . . . Everything is just
missing him."

Mercedes had turned eleven in April. For the first time ever, Cesar
had forgotten her birthday. It was then that her good behavior at school
suddenly ceased.

Cesar had been overwhelmed by the responsibilities of his busy new
prison life. The previous August, shortly after Rocco had moved into a
wheelchair-accessible apartment, Cesar had been transferred to Woodbourne, a medium-security facility. Woodbourne was the calmest of the
ten prisons he'd been in. Most of the inmates were in their late thirties
and older. Almost all of them programmed, which meant that fights were
kept to a minimum. Cesar was used to prisons where stabbings happened
daily; at Woodbourne, months passed between incidents. At first,
medium-security status unnerved him. He'd wait by his cell for a guard
to escort him to the package room until the guard said, "What are you
waiting for?"

"It's wild," he excitedly told Rocco. "You can get up and go!" For fifteen
minutes of every hour, medium-security inmates were "clear to move."
Cesar's enthusiasm for the tiny, substantial pleasures was contagious; he
was one of the few people capable of temporarily distracting Rocco
from his despair. Cesar was assigned to a dorm that housed the state's deaf
inmates. He began to learn how to sign.

Cesar also enrolled in college; the drug war had sapped the budget for
New York State inmate education, but Woodbourne had one of the
few degree programs available. Cesar's program was inmate-run. Twenty-
five men started, and Cesar was one of only six who survived the first
term. Students had one year to complete a three-year workload. The
inmates were tough professors, but if Cesar graduated, he'd receive a
Certificate of Ministry in Human Services. He loved school.

Cesar took five classes, which covered subjects like homiletics and
world religions. Three typed essays were required every week. Cesar
didn't have enough money for a typewriter, so he borrowed them from
his classmates. He had to wait until they'd finished their homework,
which meant he usually broke night typing. Under the pressure of these
unaccustomed deadlines, he'd forgotten to send Mercedes her birthday
card.

Back in the Bronx, Rocco broke night playing chess on his computer. The stainless-steel bathroom features of his new wheelchair-

accessible apartment reminded him of a cell: "I feel like I'm in jail sometimes. Toilet flushes like a jail toilet. Bars on the window. Nothing to do." Cesar immersed himself in papal history and politics; Rocco devoured gangster magazines. Rocco came across a profile of Boy George in *Don Diva* ("For the Ghetto Fabulous Lifestyle") in its special issue on kid kingpins. Pictured in a film reel on the cover, under "The Eighties," was Boy George's head. While Rocco pined for his outlaw days, Cesar had been thinking about the ways in which idle time on the street had eased his way toward criminality. He said, "For me, crime was attention. Responsibility got strapped on my chest when they said, 'There's no food in the house.' You get praise for doing wrong. I didn't see it as wrong, because helping my family is right. *How* I tended to my family was different. *Why* is because we didn't have. The sequence led to the boy that created me."

Rocco and Marlene had divorced, but Cesar and Giselle's relationship was stronger than ever. Giselle regularly visited Cesar with their baby girl. Giselle's father had left when she was young, and Giselle was determined that Cesar be a presence in their daughter's life. Cesar hated the long gaps between his other daughters' visits: "I don't think it's fair, you know. But I'm not saying it's Coco's fault. I gotta understand that she got all them kids, and she going through her own problems and sometimes I say, you know, I ain't got it that bad." But Cesar hungered for news about Mercedes that was positive. Coco tended to write for advice when Mercedes was having trouble. Lourdes's dispatches tended to seize on evidence of other people's flawed mothering. Cesar knew little about Mercedes's accomplishments. He longed to know what made his daughter happy, what thoughts absorbed her, what activities composed her daily routine. Pictures no longer satisfied his curiosity. In his letters, he made a point to acknowledge her strengths instead of reprimanding her for her weaknesses. In one recent letter, she had described her softball team. She disliked the team name—No-Smoking Kids—which she found silly, and she wished that instead of donated T-shirts, they could have real uniforms. She mentioned an outfielder who'd missed a ball—"That girl was looking stupid," Mercedes wrote.

Cesar had conducted a "positive asset search" on Mercedes's letter. He'd learned the technique in psychology. "She doesn't like the name of the team," he said. "She has a critique." He suggested Mercedes help the outfielder; perhaps they could practice together? He told her not to worry if the outfielder rejected her offer; she wouldn't be a sucker for being kind. Offering would make Mercedes feel better about herself either way. "Use that muscle," Cesar wrote. He wanted to try to make it safe for Mercedes to take risks. In thinking about his adolescence, he'd realized the punishments for his behavior never gave him clues about how to go about making improvements: "They made me pay the consequences when I did wrong, but not one ever tried to show me a solution or identify the cause."

After the superintendent's hearing, Coco had mailed Cesar a copy of Mercedes's records. Cesar pored over the notations. He said sadly, "It's like reading a book about myself." All her teachers believed she was capable. Mercedes's problem was "her attitude." But her assertiveness served her badly in only one of the two worlds she had to negotiate. Bossiness at school might have rendered her a bit of a bully, but at home, lording over little kids was a necessary skill. At school, outbursts caused chaos; at home, they somehow focused things; in either place they generated the attention she needed and craved. But unlike her sister Nikki's behavior, whose sweetness disguised anger, Mercedes's only served to underscore it. As a result, she couldn't, or didn't, move between the two worlds easily.

Cesar still blamed Coco for burdening herself and Mercedes with too many children—Coco had been "too ignorant, or too selfish," he wasn't sure which. Rather than attack Coco, however, he placed Mercedes's struggle in a wider context. Mercedes's predicament extended beyond personal history or family or attitude or teenage parenting. "Poverty is a subculture that exists within the ghetto," he said. "It goes beyond black or Hispanic, at least in my mind. Overworked teachers. Run-down schools. It looks like they designed this system to make our children fail. Socioeconomic conditions. Why are we so passive? We accept conditions that don't benefit us—economic oppression we've been suffering for years. That's the primary condition."

But Cesar mainly blamed himself. He'd been in prison for most of Mercedes's life. At first, he was going to send her copies of his syllabi to show her how busy he had been and to explain why he missed her birthday, but he decided to apologize instead. He'd still failed her—even if the reason was worthy. He wrote, "School was no excuse not to keep in touch." It wasn't often that anyone admitted their mistakes to Mercedes; the default posture of poverty was defense. Cesar told her that he hoped his degree would make Mercedes proud of him when he came home.

In Troy, children shared the same probationary space as wayward adults. The two-story office building sat opposite the local newspaper, not far from the storefront that used to house the shelter where Mercedes had stayed six years before. The city's homeless population had continued growing, and Joseph's House had since moved to larger digs. A plump receptionist buzzed Mercedes and her mother in.

Coco looked tiny next to Mercedes, who towered over her by a full head. Mercedes's long mane of brown-blond hair spilled from a bandanna of the Puerto Rican flag, which she'd positioned with the star facing front. Like Wonder Woman, she assessed the scene—a skinny white guy nervously sitting, a black woman reading a magazine. She sat down and nibbled her nails. Her door-knocker earrings swung, a cursive *Mercedes* inscribed in their cradle. Coco moved almost primly, each gesture snug with anxiety.

Miss O'Connell, Mercedes's probation officer, beckoned them through a metal detector and led them to a chilly interview room. On the wall was a tattered Xerox, *LOVE, THE ANTI-DRUG*. It read in part, "Drug Free is achieved in a series of small, personal ways."

"Do you understand why you're here?" Miss O'Connell asked without introducing herself.

"No," Mercedes said.

"Why did you leave detention without permission?" she asked.

"Cuz I didn't think I was supposed to be punished," said Mercedes.

"What else could you have done?"

Mercedes knew the drill: "Listen to Mrs. Hutchins."

"What else?"

"Asked?" Mercedes tried.

"What could you have changed to make a better situation?" Miss O'Connell asked, but it wasn't a question. "Attitude," she added. Probation tackled that.

Mercedes would be routed to Diversion, a program that aimed to keep her at home. Miss O'Connell outlined Mercedes's options: If Mercedes "didn't cooperate," she'd "choose to go to family court." There, a "judge would weigh the truth, like judges did." Then Miss O'Connell asked Mercedes to sign a voluntary form that acknowledged that she understood she had a choice. Mercedes looked perplexed, so Miss O'Connell elaborated: the voluntary form involved "rights in America."

"You have a right to accept this part of probation, so which do you pick?"

Mercedes's eyes widened and she looked at her mother. Coco uncertainly reached for the pen.

Because she was a minor, the terms of Mercedes's probation required that she follow the rules both at school and at home. "What does it mean to follow the rules?" Miss O'Connell asked.

"Listen to my mom," Mercedes said.

"That's right, listen to your mom. You're old enough to help a little bit. Set the table. Do the laundry." Mercedes's house had no table; she ate on her lap on the floor; Coco thought her daughter helped too much. Miss O'Connell quickly ticked off a checklist of questions she was supposed to ask Mercedes. "Drugs," Miss O'Connell said. "Drugs, hopefully, that's not a problem at eleven. Curfew?"

"She's barely outside," Coco said.

Ordinarily, Miss O'Connell saw her charges weekly, but since it was summer, she suggested every other week: It didn't make sense to Coco. Summer streets were the worst, and without school, the children had less to do than ever. Miss O'Connell was ready to conclude the interview: "So what are you leaving with? What's the message you are getting from me, from school, from home?"

"Try to control my temper," Mercedes said.

"You *need* to control your temper."

Then a remarkable thing happened—Mercedes asked for help: "I can't—I don't know how," she said. It was an extremely rare admission of weakness, but Miss O'Connell didn't respond. Coco, however, understood the significance of what had just happened, and she tried to keep Mercedes's request for help afloat: "How come Mercedes try to calm me down when I get upset, but she can't realize it for herself?" Coco asked anxiously. Without glancing up from her paperwork, Miss O'Connell assured Coco that Mercedes would learn all she needed to know in anger management.

That spring, Rocco's luck changed again. He'd fallen in love with Maya, a short religious missionary from the Philippines. She conducted Bible studies with several people in Rocco's assisted-living apartment building and had tried to invite Rocco, but he'd been so depressed the day she knocked on his door that he hadn't bothered to open it. But when Rocco made the connection that the pretty girl he'd spotted leaving the building was Maya, he was ready for religion.

Rocco was a dutiful student during their sessions—no wisecracking, no cursing. He offered her Pepsi and avoided his past. He finally worked up the courage to leave a love note in the pages of her Bible. After she'd discovered it, she told him, "Brother, I'm not the girl." But once Rocco had given up his romantic hope, he started speaking more freely with Maya. He unburdened himself; his humorous personality came out. One night, he showed her the X-ray film from his spinal injuries.

Around this time, Maya said, "God interfered." Maya had seen a dream interpreter on television who said some dreams were prophetic in nature, and she'd had several that stayed in her memory. In the first, she and a girlfriend went to buy shoes. They hurried; it was late, and the store was about to close. Maya quickly grabbed a pair of purple shoes, which are wedding shoes in Filipino culture. On the way home, she was pushing her friend in a wheelchair, and when they came to a hill, they switched places, so Maya could enjoy the ride down: Maya waved a shoe in each hand, she said, "rejoicingly."

In the second dream, Maya was looking in the mirror and a Latina face was reflected back. She was wearing a wedding gown, zipped halfway, and she went to find her mother to ask her to zip it. "Who am I marrying?" Maya asked.

"*Basta magiging masaya ka*," her mother said. Just go ahead, you will be happy.

In the third dream, Maya lay on a gurney in the hospital awaiting spinal surgery to make her taller. The night that Rocco showed her his X rays, Maya realized that she had had a premonition, and she cried the whole subway ride home. "I was thinking, 'Is he my destiny? I hope not.'"

They held hands a long time before they kissed. When Rocco proposed and Maya said yes, Rocco's friends warned him against it; she might be marrying him for a green card. But Rocco decided it was worth the risk.

Mercedes returned to school in time to graduate with her fifth-grade classmates. Money was tight, but Coco still surprised her with a new bicycle. Coco did her best to keep her financial problems away from her children, but Mercedes watched her mother carefully. For weeks, Mercedes had refused to let Coco take her to the mall to buy shoes for graduation. However, graduation morning, Mercedes faced the problem of walking in the sandals Coco had borrowed, having anticipated that her daughter's only other option—sneakers—wouldn't match her dress. Mercedes tottered over to the couch and threw herself down, leaned her head on one hand, and plucked at the black lace sheath that covered the crimson dress. Her white bra straps stuck out from beneath the spaghetti straps. She said she didn't want to go. "Mercy," Coco said, her concern sounding through. She wanted Mercedes to enjoy the day.

Coco had done what she could to create an air of festivity. The night before, she had styled everybody's hair—her four girls and the two white girls downstairs. She treated them all to fake fingernails from the River Street Store. She painted Mercedes's real toenails, too. That morning, Coco tried to make Mercedes laugh by dramatically karate-kicking a roach. Mercedes ignored her. Coco quickly combed her own hair out, smoothed it with hand lotion, and squinted at her reflection in the mirror over the clogged fireplace, displeased. She was wearing a short-sleeved red cotton top and black slacks. She stuck her door-knockers in and opted for a ponytail. She squirted herself with perfume and headed toward Mercedes, who craned her neck back.

"Honesty—" Coco appeased.

"I don't want it," said Mercedes.

"Mercedes, you didn't put any on—"

"I want my Tommy Girl."

"You are going to have to find it, then," said Coco, wounded. Mercedes didn't bother looking.

"I hate these shoes," Mercedes said.

"I wanted to go shopping, Mercedes," Coco chided.

"You needed the money," Mercedes said, stinging her.

"It's not your business what I need, Mercy," Coco said, biting her lip.

"Students," began Miss Scutari. She stood at a podium in the old gymnasium, looking spiffy in a white suit. "This day is for you."

"They say it's for the kids, but it isn't," whispered Coco forty-five minutes later, after a string of boring speeches by local politicos. Parents and guests were asked to hold their applause while the children retrieved their awards and certificates. Coco's eyes welled with tears as Mercedes stood. Then Miss Scutari played a scratchy recording of the class theme song she had chosen for the graduates—Lee Ann Womack's "I Hope You Dance." After the chorus sang, guests were invited outside for the final balloon ceremony.

Coco could see Mercedes in the crowd of students moving toward the exit; with the heels, she was a head taller than most everyone. Coco caught up with her daughter in the front of the building, where she was huddled forward in conversation with Kaitlin, her new friend, who was in seventh grade. Mercedes like to hang around with older children. Coco nudged her daughter closer to the graduates, who were forming a loose group on the sidewalk beneath Miss Scutari's bunch of balloons.

Coco grabbed one for Mercedes, who reluctantly received it. Mercedes held her arm rigid, as though the balloon were a misbehaving child, while the other kids bonked the balloons and plucked at the strings. Miss Scutari addressed the graduates energetically, as if all the undone work of equipping these kids for adolescence could be pumped into them in these final minutes. On the count of three, they were to shout out the refrain from their class theme song—"I hope you dance"—after which they'd release the balloons into the sky. Mercedes rolled her eyes. She seemed reluctant to extract herself from the admittedly goofy ritual, yet equally unable to enjoy its simple pleasure. The children counted, "One, two, three!" Mercedes turned away from her balloon as she released it, disowning the gesture of hope.

For all the talk in the family about Mercedes, it was perhaps Frankie who was most immediately at risk for joining a gang: he'd several times mentioned to Coco that he was considering it. His son, his mother's cancer diagnosis, and the flurry around Mercedes's suspension seemed to have caused him to reflect on the precariousness of his life. ("I *went* to high school and look at me, Mercy," he'd said, the day she'd been suspended.) His dependency on Coco shamed him. "Coco works hard, you know," Frankie said. "Sometimes I feel I'm taking advantage, but she's good to me." He seemed to be searching for a sense of purpose and at the same time to be giving up on some part of himself. Frankie still mourned his dream of playing minor league baseball. He no longer wanted to be a drug dealer; he never had. He didn't want to be dealing when his son was old enough to understand; Mercedes already did, and he'd long since stopped working out of the house. During their fights, she would say, "You a drug dealer!" How could he respond to that?

Frankie no longer said aloud that he still wanted to find a job and no longer defended himself against Coco's indictments of his uselessness, and Coco, sensing his despair, didn't insult him as often anymore. Coco doubted that any employer would hire Frankie: he was thirty years old, and the few jobs he'd held—at the packaging plant and in construction—were brief and off-the-books. Even as a drug dealer, his success wasn't notable. Weedo and Coco's cousin were dealing, and their business had "blown up," even though they hadn't been in Troy as long as Frankie had. Weedo arrogantly fanned his wads of ten- and twenty-dollar bills in Frankie's face.

Coco tried to assure Frankie that his slow way was better. While Weedo and Coco's cousin sold cocaine from a car, they blasted music with the cousin's infant daughter strapped in the backseat. Coco said to

Frankie, "They have the baby in the car. Doing their shit in the street. Frankie, you do your stuff indoors. They use their money stupidly—you take care of your family." Hungry bellies didn't feed on gold. Coco knew that her cousin's girlfriend saw little of the drug money; she'd recently shoplifted the baby's medicine. Frankie paid attention to his son, even if he couldn't dress him in brand-name; La-Monté cried for Frankie and ran to him when he stepped through the door. But Frankie remained despondent. All year long, Frankie looked forward to his summer softball league, but his team had lost every game so far. And he'd had to pawn his jewelry to pay for the uniform. Still, Frankie liked his family to watch him play.

One June evening, the girls rode their bikes to Frankie's softball game. They were running late. Mercedes raced her sisters down the stairs, bouncing her bicycle, and hit the sidewalk moving. "Stay on the sidewalks!" Coco shouted after them. Nautica zipped ahead. She kept her head low, like a racer, her elbows jutting up like the wings of a bat. Mercedes let her pass. Nikki looped around Coco. "Move along, Nikki," Coco cajoled. Lately, Nikki had become clingy. She made La-Monté's bottles and massaged her mother's aching wrists after work. At night, when Coco sat on the stairs outside waiting for La-Monté to exhaust himself with play, Nikki sometimes watched her from the windowsill.

Coco could tell from Frankie's posture beneath the field lights that the game wasn't going well. The final inning was almost over. Mercedes played softball with some other kids on an adjoining field. La-Monté demanded to walk and Nikki chased him. The Emeralds lost—again. The teams snaked their way through the handshake line; Frankie kicked dirt in the dugout. He'd only got up to bat twice. He said nothing to Coco as they headed home.

Coco pushed the stroller toward the parking lot. Cars were backing out. Nautica zoomed off on her bicycle. "Mercedes, watch Nautica!" Coco yelled. Nikki had her head turned toward Coco and Frankie and almost collided with a car. She recovered herself and pedaled to join her sisters. The parking lot emptied. The car sounds faded. Conversation wafted from a porch.

Coco dreaded going home. Roaches ruled the kitchen and the bathroom. They sapped her will to clean. Pearl grew sluggish. Coco stopped and Pearl climbed on her mother's back. "Where would you want to go if we was to move, Frankie?" Coco asked.

"I ain't going back to the Bronx," he said.

They walked quietly past *For Sale* signs, breathing in the smell of summer grass. La-Monté was wide awake, craning his neck forward from the stroller, looking up at the stars.

Back at home, the girls went inside to get ready for bed. Frankie sat on the stoop and ate a plate of food that Coco had left for him in the microwave. La-Monté pushed a toy stroller belonging to Nautica. Coco followed as he zigzagged, occasionally ushering him away from the curb. La-Monté loved the street: some days, he never set foot outside the house. The stroller tipped sideways and La-Monté fell. He grunted as Coco propped him back up—he wanted to stand up on his own. Some boys weren't allowed to play with strollers—at least not in public—but Coco didn't care if her son played with girls' toys; he was still young. Frankie shaved La-Monté's head and Coco dressed him rugged, like a hoodlum, but she didn't want him acting like one.

She smooched and hugged him with abandon. She nuzzled her nose into his chubby underarms. "You smell so good!" she sang. "My *son*." Friends chided Coco for the softness, and she retorted, "That's right. He is a mama's boy."

Frankie, to Coco's relief, didn't try to toughen him up. Frankie kissed La-Monté hello and good-bye. Whenever Frankie came home and ate, he'd balance his plate on one leg and La-Monté on the other, and they'd watch baseball or pro wrestling. Frankie never minded when La-Monté dove onto his shoulders from the back of the couch or nestled in his lap.

One of Frankie's teammates stopped by. Mercedes popped her head outside. She hopped onto the stoop and did a quick dance move as though she were swinging a golf club.

"Mercedes," Coco said. "Upstairs, now."

"All right!" Mercedes said good-naturedly. She added, "If someone asked Mrs. Cormier to baby-sit me, I bet she would baby-sit me."

"All right, Mercedes," Coco said. "Good *night*."

Sometimes Mercedes made her feel as if she had another full-time job. Coco said, "By the morning I feel like it's been a whole shift at Garden Way."

Mercedes squeezed past an old mattress in the hallway and, climbing the stairs three at a time, disappeared inside.

CHAPTER FORTY-TWO

B y the summer of 2001, Jessica was working at a security desk in the vast marble lobby of an international bank. When she received a raise to $16 an hour, she moved to a bigger apartment in the Hunts Point section of the South Bronx. She split the $750 rent with Máximo and her older brother, Robert, who had recently divorced.

Jessica wanted Serena to have her own bedroom, and Serena's white-wire frame bed was the first new piece of furniture Jessica bought. Serena's room was too small for the canopy Jessica dreamed of, but Jessica did what she could with the space. Lavender sheets and a matching comforter covered the brand-new mattress. Pink Disney curtains hung from the single window. In her own room, Jessica made do with old sheets, which she tacked up over her windows to reduce the draft. She covered her lumpy mattress with Lourdes's cast-off brown-and-olive sateen floral spread. There were framed pictures of her children on every conceivable surface.

The larger implications of Jessica's move, however, were ambiguous. Hunts Point, in Serena's words, "was straight-up ghetto." She preferred the easy freedom of her previous block. In Hunts Point, people broke night on the sidewalk, blasted music, and slept late. Serena couldn't walk unescorted to the train. She couldn't sit outside in the evening. Her Tío Robert's presence in the narrow hallways of the apartment was oppressive; even when he wasn't home, there seemed to be an awareness of his impending arrival.

After dinner, Jessica retreated into her bedroom and lost herself in one of Máximo's true-crime novels. Máximo, who worked as a security guard at a school, lived at the gym. Robert played his oldies music until his anti-depressants kicked in, then fell into an uninterruptible sleep. Serena invited Jessica to join her in the *sala*, but Jessica didn't like the types of movies Serena liked. Serena missed the closeness of Jessica's old studio. "When we all in the same room, we spent time with each other," Serena said. "Now we in separate rooms."

Serena preferred to spend her summer days at her best friend Priscilla's rather than in the empty apartment at Hunts Point. Priscilla lived with her sister, two brothers, her mother, and stepfather on the top floor of a three-decker near White Plains Road. Priscilla's neighborhood was working poor and working class—full of Albanians, Indians, Irish, Puerto Ricans, Italians, and Dominicans. Instead of the bullet-proof check cashiers, the bodegas and liquor stores shared the blocks with businesses that spoke of future-oriented days—tile and sprinkler shops, travel agencies, bakeries. The parents' workaday routines limited the teenagers' range of motion: no adults were home after Priscilla's mother went to work at two, but she kept watch on the girls by telephone. Supplemental surveillance was provided by surprise visits by Priscilla's gruff stepdad, Al, who worked for a towing company. When his red shiny truck rolled up, unannounced, the girls assumed that he was spying, but Al also liked to play video games between the dispatcher's calls.

The teenagers usually hung out with their friends on "the bench"—actually two benches—overlooking Priscilla's driveway, in the shade of some fruit trees. Priscilla's front yard set the summer stage for the drama, which was largely psychological. If the gang weren't draped over the bench, which was warped from wear, they lined the four short stairs that led up to the front door. In constant fear of missing her mother's calls, Priscilla never traveled beyond the radius of the portable phone.

The charge of "acting ghetto" delineated acceptable and unacceptable behaviors among the kids and deflated tough posturing and hypocrisies. "Acting ghetto" included bragging about violence; claiming you saw a new movie in the theater when you really saw it on a bootleg video; cursing; wearing slippers or curlers to the store. The girls labeled each other as well. "I'm the good girl, Serena's the bad one," Priscilla said. The best friends drew the line pop-culturally: Serena liked Black Entertainment Television; Priscilla preferred MTV. Serena liked rap and R&B; Priscilla, Britney Spears. *Bad* implied loud, assertive; *good* meant quieter. Serena barreled through her shyness with impulsiveness; Priscilla withdrew and fretted. Priscilla liked boys with jobs who wanted commitment; Serena liked guys who dressed like hoodlums and knew how to kiss. Priscilla had a mad crush on the landlord's son but had turned her cheek to his kiss because he wanted to date other people. She was sixteen, he was twenty-three.

Serena said, "How do you know where the first kiss will lead?"

"I'm not gonna kiss someone I'm not with," Priscilla said defensively.

"Kiss him first, and see what happens," Serena said, and rolled her eyes.

Serena had been kissing a boy named Derek, who lived in the neighborhood. He was fifteen years old, with an ex-girlfriend who was pregnant by him. Priscilla's sister, Monique, dated Derek's friend. The boys passed by nearly every hour. Once in a while, Serena and Monique ventured to the store to buy lollipops or up the block to the fire hydrant, which Derek would try to open until an old lady threatened to call the cops.

Jessica didn't approve of Derek since learning about his pregnant ex-girl. Jessica believed that his having sex with Serena was just a matter of time. "Either he'll expect it from her—cuz you know if he's sexually active, he's gonna have to have it—or he'll go to another girl," she said. Serena didn't agree, but she perceived the challenge much the same way as her mother did—as a competition between girls—and she worried about her rival's long-term advantage: "I think when the baby comes, there's gonna be a lot of problems. Cuz he's gonna go to see the baby, and I'll think he's gonna see the mother," she said.

Serena had other, pressing problems. She was teetering on the edge of academic disaster; if she failed summer school, which seemed increasingly likely, she faced the embarrassing prospect of a third year of ninth grade. Jessica assumed that Serena's educational failure was part of her daughter's personality—"That's just Serena," said Jessica. Virginity was another thing entirely. But if Jessica complained that Serena spent too much time on her social life, Serena retorted, "You jealous I'm the one having fun?" If Jessica mentioned pregnancy, Serena said, "*You* the one never should have had kids." Jessica complained bitterly that Serena put friends before family. Serena coldly reminded Jessica about a lifetime of being pushed to the side for Jessica's men. When they were younger, Serena had always remained behind, longing for Jessica, waiting; now that Jessica had finally created a home for her, it seemed to Jessica that all Serena wanted to do was leave.

Lourdes expressed more confidence in Serena, whose success she viewed in opposition to both her own and Jessica's experience: "I haven't gotten nowhere because, from being a mother, I became a mother again for my grandchildrens." Lourdes spoke her mind to Serena, who laughed nervously at her grandmother's directness: "Honey, the boys that are growing up now, it's only for your pussy. A girl has to be smart now. Study. Be somebody. So when you become somebody, you don't have to have this straggly shit on your lips, sitting on your ass, to see if they could support you. You could support yourself. They respect you, because they know they could lose you right there and then. You don't need *them*, you understand?"

Serena wasn't the only one who seemed to be passing Jessica by. Shortly after Jessica met Máximo, she'd introduced Elaine to John, one of Máximo's friends; Elaine and her former boyfriend had split, but remained on good terms. Elaine and John became a couple; now they led such a busy social life, Elaine had to carve out time for Jessica. John treated Elaine to dinner. He took her dancing. John had already introduced Elaine to his mother and his six-year-old son.

Jessica had yet to meet any of Máximo's children. They'd become engaged—but only because she surprised him with a ring at a seafood restaurant on City Island. Now she suspected he was cheating on her, although he denied it. She said she'd traced his cell phone calls and spoken with two girls who said they were involved with him. Neither sounded surprised to hear from Jessica; they'd been suspicious of his living arrangement; humiliatingly, Máximo had told them he was living with an aunt.

John, on the other hand, had publicly claimed Elaine with his anniversary gift—a thick gold chain, studded with her sons' birthstones, and earrings that matched. "What's ten years from now? A house? A car?" Elaine joked. "Westchester County, baby," she said.

Jessica's move to Hunts Point was a demotion by comparison. Once, Jessica's little cousin Daisy had been dumped there in the dead of night by a disgruntled date. Prostitutes milled around the corner from Jessica's apartment. Even Spofford Hall, Cesar's old juvenile detention center, had graduated to a better neighborhood. The stench of fumes from the incinerators seemed ominous, like the risks the area posed for both mother and daughter—invisible, yet pervasive. For Jessica, though, the ghetto's familiarity might have been its greatest threat—the danger that felt like home.

Boy George's letters had finally reached Jessica. "So tell me, how was your transformation from convict to Jane Doe Citizen?" Was freedom similar to being reborn? What kind of food did she eat? Had she finally learned to drive? "I've had all types of things run through my mind upon a possible release date. I believe I've thought of 1000 things I'm going to put on my priority list, buy a couple of dogs, get a couple of nice cars, take a vacation, raise a baby boy, just *live*, Jessica."

He'd heard that she'd finally reunited with Serena, and he congratulated her. He hadn't heard much about Luciano, his firstborn, since his arrest. George had effectively disowned his other boy. The teenager had ignored the primary lesson his father's grim life could teach. "He's into some heavy hoodlum shit," George said with disgust.

In fact, George's son was the rule rather than the exception. George's old Chinese supplier, who was also still in prison, marveled at the staying power of Boy George's legend. "Twenty-two-year-olds coming in from the Bronx still idolize him: so young, so much money, girls, cars. He becomes like a bedtime story," the supplier said. Like George, the supplier was baffled by the youngsters' shortsightedness. "I feel sad by the fact that these kids don't know what they are getting into. He's doing life in jail—what about that point?"

Jessica read George's letters aloud to Serena. Serena blamed George for the anguish she and her sisters and brothers had been through; she wrote to him and told him how much she'd hated her mother's incarceration. Jessica forwarded the letter to George, wrapped inside her own. He responded to mother and daughter separately.

In his letter to Jessica, George acknowledged that he'd abused her and told her how humiliating it had been to hear the wiretaps ("To say that I was deceived," he wrote, "that would be the understatement of the millennium"). He marveled at the brazenness of her cheating and mused, "I knew you were just crazy cause God couldn't save you if I would have found out. Who knows scholars would probably say he did, and that's why I was arrested." He reminded her that she had deserted him just when he needed her most. But his concerns about the future outweighed his grievances about the past. He encouraged Jessica to stay on track and suggested that she periodically reassess her progress and her goals. "You are a good person and a smart person who has suffered," he wrote. "Now hold your head up and move on." He hoped she could let go of the bitterness she held for him.

In his letter to Serena, George asked her to set aside her preconceptions and reintroduced himself: "My name is George." He acknowledged that he truly loved her mother, but that they both had been living the fast life and couldn't commit themselves to one person. "If I could've seen into the future I swear I would have declined to meet your Mom, but destiny took its course and so did the misunderstandings. Serena, just as there is evil in my past deeds with your Mom, so too there were good ones." He apologized for the pain he had caused her and her sisters and acknowledged that she might not accept his apology. The cordiality of his parting words recalled the George who'd driven up to Tremont thirteen years before: "I hope that one day upon my release I can be of assistance to you."

When Serena's sixteenth birthday rolled around, she had been at Priscilla's for almost two weeks and Jessica wanted her to come home; Serena wanted to celebrate her birthday there. Máximo advised Jessica to try reverse psychology. "Act like a bitch; have an attitude; play her own game; show Serena that you're not interested," he said. But Jessica thought Serena already believed she wasn't interested. "What Jessica did to her mom, Serena's doing back to her," said Máximo. "She throws the past at her, and Jessica will give in too easily. Jessica had all that time incarcerated to dwell on what she did. Serena, as a young child, was always grabbing Jessica's leg and saying, 'Don't go'—that plays a lot on her mind. All that time, Jessica ain't going to make it up to her."

It was a sunny summer day in 2001 when Jessica walked to Southern Boulevard to buy the party supplies for Serena's surprise sweet sixteen. Jessica had abandoned the formal celebration—Serena had flunked out of summer school—but Jessica wanted to acknowledge that Serena had made it to the age of sixteen with her virginity intact. "I've got to give her credit for that, come on," Jessica said. The party would be a small family affair, but Jessica had rented a limousine for afterward.

That morning, Jessica first went to the ATM—she'd promised Serena $100 for a new outfit and she wanted to get a money order for Cesar's commissary account. With the baby, Giselle was struggling. Jessica, too, constantly worried about cash: she had to order a cake, party favors, corsages, a keepsake, and pay the balance on the cell phone she'd put on layaway for Serena's gift. An old prison pal let Jessica charge the limo on her credit card, which gave her a month's reprieve on the $300 bill. If Jessica calculated right, she could pay for most of the party and still cover her monthly expenses. Elaine had offered to pay for the food. Lourdes would cook.

Jessica climbed the steep stairs to the party store, which felt like a relic from another era. The cartoon figures for the party favors dated no later than the Ninja Turtles. Garfield hadn't even replaced Felix the Cat. No Powerpuffs, no Stone Cold, only the staples—Barbie and Tweety Bird. The Saran Wrap–covered display of fake-flower corsages was powdered with dust. A middle-aged woman was sitting behind the counter wielding a glue gun, affixing miniature bottles and pacifiers to an enormous corsage. Her husband mulled over a crossword puzzle in the breeze of an industrial fan, balloon streamers whipping above his head. Jessica wandered through the graveyard of milestones. Precious wedding trinkets were tucked safely in an enclosed glass case, but toy babies were accessible everywhere—on open shelves, beneath the counter, in plastic bins, in the protruding bellies of clear plastic storks.

Jessica decided on traditional ribbon corsages and votive-candle favors.

She chose Serena's keepsake with extra care—a girl, pert at a vanity, holding a brush, turned away from the mirror, with a vacant expression on her face. Everything would be in Serena's favorite colors—pink and lavender. As the lady tallied the bill, Jessica perused a clutch of photocopied pages, like a tattoo book, and chose a design for the balloons: a solo Minnie Mouse to match the cake.

The Minnie Mouse theme was reminiscent of Serena's sixth birthday, the last party Jessica had given her. Jessica had been twenty-three then, free on bail while awaiting sentencing. Serena had worn a brown mother-daughter dress, with flowers planted along the trim, even though Jessica wouldn't wear hers because she was going out partying afterward. The next morning, Lourdes told Jessica how Serena had refused to take off the dress after they had gotten home; she'd even slept in the thing. Now Jessica could barely get Serena's attention.

Serena was back at the apartment, waiting for Jessica's return so that she could go shopping for a birthday outfit. Her cousin Tabitha was there for the weekend, and her friend Monique had spent the night. Serena called Jessica's cell phone. "When you coming back with the money?" she asked.

"And good morning to you," said Jessica. It was after one o'clock.

As Jessica headed for home, no man called out or turned to watch her pass; she'd gained another thirty pounds and felt self-conscious about her figure. But when Serena and her girlfriends hit the sidewalks a few minutes later and retraced Jessica's steps to Southern Boulevard, the attention was fierce.

"*Que familia bella*," said one man. That's a beautiful family. The girls walked in the shadow of the Bruckner Expressway. They passed the old man scooping mango ices from his silver cart. They floated through a smoky cloud of sidewalk shish kebabs. Tabitha and Monique wore halters; Serena wore a baby-blue T-shirt. All wore tight jeans and topknot ponytails. They ducked into Jimmy Jazz. Serena held a pair of Mudd jeans at arm's length and, without ceremony, bought them. The store didn't have a dressing room.

It had plenty of T-shirts, though, with a chorus of messages not much different from the sidewalk calls. *Angel Outside. Rebel. Princess. Too Sexy to Stop Here*. Beside a cell phone: *Call Me*. Beside a strawberry: *Pick Me. Kiss Me*—a rainbow over lips. *Boys Lie*. Monique pointed to one that read *I'm so sorry. You looked cute from far away*.

"That's something you'd say," Monique said to Serena. But Serena wasn't bold with the sneaker clerk. She badgered Tabitha to ask for a pair of zebra-striped Jordans in her size and beckoned her cousin over to the cashier so she wouldn't have to stand in line all alone, feeling stupid. At the register, a vast rack of sneaker laces hung like a million mini-nooses. Serena, who was as short as Coco, had to stand on her toes to pay the clerk.

Robert met the girls at the corner with the car; he didn't want them walking home. Jessica, who sat in the passenger seat, reached for Serena's bag as the girls crowded in. "Let me see," she said. "More sneakers?" She pulled them out and inspected them critically. "They ugly."

"They're mine," Serena said.

"Don't go complaining to me when you can't find nothing to match," Jessica said, tossing them back in the box. Neither did she approve of Serena's jeans. They cost $30.

"She found the same ones cheaper," Tabitha said.

"Why you pay thirty dollars for them, then?" Jessica asked.

"Because I already got them, I didn't *know*," Serena said. Jessica wished that Serena had spent the money on an outfit; she wanted Serena to look pretty at the party, not regular.

"Don't go asking me—" started Jessica.

"Ai, Mommy," Serena said, exasperated. "My father's coming to pick me up at twelve." She was referring to Jessica's ex-boyfriend George. George still called Serena. "I ain't calling for you," he'd tell Jessica. "Put my daughter on." He'd promised to pick up Serena that night, at midnight, after he got out of work. Serena assured her mother that George would help her out with money for an outfit.

"You better get money from George. Cuz you don't have nothing," said Jessica.

"I'll fight for it," Serena promised as she gathered her things to get out of the car.

"You better take out your boxing gloves," Jessica said.

"No boys in the house!" Robert warned.

Jessica called out after Serena, "Vacuum your room!"

CHAPTER FORTY-THREE

On the morning of Serena's birthday, Priscilla's thirteen-year-old brother gave her a half-eaten bag of M&M's. Reluctantly, the five-year-old handed her a Twinkie. "You gonna eat it?" he asked.

"Not now," Serena said.

"Can I take it back?" he said.

The day was windy. Derek surprised Serena with a bouquet of flowers down by the bench. Serena was wearing jeans and one of Monique's halters, which she partly obscured with a black sweater. He glanced down at her cleavage. "Button up," he said.

Derek's Charlie Brown T-shirt dropped below his knees. He had extremely long, curled-up eyelashes and the makings of a beard. He was always on the move—hopping over the fence that lined the driveway, striding down the sidewalk to get high near the school, dancing around Serena like a Harlem Globetrotter dazzling a basketball. The need between them rose and fell in shoves and bear hugs. Desire got presented as a mock threat, affection as a taunt; touch was so conditional that half the pleasure was in the tease.

"Come here!" Serena shouted. He'd try to kiss her. "Stop!" she'd yell. But then if Derek walked away, she'd chase him down and drag him back.

"You making it too easy for him," Priscilla said critically.

By late afternoon, the wind chilled, and Derek got a kiss. Serena pulled on an oversize sweatshirt. She tucked her knees beneath her and sat on the bench. She pulled Derek's hands into the tunnel of extra sleeve. "Your hands is sweaty! You nervous?" she said sweetly.

A few hours later, Jessica stopped by Priscilla's carrying Serena's gift. She hesitated outside by the fence. Serena and Derek were sitting on the steps of the front porch, shaded by the grapevines that made a room of leaves.

"Your mother, Serena," Priscilla whispered. Serena broke free, ran over, and sprung open the gate. Serena had clipped her hair back, and stray curls framed her open face. The dark brown strands still showed reddish tints from the summer that Jessica had dyed it blond. Serena was glad to see her mother. Her eyes were bright.

"You look all busted," Jessica said.

"Nah," Serena replied happily. She lifted up her sweatshirt to show her mother the halter.

Jessica raised her eyebrows and laughed. "You'd better leave that on," she said.

"Derek told me to put it on," Serena said agreeably. Jessica and Serena hugged. Jessica rocked side to side.

"Ooh," Jessica sighed sentimentally.

"Ma!" Serena said, embarrassed.

"Sixteen years ago you weren't even a thought," said Jessica affectionately. "Seventeen years ago!"

"Ma," Serena said. She grabbed the bag with Jessica's gift. She read the card from Máximo and the one from Jessica.

"You're welcome," Jessica said, hurt.

"Thank you," said Serena, and kissed Jessica's cheek. Serena hurried over to her friends and showed them the cell phone. Jessica stood awkwardly in the driveway. She was still wearing her work outfit: a white polyester blouse and navy polyester suit. She clutched her purse beneath her arm and toyed with her pendant, an oval piece of jade. She sat on the warped bench. "Serena!" Jessica yelled. Serena didn't hear her. "*Serena!*"

"Whaa!" Serena said.

"Serena, get over here," Jessica said harshly.

Serena plopped down beside her. Derek approached and left almost as quickly, as if he were making a U-turn on a skateboard. Jessica called after him, "Your parents don't believe in giving you condoms?" She turned her head away, feigning a disgust she knew he couldn't see. She'd spotted his hickey.

Serena started after him. "Serena, come here!" Jessica said, calling her back. "What'd I tell you? What'd I tell you?"

"Whaa?" Serena moaned.

"I told you. I don't like that. I don't like you giving boys hickeys. I—"

"What about you and Máximo?"

"Me and Máximo?"

"I don't like it, and you don't care."

"I am thirty-three years old. I don't have them on my neck. I am a grown woman. I work and I pay bills."

"I don't care. It's none of your business."

"Serena! Please!"

"Ma, look at you. Catching an attitude," Serena said, then caught one herself.

"I told you I didn't like you giving boys hickeys. Tell him to come over here. Tell him, *now*," ordered Jessica.

"Why, you gonna say something to him?" said Serena, alarmed. "What you gonna say to him? It's *me*."

"And what's that?" asked Jessica, flicking Serena's neck, where a strawberry spot had begun to fade. "I don't like that," Jessica hissed. "Gimme the phone. I'm gonna tell Máximo to come and get me and take me home."

"Ma, you are wrecking my birthday for real," Serena cried. She ran into the house. "My mother is ruining my birthday!" she howled to Priscilla, who stood in the kitchen baking Serena a birthday cake. Priscilla went downstairs to smooth things out: yes, Jessica could threaten to cancel the surprise party, but what good was punishment for something Serena didn't even know about?

Jessica thought she understood Serena's motive for the hickey. "When he goes to see the baby's mother, Serena wants her to know where he's been. My daughter ain't stupid," she said.

Serena rejoined her gang on the stairs just as Máximo pulled up for Jessica, who stepped into his car, slammed the door, and left. A blast of Metallica punched out the window as they sped away. Night fell, and the steps where the kids sat became a tunnel of love.

Derek rested his back against the house, and Serena, who sat between his legs, leaned her back into his chest. Derek tenderly chided her about the hickey. He hadn't wanted one. He knew that he was going to meet Jessica, and he felt the hickey was a sign of disrespect.

"I don't care," Serena said.

"She did care, though. I felt stupid," Derek said.

"I wish she wouldn'ta been stupid and leave. She walks all around with hickeys all over her and I don't like it, and I tell her, and she don't care. So why I gotta care?"

The surprise birthday didn't surprise Serena; Kevin had broken the news when he'd asked Serena for directions to Lourdes's. Jessica was livid, but at least her daughter didn't know about the limousine, which would appear at the party's end. The guests lolled beneath the balloons and a misspelled banner reading "Happy Sweet Sixxteen!" For Serena's entrance, Máximo blasted "Suave," Lourdes's dancing song; Lourdes upstaged Serena, leading her granddaughter in, with Jessica self-consciously pulling up the rear. Serena immediately picked up a baby to deflect attention. A friend of Serena's from upstate had brought down

Milagros and both sets of twins. Brittany and Stephanie had demanded that Milagros dress up, and she appeared in a halter and tapered jeans. Robert arrived in a shirt and tie. Máximo came straight from the gym in sweats, which irritated Jessica. Serena wore a patchwork denim miniskirt and halter with her new sneakers. When Elaine bustled in, she said, "You're half-naked! Turn around!" Serena turned slowly. "Where'd you get it?" Elaine asked, then raised her hand and high-fived her niece.

Kids leaped after the balloons, some of which had been tied to a fan. Lourdes sweated in the kitchen. Jessica passed out the corsages; Serena cut the cake. Meanwhile, Priscilla fielded increasingly distressed phone calls from Derek, who was trying to figure out whether or not he should come; Serena couldn't decide herself. Lourdes, after learning that Derek's ex-girlfriend was pregnant, had warned Serena that she was going to have a talk with him. "Now is not the place," Serena argued. "It's hard enough to come and not know nobody." Before long, everyone was putting in their two cents. Serena burst into tears, then locked herself in Lourdes's bedroom; Emilio was already hiding out there, with all the furniture that had been dragged away to make room to dance; Roxanne's new baby lay asleep on a towel on the floor.

Serena sobbed into her hands. She imitated her grandmother, her mothers, her aunt: "What makes you think if he got one girl pregnant, he's not going to get you pregnant?" She answered herself, "Who says I'm going to spread my legs?" Priscilla knocked and reported in: Derek was on his way! Serena worked herself up into a frenzy: "They are so worried about me having sex. She has fourteen grandchildren. Why *me*? They don't care if their sons do it, only their daughters. If I was a grandson, do you think they would all be pressuring me?" she cried. "If I want to have sex, I'm going to have sex. Everybody has sex. They all want me to change. I don't care what my family, friends, or nobody says about me, I am the way I am and I don't care!"

She would be pregnant within six months.

That evening, when the limousine arrived, Jessica and Elaine escorted Serena outside, covering her eyes. Monique and Derek showed up in a livery cab just as Serena's sisters and cousins and friends excitedly filled the seats.

"Sorry, too late, go home!" said Priscilla, dismissing her sister. Serena did the same to Derek. Derek stormed away. Monique followed him. Serena climbed into the limo in a huff. Jessica watched Monique and whispered to Elaine, "What's her problem?" The adults crowded around the limo window to send the children off. The coolers had beer and soda.

"No drinking!" Jessica said. "I forgot to ask them to take it out!"

"Have fun!" Elaine said. Her sons, Angel and Edriam, and their friend Josh were going along. Serena had known Josh from childhood.

Jessica warned, "Remember to be back by twelve or else they'll charge it to the credit card! Don't break anything!"

Someone passed Brittany the clutch of pink balloons. The divider between the driver and the kids dropped down. "Where do you want to go?" the chauffeur asked.

"Times Square!" Serena replied. They snapped pictures.

"Smile!"

"Say *welfare!*"

"Welfare!" they shouted.

"Say *food stamps!*"

"Food stamps!"

"Say WIC!"

"WIC!"

They tested the buttons. They clicked the divider up, then down, then up, then down. Turned on the heater, then the air conditioner, then flashed a neon strip of light. Ice cubes sailed back and forth. Serena handed around cans of Coke, with the Blimpie's napkins provided by the limo company.

"Lower the music!" she yelled as she dialed Derek on her new Minnie Mouse cell phone. "Hello," she said. "What you doing? . . . Yo, son, don't catch an attitude. Bye!" She hung up.

The limousine turned off the West Side Highway and moved toward Forty-second Street and inched through the tourists. "Times Square," the chauffeur announced. Josh stuck his head out the window.

"We're going to get in trouble," Stephanie said.

"Ya'll get your head in the window!" Serena said.

"Ya'll get a limo to cover up?" said Josh, astonished. He called out to a stretch limousine as it glided by.

"That's a Navigator," said Angel.

"Why don't I have one of those? I could have fit everybody in there," Serena said morosely. Brittany and Stephanie each had a window. "Let me sit by the window," asked Serena. They refused. "My greedy sisters being greedy with the windows," muttered Serena. Stephanie finally gave in.

The driver needed to move along or park the car. Did they want to take a walk?

"Why we gonna get out and walk?" asked Tabitha.

"Nobody gots money," Serena said.

"Let's go rob a bum," Josh joked.

"Stoopit," said Serena.

"Where would you like to go?" asked the chauffeur.

"Somewhere far!" Tabitha said.

"New Jersey?" Priscilla asked.

"Can we get out of Manhattan?" Josh asked. "Let's go to a bridge."

"There's mad bridges," said Serena. The kids paused uncertainly.

"The Brooklyn Bridge?"

"The George Washington Bridge?"

They wanted to leave the familiar world behind, but no one knew the direction out. "Mister," Josh asked the chauffeur. "You must know everything. You been everywhere. Where should we go? The waterfront?"

The chauffeur didn't respond. Someone suggested the bench, and so they cruised back up to Priscilla's. Nothing was happening at the bench. "Where do you want to go?" the chauffeur asked again.

"Tremont," Tabitha said. She still lived there, in Rocco's old building. She wanted to see her boyfriend. She borrowed Serena's cell phone to alert him and instructed the chauffeur, "Tremont near the Grand Concourse and Anthony."

The old neighborhood had changed in small ways, imperceptible to outsiders. Some of Tremont's hungry spiritedness had been subdued. Instead of its edgy hustle, Jessica's old block had the dusky veneer of a dying industrial town. Under the policies of New York City's prosecutorial mayor, police had frog-marched the dealers off the streets; some of them were now working indoors. Others had moved north, upstate, to small cities like Troy. But the quiet wasn't calm: it was as though the whole neighborhood were fronting.

The super of Jessica's old building had passed his job down to his son. The old apartment wasn't quite an apartment anymore: the son had broken up the units and rented out single rooms to a collection of unattached men—motherless men; husbands whose women had given up on them, or men who had given up on themselves; immigrants. The limousine pulled up in front of the old steps, right where Boy George had collected Jessica, and where Cesar and Rocco and Mighty and Tito used to watch girls and hang out; now only a few boys were there, leaning against a car.

Serena and Tabitha climbed out of the limo into the balmy summer night. The streets seemed strangely empty. Tabitha's boyfriend spotted her from the opposite side of Tremont. He tried to keep his cool pose as he approached, slipping between the passing cars, but the agility of his movements belied his eagerness. Tabitha flew toward him as though she were running for her life. He lifted her and twirled her around and placed her safely on the sidewalk. They lingered in the shadows.

"C'mon," Serena said, ushering out the stragglers. "Let's go for a walk." Her stomach hurt; she needed air. She wondered if the nausea came from the ride or from the "hoochie drink" her Tío Robert had prepared for her the night before. Her sisters and cousins and friends stepped onto the sidewalk. For a moment, they looked lost. The limo driver stepped out, too. "Don't go far," he said.

Serena peered east, down Tremont, toward Anthony. Tabitha and her boyfriend were just turning the corner, headed toward Mount Hope. Serena led the way, following the lovers. She passed her old elementary school. Elaine's oldest son suggested a visit to his grandmother, who lived nearby. She wasn't home. Aside from Tabitha's mother, they didn't know anyone else in the neighborhood, although most of them had been born there. Their time was running out: soon it would be midnight. Serena herded the procession of sisters and cousins and friends back to the car.

Jessica fumed when she learned about the stop on Tremont: "I wouldn't have paid for a limo if they wanted to go for a *walk*." Even if they wanted to walk, why pick Tremont? And if they had to choose Tremont, why walk east? "Anthony? Mount Hope? That's a drug-infested block, there's shootings there," Jessica said. "They could have at least walked in the opposite direction, by the Concourse." In the Bronx, you always had to watch where you were going. The smallest moves in the wrong direction could have enormous consequences.

CHAPTER FORTY-FOUR

Coco's family wasn't at Serena's birthday party, but they heard about it, and it made Coco feel bad for all she couldn't do. She had wanted to rent a limousine for Mercedes's fifth-grade graduation, but there had been the suspension, followed by probation and counseling, and then the roof had caved in—literally. A whole chunk of Coco's kitchen ceiling came down, after a weekend's rainstorm. And then roaches—wave upon wave of roaches—made use of the sudden hole. Coco left increasingly desperate messages for her landlord, but the landlord never called back. "That lady have a habit of not returning calls," Coco observed dryly. Then Coco and Frankie broke up again, but this time they'd even parted on kind terms, exhausted from the recriminations and arguing. Next, Coco lost her job: Garden Way closed. Not long after, the authorities discontinued Pearl's SSI benefits; "She does too good in school," Coco said. Within weeks, Rent-A-Center retrieved the velveteen green sectional couch that had effectively furnished the living room, and cable cut off access. Frankie brought milk and Pampers for La-Monté and called every night to calm him because he had trouble falling asleep without his father; then the phone company shut off the phone. In the barrage of trouble, Coco's worries about Mercedes had once again been eclipsed.

By the end of July, the infestation was so bad that roaches were crawling out of the ketchup bottle and inside the TV screen. Everyone slept on the raft of the double-sized bunk bed in the center of the living room; Coco had dragged it away from the walls so that the roaches couldn't crawl directly onto the children. But even with the moat, nobody was sleeping much; every time someone had to pee, Coco had to stomp the way to the bathroom, flicking on lights—where there were bulbs—disrupting the roaches with her own maternal parade. The damp bathroom was so bug-ridden that the children didn't want to use it: Pearl shunned her beloved tub; Nikki, who was ten, began to wet her pants again, which she hadn't for years; then Naughty, who'd never had the problem, caught it.

Mercedes bravely slept on an old couch. In the morning, unasked, she approached the hallway closet, where Coco had stockpiled the children's clean clothes. Nikki, Nautica, and Pearl—afraid to stand on the floor—stood and watched from the couch: opening the door inevitably unleashed a shower of roaches. But Mercedes just hopped back, let them fall, stomped to make them scramble, and then began shaking out the clothes so her sisters could dress.

Mercedes hadn't expected a limousine ride for her graduation. But what she'd wished for on her last two birthdays was equally impossible—she wanted her parents to be together, and she wanted her father home, in the house.

Last year, before the arrival of Cesar's new baby daughter, Mercedes's birthday had been just right. Coco took her and Nautica to visit their father, and their parents got along. Cesar had matured notably in the fifteen months since he'd last seen his daughters, and his change of heart was evident.

Ordinarily, when Coco did manage to bring them, Cesar made his displeasure at the rarity of her visits known, and Mercedes had to anxiously defend her mother against her father's silent treatment and his quips. That day, however, Mercedes had been relieved of the duty of diplomacy. After Cesar had kissed and hugged his daughters, he'd welcomed Coco. "Wow, man," he'd said warmly, "you got fat."

The visit took place in the honor room, where inmates had more freedom of movement. Inmates were allowed to use the honor room if they'd gone sixty days without a disciplinary infraction, and Cesar easily qualified. He'd been programming consistently—he'd already taken Alternatives to Violence, Frontline Anti-Aggression, Latinos en Progreso, General Business, Printing, and Parenting. He volunteered for a diversion program that brought teenagers into the prison, in the hope of keeping them outside.

Coco relaxed as soon as she realized that Cesar wasn't going to lecture her. Then Mercedes relaxed, and Nautica, who was six, amused them all by running around, dancing crazy, singing silly. "She was like a little Energizer Bunny," Cesar said. Nautica's abandon teased out Mercedes's levity. Mercedes had become buried in self-consciousness—at ten, she already thought she was too tall, that her eyebrows connected unappealingly, that her stomach was fat. Her head now reached up to Cesar's chin. Cesar was stunned by Mercedes's height. He thought she was perfect. But he hadn't remembered Coco as quite so short. One of his friends mistook Coco for his daughter. "No, man," Cesar told him, "that's the mother of my kids."

The girls admired their father's biceps and made fun of his Afro. He'd explained that he was growing it out until Giselle gave birth, just as he'd done before Nautica was born.

"I'm always going to be the oldest one," Mercedes said.

Cesar smiled. Mercedes and Nautica picked his Afro with their fingers and twisted small clumps into ponytails. Coco couldn't help but laugh.

"You find this real entertaining, right? Hilarious?" he said companionably.

The old Cesar wouldn't have stood for it—not in public, in front of other men—his head sprouting a garden of dizzy antennae pointing every which way. When the girls performed songs and cheers, he clapped and sang freely. He danced, which sent his daughters into gut-clutching giggles, and played round after round of patty-cake.

He later said, "I don't want to be on a visit with them and they want to play and I go, 'No, sit down. No, be quiet. No.'" Everything was Yes. Yes to countless games of cards and checkers and tic-tac-toe. Yes to all the candy Nautica retrieved from the vending machine; at home, Nautica and her sisters only got a quarter, and she had to decide between the miniature bags of Skittles and the jellies she loved. Mercedes and her father shared four packs of his favorite barbecue chicken wings, which she heated for him in the microwave. They took pictures when the click-click came—all four of them, together. They acted like a family. Coco later said how strange it was—how if they'd been on the outside, even on a birthday, they would never have spent the day like this.

Toward the end of the visit, Nautica begged Cesar to give her a pony ride, as he had when she was little, where he bounced her like a piece of popcorn on his knees. He did—for a good ten minutes. Then he held her lengthwise like a barbell and pushed her into the air. Mercedes watched, her awe and longing clear. When Cesar began to spin Nautica around, Mercedes couldn't contain her desire. "Can you do that to me?" she asked breathlessly.

She caught herself as quickly, and her expression turned stony. The hope became a dare. Since she was a baby, no one had been able, or willing, to carry her. She weighed 130 pounds now.

Cesar placed Nautica down and squatted before Mercedes. Drawing out the moment, he rubbed his chin. Then, very seriously, he examined his big hands. He measured the width of his grip below Mercedes's knees. Mercedes had braced herself for rejection; then, the next thing she knew, she was up in the air. She went rigid with excitement and terror. "No, Daddy!" she shrieked giddily.

He adjusted her on his shoulders. She clutched his hair and dug her legs into his armpits. Then he paraded his daughter around the honor room and into the regular visiting area, where they took another lap past the inmates, who smiled and nodded as Cesar introduced his oldest girl. He pushed out the door to the enclosed cement courtyard. An April wind had whipped up, and everything was flying, so he quickly ducked back inside, exaggerating the drop as they went over the threshold.

"*Daddyyy!*" Mercedes squealed, nearly losing her balance. She regained it as he steadied. He headed back to their table, where Nautica grinned and Coco gazed up at them, like a little girl in awe of a Christmas tree. Mercedes was trying not to smile but she couldn't help it. "I'm going to fall! Daddy! I'm too heavy!" she said urgently.

"Relax, I ain't going to drop you, don't worry," Cesar assured her. He'd been lifting weights almost daily for the last five years. To himself, he said, "Listen, you light as a feather to me."

This is a book of nonfiction. I was present for much of what is depicted here; some scenes were recounted to me. Hundreds of hours of written and tape-recorded interviews were supplemented with other research, including court transcripts; medical, academic, financial, legal, police, and prison records; and personal letters and diaries. I have generally referred to the Administration for Children's Services by its former name, BCW (Bureau of Child Welfare), as that was the term commonly used by the subjects of this book. Some of the dialogue has been taken from government wiretaps transcribed by me. Recollected experiences and exchanges were assembled through primary- and secondary-source interviews and visits to locations. In those cases where someone is said to have "thought" or "believed" something, those thoughts and beliefs were described and recounted to me by that person. There are no conflated events or composite characters in this book. Only the names of some individuals have been changed.

Some of the people in this book have not been charged with or admitted to crimes ascribed to them by others; Boy George was never tried for the murders attributed to him during his trial. Much of the information about those murders, as well as the heroin milling process, is culled from court testimony, with further independent corroboration from millworkers and other employees. I attended most of Boy George's trial, two related trials, and several sentencings. For further background, I studied criminal law, drug policy, and the Federal Sentencing Guidelines during a year's Knight Journalism Fellowship at Yale Law School, and spent a summer as an intern in a New York State court that handled only A-1 felonies. The majority of the fieldwork for this book, however, consisted of open-ended days and nights in those places where poverty takes poor people: prisons, police stations, countless legal- and social-service institutions, homeless shelters, emergency rooms, the street.

Clearly, I could not have written intimately about this particular American experience of class injustice had the many people in this book not opened their lives to me. While the telling of this story is, finally, my own, I hope it honors their insight and generosity. I met George at the start of his criminal trial. What began as a portrait of a remarkable young man became a complicated family saga, which engaged eleven years of my life. I'm grateful to George for his impatience—his repeated attempts to make me see the bigger picture. My immense gratitude to Jessica, who bravely shared the highs and lows of her extraordinary life. Coco, in the deepest sense, made a home for me. I cherish her friendship and her capacity for joy. Cesar educated me. Our conversations continue to stimulate my thinking about both the worlds he inhabits and the ones we share. I look forward to a day when we can talk freely on this side of the wall.

My decision to write about Coco's daily struggles baffled her neighbors, family, and friends. "Why Coco?" I was asked again and again. "Coco's just regular," people said. "Plenty of girls is worse off." Certainly, I have found this to be true. The hardships of these young people and their families are not unusual in their neighborhoods. Neither are their gifts.

ACKNOWLEDGMENTS

Many people and organizations, only some of whom I honor here, contributed to an environment within which my ability to do creative work was nurtured and sustained: Dorothy O'Connor, one of my earliest teachers; Sheila Rockwell, who literally drove me to Smith College, a rare institution whose tensions sharpened me and whose educators equipped me for a spacious world, especially Maria and Ron Banerjee, Martha Fowlkes, Carla Golden, Philip and Dorothy Green, and Marian Macdonald. Thanks to Richard Todd, my first editor, with whom I began this work; Roberta Myers, for giving me wide berth exactly when I needed it; Amy Virshup, for the initial assignments at *The Village Voice*; and Adam Moss, at *The New York Times Magazine*, for his ongoing interest and goodwill. Both the Barbara Deming Women's Memorial Fund and Cottages at Hedgebrook believed in me early on; much later, at *The New Yorker*, Henry Finder reeled me in. Also at *The New Yorker*, I am grateful to Jay Fielden and Andrew Young.

The Knight Foundation and Yale Law School gave me a fellowship that armed me for one side of the legal world. Rona Jaffe, the Commonwealth Fund, the Carnegie Corporation and the Mrs. Giles Whiting Foundation made possible a critical year at the Bunting Institute under the artful directorship of Florence Ladd. There, my sister-fellows enriched my understanding of passion and community. The Radcliffe Research Partnership Program connected me with the inspiring Sarah Dry and Alison May. Jennifer Forrider and Robert Schirmer provided welcomed technical assistance; Hilary Russ, cheer along with the extra fact-checking. The Blessing Way Foundation, Echoing Green, the Richard Margolis Award, and the Open Society Institute generously gave me additional financial support. Edward Albee, Sophie Cabot Black, the MacDowell Colony, the Millay Colony, and Blue Mountain Center kindly provided me with necessary solitude.

Robert Simels good-naturedly let the story happen. My appreciation to the wonderful women of Thorpe House, especially Sister Christine Hennessy; Ramapo Anchorage Camp, for the staff training that taught me the magic of their pragmatism; Willie Cebollero; Henry DiPippo; Patrick Fitzgerald; Les Wolff; Vinny Lopane; John Harris; Leslie Crocker Snyder; Steven Duke; Brett Dignam and the enlivening students of the prison clinic at Yale Law School, especially Jonathan Hafetz and Johanna Schwartz; Rick Mason; and the staff at the National Archives and Records Administration in New York. Many sources took real risks in talking with me whom I cannot mention by name—without your trust, this book would not exist.

Other courageous and patient people not only gave of their time but shared their lives. In particular, I would like to thank Mercedes, Serena, Iris, Elaine, and Robert, who revisited painful times in telling me what I needed to know. Warmest thanks also to Foxy and Lourdes, who raised me up by welcoming me into their families; to Milagros, for her friendship and hospitality; and to Rocco, not only for the pleasure of our countless interviews but for his wise counsel about my dad. May this book do some justice to your experiences.

At ICM, thanks to Katharine Cluverius. My agent, Sloan Harris, good-humoredly steered this project through its terrific travels, until it found its rightful home. At Scribner, heartfelt thanks to Nan Graham, for not needing to be convinced. Gillian Blake, my editor, saw the promise of a book long before it was one and expertly read countless incarnations of the manuscript. Her graceful ushering of *Random Family* through to its completion gave me all the elbow room I needed, and her guidance over these past years remains a balm. Also at Scribner, thanks to Laura Wise, who is a consummate professional. Leslie Jones saved me from my mistakes. My appreciation to Rebecca Sumner Burgos, Betty Kramer, Rachel Sussman, and Julie Truax for their helpful readings of the manuscript.

I am fortunate for the company who has kept me along the way: Laurie Abraham; Jane Evelyn Atwood; the Azzolini-Kirns; Brett Berk; Melanie Bishop; Kenneth Bobroff; Linda Bowers; Colleen Craite; Lori DiGiacomo; Beth DiNardo; Susan Eaton; Gerald Freund; Amy, John, and Jillian Giangrande; Gus Giangrande; Lucy Grealy; Leston Havens; Lillian Hsu-Flanders; Sonny Kleinfield; Judith Lahti; Daniel LeBlanc; Gerard LeBlanc; Barbara Lewis; Linda Martin; Guy Mastellone; Jerica Mazzaferro; Tal McThenia; Victoria Shaw; Ilena Silverman; Dorothy Thomas; Susan Todd; and Kimberly West-Faulcon.

Special thanks to Pamela Talese, for her careful eye; Will Blythe, for his hunger; my mentor, Mark Kramer, for his delight in the arduous process of teaching me how to write and for championing my work these many years. All graciously read several drafts of the book.

My gratitude to the home team runs deep: Ann Patchett, for her steady faith and humor; Kristine Larsen, for her playful intelligence; Laurel Touby, for her ready spirit; Edwin C. Cohen, for the many ways in which he has sheltered me; Deborah Gunton, for her precious drive; and my parents, for the lessons in their labors of love.

Dearest thanks to Alice Truax, my editor, whose involvement in this project has been a profound blessing in my life. She gave each line her full attention and brought out a better book from me. The failures are entirely my own.

How can I thank you, my heart and ally, Arthur Joseph Giangrande? I am a very lucky girl. And so glad that it was your strong hand, the one I held every step of the way.

P.S.

Ideas,
interviews
& features ...

Profile of Adrian Nicole LeBlanc

by Travis Elborough

TOWARDS THE END of the interview, after
we've been talking about responses to the
book for a while, Adrian Nicole LeBlanc
fetches, and then reads out, a letter she has
received 'literally yesterday'. It's from a man
who describes himself, and his address
confirms it, 'as "a prisoner" but nonetheless a
prisoner with a heart and a family'. Having
initially picked up the book because he'd
heard it was all about the drug dealer Boy
George, her correspondent says he was
touched by Coco's story and wants to offer
her financial support. 'He may just be trying
to pick her up and I mean, what's he going to
do? Send her $20? But I get letters from poor
people, and money from poor people all the
time and nothing,' she says with undisguised
regret, 'from anyone who could actually
help them in any really substantial way.'

Like her letter-writer though, LeBlanc's
own starting point was Boy George – as she
states in her author's note. A journalist for
Village Voice in New York during the late
eighties, she'd already covered a number of
drug cases when she came to report on
George's trial in 1989. 'I was spending a lot of
time in the criminal court system and I became
interested in understanding what it meant if
you were young and earning your income
from drug dealing. Drug arrests back then
were such a big thing and I was really trying to
understand the impact they were having on

whole families. Drug dealers really were the media's incarnation of evil – before terrorists took their place, that is. The drug war was a morally charged campaign, incredibly righteous. The ordinary kids interested me in that context because it was clear that there was something extremely mundane about their own relationship to the business. You could almost see it in the courtroom because the narrative that the prosecutors would use was all pumped up and then these kids looked totally bored and the two just didn't connect. But the enormity of George's situation really dwarfed everything for a while.'

Concerned, at least in part, about inadvertently contributing to Boy George's burgeoning ghetto-fabulous mythology (she maintains that if she were writing now, she would probably employ even greater subtlety when detailing his material acquisitions), her original plans for a book on George gave way to something far broader in scope. If the book's title is aptly descriptive, it equally points to the way in which its composition started to take shape. 'I met George and through him Jessica, and it kept veering off. I would have a hunch or ask a question and the thing would take another turn. And then I met Cesar and Coco and the narrative splintered even further from there.' There was, of course, the South Bronx, and faithfully chronicling the lives of some ▶

❛ Drug dealers really were the incarnation of evil – before terrorists took their place, that is. ❜

LIFE AT A GLANCE

BORN
....
1963

EDUCATION
....
BA in sociology from
Smith College, a Master's
of Philosophy and
Modern Literature
from Oxford University
and a Master of Law
Studies from Yale Law
School.

CAREER
....
While attending Smith
College, LeBlanc began her
reporting career at the now
defunct *New England
Monthly*. She has written
for the *New Yorker*, *Esquire*,
Elle, *SPIN*, *The Source* and
the *Village Voice* and is a
frequent contributor to
the *New York Times*
Sunday magazine.
Currently, she is a Visiting
Scholar at the New York
University School of
Journalism. *Random
Family* is her first book.

Profile *(continued)*

◄ of its most overlooked and marginalized inhabitants would occupy LeBlanc for the next ten years. 'The other piece of this is that I was really learning how to be a journalist as I was writing it but there were incredible advantages to my ignorance. I had no expectations, I didn't know that it was such a hot spot.'

Unlike many previous studies of urban poverty – George Orwell's *Down and Out in Paris and London* or, recently, Barbara Ehrenreich's *Nickel and Dimed: Undercover in Low-Wage USA* – LeBlanc is entirely, noticeably, absent from her narrative. However, she speaks warmly of Ehrenreich's book. (Ironically Coco, she tells me, was recently made an employee of the year at one of the companies Ehrenreich worked for. 'One of my editors said, "That's great, it just goes to show how hard work pays off." Yes and no. No to the obscenity that she's employee of the year, one of 4 out of 40,000 employees selected, and she still can't earn a living wage.') Although LeBlanc admires *Nickel and Dimed*, she could never sanction the idea of putting herself in her book. 'There were times when I was writing it, certain scenes I'd hoped to keep in that were contingent on putting me in, so they had to go. I felt that if I had appeared in it, I would be accepting the idea that their world needs a translator, a bridge to guide the middle-class reader on a ghetto tour. I thought the achievement, if I could do it, would be just to say, here it is on its own terms, and plunk you down in the middle of it, like covering anything else, Wall Street, or Cannes.'

As any reader cannot fail to notice, her unique vérité style lends an astonishing and disarming immediacy to the book (it is not surprising to discover William Faulkner and Nelson Algren 'for dialogue' among LeBlanc's literary favourites). Her writing is visibly the product of immense, and committed, journalistic legwork. By a process of what could be described as sustained osmosis, LeBlanc absorbed the minutiae of her subjects' daily existences. 'To begin with I was tentative about doing the work because it felt like, on top of all you're going through and everything else, here I am with my twenty questions. Hi, you're getting evicted and here I am needing more. Here I am on the back of another horrible night.' With Coco, with whom she has developed a lasting bond, she says, 'We clocked in so many hours together that when she calls me on the phone I can tell immediately by her voice when something is wrong.' One section, she informs me, that a number of parties have reacted to with a certain alarm, or in some instances outright distaste, is the part where Richie and Foxy burn through a $70,000 insurance windfall. 'So many people have been freaked out by it; you know, "He had a certain chance and he took another," but at the time that it happened I was so immersed in their world I could totally understand doing that. It became a sort of marker to my own experience.'

The downside to such immersion, ▶

LIFE AT
A GLANCE
(continued)

AWARDS
....

LeBlanc has been the recipient of numerous awards, including a Bunting fellowship from Radcliffe and a MacDowell Colony residency.

What is your idea of perfect happiness?
Hmmm. When I'm reporting and time disappears. Riding on my boyfriend's motorcycle anywhere outside of the city, or walking around any city with my boyfriend. Swimming naked in natural lakes.

What is your greatest fear?
I don't have a greatest fear. I have many. I suppose I'm counterphobic.

What objects do you always carry with you?
Notepad and pen and a book.

Where do you go for inspiration?
The swimming pool. The coffee shop. The sidewalk, where bunches of people are.

Which living person do you most admire?
Arthur Joseph Giangrande – the strongest person I am lucky to know.

Who are your favourite authors?
I can't answer this but, right now? James Baldwin, Dostoyevsky, Joseph Conrad – especially *Lord*

◄ she admits, was that extended periods in that environment slowed down many of her natural responses, particularly to the violence, which was virtually omnipresent – 'a community dynamic', as she puts it. 'Now I realize to an extent I was withholding certain parts of my personality; in a lot of those early meetings with the family, I was really just trying to figure out what was happening. I did,' she later adds, 'get really affected by what I witnessed. It made me numb and put me in a kind of stupor.' She recalls an evening where she was staying with Coco at her flat when two men tried to break in and rape them; LeBlanc explains that it was only when she, quite casually, related the event to her understandably concerned boyfriend the following day over coffee that she realized the danger she'd been in. 'There were times when I could intellectually apprehend things, but there was sludge between my intellectual apprehension and the visceral reality was like a sort of trauma. I am not saying, in any way, I was anything near experiencing what these folks were going through but when you are there you understand why people appear unresponsive.'

She draws an analogy from her own experiences of caring for her father, a Massachusetts union organizer who died from cancer. (Her mother, incidentally, worked at a residential drug rehabilitation centre.) 'My dad was sick for about two years. For the first six months we changed the sheets every day and everything was tender and attentive. Then we started getting tired, and perhaps we'd change the sheets every other day, and maybe were a little quicker when we gave him a bath. Now if you enter into the family situation after, say, sixteen months, you might think, "Hey, they're pretty rough." The cumulative stresses take a toll and are incredibly complicated. When I was taking care of him the sensible thing, of course, would have been to have taken care of myself, eaten well, exercised and gotten some sleep. But what was I doing? I was smoking again, I couldn't sleep and I was eating crap. But had I left the environment for three weeks, I could have come back and seen that.'

It's precisely for this reason she is so angered by the willingness of those who have absolutely no understanding of the mundane struggles of Coco *et al* to condemn the poor for their actions. 'People say, "Why, they should try to do this" and "They should try and do that", but you have to actually see *something*. You have to see a twenty-eight-year-old man with a job that seems like it's doing something to change his life. There is a complete absence of young men working in these communities; outside of drug dealing, they rarely see young men working. You see people on the street and then there is a gap and then they see old men, old being forty-eight or something. And I don't even know what that does to the orientation of a young boy.'

She believes people are morally righteous ▶

Q & A
(continued)

Jim, Faulkner and Nelson Algren for dialogue, Márquez Márquez Márquez, Alice Munro, W. H. Auden, Elizabeth Bishop and Joan Didion.

What are you writing at the moment?
A book about stand-up comedians, which I think is a book about American male identity. Or rendering damage creatively.

Profile *(continued)*

◀ about poverty because it is 'sad and painful and scary' and in the States the fact that so many of those responsible for providing for the poor are themselves often borderline poor doesn't exactly help. 'I think their fears of becoming these people in a way, or having been them and got out, animates a very strange ethical situation.' It is easier all round, she believes, for most to judge Coco than feel the loss of Mercedes' life. 'A kid like Mercedes, who from the minute she was born was identified as a kid in need of help, and *really* no help was ever given. That child, statistically, by any category, was a child who needed extra support. She should have had all kinds of help, been sent to summer camps and all kinds of after-school stuff, right? Because you identify kids in that community with incarcerated parents, she's at risk for drug use, early pregnancy, family violence – but nothing. Now, is that because the caseworker never had time to get to know the case? Could things have been better if there had been one caseworker who had gotten to know the family instead of twelve that kept getting shifted around?'

That her random family don't blame anyone else for their ills, especially when so many others are willing to blame them, still amazes her. 'Cesar, when he read the book, criticized me because he felt I was much too much of a bleeding heart. He really feels his life was his own doing. He admits he had it bad, but says he knew that when he was

6 She believes people are morally righteous about poverty because it is "sad and painful and scary". 9

running away from some guy he had just mugged that what he had done was really wrong.' Many of the doubts she may have had about the book's reception, locally as it were, were dispelled at a reading in the Bronx shortly after publication. 'It really was like a religious revival thing, people were shouting, "You Tell It!"' The need to recognize the joys and strengths of these families – not only their problems and pains – was celebrated, and more thoughtfully understood. The expanse can help journalists wrestling with the personal anxieties of the profession. Young journalists frequently ask LeBlanc how to make connections among the poor, how they should dress, or how they can get people to accept them. 'Whenever I started to slip into a level of dysfunction as a result of the amount of time I was spending in this environment *they* pulled me back up to do what I was supposed to do. Coco wanted me to write about her so people could understand how she wanted things to change. Now she wants me to write another book about her because she says she's still struggling. So, I always have to remind journalists, subjects don't want you to come in and be cool, they don't want you to come in and hang out, they want you to come in and do your thing – write about their lives.' ∎

> ❛ Cesar criticized me because he felt I was much too much of a bleeding heart. ❜

A Critical Eye

IF, AS IS often said, a person can be judged by the company they keep, then an equivalent for books is surely the comparisons reviewers make. It is hardly surprising that *Random Family*, described as 'enthralling' by the *New York Times*, 'remarkable' by *Newsweek*, 'a tour de force' by *Vogue* and 'a stunning ... glimpse into the sorrow and pity of America's inner cities' by *Elle*, was justly viewed to have held its own with some of the biggest wigs ever to have put pen to paper, unfurled a notebook, or slotted a ribbon into a typewriter. The *Los Angeles Times* was not alone in finding parallels to George Eliot and dubbed *Random Family* a 'non-fiction *Middlemarch* of the underclass'. On this side of the pond New Puritan novelist Nicholas Blincoe, writing in the *Daily Telegraph*, whilst stressing the originality of LeBlanc's style and approach, concurred, finding this '400-page towering achievement ... closer ... to Defoe's *Journal of the Plague Year* or even George Eliot's *Middlemarch* than it is to most examples of literary journalism. Rather than looking for a story,' he concluded, '*Random Family* gives us a whole way of life.' Marianne Brace, in the *Independent on Sunday*, saw LeBlanc as 'a modern-day Mayhew' and believed her 'ghetto-blaster of a book, sympathetic and unsentimental', would make us all 'think deeply about America's desperate urban poor'. The *Observer*'s Geraldine Bedell felt that as 'an extraordinary social document which is also a riveting read' it really was 'a contemporary *Down and Out in Paris and London*'.

For the *Scotsman*, though, it was new tricks rather than old dogs that caught their eye in what they dubbed 'a monumental work of narrative journalism'. LeBlanc, their reviewer claimed, had taken 'poverty . . . the oldest story in town' and written 'about it in a way that makes us look at it anew.'

Bryan Appleyard in the *Sunday Times*, meanwhile, was struck particularly by LeBlanc's immersive literary device. 'She sinks,' he wrote, 'into the world of her subjects, identifying exactly and in intimate detail the successive trials by which they are afflicted.' The resulting evocation of character he found 'immaculate', as was 'the sheer precision of her observation'. It was, he stated, 'a brilliant book'. The last word must, however, go to Decca Aikenhead who finished her review in the *New Statesman* with this winning endorsement: 'I had always thought the phrase that critics occasionally use – "If you buy just one book this year, make it this one" – quite meaningless, until I read *Random Family*.' ∎

Bronx Cheer
by Travis Elborough

THE BRONX TOURISM COUNCIL'S helpful website (Ilovethebronx.com) has a little note for visiting travel writers. 'Call us,' it implores would-be Bill Brysons, 'for more information on Bronx stories with happy endings.' E. L. Doctorow, Colin Powell and Kiss guitarist Ace Freeley are among the former residents offered as prime examples of boys-and-girls-done-good, celebrated in the borough's Walk of Fame. Jennifer 'Jenny from the Block' Lopez, Al Pacino and Leon Trotsky have yet to be honoured but give it time; the scheme has only been running since 1998 – a year after the Bronx earned an All-America City Award in recognition of its renewal.

You can only really applaud their efforts; until very recently the Bronx had, in the words of one local commentator, served as little more than 'a media metaphor for urban blight'. President Carter, visiting the burnt-out wasteland of Charlotte Street in the South Bronx in October 1977, pronounced it 'the worst slum in America' and promised to help. The *New York Times* at the time remarked that the South Bronx was 'as crucial to an understanding of American urban life as Auschwitz is crucial to an understanding of Nazism.' Ronald Reagan, on his presidential election campaign trail in August 1980, popped by to tell assembled locals and newscasters that he 'hadn't seen anything like this since London after the Blitz'. Residents, perhaps recalling that

> ❝ Until very recently the Bronx served as little more than "a media metaphor for urban blight". ❞

Reagan spent the war in Hollywood making propaganda films, told him to 'Go back to California.'

For much of its history, though, the neighbourhood was regarded as well-to-do, leafy even. (It has 6,000 acres of parkland 'and a greater percentage of green space than any other urban area in the country', apparently.) The borough takes its name from its first white settler, Jonas Bronck. A Swede with the Dutch West India Company, Bronck purchased a 500-acre tract of land beside the Harlem River from the indigenous Mohegan tribe for 'two guns, two kettles, two adzes, two shirts, one barrel of cider, and six bits of money' in 1639. Bronck informed his Dutch masters that it was 'a veritable paradise and needs but the industrious hand of man to make it the finest and most beautiful region in all the world'. Like Brick Lane for London, the Bronx provides a microcosm to view the shifting migrant population of New York. Dutch settlers were replaced by Irish and German immigrants, who in turn were joined by Italians and Jews from Eastern Europe in the early twentieth century. Following the Second World War, African Americans, Afro-Caribbeans and Latinos – mainly Puerto Ricans encouraged to settle on the 'mainland' by a state-sponsored migratory scheme called Operation Bootstrap – moved into the borough in greater numbers. Many had ▶

‘ The borough takes its name from its first white settler, Jonas Bronck. ’

Bronx Cheer *(continued)*

◄ been made homeless by gentrifying slum clearances in Manhattan.

During this period the Bronx suffered plenty of redevelopments of its own. The Cross-Bronx expressway, a monstrous six-lane road development forced through by New York's Machiavellian Construction Coordinator Robert Moses, is an indignity few could forget or forgive. The Cross-Bronx took years to complete, cut a swathe through several neighbourhoods and displaced thousands of families. A multi-million-dollar Model Cities grant for new housing in 1967 was poorly managed and planned – a slew of projects were eventually iced by Nixon in 1973 before they got off the drawing board. As the economy stalled, jobs fell away and the housing situation was further exacerbated by a rent-control system that effectively made it uneconomic for private landlords to repair their properties. By 1969 a quarter of the Bronx's rental properties were classified as 'dilapidated or deteriorating'. As New York teetered towards bankruptcy in the 1970s, the Bronx was beset by a series of conflagrations, as landlords resorted to arson to cash in insurance policies on worthless buildings. Drugs and violent crimes soared, reaching their peak in the years covered in LeBlanc's book. In 1990 alone there were 653 homicides in the borough.

You may remember that in Tom Wolfe's withering satire of the Reaganite years,

❝ Like Brick Lane for London, the Bronx provides a microcosm to view the shifting migrant population of New York. ❞

Bonfire of the Vanities, his Wall Street yuppie Sherman McCoy panics, with disastrous consequences, after taking a wrong turn and getting lost in Bruckner Boulevard in the South Bronx. Bruckner Boulevard is now home to chi-chi antique dealers. Clinton, following Carter and Reagan, took a brief sojourn to the South Bronx in 1997. Standing on a ranch-home-bestrewn Charlotte Street unrecognizable from Carter's or Reagan's day, he praised the local community groups for their role in transforming the area. The Bronx as 'they' say is 'Up'. *Random Family* speaks for the un-Up, the generations still blighted by the fallout from the un-Up days. Figures from the New York City census in 2000 show that the Bronx has the highest number of households with an income of less than $25,000 (46%) and the highest number of residents over 25 who did not graduate from high school (38%). The Bronx District Attorney's office in October 2003 recorded the lowest homicide rate since 1966, but the borough, which has 16.6% of New York's population, 'had almost 23% of the City's murders, and nearly 24% of its felony assaults'. Jessica, Coco and Cesar's stories may not have happy endings, but all too often their voices have been ignored. If we are serious about understanding poverty and bringing about change, the past confirms we could do a lot worse than listening, honestly, to what they have to say. ∎

❛ The Cross-Bronx expressway, a monstrous six-lane road development, is an indignity few could forget or forgive. ❜

If You Loved This,
You'll Like . . .

Nickel and Dimed: Undercover in Low-Wage USA *by Barbara Ehrenreich*
A shocking exposé of the low-wage slavery in
supposedly the richest country in the world.

Cold New World: Growing Up in a Harder Country *by William Finnegan*
New Yorker writer Finnegan's book explores
the lives of underprivileged adolescents
across the four corners of America.

The Other America *by Michael Harrington*
This classic work on the American poor, first
published in 1962, remains all too relevant
today.

There Are No Children Here *by Alex Kotlowitz*
Chicago's gang-plagued West Side is
chronicled through the lives of two young
brothers who grow up dodging bullets much
as other children might chase baseballs.

Westsiders *by William Shaw*
Seven aspiring rap stars dream of rhyming
their way out of poverty-stricken South
Central in Shaw's compelling portrait of the
LA hip-hop scene.

Below the Breadline *by Fran Abrams*
In the tradition of George Orwell's *Down
and Out in Paris and London*, Abrams
investigates Britain's underpaid underbelly.